inspire

family

spa

trellis

summerhouse

balcony

oasis

climbers

create

decking

ergola

cottage

terrace

wheelbarrow

build

water

conservatory

wildlife

pond

easy

D1429000

escape

enjoy

success

play

relax

barbecue

entertain

design

create

grow

enjoy

outdoor living

with over 1900 colour illustrations

the inspirational new step-by-step guide
to today's outdoor living space from **B&Q**

be safe ©

Individual skills and site conditions vary widely, and some of the projects detailed in this book involve a degree of risk. Although B&Q has made every effort to ensure that the instructions are accurate, they are provided for general information only and you should always read and follow any manufacturer's instructions and, where appropriate, seek the advice of professionals.

In particular:
- Before working with electricity or water you should consult an appropriate professional. When working with electricity always turn the power off at the mains.
- New Building Regulations relating to electrical work in the home and garden came into force on 1 January 2005 in England and Wales. It is essential that you check these regulations before proceeding with any electrical work. Contact your local authority's Building Control Department for guidance.
- Always read any relevant manuals or instructions for using tools and follow the safety instructions.
- The law concerning Building Regulations, planning, local byelaws and related matters can be complicated and you should take professional advice where appropriate. In connection with building work, B&Q cannot advise on planning permission or Building Regulations issues.

The techniques suggested in this book should not be used by anyone less than 18 years of age. To the extent permitted by law, B&Q accepts no liability for any loss, damage or injury arising as a consequence of the advice contained in this book. References to legislation and regulations are correct at the time of going to press.

feedback and further advice
B&Q welcomes your comments on this book and suggestions for improvements. Contact us by sending an e-mail to: thebook@b-and-q.co.uk

To find your local B&Q store, or for design and planning advice, indoors and out, visit **www.diy.com**

outdoor living
The inspirational new step-by-step guide to today's outdoor living space from B&Q

Commissioned by David Roth, Marketing Director, B&Q

Project Director Nicholas Barnard
Consulting Editor Ken Schept
B&Q Project Manager Geoff Long
Managing Editor Amanda Vinnicombe
Assistant Editor Lara Day
Art Direction and Design Aaron Hayden
Designer Clare Barber CB Design
Production Manager Philip Collyer
Photographers Dan McNally and Lucy Pope
Illustrators Peter Bull Art Studios and Stuart Blower

This edition first published in the United Kingdom in 2005 by B&Q plc, Portswood House, 1 Hampshire Corporate Park, Chandlers Ford, Eastleigh, Hampshire SO53 3YX

© 2005 B&Q plc

Edited, designed and produced by Thames & Hudson Ltd, London, and B&Q plc

British Library Cataloguing-in-Publication Data
A catalogue record for this book is available from the British Library
ISBN 0-9535243-3-7

This book is printed on 130gsm Perigord, manufactured in southwest France by Condat in a plant with ISO 14001 environmental accreditation. The components of this paper are elemental chlorine-free (ECF) pulp plus filler and coating, all of which are recyclable.

Printed and bound in the UK by Butler and Tanner

introduction

design

create

grow

plant chooser

enjoy

Wendy **Atkins**
Sally **Clifton**
Mark **Turner**
Pete **Riding**
Dave **Sparks**
Ellen **Morgan**
John **Humphries**
Jason **Ellery**
Sally **Ockenden**
Andy **Maulin**
Richard **Wareham**
Neil **Watson**
Marie **Glassborow**
Geoff **Long**
Adrian **Hughes**
Dan **Bird**
Steve **Guy**
Jean **Linehan**
Jacqui **Henry**
Dorothy **Agnew**
Nick **Thornton**
Sarah **Kemish**
Mick **Callow**
Maria **Sealey**
Alistair **Sanderson**
Terry **Wade**
Lesley **Munro**
Linda **Taylor**
Claire **Cooper**
Duncan **Whitfield**
Mike **Williams**
Trevor **Moody**
Malcolm **Gray**
Nick **Soutter**
Paul **Roebuck**
Arthur **Weir**
Alan **Teahon**
Ian **Howell**
Claire **Sparkes**
Keith **Maggs**
Gill **Harris**
Annie **Johnson**
Keith **Reed**
Paul **Haynes**
Peter **Marten**
David **Gray**
Iain **Lynch**
Lyndon **Goddard**
Sophie **Gehin**
Keven **Huelin**
Kay **Hedges**
Sue **O'Neil**
Tim **Clapp**
Dawn **Edwards**
Andy **Melpous**
Anthony **Perry**
Dawn **Plumbly**
Steve **Brockway**

8

outdoorliving

The title says it all

The inspiration for this book came to me while relaxing on my new deck. It overlooks a modest play area that we built for our kids and a thicket of trees where we dream of creating a contemplation garden.

My name is David Roth. I am the Marketing Director of B&Q. My own family garden informs the core message of this book: just outside the door many of us have a space full of untapped potential – a space to create, design, grow and enjoy. Especially enjoy.

outdoorliving presents all the knowledge and inspiration you need to make your outdoor space truly part of your living space. Whatever your home – country cottage, suburban semi, city flat – and whatever your passion – plants, partying, peace and quiet – we show you how to create the perfect outdoor room for you.

To demonstrate how it can be done – we did it! Drawing on the huge expertise of B&Q customer advisers and suppliers, we designed, built and planted nine inspiring garden projects, specially for this book. They include:

• **A family garden** – where kids can play safely and adults relax in comfort, surrounded by cheerful, easy-care planting.

• **A socialising garden** – a grand space for eating, drinking and partying, complete with an elegant patio, generous deck, summerhouse and spectacular water feature.

• **A contemplation garden** – a secluded, secret space to get away from it all and be at one with the colours, sights, scents and sounds of nature.

• **An exotic garden** – a small urban backyard transformed by cedar-stained decking, tropical planting and the therapeutic swirl of a spa set beneath an arbour covered in climbers and a twinkling net of fairy lights.

We did it – so can you! Every project is illustrated with step-by-step photographs and drawings that take you through the job in a clear, easy-to follow fashion.

But that's not all. We also explain the process of garden design – from first inspiration all the way to scale drawing. We take the mystery out of gardening in a chapter that explains everything from lawn care to planting trees. We include a catalogue of recommended garden plants – widely available, easy to grow, all with something special to offer. And we show you how to enhance the comfort and style of your outdoor space, so that it will become an ever greater part of your life.

outdoorliving was developed by a collaboration of experts from B&Q and the world's leading publisher of illustrated books, Thames & Hudson. It follows our award-winning **You Can Do It The complete B&Q step-by-step book of home improvement**. These two books are part of the expanding B&Q library of home improvement publications. Together they form a partnership providing inspiration and advice indoors and out.

outdoorliving – one more way you can make your home better with B&Q.
Creatively
Confidently
Affordably

You can do it...

David Roth   Marketing Director, B&Q

You Can Do It
The complete B&Q step-by-step book of home improvement

understanding **colour**
All the know-how and inspiration you need to succeed with colour in your home

Includes the Instant **Makeover** CD–ROM

introduction

We are a nation of gardeners. It's an old saying, but it's true: we have a great love for plants. But times have changed, and there is more to the outdoor room than pottering in the potting shed.

the outdoor room

Outdoor living through four seasons

OK, our climate isn't exactly Mediterranean. But while we may not be able to sunbathe all year round, that doesn't mean turning our backs on the outdoors for eight months of the year. Even winter sun can be warm enough to sit outside in, provided you are screened from the wind. A little more shelter – a pergola, summerhouse or protected patio or deck – coupled with a little more privacy – screens, fences and year-round foliage – will make any outdoor space much more enticing. Add a barbecue, patio heater and some lighting, and you can enjoy your outdoor room long after the sun has set for dining under the stars.

You can do it

Another thing that keeps people indoors is the belief that to create a garden they must master great horticultural manuals, and spend hours bent double over weed-infested beds. But it doesn't have to be that way. For some people the pleasure of gardening is an end in itself, while for others the priority is to create an outdoor living space – somewhere to relax, cook, eat or socialise. Whether or not we are cash-rich, most of us these days feel time-poor. That means we want maximum returns for minimum effort: low-maintenance solutions that will allow us to spend our time outdoors relaxing, not working. Solutions that this book will provide.

Do it your way

No two people are alike. When we visit other people's homes, or invite guests into ours, it is the individual touches that make the impression: the choice of objects and the way they are arranged, how colour, texture and light are combined to create a cosy atmosphere, or a sense of the romantic or dramatic, or a feeling of calm. The outdoor room offers exactly the same opportunities to express your own individual style.

What's different with a room outdoors is that it offers a far wider range of sensory experiences: the scent of plants, the feel of the sun on your skin or the breeze in your hair, the sound of water in a fountain or the tinkling of a wind chime. Food cooked on a barbecue and shared around a table in the sun offers a wonderful taste sensation. Even better if accompanied by your own freshly picked herbs and salad leaves. With a little know-how (and consideration for the neighbours), you can position speakers in your outdoor room to let you enjoy a concert in the open air or conservatory.

Impressing your own personality on your outdoor room will turn it into a personal space, somewhere you will treasure time spent alone or with family and friends.

Seeking inspiration

Whether you live in the town or the country, have
a backyard, front lawn, patio, balcony or roof
terrace, an outdoor room is a valuable extension
to your living space. The style you choose for it is
up to you – there are plenty of ways to get inspired.

A style of your own

There is a wealth of publications and television programmes
to dip into for ideas when planning an outdoor room, and don't
forget your holiday snaps: a sunny terrace, pots of cheerful
geraniums, a brightly painted summerhouse, a tiled pool –
pictures that bring back happy memories can also suggest
features that you might bring into your own design. Magazines,
television and – if we're lucky – overseas travel have allowed us
to experience an enormous range of arts, crafts, architecture
and interiors from the terraces of the Mediterranean to the
souks of North Africa, and from the quiet calm of the Zen
gardens of Japan to the vibrancy of the Caribbean.

Closer to home, as well as the leading annual garden shows
such as Chelsea and Hampton Court, there are hundreds of
inspirational gardens in Britain to visit. From the futuristic Eden
Project or the once 'lost' gardens of Heligan in Cornwall to the
spectacular new Alnwick Gardens of Northumberland, these
are scattered throughout England, Scotland, Ireland and
Wales. Thousands more private gardens in towns, cities
and countryside open for charity once or twice a year under
the National Gardens Scheme (www.ngs.org.uk).

Gardens past, present and future

The ancient Persians created some of the world's very first gardens, and they have been an inspiration ever since. In fact their word for garden is the origin of our word paradise. A Persian 'paradise garden' was an enclosed or walled garden, filled with the sights and sounds of water, cool shade and the perfume of sweet-smelling flowers. It was a place of calm retreat from the heat of the desert outside. Today, our 'desert' is more likely to be made of concrete than sand, but our need for an oasis of peace and quiet is greater than ever.

Another lasting influence are the monastic gardens where medieval monks grew flowers, culinary herbs for their kitchens and therapeutic herbs for their infirmaries. In turn these inspired the 'physic' gardens first established in the 16th and 17th centuries. You can still visit the famous Chelsea Physic Garden in the heart of London, founded by the Society of Apothecaries in 1673. These monastic and medicinal gardens were the ancestors of our modern herb gardens.

Not all gardens were places of escape and tranquillity. Britain's great Tudor and Elizabethan houses – places such as Sudeley Castle in Gloucestershire or Penshurst Place in Kent – had gardens designed to be lived in and enjoyed throughout the year. They had shaded tree-lined alleys and rose-covered arbours for strolling beneath in summer, mazes and elegant statuary to impress the guests, and grand banqueting platforms for al fresco dining. These outdoor rooms were the setting for mock tournaments, music and theatrical performances, and general revelry.

Not everyone lived in a monastery or grand house of course. Ordinary country dwellers used their gardens to grow herbs and vegetables, to keep bees for honey and chickens for eggs. There might be a little space for flowers but essentially a garden was an aid to survival. These days, thankfully, most of us have more choice. Growing food can be incredibly satisfying – but you might prefer an outdoor room designed as a space to eat, drink and be merry. Either way, the gardens of the past live on in the inspiration they provide for today's outdoor room.

Greener
gardens

Encouraging wildlife, being wary of chemicals and wise with water: these are just some of the ways you can do your bit in the garden to avoid depleting and damaging our environment. And thanks to initiatives by consumers, governments, manufacturers and retailers such as B&Q, there is now a wide variety of products available that will help you achieve those goals.

Sustainable sources

In our choices as consumers we all have the power to make a difference. When buying wood products, from decorative bark to deck timbers, furniture, sheds and fences, always check where the materials came from. Look for products made from recycled materials or that bear the logo of the FSC (Forest Stewardship Council), the UKWAS (UK Woodland Assurance Scheme), the Indonesian LEI (Lembago Ecolabel Institute) or the MYCC (Malaysian Timber Certification Council), which certifies that the wood used comes from sustainable sources.

The extraction of peat, which is contained in many multi-purpose and specialist composts and soil improvers, can be very damaging to wildlife and the environment. Many peat bogs support a large and diverse variety of insects, birds and plants, as well as hundreds of kinds of mosses, liverworts, lichen and fungi. Peat bogs need to be drained of their water to harvest peat, often causing the fragile habitats these species depend on to be destroyed. So be sure to choose peat-free options for your garden, which are now widely available.

Many beaches and natural rock formations have been depleted by people collecting stones to decorate their gardens. So check too that any ornamental stones, cobbles, pebbles and grit come from recognised quarries.

Finally, when buying bulbs, always make sure that they are from cultivated stock and not from the wild.

Garden chemicals

Many of the insects in the garden are our allies – but not all. In the past, people were quick to combat pests and weeds with hazardous chemicals and pesticides. Britain now has some of the world's toughest pesticide regulations, and many once common products have been removed from the shelves. Even so, scientists and gardeners remain concerned about the 'cocktail effect': when chemicals seem perfectly safe in isolation, but cause unpredictable problems if combined. There are also worries about the build-up of chemicals in the soil, which inevitably find their way into fruits, vegetables and water. All the more reason to use chemicals in the garden with great caution.

However, sometimes even responsible gardeners choose chemical pesticides or weedkillers. If you do, be sure to use them safely, and always follow any instructions on use, storage and disposal (see page 254)

Paints and solvents

Paint and wood treatment products often release VOCs (Volatile Organic Compounds), chemicals which contribute to atmospheric pollution and may aggravate asthma. Many preservatives, paints and stains are now clearly labelled to indicate whether they release low, medium, high or very high levels of VOCs, enabling you to make informed choices when you buy.

When you have finished painting, always make sure you dispose of paint products responsibly, never into drains or watercourses. Ideally, buy the amount you need and use it up; or give it to someone else to use, or donate it to charity. Contact your local Environmental Health Department for details of disposal or recycling facilities for paint. Remember that choosing water-based paints means you can wash your brushes out in water, and so can avoid using and disposing of white spirit; but do remove as much paint as possible from your brushes and rollers before washing them, to minimise the amount of paint that goes down the drain.

Encouraging wildlife

Colourful butterflies, choruses of birds, busy insects: wildlife in the garden will give the whole family something to watch, listen to and learn about. Better still, these creatures' interactions with one another can help you create a naturally beautiful garden, without the need for chemicals or pesticides. Growing flowering herbs such as santolina, lavender, sage or rosemary attracts ladybirds, lacewings and hoverflies, which all prey on greenfly and other pests. Useful visitors also include tits, which love aphids, and thrushes, which feast on slugs and snails.

Wildlife-friendly pest controls

Encouraging natural predators that will eat pests is the number one alternative to chemicals. On top of prevention, there are alternatives to chemical controls. For example, try using copper-tape slug barriers around pots of tender annuals (see page 255). Or leave out strategically placed 'traps' overnight – grapefruit rinds or shallow dishes filled with beer. These attract slugs and snails: you just have to round up and destroy the captives first thing in the morning. If you have the stomach for it, you could even go out there with a torch after dark and pick them off your plants.

Water

Britain is fortunate to enjoy a temperate climate: cold, but not arctic, in winter; warm, but not scorching, in summer. And it rains all year round. So there is really no need to put premium-quality purified drinking water on our gardens. A single rain butt catching the run-off from roofs and gutters can often be enough to supply the needs of the average garden (see page 253). Water is constantly being lost from the ground through evaporation. On beds and borders you can help to slow that process by spreading a thick layer of mulch over any exposed soil (see page 191). Natural mulches such as chipped bark or cocoa shells will add nutrients to the soil as they break down. Or you could use your own garden compost made from plant cuttings and uncooked vegetable waste (see pages 192–93).

Most water companies in England and Wales now require customers who use sprinklers or any unattended garden watering device to have a water meter installed. Contact your water supplier for details.

wise watering

- Water thoroughly, and preferably no more than once a week
- Water plants in the evening to minimise water loss through evaporation, especially in hot weather
- Potted plants are dependent on the water we give them: grouping them together helps to hold in moisture. Move them out of the sun during long hot spells
- Stand pots on a layer of moist gravel to increase humidity – this works for house plants too
- Line sides of terracotta pots with plastic to retain moisture
- Mix water-retentive crystals with the potting compost of containers and baskets to slow drying out
- Don't water unnecessarily: some plants thrive in hot, dry conditions that mimic their native climate; the flavour and scent of many herbs is enhanced by dry growing conditions
- No time to do the watering yourself? Install an irrigation system, which will direct water to exactly where it's needed
- If you do use a sprinkler, an oscillating type that swings back and forth will distribute the water most efficiently

Gardens for all

Outdoor living should be for everyone. Gardens can give just as much pleasure to people with physical or sensory disabilities. With careful planning and creative thinking, you can make the benefits of an outdoor room available to all who might enjoy it.

Stepping out

For people who are less steady on their feet, it's vital that surfaces are level and non-slip. Sudden small changes in level, for example from flat paving to raised cobblestones, can easily become a trip hazard. The same is true of small depressions, which may also trap frozen puddles in winter. Wooden deck boards should be laid with the grooved side up, and new concrete paths topped with gravel when still wet, or tamped to a rough non-slip finish. There are specially formulated patio cleaners that will remove slippery moss and algae growth, and patio sealants that will help prevent it returning.

Handrails running along the side of paths can be a huge help. They can also serve as tapping rails for a blind or partially sighted person. And don't forget to keep pathways clear of tree branches and other low-hanging obstacles.

Planning for different users

Different disabilities create different needs, so think carefully about any individual who will use your outdoor space: contrasting surface textures, such as the changes from paving slabs to loose gravel to grass, can be very helpful to people with a visual impairment, signalling a change in direction or the location of a feature such as a seat. But loose surfaces are not suitable for wheelchair users, and a lawn can be awkward and muddy. Paths need to be wider to accommodate a wheelchair – a width of 1.5–2m is ideal, allowing a pedestrian and wheelchair user to pass comfortably. In a small garden that may be excessive, but there should still be plenty of space for a wheelchair to turn at points within the garden and outside the door into the house. Raised path edging, securely laid in mortar, will prevent wheelchairs straying from paths and possibly tipping. Be sure to check that gates and doorways are wide enough for a wheelchair to pass.

Stepping up and down

It's necessary to move from one level to another at some point in order to get around most gardens. When it comes to steps, it's the details that can make all the difference to a physically impaired person. The risers – the vertical faces of the steps – should all be the same height, no lower than 100mm or higher than 150mm. The treads – the horizontal part – should never be less than 300mm from front to back. Rounded edges and non-slip treads will also help to minimise the risk of falls and injuries. Handrails will not only give extra support and safety, but they'll encourage a feeling of confidence and independence in the user.

Steps can of course be completely impassable for many wheelchair users. So where possible, replace them with a ramp on a gentle slope of no more than 8%.

Easy does it

For the gardener with a disability, narrower beds and borders are much easier to manage: no more than a metre deep is best. If getting down to ground level is awkward, raised beds and planters can be much more comfortable, especially if all areas are within easy reach. When deciding what to grow in them, take into account the eventual height of the plants you choose. There are lots of lower growing plants, including herbs, alpines and summer bedding, that will thrive in raised beds and containers and are ideal for gardeners unable to reach up high. Espalier or cordon-trained fruit trees (see page 244) are fantastic in any small garden and can be reached from a wheelchair or garden seat.

The right tools can also make a huge difference. There are dozens of easy-grip, lightweight, angled and long-handled tools that will enable disabled people to enjoy gardening to the full (see pages 178–83).

Remember too that there are lots of features that will add interest to a garden without adding to the workload of maintaining it: a bird table, for example, or water feature. See pages 32–33 for other tips on creating a low-maintenance garden.

Sensory delights

It's possible to create a rich sensory environment in the garden that will open up a whole new world of experiences. Sights, sounds, textures, tastes and smells all contribute to the joys of outdoor living for people with or without a disability.

Scent

Your sensory garden might be enjoyed from a bench beneath a shaded alcove of roses, jasmine and honeysuckle, whose delicate scents will restore the most frazzled of spirits. Or it might hold the unexpected pleasures of scented foliage such as rosemary, thyme, mint or lemon balm, grown where they will be brushed against or trodden on to release their fragrance.

Sound

A garden can be music to the ears: the swish of the breeze through long grasses, the tinkle of a windchime, the gentle hum of insects, the crunch of footsteps on gravel, or the meditative quality of moving water, whether a rushing cascade or a trickling fountain. Sound can also be a practical help to people who are visually impaired, providing fixed aural landmarks that will help them find their way around.

Touch

From the felt-like softness of lambs' ears (*Stachys byzantina*, see page 308) to the tickle of furry catkins, the tactile aspect of a sensory garden is irresistible. You can tickle the tastebuds, too, with garden-grown treats – just grow fruit-bearing trees and bushes somewhere easy to harvest. Or simply sit on soft grass and feel the sun and breeze on your skin.

Colour

Flowers, shrubs and trees can all bring seasonal colour to the garden, while ornaments, pots and containers, and decorative paints and stains can colour the space all year round. Use colour to create mood: cool, harmonious colours are calm and relaxing; hot and bright colours are vibrant and energising, and can give particular pleasure to people with partial sight. See pages 42–45 for more ideas on using colour outdoors.

Safe and sound

Avoiding accidents outdoors is largely a matter of common sense.
But do give some time to thinking through where potential dangers may
lie in your garden, especially if you have a young family or friends who
visit with children. Just a bit of care and forethought will go a long way
towards preventing accidents in your outdoor room.

Hazardous garden products

Does your garden shed contain a collection of old and half-
empty containers of paints, thinners, weedkillers, pesticides
and fertilisers? If this sounds familiar, beware: you may be
harbouring a store of toxic chemicals. What's more, some of
them may no longer be legal. Many garden chemicals, including
common ones like creosote, have recently been banned. Don't
be tempted to pour chemicals down the drain. The only safe
and legal way to dispose of them is at an official local authority
rubbish dump. Visit www.pesticidedisposal.org for a list of
approved sites, or contact your local council for advice.

For those products you do need to keep, make sure that all
containers are clearly labelled and have tight-fitting lids, and
that cans are not rusting, bulging or leaking. Chemicals –
diluted or undiluted – should never be stored in drink bottles or
food containers, or anywhere within reach of children. Always
read the label for directions on use and storage, and check the
safety instructions in the store, before you take a product to the
till. That way you can pick up any protective gear – gloves,
goggles, breathing masks – at the same time, and you won't
be tempted to go without.

If you use a shed or garage to store chemicals, make sure
it's secure, well ventilated and properly lit. And don't smoke
in there, as chemical fumes can easily ignite.

Keep it clean and tidy

Most garden injuries are caused not by the tools or plants
themselves, but by our mishandling of them. A regular routine
of cleaning and maintenance will help keep hazards to a
minimum. We wouldn't trip over wires and hose pipes if
we didn't leave them lying around, and neither would we slip
on paths if they were clean and adequately lit. Neglecting
maintenance won't just damage your health. It may hurt your
wallet. A few spots of rust on a metal hinge may look innocent
enough, but they could easily cause your gate or garden
furniture to collapse. Spend some time looking around your
outdoor room: inspect potential trouble spots and deal with
them early.

Using and storing tools

When you buy a new tool for your garden, always read the
instructions and follow them. Put on any protective gear
provided, and make sure you understand how to stop, start
and use the tool safely. When not in use, hand and power tools
should be put away tidily, well out of the reach of children, as
curious fingers cause accidents. And whatever work you do in
the garden – whether it's digging, hoeing, mowing, raking or
watering – opt for sturdy footwear.

introduction

Water in the garden

Ponds are fantastic for attracting wildlife, and paddling pools are great for splashing around in. But for a young child they can be lethal. Constant supervision around a paddling pool may be realistic, but a permanent pond can be too great a risk. Small ponds and pools can be made safe by installing a rigid galvanised iron grille just below the surface of the water. However, this is an expensive solution as such a grille must be specially designed and fitted. An alternative is to erect fencing and a gate with a childproof lock. Or you could simply decide to play safe and fill it in while the children are small. That doesn't mean you cannot have water in the garden: there are many small water features on the market, powered by solar panels or low-voltage electricity, that gently trickle a small amount of water into a shallow reservoir hidden underground.

Safe barbecuing

No outdoor room is complete without a barbecue (see pages 352–59). Here are some tips for enjoying your barbecue safely.

---

safe barbecuing

- Burning charcoal or gas produces poisonous carbon monoxide, so position a barbecue away from a doorway
- Always place it on a flat, stable and hard surface, clear of fences, buildings or overhanging trees
- Only light it using solid or liquid barbecue firelighters that are sold specifically for that purpose
- Don't move a barbecue once it's lit
- Never leave a barbecue unattended
- Too many cooks can spoil a barbecue: only one person should be in charge of the cooking
- Avoid drinking alcohol before or while barbecuing
- Barbecue chefs should be dressed for the occasion: avoid trailing sleeves or ties; wear flame-retardant gloves (ordinary oven gloves aren't safe enough); and use long-handled tools to turn food over
- Check that meat is cooked right through before serving; it may be charred on the outside but still raw in the middle
- When the party is over, let your barbecue cool down overnight before you touch or clean it. Don't let children play unsupervised until it is completely cold

---

Safe electrics

Any electrical equipment that runs at mains voltage and is used outdoors must be protected by an RCD (residual current device) rated at 30 milliamps. This will cut off the energy supply in a fraction of a second if it detects an earth leakage, caused, for example, by accidentally cutting through an electrical flex with a hedge trimmer or other tool, reducing the risk of a fatal electric shock. An outdoor socket must be protected by an RCD; indoor sockets used to power outdoor appliances can have a plug-in RCD (pictured). Even with an RCD, it remains very important to observe basic safety precautions: unplug all electrical tools when not in use, and never, ever clean or adjust them while they're plugged in.

New regulations

Since 1 January 2005, new laws have required anyone carrying out electrical work in a home or garden in England or Wales to notify their Local Authority Building Control Department, which has responsibility for ensuring the work is inspected and tested. See page 373 for further details.

Harmful plants

A surprising number of plants contain toxins. While some of these are actually dangerous to humans, many more cause minor yet uncomfortable effects like skin irritation, including popular garden plants such as euphorbia (below). Check labels when you buy for any warnings, and if in doubt, leave it out.

Often, however, it simply isn't possible to eliminate everything potentially harmful from a garden. A mature yew tree, for example, may be protected by law – despite its poisonous berries. Children will often confuse bright berries, bulbs and seed pods with sweets or familiar vegetables. It's up to adults to teach them what can and cannot be eaten.

Dense prickly shrubs are not advisable in beds where children are likely to lose a football. However, they can be a useful deterrent to intruders. Wear long sleeves and gloves when pruning to help keep your arms from getting scratched.

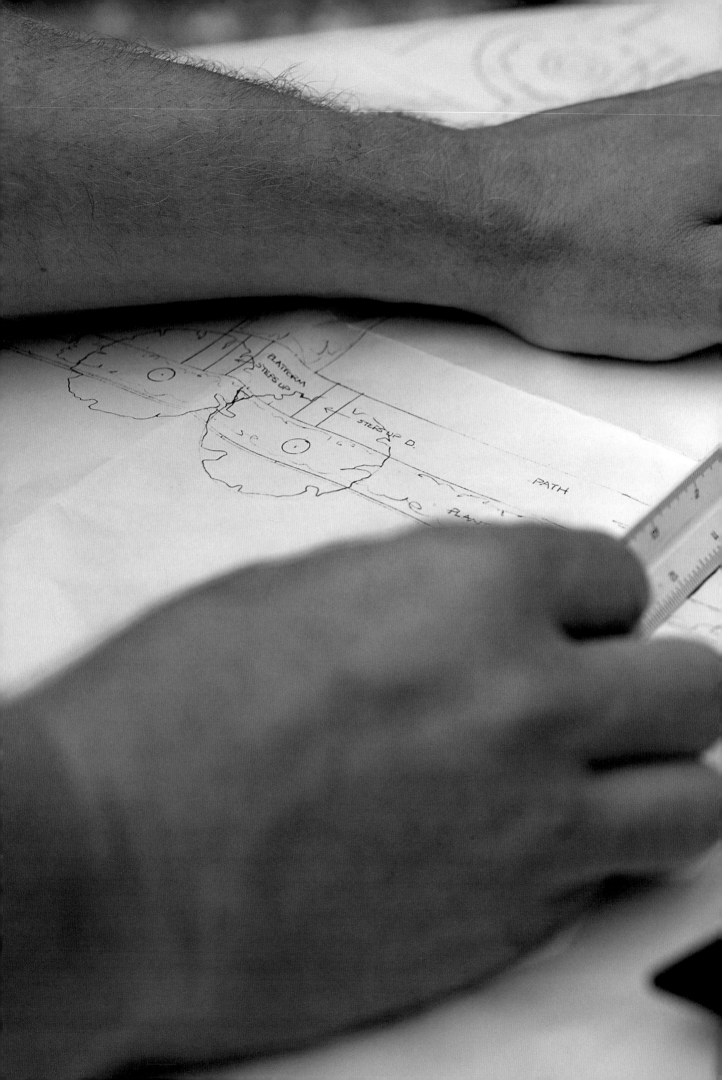

Play, cook, entertain, eat, relax, exercise, escape, grow flowers, fruit or vegetables – what do you see yourself doing in your outdoor space? The way to create a really successful outdoor room is to start by thinking about who will use it, when and how. Your garden holds so much possibility: with careful planning, you will be amazed how much you can achieve.

an outdoor room for you

Your ideal space

The very first step in any new garden design is simply to sit in the space you want to change. Look around you, look at your property, look at those surrounding you. Are you surrounded by wall-to-wall houses that you'd prefer to see less of? Or do you have a wonderful view you could gaze at for hours? Are you happy with some of the garden's existing features, or do you dream of a complete makeover? Think about who you are and how you live. Do you picture yourself relaxing with a chilled glass of wine and a good book on a sunny summer's day? Or are you more likely to have earth-encrusted hands and a home-grown salad for supper? Do you long for a secret garden retreat, a place to escape from the world and all its pressures? Maybe you envisage yourself surrounded by friends and family, enjoying laughter and long lazy lunches on the patio. Or perhaps you have children who want to play football or have fun in the fresh air.

Outdoor fun and relaxation

Younger children love being in the great outdoors, especially if there is something to tempt them out there: sprinklers and paddling pools, climbing frames and playhouses, open spaces to run around in and mysterious nooks and crannies where they can make secret dens. A summerhouse or wooden garden building can be transformed into a teenage palace for weekend sleepovers and hanging out with friends; it might even enable you to banish their loud music and mess from the house.

But today's outdoor room is not only for those with a family to occupy. The stress of commuting and spending long days at work can be hard to shrug off. Even if it is nothing more than a few square metres of patio or a balcony, a garden can be transformed into a restful place in which to unwind. Comfortable seating, subdued lighting, fragrant flowers and herbs, plants that sway and rustle in the breeze – all will contribute towards resting the mind. If entertaining colleagues and friends comes high on your list of priorities, you can indulge in al fresco dining in chic contemporary surroundings. A generous patio or deck will give plenty of seating room, while a spectacular water feature, statue or dramatic lighting will create a talking point and give a stylish focus to your outdoor space.

Gardens for getting together

If your friends and family are always dropping round, if you love to
eat and drink and share good times, then your outdoor room should
be a sociable space, designed for getting people together.

Sharing the pleasure

Your garden can be many things: an expression of your taste
and personality, a creation to be proud of and a space to share.
This environment filled with colour, scent, texture and sound
can give huge pleasure to your friends and family too.

When planning a garden, it adds an extra dimension if
you take a moment to picture yourself celebrating a friend's
birthday out there. People love to dress up for a party, and so
they need to feel clean and comfortable. Think about surfaces:
lawns can remain muddy and damp long after the sun comes
out, whereas a patio or deck will dry off in half an hour, making
your plans much less vulnerable to the odd shower. Think too
about providing shelter from both sun and breeze. A parasol
will shade the sun – especially important when sitting down
to dine outdoors, when the direct glare of the sun can become
very uncomfortable. A summerhouse can be a delightful
escape from a brisk breeze without needing to retreat indoors
or bundle on coats and jumpers. A patio heater will take the nip
out of the air, especially as a balmy summer's afternoon turns
into the cool of the evening. And as darkness falls, your guests
will love to huddle around the warming glow of an outdoor
fireplace or chiminea.

For bigger gatherings – and bigger gardens – think about
creating a collection of spaces, so people can split into smaller
groups and multiple conversations. Grown-ups and kids alike
adore seeking out private nooks and corners. Entice your
guests with invitations to explore: an arch, path or walkway that
leads to an area hidden from view. Allow lots of seating space –
not just chairs, but maybe low walls to perch on, a bench, swing
seat or tree seat. A few cushions will soften all-weather
outdoor furniture in metal or wood.

One of the most effective ways to transform a garden into
party mode is lighting. Who can resist the magical lure of fairy
lights strung through the branches of the trees in the garden?
Solar-powered lights will do away with the need for an outside
power supply. Placed either side of a path, they can light the
way, drawing people further into the garden, perhaps to a pond
with underwater lighting illuminating the lilies from below.

A garden designed for get-togethers will encourage them.
It will draw people outside and inspire spontaneous barbecues
and impromptu picnics. Adults will follow kids, kids follow
adults, as everyone spills forth to enjoy the pleasures of
your outdoor room.

Gardens for getting away

The garden can be the perfect place to relax, soothed by the sounds, scents and colours of the natural world. It's a space to get away from everyday pressures, recharge your batteries and recover your sense of perspective. That might mean simply sitting and reflecting in a quiet corner; or it might see you harvesting fresh salad leaves for supper. Everyone is different, and our gardens can reflect that too.

Gardens for relaxation

One of the easiest, cheapest and most satisfying ways of calming your frazzled state is spending unpressurised time in your outdoor space. There can be few things better than finding a quiet spot, away from everyone, where it's possible to sit and catch your breath for a moment. Switch off your mind and let your senses take over: listen to the gentle trickle of water tumbling from a fountain; walk barefoot across soft grass; feel the breeze on your skin. The benefits of lavender oil, favoured by aromatherapists for its relaxing properties, can be obtained simply by planting a bush beside a seating area; as you brush a hand over it, its calming scent will surround you.

The more you relax and find stillness outdoors, the more you will observe – and the more all the creatures who inhabit your garden will carry on as if you weren't present. Birds, insects, squirrels, fish, frogs – you might be surprised and delighted by how busy it can get out there. The gentle sounds they make can soothe and relax you, making your garden a magical place and a healing force in your life.

Planning to relax

It's important to design a garden not purely from an aesthetic or practical point of view, but with a mind to spending relaxation time in it. How a person chooses to relax, what they find restful, varies from one individual to another. For some it means doing nothing at all, while others need activity to clear the mind and refresh the spirit. Consider which type you are – it might be both – and create your outdoor space accordingly.

For those who like to do

The inactivity of a desk-bound job can leave you with bundles of nervous energy that needs to be burned off. Joining a gym is one answer, but why not invest the membership fee into a garden instead? A garden is constantly available without the need to travel, and can be planned according to the activity level you desire. You might have a lawn that needs mowing and feeding, lots of plants that require snipping and pruning, hedges that need cutting and leaves that need sweeping. You could plant a vegetable and fruit plot and enjoy the rewards of your efforts with a home-grown healthy supper. You could even create a dedicated space for outdoor exercise or yoga.

For those who like to relax

A garden can provide a special place to be at one with yourself and nature, away from the world's pressures and demands. Plan in fences, hedges and tall plants to shield all or part of the space from prying eyes. A sunken area such as a deck surrounded by tall planting will instantly create a sense of immersion in nature and separation from the rest of the world. Add in low-level lighting, a gazebo or pergola clothed with perfumed plants – roses which release their scent during the heat of the day, jasmine to perfume the cooler night air – and you have a place to unwind in, whatever the time of day. Seating plays a vital role too. Concentrate on comfortable furniture for lounging in. You might install a suspended swing seat, or a hammock, available nowadays complete with hanging frame, doing away with the need for trees or poles on which to secure it. Add a pebble fountain to bubble gently in the background, maybe even a spa, and the strains and stresses of life are sure to ebb away.

The best of both worlds

Deciding how much activity and relaxation you want is all part of designing the garden that works best for you. A balance between the two can be achieved in the most modest-sized plots. If you have the space, you could create a series of 'rooms' within one garden. Partitioning even a small garden in this way doesn't in fact create a feeling of claustrophobia, but has the opposite effect. Quiet secluded spots at the bottom of the garden are an ideal place to escape to, all the more so if they cannot be seen from elsewhere in the garden.

Finding your garden style

The style of garden that suits you best is a matter of individual taste, reflecting your particular likes and dislikes, the style of your home and how you live. You could be influenced and inspired by any number of garden traditions, from this country and around the world.

The classical garden

The splendid formal gardens of many of Britain's stately homes typify the classical garden, none more so than Hampton Court Palace. But you don't need acres of land to achieve the look for yourself; this is a style that suits the average-sized garden very well indeed. Neat circles, straight lines and symmetry are the order of the day, with beds often flanked by low hedges of clipped box or lavender. Planting schemes are often very simple and monochromatic, emphasising structure and creating a restful, relaxing space in which to sit. With careful planning and plant choice, this style of garden can be very low-maintenance. The more topiary there is, the more clipping will be needed annually, but choosing plants with a slow growth rate will reduce this; box needs only one or two trims to keep it neat and tidy. For tall, standard topiary forms, bay or holly will look good all year round with only one cut.

The cottage garden

An abundance of flowers and colour, rustic arches and fencing of woven willow all typify the traditional cottage-style garden. These are the gardens of romance and chocolate boxes, with annuals, perennials, shrubs, roses and vegetables all jostling for position. Created with pastels, they can be very soothing on the eye, but an altogether more energetic feel can be produced using hot, vibrant colours. Despite looking very relaxed, with everything crammed in together, such gardens are actually among the most labour-intensive; it takes a great deal of effort and control to achieve that look of casual abandon. See pages 64–73 for how to create your own version of the traditional cottage garden.

The contemporary garden

Contemporary gardens are not just about straight lines and gleaming stainless steel; they simply use modern all-weather materials, often in unusual ways, to create chic, living, up-to-the-minute art. Although this style works well regardless of the size of the garden, it can be one of the best approaches to adopt for smaller spaces. Courtyard gardens, modest backyards and balconies can all be successfully brought to life simply, cheaply and very stylishly, creating gardens that require a minimum of maintenance. The materials used – slate, glass, steel, concrete – require very little attention once installed. Planting is usually restricted to a few large dramatic plants and groupings of species such as bamboo. Once established, these need little more than watering and the occasional feed. Installing automatic watering systems does away with the former task, while slow release fertiliser applied in the spring takes care of the latter in one easy annual step. Planting through weed-suppressing membranes (see page 33), then mulching with one of the many loose mulches now available, can make this an almost maintenance-free style of garden.

The Mediterranean garden

This garden tradition is all about people being together, with family and friends dining al fresco, recalling happy memories of times spent on holiday. Colour plays a vital role in this style, as does light. Walls are often rendered and painted: warm shades of terracotta, bright sky blue, or simple crisp whitewash all work equally well. Succulents, olive trees and geraniums all add to the picture. These are often grown in terracotta pots, allowing them to be moved somewhere warm for the winter. Patio tables and chairs, frequently made of metal with a distressed paint finish, recall those found at Mediterranean roadside cafés. Paths and patios are made from terracotta slabs or soft honey-coloured stone. The essence of this style is relaxed and informal, with less emphasis upon the horticultural aspect of gardening and more upon creating an outdoor living space. In the UK, however, it's important to bear in mind that this sort of treatment needs a sheltered south- or south-west-facing spot. Gardens with a cold northern or eastern aspect would appear very gloomy, and the planting would not thrive.

The Japanese garden

The essence of a Japanese garden is contemplation. It is the polar opposite of the chaotic modern lifestyle. Less is definitely more; this style of garden is characterised by a simple enclosed space, with gravel and a few carefully positioned boulders. Traditionally, the gravel would be raked over and new patterns created daily, symbolising a spiritual cleansing and a readiness to face the dawn anew. Rhododendrons, bonsai and bamboo are classic ingredients of this garden. Water is another important element, not in the form of a gushing fountain, but the serene drip of a deer scarer, a bamboo pole balanced to tip to and fro with the flow of the water. This may not be the best choice of style for those with an energetic young family, but it's certainly ideal for busy people with little time to maintain a garden.

You can do it...

Seeking inspiration

Annual shows like the Chelsea Flower Show are a wonderful way to find up-to-the-minute garden inspiration. In the display gardens created for such events, you can see for yourself the work of some of today's best garden designers.

B&Q

The low-maintenance garden

All gardens, regardless of size, need some form of regular upkeep. Planning how much time you can devote to this is an important stage in garden design. Some elements require a lot more work than others, so your decisions now can make a big difference in the long run.

The truth about lawns

Once a garden is built and planted, the single most demanding element on your time and effort will almost certainly be the lawn. Even the most natural lawn, complete with a sprinkling of weeds and flowers will, at the very least, require mowing once a week during the growing season. An immaculate expanse of turf will need considerably more care. Having a hard edging that sits flush with the ground will at least eliminate the need to trim the edges: you can just mow straight over the top (see page 267). You could consider converting all or part of your lawn to a wildflower meadow, which is less work to maintain than a conventional lawn (see pages 274–75).

Easy-care surfaces

All gardens need some areas of all-weather hard surfacing – patios, paths and drives. The less earth in your garden, the less work is required: it's a simple equation. But that need not mean great expanses of ugly concrete. Paving slabs, bricks and blocks come in a wide range of tones and finishes. Plants in pots, ornaments and furniture can all add interest and colour to areas of hard surfacing. Decorative gravel is another option: this provides a durable surface, but one through which plants can be planted directly into the soil, meaning they will need less looking after (see page 203). Because of the noise it makes when walked on, gravel can also be a deterrent to thieves.

You can do it...

Low-maintenance checklist

Surfaces
A lawn is usually the most labour-intensive element in a garden. Paved or gravelled areas need least work.

Boundaries
Walls can be expensive but are virtually maintenance-free.

Beds and borders
Prepare the ground thoroughly; ensure all areas can be accessed without walking on the soil; mulch bare earth in spring.

Planting
Choose self-clinging climbers, slow-growing evergreen shrubs, and vigorous ground-cover plants.

Weed prevention
Plant through a layer of weed-control fabric.

Watering
Mulch to retain moisture in beds; add water-retentive crystals to containers; install an automatic watering system.

B&Q

Creating boundaries

Wall, fence or hedge? A new wall is the most expensive option, but once built, it is by far the best investment in terms of time management. It will require little or no maintenance. Fences, even if pressure-treated, will require regular application of timber preservative to prolong their useful life.

Hedges come in all shapes and sizes, some more manageable than others. When planting a new hedge it is essential to give honest consideration to the time you want to spend cutting it. Box will take some years to reach its mature height, yew even longer, but these will require only one or two trims per year. The ever popular Leyland cypress grows much more rapidly, but often needs three or more cuts a year to keep it within acceptable boundaries. Investing in a power hedge trimmer will make the task of cutting any hedge a great deal easier (see page 183).

Pots and containers

Plants in pots are a great way of softening the look of areas of hard surfacing. Topiary or shrubs in containers require very little in the way of routine attention apart from watering, feeding and trimming; they will, however, need a little more care in the spring when they should be top-dressed with fresh compost or re-potted as necessary. Pots and hanging baskets planted with seasonal bedding will need more attention. Water-retentive crystals mixed with the potting compost will delay drying out. Even better, install a watering system with an outlet to each pot; add a programmable timer switch and you won't even have to remember to turn the water on and off (see page 252).

Weed-free beds

Weed-control fabric suppresses annual weeds, while allowing air and water to pass through to the soil. Easy to apply and easy to disguise, this is a great fast-track to low-maintenance beds and borders.

1 Prepare the ground in the usual way, by digging and working in soil improver and fertiliser (see pages 190–91). Lay the fabric over the entire area and place your plants, still in pots, in position on top. Make cuts in the shape of a cross in each planting position and tuck under the flaps.

2 Plant through the holes. This method is ideal for slow-growing, low-maintenance evergreen shrubs such as pieris, holly and gaultheria.

Manageable beds and borders

The most important stage in creating a new bed or border is the preparation. Take the time to clear perennial weeds (see page 254) and you will save yourself years of work and frustration. Bear in mind that small areas are easier to maintain than large ones. If possible, lay out beds and borders so that they are accessible without the need to walk through them. This makes it possible to work on them even when the weather has been wet, and by not compacting the soil, you will avoid the need to dig them; a hoe or cultivator (see page 181) will be enough.

Selecting plants

Choosing the right plant for the growing conditions is the biggest time-saver of all. Rose-beds need far more attention than shrub-beds, especially if the shrubs are slow-growing evergreens (see pages 297–303). Annuals may need staking in spring and clearing in autumn; instead, go for perennials, including vigorous ground-cover plants that will keep weeds at bay (see page 314). And select self-clinging or twining climbers such as ivy, virginia creeper or clematis, which will happily scale a vertical surface without extra support (page 204).

Mulching

Once a border is planted, the single most effective step you can take to reduce the work of maintaining it is to apply a generous layer of mulch such as chipped bark, garden compost or cocoa shells (see page 191). Do this annually, in early spring, and you will reduce the need for both watering and weeding throughout the coming year. Even more effective is to plant through weed-control fabric (see below).

tools materials
- **gardening gloves**
- **spade**
- **fork**
- **craft knife**
- **trowel**

- soil improver
- fertiliser
- weed-control fabric
- plants
- loose mulch

3 Cover the area with chipped bark, gravel or other mulch to a depth of about 7cm. Any weeds that germinate in this layer will have a very shallow root run, making them simple to remove.

We all have wishes and dreams for what we might like to do with our outdoor space – here we show you how to turn those visions into a successful and workable garden design.

be your own garden designer

Finding inspiration

Inspiration for gardens can come from many sources – books and magazines; holidays; TV, films and paintings; other gardens, public and private. You could take a tip from interior designers and create a mood board – a collection of snapshots, cuttings, swatches and inspirational images, all stuck together on one big sheet of paper or card. This can be a great way to develop an overall theme for your garden.

Once you have thought through how you want your garden to look, and who will use it, when and how – what next? This is the time to start putting the various elements together to create your own garden design.

Design in practice

Designing a garden isn't rocket science, but there are lots of tricks and know-how that will help you make a success of it. On the one hand it's about indulging in dreams and fantasies, as outrageous as you like; on the other it's about squaring up to realities – everything from the conditions of your site and the limitations of your budget, to mundane questions of where the lawnmower, washing line and dustbins will go.

The climate of your garden will inevitably play a big part in your plans. That means both where you are in the country, and the individual conditions of your outdoor space – which direction it faces, how exposed or sheltered it is, how much sunlight it receives, what type of soil you have, and whether it drains efficiently or not. All these circumstances need to be observed and respected if your plans are to be a success.

Don't expect to get it right first time. Scribbling and sketching, rubbing things out and starting again is all part of the process. Taking time to think through your ideas first, before starting work or going shopping, will save many headaches in the long run. It will enable you to think through the practicalities of realising your vision with the minimum of cost, time and trouble.

Taking charge

Being the designer of your own garden gives you all the choices. Even if, once designed, the project is too large to contemplate undertaking yourself, or there just isn't the time, a fully thought-out design will put you in the driving seat, steering the contractors.

WATER FEATURE

1:25

0

25

How to think like a designer

Designers constantly strive to make connections between the different features in a garden – echoing its shapes from one side to another, and linking elements visually and with walkways. This is how they ensure that all the various parts of a design form a coherent whole.

Interest and surprise

The best and most interesting gardens are those where it is not possible to see the entire garden at once. Areas hidden from view, curving paths which lead the eye down the garden, and focal points in the distance all encourage exploration and discovery. Parts of the garden concealed by hedges or fences, or linked by archways that partially screen them from view, create a sense of mystery and curiosity – even if they are just areas that house the rubbish bins.

A place to sit

Seating areas in a garden can be about much more than just chairs or a bench. Positioning them among interesting planting will make them a far more enticing place to pause and relax. And don't just think in terms of the visual: fragrance plays an important part here too. You might plant scented climbers to grow up and over a pergola or trellis. Or herbs planted within a gravelled area or nearby bed will release their perfume when brushed against with hands or feet. Think also about what you will be looking at. Any seat should come with a view, something that either draws the eye up or down the garden or provides a focal point upon which to gaze.

Framing a view

A small garden will appear bigger if the boundaries between it and the outside are blurred. Framing a view is one way to do this. A mature tree in the distance will seem to be drawn in and become part of the garden if the planting is planned to leave a space through which it can be glimpsed. Gardens that back onto open countryside or parkland will appear more spacious if the boundary is kept low, allowing a view of the landscape beyond.

Creating an illusion

Fooling the eye into seeing something that isn't there is a great way of making a garden not only more interesting but seem bigger. Fixing a door to a solid wall will create the illusion that there is more garden beyond. A visual 'hole' can be created in a wall at the back of a flower-bed with a circular mirror that will reflect the planting. A mirror can also be used to make a shallow bed appear twice the depth, or to create the illusion of a room beyond if fixed to a garden wall and framed with an archway. (But don't position mirrors too high, as birds can become confused and fly into them.) Different colours can affect our perception of distance. A bench or wall at the end of a garden will make the boundary seem further away if it is painted white or pale blue than if it is a darker colour (see page 44).

WATER FEATURE

How to think
like a designer

When garden designers first consider a plot they don't home in on the problems – the boggy bit under the washing line, the fence that wobbles in the slightest breeze. They look at the size and shape of the space, its aspect (the direction it faces), and the style of the house and surrounding area.

Looking at the big picture

Everyone has particular likes and dislikes, in gardens as in anything else. But when designing a garden, it's very important to look at the whole picture – plants or features that you like in isolation may not fit into a broader scheme that is in sympathy with its surroundings and its situation. For a really successful garden, it pays to plan the space as a whole, not as separate and self-contained bits. This applies even if you're intending to make over only one section, either because you don't need to start from scratch or because your budget won't stretch to doing all the work in one go. If there is a secret to good garden design, this is it: it isn't just about fitting a collection of plants and features into an available space, but about bringing them together in a way that feels harmonious and deliberate. A good garden is always greater than the sum of its parts.

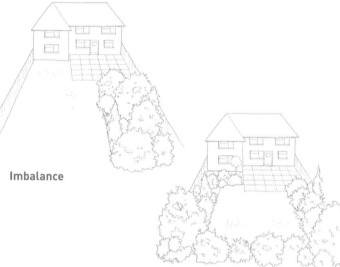

Imbalance

Balance

Getting the balance right

Achieving balance is one of the most important aspects of garden design. But it's one of those things that is usually only obvious when it is lacking: one part of the garden seems busy and cramped, another empty. This is simple enough to avoid: pay equal attention to all areas, and avoid concentrating on one part at the expense of another, or leaving any obvious gaps. When planning the planting, remember to consider the changing seasons. If one side is planted mainly with evergreens and the other side with herbaceous perennials, the garden might look wonderful in summer but become decidedly unbalanced in the winter once the perennials have died back.

Proportion

Linked with balance, and equally important, is proportion. A huge timber pergola marching up a narrow garden will merely emphasise the narrowness and overwhelm the space. If you want to plant a tree in the middle of a large lawn, on the other hand, choose one with good height and spread, as a tiny tree in a vast lawn can look like a toy. The same applies to any other feature – the bigger the space, the more imposing whatever you put in it needs to be, or it will get 'lost'.

Shaping the space

Seen from above, almost all gardens are composed of a mix of circles and rectangles or parts of these shapes. Cutting out several squares, circles and rectangles in varying sizes and playing with them on a flat surface will help you develop ideas for the layout of your garden, and how this might affect its feel and flow. Try overlapping them to see what works best with what. A square garden doesn't have to have a square lawn, nor do patios have to be rectangular or square.

Formal or informal

Formality in gardens is associated with sharp straight lines, crisp corners and neat circles. The layout of a formal garden may not be symmetrical, but it will be orderly and geometric. Planting is restrained and relatively minimal: tidy box hedges surrounding beds containing just one or two different plants, with clipped topiary carefully positioned to punctuate the space.

Informality in gardens, on the other hand, is associated with organic, curved and irregular forms. Planting is much more free and easy. Borders are mixed and climbers scramble up and over vertical structures and surfaces.

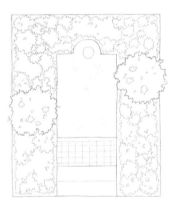 

Formal **Informal**

Symmetry in garden design

Gardens with symmetrical layouts usually do look more formal, especially if their shapes are rectangular or square. Despite the sometimes harsh lines, symmetrical spaces are very restful upon the eye, as the brain has to work only half as hard to analyse the overall image. However, a formal, symmetrical design will tend to emphasise boundaries rather than blurring them. The average-sized garden will usually appear bigger if planned and planted asymmetrically.

Symmetry **Asymmetry**

Designing to a grid

One approach to designing a garden is to plan it on a grid based on the facade of the property. This involves taking careful measurements across windows, doors, areas of masonry and any other feature, then drawing evenly spaced lines out from these on a plan. Graph paper is very useful for this. There may be fence posts that divide the space evenly along the length of the garden; if not, then simply use the same measurement in each direction and make a grid of squares. Take some photocopies of your grid and sketch in different layout ideas, always being guided by the lines.

Designing to a grid in this way can be a useful discipline, especially for the inexperienced, and will help to produce a garden that looks and feels right for your home.

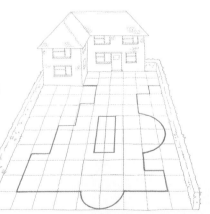 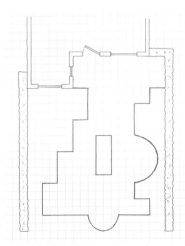

How to think like a designer

Designers constantly strive to make connections between the different features in a garden –
echoing its shapes from one side to another, and linking elements visually and with walkways.
This is how they ensure that all the various parts of a design form a coherent whole.

Interest and surprise

The best and most interesting gardens are those where it is not
possible to see the entire garden at once. Areas hidden from
view, curving paths which lead the eye down the garden, and
focal points in the distance all encourage exploration and
discovery. Parts of the garden concealed by hedges or fences,
or linked by archways that partially screen them from view,
create a sense of mystery and curiosity – even if they are
just areas that house the rubbish bins.

A place to sit

Seating areas in a garden can be about much more than just
chairs or a bench. Positioning them among interesting planting
will make them a far more enticing place to pause and relax.
And don't just think in terms of the visual: fragrance plays an
important part here too. You might plant scented climbers to
grow up and over a pergola or trellis. Or herbs planted within
a gravelled area or nearby bed will release their perfume when
brushed against with hands or feet. Think also about what you
will be looking at. Any seat should come with a view, something
that either draws the eye up or down the garden or provides a
focal point upon which to gaze.

Framing a view

A small garden will appear bigger if the boundaries between
it and the outside are blurred. Framing a view is one way to do
this. A mature tree in the distance will seem to be drawn in and
become part of the garden if the planting is planned to leave a
space through which it can be glimpsed. Gardens that back onto
open countryside or parkland will appear more spacious if the
boundary is kept low, allowing a view of the landscape beyond.

Creating an illusion

Fooling the eye into seeing something that isn't there is a great
way of making a garden not only more interesting but seem
bigger. Fixing a door to a solid wall will create the illusion that
there is more garden beyond. A visual 'hole' can be created in a
wall at the back of a flower-bed with a circular mirror that will
reflect the planting. A mirror can also be used to make a shallow
bed appear twice the depth, or to create the illusion of a room
beyond if fixed to a garden wall and framed with an archway.
(But don't position mirrors too high, as birds can become
confused and fly into them.) Different colours can affect our
perception of distance. A bench or wall at the end of a garden
will make the boundary seem further away if it is painted white
or pale blue than if it is a darker colour (see page 44).

Planning paths

Paths are not merely ways of getting to places; they are the route map of a garden, and add a lot to its shape and character. They may be straight or meandering, but they should always have a destination, ideally something pleasant: dead-ends are pointless and frustrating in a garden. In a long narrow garden, a path running directly up the middle or down one side will lead the eye straight to the end and make the space appear longer and narrower than it is. For a garden like this it is much better to take the path on a diagonal, or include horizontal sections, or curve it into a flowing line. A short garden can be made to appear longer by subtly tapering a path so that it narrows towards the end. Whichever style of path you decide on, mark it out first with spray paint, sand or a length of hose so that you can look at it from different angles, and play around with its route and appearance until you get it right.

Vertical planning

The vertical element of any garden design is an important extra dimension. Height gives an immediate impression of maturity and grandeur. It can be used to emphasise points within a garden, and to guide the way in which it is navigated: a path beneath a pergola is delightful to walk along and unlikely to be strayed from. Vertical elements such as hedges, fences and trellis may be used as partitions to create separate 'rooms' within a garden, providing shelter, privacy and support for climbing plants. A statue, urn, planter or even a water feature raised above the surrounding landscape will act as a focal point, a vertical visual punctuation mark in the garden.

An area of low planting within a bed or border can be lifted and transformed with the addition of one or two tall, vertical plants. These may be colourful annuals or biennials (see pages 321–23) or perhaps something more formal such as a clipped box spiral. A wirework obelisk placed within a border and planted with a climber such as a clematis (see page 306) will give instant vertical impact even before the plant has grown and covered it. Statues and ornaments can also provide vertical accents among the planting of a bed or border.

Achillea 'Feuerland' Yarrow

Designing
with plants
new beds and borders

Stocking the garden with plants is one of the most rewarding aspects of gardening. It's always useful to do some planning first, so that when you're ready to buy, you can go armed with a planting plan that also serves as your shopping list.

Imagining your garden

Planting plans, whether hand drawn or computer generated, give you the chance to walk through the garden in your mind, envisaging the different shapes and colours, light and shade, how one part of the garden links with another, where you would like to pause for a while. Taking time to plan this imaginary landscape will help you develop your vision and make it more likely to succeed. If you are short of inspiration, visit gardens that are open to the public and look through books and magazines. You could of course go and browse plants for sale, but remember that not all plants are available at any one time.

Drawing it out

You don't have to be a skilled artist to sketch a planting plan. Plants can be represented by simple blobs, squiggles and circles. Play around with the drawing, remembering that plants need to work together not just in terms of colour and shape, but also with regard to growing requirements and eventual size. When planting more than one of the same specimen together, garden designers always prefer to plant in odd numbers, as this tends to create a more natural effect.

Where to start

Any planting scheme has to begin with the big, permanent planting. This includes trees, hedges and shrubs – the things that are the most difficult to move once established. Think about whether you want to use planting to block views of neighbouring houses or to partition the garden. Likewise any shrubs that are to serve as the backdrop to the rest of a planting scheme, or as a focal point in their own right, need to be positioned before anything else.

Designing a border

Beds and borders should have simple, flowing outlines; introducing quirky kinks or too many curves and bends can not only look very fussy but will take twice as much time to maintain as areas with plainer lines. Try to envisage the overall shape of the border when the planting is mature, seen both side-on and from the front. Traditional planting graduates in height from front to back of a border, and while this is still a good rule of thumb it can sometimes look a bit predictable. To avoid that, position a few tall, upright plants towards the front of the bed, where the planting is otherwise lower. And aim to graduate the height of plants along the length of a border: a symmetrical shape, with taller plants at each end and lower-growing ones towards the middle, can be very successful.

Side view of a traditional border

Front view of a symmetrical border

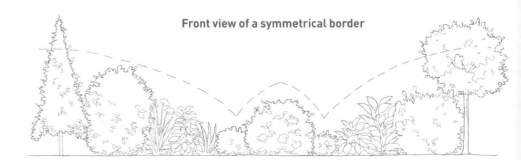

Right plant, right place

Your personal likes and dislikes will obviously play a huge role when it comes to planting a garden, but it is pointless to try to grow your favourite plants if the soil and aspect are wrong for them. Adding horticultural grit, digging in lots of moisture-retentive soil improver or creating shade where none existed before will all produce significant environmental improvements, but they won't turn a shady corner into a hot dry bed. So it's usually better to work with the existing growing conditions: the plants will be happier and will require much less ongoing time and attention. Do remember, however, that as new shrubs and trees mature, one of their effects is to create shade, and this does need to be anticipated when planning a garden.

There is such a wide range of plants available for every kind of soil and aspect that there are many factors apart from growing conditions to consider when making your choices.

Structure, texture and contrast

A plant can mark a change or transitional point from one part of the garden to another. It may add height, or screening, or divide one area of the garden from another. Or it may provide a focal point within a border or something to draw the eye up the garden. Designers often talk about 'architectural plants' – eye-catching plants that stand out for their dramatic shapes and dominating presence, making a real statement in the garden. Evergreen topiary shapes will contribute drama and structure all year round.

Consider also the texture of plants, especially their foliage. This may be shiny or furry, feathery and spreading, or upright and strap-like. Groups of plants with contrasting textures can be very effective in a bed or border.

Sound and scent

The sound of the breeze rustling through tall grasses or bamboos can add a whole new dimension to the experience of a garden. Scent, too, is a very important element in planting schemes. Fragrant plants can give particular pleasure when grown near to sitting areas. Plants that release scent when their foliage is brushed, such as Mediterranean herbs like rosemary and lavender, make an ideal choice alongside a path.

Vigour and eventual size

When faced with a bare patch of ground it is easy to cram in too many plants, which can end up swamping each other. To avoid this, check what the eventual size of each plant will be and take this into account when creating your plan. You can always fill the gaps with annuals for the first year or two. Speed of growth is also important: some plants are much more vigorous than others, and may quickly smother slower-growing neighbours.

Seasonality

All plants change through the seasons, providing more colour or interest for a particular part of each year. Evergreen shrubs, trees and climbers may fade into the background in summer, but come into their own in the winter months. It's important to balance them with deciduous and perennial planting, however, as too many evergreens can create a gloomy, dull effect. Don't forget to include plenty of spring bulbs in any planting scheme: these will bring life and colour to the garden early in the year.

Maintenance

Growing lots of plants that need staking, pruning or clipping can become tiresome if you have neither the time nor the inclination to do it. Some plants can almost look after themselves: slow-growing evergreen shrubs, for example, and also many 'ground-cover' plants (see page 314), which can provide colour while also helping to suppress weeds.

Planting in colour

Nature's colours add a wonderful decorative quality to a garden. They can be used to complement a design or create a mood; they can also affect our sense of distance and perspective.

Colour and light

The prevailing light in a garden plays a large part in how we perceive its colours. In the full glare of the sun, hot vibrant colours will zing with extra brightness, while pastels appear paler, gaining the washed-out look of old watercolour paintings. Colour can be used to bring light to shady spots and tone down areas that take the full glare of the sun, much as it might be used when decorating indoors. However, the stronger light and shade, and the predominance of foliage in the garden, mean that colour often works differently outdoors. Planting white flowers in a shady place, for example, will actually emphasise the gloom, whereas yellow flowers brighten it up, as if bringing sunshine to shade. Blue is another colour that can brighten a dark corner: in the sun blue flowers often look bleached, but in dappled shade they become almost luminous.

The colour wheel

The colour wheel is the tool designers use to illustrate the relationships between the colours of the spectrum. Red, yellow and blue are the primaries – colours that cannot be made from mixtures of any other colour. Between them on the wheel are secondary colours, mixed from equal amounts of the two nearest primaries, and tertiary colours, mixed from unequal amounts.

Colours that are beside or near each other on the wheel are closely related: together they form harmonious combinations. Those opposite each other are entirely unrelated: designers call them contrasting or complementary colours, and together they produce vibrant combinations.

Using the colour wheel

Whatever your tastes, there is no right or wrong when it comes to colour. Experiment to find out what works for you. When planting a border, you might use harmonious colours to create a restful, easy-on-the-eye display; or contrasting colours to produce a lively, vivid effect. The impact of such combinations will depend on whether you are using soft pastels or rich strong colours. Contrasting colours in pastel shades will be a little more eye-catching than a display of harmonious pastels. And even the brightest yellow, orange and red will be more restful together than, say, orange and blue. But remember, of course, that the flowers are not the only element providing colour in a bed or border: the reason hot red makes such an impact in the garden is that it contrasts with the green of surrounding foliage. Shades of blue or yellow, on the other hand, are in harmony with the foliage.

Shades of green and brown

While some flowers bloom continuously, many others bring just a fleeting moment of colour to the garden, however glorious. The two predominant colours outdoors are green and brown, regardless of season. Green is often regarded as a mere background colour, but in fact foliage plays the biggest part in any planting scheme. And it's not just green: foliage can bring an enormous range of tones and textures to a garden (see page 45). Evergreen trees and shrubs come into their own during the winter months. Twigs, branches, tree trunks and soil are even more likely to be overlooked. But again, these can add interest in their own right: think of the peeling white bark of Himalayan birch (*Betula utilis* var. *jacquemontii*, see page 295), or the red stems of dogwood (*Cornus alba* 'Sibirica', see page 300), which can bring vivid colour to the garden in the dead of winter.

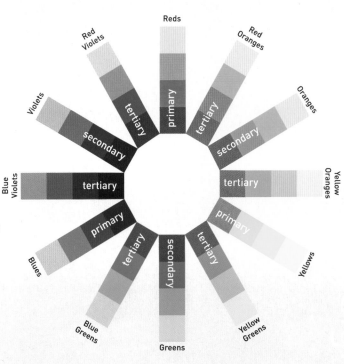

Planting in colour

As with so many aspects of garden design, the way to succeed with colour is to keep it simple. Whether you decide to go for hot brights or cool pastels, vibrant contrasts or calm harmonies, stick to a restricted palette for the best results.

Making colour work for you

Colour can have a marked impact on our perception of distance. Hot colours – red, yellow, orange – push forwards, seeming closer than they actually are. Cool, pastel colours and all the whites appear to be further away, elongating a view. This is an important consideration when deciding what to plant, especially in a small garden, as filling a tiny space with lots of vibrant colours can enclose it further, making it feel claustrophobic. In such a garden, concentrating upon foliage plants with the odd dash of pale, cool colour will produce a far more open, restful atmosphere.

If you have sufficient space, colour can be used to create separate zones or 'rooms' within the garden, each with an appropriate mood. You might make a bold statement with energising brights in an area dedicated to socialising, eating or entertaining. In an area set aside for retreat and relaxation, cool, harmonious colours will help establish a calm atmosphere.

Contrasting planting

Few flowers are only one colour when you look at them closely, which means that the colours within a single flower can inspire a whole planting scheme. Occasionally nature itself throws together some amazing colour combinations. This iris (*Iris ensata* 'Hercule') could be the keynote of a contrasting planting scheme mixing deep and purples with brilliant yellows and oranges.

Harmonious planting

For a softer, more romantic effect, consider a harmonious planting scheme based on a group of colours that lie next to one another on the colour wheel. Here the rich dark green of box topiary is surrounded by silvery greens and aqua blues, with small highlights of yellow. The overall mood is calm and contemplative.

Pastel planting

Pale colours are pretty and charming in the garden. But beware the temptation to plant exclusively white flowers, at least not over a large area. The effect can be disappointingly dull. Instead mix white with soft pastels – lemon, peach, pink and blue – for a more interesting and varied look.

Hot and bright planting

Hot reds and oranges are exotic and eye-catching. They can add a vivid flourish to a planting scheme. However, they do work best in full sun, as red tends to get lost in shade. It also quickly loses its impact from a distance, so position red flowers alongside a path, or around a window – somewhere where their brilliance will be seen up close.

The value of foliage

It's definitely worth getting into foliage. The colour green varies according to the balance of blue and yellow present, ranging from soft bluish-green through to acid yellow-green. Different shades can emphasise or diminish the colour of flowers around them. Silvery-blue leaves 'lift' white flowers, making them appear whiter than they are, but the same foliage will darken the colour of deep purple flowers. Acid greens bring out the yellow in white flowers, making them appear creamy. And of course foliage may not be green at all: many lavenders have silvery grey foliage (see page 298); sea holly is blue (*Eryngium*, see page 308); some heucheras are deep purple or bronze (see page 316); and the ornamental grass *Ophiopogon planiscapus* 'Nigrescens' (see page 314) is a dramatic black.

Sunny yellow

The evergreen golden-yellow leaves of *Choisya ternata* 'Sundance' will brighten a sheltered, sunny border.

Serrated texture

The shuttlecock fern, *Matteuccia struthiopteris*, brings a light and feathery texture to a damp, shady spot.

Variegated colour

Multi-coloured foliage can be as ornamental as flowers. The bottle green leaf of *Hosta fortunei* var. *aureomarginata* is fringed with creamy white.

Rich shiny evergreens

Dark, glossy evergreens such as laurel provide a backdrop to many planting schemes.

Deep red leaves

The dark red-purple leaves of *Cotinus coggygria* 'Royal Purple' (smoke bush) turn scarlet before they fall from the tree in autumn.

Designing
hard landscaping

Of all the elements of garden design, the hard landscaping is the most important to get right. Not only does it define the shape of the space, it can also be the most expensive part of a garden, the most permanent and the most difficult to change if mistakes are made.

The bones of the garden

Paths, patios, steps, decking, walls – hard landscaping is the skeleton of a garden. It can often define its style and shape to a greater degree than the planting. Time spent drawing and re-drawing at the planning stage can save weeks rectifying expensive mistakes.

Planning patios and paths

If you have enough room, try to allow about a metre of space around any piece of furniture and at least two metres around a table that will be used for dining. Bear in mind that any surrounding planting may encroach on a patio or deck during the summer months: either choose small plants or allow for this when measuring. Paths should ideally be at least a metre wide, 1.2m if possible. If that would seriously compromise the proportions of your garden then at least try to ensure that they are wide enough to accommodate any wheelbarrows, rubbish bins, pushchairs or other items that may have to be transported through the garden. To accommodate a wheelchair paths need to be a little wider – 1.5–2m will allow a pedestrian and wheelchair user to pass comfortably (see page 18).

Continuity or contrast

Matching the colour of hard landscaping materials to the colours outside and inside the house, even in varying shades, will create a cohesive, restful impression. A red brick house will sit companionably alongside a brick patio or a deck that has been stained a similar colour. In contrasting materials and colours, outdoor and indoor spaces will retain their separate identities. So for example you might position a teak deck surrounded by orange and red flowers outside a muted pastel-painted room with a light wooden floor. Bear in mind, however, that blurring the divide by taking inside colours outside will tend to make both the garden and the house feel bigger.

Choosing materials

It can be easy to get carried away when faced with the vast available choice of hard landscaping materials, from ornamental aggregates to paving and decking. But do try to resist the temptation to mix up lots of different textures and colours. You will achieve a more coherent and uncluttered result by using a restricted selection of materials for paths, patios and edgings throughout the garden. One or more of these materials might closely echo the brick or stone with which your house is built. Practicality is also important: make sure that a material is designed for the use you intend for it, that it is strong and durable enough, and is safe.

Patterns and illusions

Bricks, blocks and slabs can be laid in attractive patterns of circles, diagonals or squares. These can provide a striking decorative feature in a garden, and have the benefit of being virtually maintenance free.

Our eyes naturally tend to follow straight lines. This has the effect of emphasising proportions in the direction of the lines: thus bricks, slabs or deck boards laid lengthwise will seem to elongate the area they cover, whereas laid widthwise they widen it. This can be very useful if, for example, you have a long, narrow garden: by creating linear patterns from side to side, you will 'improve' the proportions of the space.

choosing hard landscaping materials

Slabs	Paving slabs are the ideal choice for creating an all-weather, hardwearing surface. There are slabs suitable for drives, patios, paths and steps. Concrete slabs are available in a huge choice of colours, textures and shapes, or choose quarried sandstone for authentic natural texture. A paved circle made from pre-cut slabs can form a striking centrepiece to a garden design. Maintenance of paving is minimal – simply sweep clean or pressure wash.
Bricks and blocks	Bricks and blocks are versatile detailing materials; use them as edgings to complement slabs or gravel areas, or to create patterns around features such as sculptures or fountains. They may also be used to cover larger surfaces such as patios, paths or drives.
Gravel, pebbles and chippings	Available in an extensive range of colours, stone size and texture, decorative aggregates are easy and quick to lay. They are best suited to areas surrounded by a retaining hard edging such as paths or small formal courtyards, as loose materials will tend to spread. Gravel paths are noisy to walk on, making them a useful deterrent against intruders.
Stepping stones	Stepping stones are both decorative and practical. Laid across a bed, they make an informal pathway, allowing you to weed and tend the plants even when the ground is wet. Laid over a lawn, stepping stones will protect the grass from wear.
Edgings	Decorative edgings can be used to mark the boundary between contrasting surfaces such as grass and gravel, or flowerbeds and paving. They will also retain loose materials or earth. They are available in a wide range of colours, textures and shapes - or create your own with bricks or pressure-treated timber.
Walling	Moulded walling makes easy work of building garden walls, and a change from conventional brickwork. Choose from a range of finishes, including rustic blocks and classic dry-stone walling. Or for a simple modern look, try rendered concrete blockwork.
Decking	Popular and versatile, decking is a 'softer' alternative material for patios and terraces and is particularly suitable for multi-level or raised areas. It's easy to change the finish of the wood with coloured stain or oil, and a deck made from pressure-treated timbers is simple to maintain – brush clean and remove stubborn grime with a pressure washer.

Hard landscaping on a slope

Garden steps should always be designed with safety in mind – narrow treads and risers that are either too tall or too shallow are an accident in the making, so make sure that they will be sufficiently wide and deep: the tread (the horizontal part) should never be less than 300mm from front to back, and the riser (the vertical face between the treads) should be no lower than 100m and no higher than 180mm.

Terracing combined with retaining walls and raised beds is one solution when faced with an awkwardly sloping site. However, this is major work and can be expensive. An easier, more affordable way to create a level, all-weather surface is with an elevated deck built on posts.

See **You Can Do It: the Complete B&Q Step-by-Step Book of Home Improvement** for more detailed advice on hard landscaping on a slope.

Starting with what you have

Few people inherit a totally bare patch of ground. Even in new housing developments there will at least be a surrounding fence and a path or two. Established gardens may contain trees or shrubs that could give instant maturity to a new scheme. Deciding which features to keep and which to change is the starting point of any garden plan.

Establishing boundaries

Some property deeds clearly mark the boundaries and state whose responsibility it is to repair and maintain them. Unfortunately, with many older properties the situation is much less clear. Traditionally, if the fence posts were on your side, then the fence was your responsibility. If a badly-maintained fence bordering your property belongs to your neighbours then talk to them to establish how to go about maintenance or repair. If they are not willing or able to do it themselves, you could erect an alternative fence in front of the old one, provided it lies within your property. You may lose a few inches of land, but you'll have the new fence you wanted. If the only problem is the appearance of a fence, you can disguise it by stapling on some roll-out fencing made of willow, hazel or bamboo (see page 115). But bear in mind that if it's not your fence, you will have to take it off or lose it should the neighbours eventually opt for replacement. Be considerate, and make a point of discussing your plans for the garden with your neighbours; chances are, they will then do the same for you.

Clearing overhanging growth

Even if your neighbours' trees and shrubs are spreading into your garden, it's important to remember that they don't belong to you. If you draw a vertical line straight up from the boundary, anything on your side is classed as overhang and you should be able to cut it back. However, you must contact your neighbours before taking action. Inform them of your intention to prune the overhang, setting a date that gives them plenty of time to respond. Be sure to do it at a time that will minimise harm to the plant (see pages 240 and 245). Check that any trees are not subject to a Tree Preservation Order (see opposite). And offer the prunings to your neighbours – they belong to them, not you.

Observing the seasons

When you move into a house it's a good idea to live with the garden for a year, to discover what the changing seasons bring. There might be a wonderful display of spring bulbs out there that you won't know about until they appear. And you'll have to wait until winter sets in to spot any sodden boggy patches or frozen frost pockets. A whole year spent watching and waiting may seem like a frustrating prospect, but it could save you a lot of money and effort. See it as time to research and plan, and to develop a feel for the space and its potential.

Planting worth keeping

A large shrub gives even the newest garden a sense of maturity, so give careful consideration before you decide to uproot one. Most mature shrubs can be rejuvenated with some judicious pruning and feeding. Getting the timing right is essential. As a general rule of thumb, if the shrub flowers early in the growing season, it is pruned directly after flowering; if it flowers later in the summer then it is pruned in the winter (see page 240 for further detail on pruning). However, if a shrub is too unruly to live with even for a few months its stems can be hard-pruned back to an outward-facing bud. This could mean that it won't flower for a whole season but that may be a price worth paying for a healthy and manageable flowering shrub.

The value of trees

While root damage to property can be a serious problem, the felling of a large, mature tree will inevitably have an enormous impact upon the surrounding environment. In urban districts, most trees have legal protection. Tree Preservation Orders can be applied to individual trees or to an entire area. Planning consent for new developments often stipulates the planting of trees, especially if old ones have been removed. These trees, regardless of their age or size, are instantly protected by law. It is therefore essential to apply to your local or district council to find out if there are any restrictions before taking action to remove or prune a tree (see page 373). The onus to check is on you; if you break the law you could face a hefty fine.

Climate and conditions

Awkward shapes, frost pockets, boggy ground, howling winds, roaring traffic: for many of us, reality falls far short of the gardens of our dreams. But there are always ways to make the best of what you have.

Accentuating the positive

Very few people start out with the 'perfect' site, whatever that may be. Working with what you have, seeking to enhance the good aspects and play down or disguise the bad: these are sensible approaches to bring to any garden, whatever its inherent merits or flaws. No problem is insurmountable, even if some take more time and money to solve. There are plants for all situations and soil conditions, and apparent difficulties can even sometimes be turned to your advantage.

The UK climate

Despite ours being a rather small island, the differences in climate from north to south can make the growing season vary by two months or more. The contrast between east and west is just as noticeable. The mild winds blowing off the Atlantic bring warmer, damper weather to the western side. The altogether harsher wind that blows off the North Sea onto the eastern coast brings less average rainfall, but lower winter temperatures. The middle of the country, with no coastal air to cool it down or warm it up, experiences extremes of the highest summer temperatures and the lowest winter temperatures.

Wind at the top of a hill will blow away winter frost

Sheltered areas at the bottom of a hill can become freezing frost pockets in winter

Cold air sinks to the lowest point

The importance of location

It is possible to find variations of climate even within a local area. Houses on top of a hill get more wind; the breeze that cools you down in summer day will also blow away the winter frost. Houses at the bottom of a hill, although sheltered from buffeting winds, will in the winter be at the mercy of freezing air that sinks to the bottom of the hill; on some overcast winter days, this can mean that the garden never thaws out at all.

Climatic variations within a garden

Even within a garden there are variations in climate, known as micro-climates. One aspect of this is moisture levels, which will always differ from one part of a garden to another, with the foot of a wall being the driest spot of all. The house wall creates what gardeners call a 'rain shadow'; anything growing here is totally dependent on you for water. The direction each part of the garden faces determines the amount of light it receives. The differences may not be all that noticeable in summer but can be very significant in winter (see page 53). The base of a north-facing wall will be the coldest part of the garden in winter.

garden solutions

Poor drainage	Work horticultural grit into the soil. If the problem is persistent, consider laying land drains which run off to a soakaway or to a main surface-water drain (see pages 196–97). Alternatively, you could create a bog garden with water-loving plants (see page 318).
Shaded areas	If the shade is cast by large trees, it may be possible to thin the canopy to let in more light. Unavoidable shade should be treated as an opportunity to grow plants that wouldn't survive in a sunnier garden.
Poor soil	Add lots of compost and organic matter (see pages 190–91). Or import new topsoil – this is often necessary in the gardens of newly-built houses.
Tree stumps	You could turn a tree stump into a rustic seat, or grow ivy over it. However, rotting wood can encourage fungal disease which may cross to neighbouring plants. To remove it you will need to hire a machine and a worker for a day to grind out the stump.
Traffic noise	Noise will be filtered and reduced by planting a dense hedge or erecting a fence and training climbers over it. Gentle sounds such as flowing water can help push it into the background.
Lack of privacy	A hedge or fence, large shrub or tree can all provide screening, as will trellis panels, arbour or pergola, with or without the addition of climbing plants. A parasol or gazebo will protect you from view as well as from the sun. Or consider erecting a summerhouse or garden building.
Long, narrow site	Lay paths on a curve, or partition the garden horizontally to emphasise the width and create separate 'rooms' that prevent the entire space being seen at once. Make sure linear patterns in paving or decking run diagonally or side to side, not straight towards the end of the garden.
L-shaped site	Use the area around the corner to hide things: it's the perfect location for a shed, compost heap or rubbish bins. Alternatively, it could be used to create a vegetable garden, or a quiet spot away from it all, maybe with a different style and colour theme from the rest of the garden.
Security and crime prevention	Furniture can be bolted securely to the ground using specially designed kits. Motion-activated lighting will automatically come on if anyone is lurking outside. Using spiky plants as hedging will deter intruders, as well as cats. The noise made by walking over gravel paths and driveways is a deterrent to thieves. See also page 372.

Windy sites

The direction and strength of the prevailing wind can limit what you are able to grow. Solid barriers are not the best solution: wind will roll over the top of a masonry wall and down the other side, blasting whatever lies at its foot. More effective are trees and tall hedges, which filter the wind, breaking its force. A new hedge will need protecting in its infancy, but once established it will provide shelter for you and your plants, and a home for wildlife. Evergreen hedges are effective year-round, but some grow very fast and need a great deal of trimming to prevent them getting out of control; they also have a tendency to be 'burned' by cold winds, especially if planted on the coast. A deciduous hedge would be a better option.

Sloping sites

Terracing, retaining walls and steps are an obvious solution in a sloping garden, but they can be a very expensive one. More affordable would be an elevated deck, providing an all-weather flat surface for sitting or dining outdoors.

Much depends upon the gradient of your slope. Provided it is not too steep to mow, then a slope can be seeded or turfed to create a lawn. You might lay a stepping stone path through it, with log or paved steps running down the steepest sections (see **You Can Do It: the Complete B&Q Step-by-Step Book of Home Improvement** for advice on how to build steps on a slope).

For sites that are so steep they are tricky to access it may be better to create a low-maintenance evergreen planting scheme that will pretty much look after itself.

Gardens by the sea

Coastal areas enjoy higher winter temperatures and fewer frosts, but winds coming in off the sea are laden with salt. As well as erecting some form of barrier against the wind, you'll need to grow tougher plants. A plant's protection is the outer skin of its leaves; the thicker and glossier this is, the hardier and tougher the plant. Plants with hairy or furry leaves are the most resilient, able to survive in the most exposed spots.

Light and aspect

Observing the light and shade of your garden is a key stage in planning a new design. The direction it faces – its aspect – is a big influence on how much sunlight it receives.

Valuing shade

Shade in a garden is often viewed as a problem, yet in summer a shaded area gives us opportunities a sunbaked garden can never provide. Many plants would die in the harsh glare of unbroken summer sunshine. Colours fade, shadows are lost, and the amount of time we can spend outdoors is limited by our ability to withstand the heat.

Understanding aspect

All gardens contain a series of micro-climates that are partly determined by the compass direction each area faces. These offer different levels of light, warmth and moisture.

South-facing areas These enjoy the hottest sun, enabling sun-loving plants to thrive. South-facing walls intensify this by storing heat and reflecting it back on whatever grows in front of them. Watering will be necessary for all but the toughest plants, so work in plenty of moisture-retaining soil improver before planting. Mulching will also help. A soaker hose or automatic watering system (see page 252) will reduce both the effort of watering and the amount of water used.

North-facing areas These may never receive direct sunlight, so conditions will be cool and shady. But don't despair: see them as an opportunity to grow plants that prefer a shady spot.

East-facing areas An easterly orientation can be the most challenging – hot and dry in the summer and bitterly cold in the winter. The same shade-lovers that do well in north-facing spots will grow here too, but evergreens may be scorched by the winter and spring winds. Spring-flowering shrubs will need some protection from the early morning sun as flowers carrying frost from the night before will thaw out too quickly and drop.

West-facing areas Western aspects enjoy the best of both worlds, being neither too hot nor too cold. Almost any plant will thrive here, including some of the more tender ones.

Siting a patio

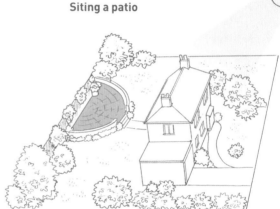

If the rear of the house faces north, position a patio at the end of the garden to get maximum sun

A patio beside a south-facing house wall will get maximum sun

8am   10am   12pm

Summer and winter shade

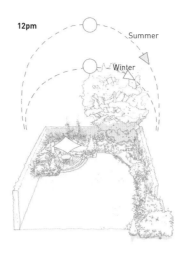

Because the winter sun is lower in the sky, the shadows cast by fixed features become much bigger.

Observing your garden

Spend some time watching the changing light in your garden. The photographs below show the passage of the sun through a southeast-facing garden in June. High hedges and trees on all sides diffuse much of its light, creating dappled shade, though the patio catches the full sun at midday.

Positioning seating areas and patios

If a patio is mainly for sitting out and sunbathing, you will want to site it so that it gets the maximum sun. But if you prefer to have somewhere cooler to dine in mid-summer, then select a shadier spot. Bear in mind that it is easier to create shade than sunshine. Climbers trained up and over a pergola or arbour will cast a natural dappled shade. Choose deciduous species and the leaves will drop in autumn, allowing through the welcome rays of the weaker winter sun. A simple parasol or gazebo will provide temporary relief from the summer sun.

Shade in summer and winter

Light travels in a straight line from the sun; anything that stands in its way will block or diffuse it, creating a shadow. Because the position of the sun in the sky changes from high to low between summer and winter, the shade cast by immovable features such as houses and high walls or evergreen hedges will expand and retreat with the seasons. What may be a bright patch through the summer can become very gloomy in winter if there is a barrier high enough to block the sun's lower path – one more reason why it is always worth living with a garden for a full year before going ahead with a new design.

Making the most of shade

If you have a naturally shady spot in your garden, consider what causes it and whether it varies with the seasons. The dappled shade cast by a deciduous tree is very different from the solid block cast by a huge evergreen hedge. Either way, there are plants to brighten the gloom. Indeed, a shady spot opens up a whole wealth of possibilities to grow plants that would die in full sun. You'll need to establish the condition of the soil – is it prone to dampness or almost permanently dry? Moist shade is easier to plant than dry, but working a lot of soil improver into a dry patch will help considerably. Many yellow-leaved and variegated shrubs that would scorch in full sun will bring a golden glow to all but the deepest shade. Foliage plants such as ferns and hostas will grow dense and lush in a moist shady area. Spring and summer colour can be provided by bluebells and foxgloves. And there are many climbers that will soon clamber up and over a shady wall (see page 305).

In addition to planting, you could create a seating area to retire to when the sun gets too hot. It doesn't have to be decked or paved, just a strategically placed bench or even a hammock.

2pm   4pm   6pm

You've decided what to keep in your garden and what to remove; you've spent time studying its light and conditions, its strengths and flaws; you know what style of garden you want and and the mood you want to create. You are armed with dreams, wishlists, cuttings, photos and sketches. Now is the time to pin down your vision on a scale plan of the garden. And that is not as difficult as it sounds.

making plans

Putting it down on paper

This is the point at which all your ideas come together as a coherent and workable garden plan. 'Why bother?', you might ask, especially for a small patch. But proper planning can be even more important if all your needs and aspirations are to be met within a restricted space. Planning enables you to play with the possibilities, and to work out how your dreams and desires can be combined with practical necessities such as storage and access. You are much more likely to spot errors when they are laid out on paper, and so should also avoid expensive mistakes or throwing money away on passing whims.

The first stage is to make a rough two-dimensional plan of the existing garden, including everything that is to be retained and omitting anything that will be removed. Draw in the house, complete with the positions of doorways and windows. Add any trees, garages, paths and gateways, existing power supplies, outside taps, drains, manhole covers and drainage inspection chambers. Don't worry too much about getting things drawn to scale just yet; this preliminary sketching is just to get an overall feel.

You are unlikely to get it right first time (even professionals don't usually manage that), so make sure you have plenty of paper to hand. And if drawing is really not your thing, don't be put off: try taking a photograph of the space and sketching on tracing paper laid over the top. This can be a great way to get started.

Checklist of practicalities

Life's practicalities have to be catered for if the garden is to become a useful space. Washing lines have to be reached, rubbish bins have to be stored, wheelbarrows, pushchairs, lawnmowers and bicycles all have to be manoeuvred. Make sure that paths, gateways and arches are all wide enough to accommodate the widest thing that will have to pass. If you intend to lay a patio or any other hard-surfaced area, remember that you will need to preserve access to stopcocks and manhole covers.

Making use of technology

If you have a computer, it can be well worth investing in a garden planning programme. Not only will this remove the need to draw by hand but it will enable you to take a virtual tour through the garden at the planning stage. Such programmes include vast selections of plants, and will show you how to work out planting distances, how colours work together and how big trees will grow. When you have experimented with all the different options and decided what will go where, you simply print out your complete garden plan.

Surveying a site
and drawing a plan

In order to convert your sketches into an accurate scale plan you will need to make a detailed survey of the garden.

Measuring up

Start by measuring the width and length of the plot, the width of the house, including windows and doorways, the height of walls and fences, any patios, paths or features that are to be retained, the estimated height and canopy radius of trees, and any buildings that are to stay, including sheds and summerhouses.

Plotting boundaries

You will need to plot the exact lines of your boundaries – and these are rarely perfectly straight. One way to do this is to run a string line along the side wall of the house and extend it all the way to the end of the garden; pull it taut and make sure there are no kinks. Then measure the distance between the line and the boundary at metre intervals all along its length. If this distance changes, then your boundary is not quite straight – but the measurements you have taken will allow you to plot its line on your plan.

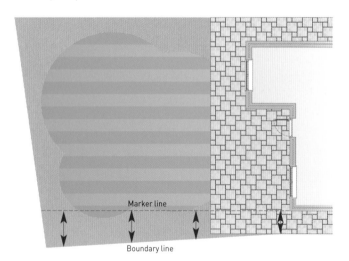

Marker line

Boundary line

Locating pipes and services

Accidentally damaging a water main or electricity cable can be dangerous and expensive. It's easy enough to lift manhole covers and see which way pipes run, but this is only reliable over short distances. All the main utility suppliers should be able to provide records of what lies where. But if these are incomplete – as may be the case with older houses – hiring a cable avoidance tool (CAT) from a tool hire company will be essential. These hand-held or push-along devices (see page 78) can locate all underground service pipes and cabling. Use a marker spray paint to show them on the ground, and also make your own detailed map for present and future reference.

ideal tool
Long-reel tape measure
This will make easy work of taking accurate measurements of a garden, especially if you have someone to help you by holding the other end.

Plotting fixed points

Once you have measured the house and plotted the boundaries, you need to work out the precise position of fixed features such as trees or manhole covers. The most accurate method for doing this is a process known as triangulation. Choose two fixed points as your base points – the outer corners of the house are usually ideal. Then measure the distance of the feature from each point. When it comes to drawing your plan, set the radius of a pair of compasses to the first (scaled-down) measurement, place its point at the corner and draw an arc in the area of the feature. Do the same from the other corner. The feature lies at the exact point that the two arcs intersect.

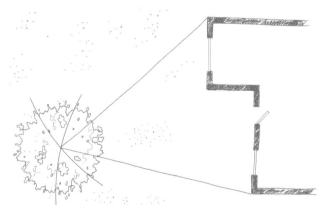

Using triangulation to plot the position of a tree

Taking levels

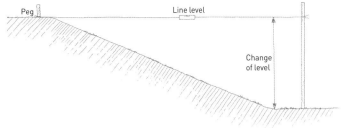

Peg · Line level · Change of level

Drawing to scale

This isn't as complicated as it may seem – it will come together very quickly with the help of some graph paper, a compass and a ruler, or a scale rule if you have one. The size of the garden dictates the scale – the smaller the area, the larger the scale and vice versa. Keeping it within the bounds of an A3 pad will make life easier – you won't have to wrestle with large sheets of paper in the wind, and photocopying will be easier. A scale of 1:50 (1cm on the page representing 50cm on the ground) will work for smaller gardens (up to 14m x 20m); for a larger site (up to 28m x 40m), you will need to reduce the scale down to 1:100 (1cm on the page to 1m on the ground). Write a note of your scale on the plan: this will help when estimating materials.

Creating a masterplan

Once you have worked out your scale, draw the outline of the plot. Draw in any buildings, including the house, and any existing features that are to be retained, including trees. Mark in services, drains and manhole covers. Use a compass to check which way is north and mark this with an arrow. This is your masterplan. Make several photocopies of it, and use these to draw in all further additions and features, keeping the original clean. This means that mistakes and rethinks can be thrown out without having to start from scratch.

Measuring changes of level

It's highly unlikely your garden will be completely flat – very few are. If you are planning any new hard landscaping – steps, patios, paths or decking – you will have to measure changes in level across the site. The simplest way to do this is to hammer pegs into the ground at the lowest and highest points and balance a straightedge and spirit level between them. Or run a taut string line and hang a line level from it. Adjust the pegs until you get a level reading; the change in level is the difference between their lengths. If you are planning to build a feature over different heights, such as steps, it will help you to draw a cross-section of your plan showing the changes of level.

ideal tool

Laser level
A laser level with adjustable tripod will accurately transfer levels over long distances.

Easy experimenting

An easy way to transfer your vision to paper is to make scale cut-outs of everything you would like to put in the garden, including sheds, summerhouses, hedges and flower borders. These can be placed on the outline plan and moved around so that you can establish what works best where and how the garden flows as a whole. As these are placed upon the plan, take a mental stroll through the garden, considering how each area or feature links with the next. Does it feel right or are there awkward areas that need adjustment? Does the garden look balanced or are some parts full and others vacant? When you are completely happy, draw the features on the plan.

Drawing planting plans

Details of any planting can be made on the same plan but it is often easier to draw a separate one on tracing paper, so that a simple flip of the paper will allow you to see how the design changes when the plants are added. The planting plan should show the distances between new plants, taking into account their eventual size. Remember to place evergreen trees or shrubs evenly throughout the scheme as any imbalance will be very obvious during the winter months. Include seasonal planting: bedding, herbaceous perennials and bulbs.

If you find it difficult to visualise the planting it can help to make two plans, one viewed from above, one from the side. This will help you gauge the overall height and shape of your beds, and see where vertical elements are needed to 'lift' a flat spot.

Drawing construction plans

Any feature that requires detailed, accurate measurement, such as steps, a patio or deck, should have its own individual set of plans. These should be drawn to a much bigger scale, ideally 1:10, which will enable you to draw in far more detail.

Budget and practicalities

Once you have worked your ideas into a real garden plan, you are ready to face the challenge of building your new garden.

Managing the costs

Creating a new garden often means spending a lot of money. Breaking the project down and completing it over a period of time – months or years – is one way to make that expense more manageable. Prioritise the jobs that need to be done to make the garden a usable space. Which can you afford to do now and which could be completed at a later date?

Large areas of hard surfacing can be prohibitively expensive. But you can reduce your costs considerably by opting for concrete slabs or the latest, very convincing imitation stone slabs. The excavation, preparation and installation of drainage and the laying of hardcore is the most disruptive and messy work; once done the area can be topped with gravel. This can be raked off and replaced with paving or slabs at a later date when your budget allows.

Planting on a budget

When it comes to trees and shrubs, the bigger and more mature they are, the more expensive they will be. Buying small will save you a significant amount of money. Any gaps in borders can be planted with annuals while you're waiting for them to fill out. Growing from seed and cuttings is much cheaper than buying established plants, but you may have to wait a year for some perennials to come into flower. Almost all herbaceous perennials will bulk up within a season or two, so if you can live without instant impact, buy smaller, cheaper plants and wait for them to spread. And it's much cheaper to buy bags of bulbs and plant them dry than to buy them flowering in pots.

Don't, however, be tempted to economise on soil preparation, especially when creating new beds: grit, soil improver, topsoil, mulch – the boost these give to new planting is invaluable (see pages 190–91).

Arranging access

The importance of access to a garden is too often overlooked. If you are planning extensive new landscaping – digging a large pond, installing decking or large areas of paving – there will be a lot of materials and equipment to be transported in and out of the garden. If the only access is through the house, it's all the more important to plan the logistics carefully and realistically. Where will all the soil from an excavated pond go? Can you incorporate into your design a feature that will make use of it, for example a raised bed? Even so, remember that only topsoil can be used for a bed; digging a deep pond will produce a lot of sub-soil that will have to be removed from the site. Is there space for a skip to be delivered and collected?

You can do it...

Consider the neighbours

If creating your new garden will involve the use of large, noisy machinery over an extended period of time, or if access for workmen and equipment is over a shared driveway, do let your neighbours know before work begins. Courtesy and cooperation will help the whole operation to go much more smoothly.

B&Q

Checking the regulations

Planning regulations vary from area to area (see page 373). There are usually very tight restrictions on what may be done to listed buildings or properties in conservation areas, and that includes their gardens. However, even new housing estates are subject to regulations governing, for example, the height and ground area of garden buildings – this may even include sheds. So it's always worth checking with the Planning Department of your local council first. If you wish to fell or prune a tree, ask the local council whether there are any Tree Preservation Orders in force. Find a qualified tree surgeon for any permitted work; they can have waiting lists so it is best to book early.

Sequence and timing of work

For all hard landscaping it is usually best to start at the point furthest from the intended access point, so that finished work is not dirtied or damaged as the rest of the garden progresses.

The hard landscaping in a new garden should be completed first, if possible during the winter months so that the garden will be ready for planting in spring. However, if drainage is a problem, a wet winter may hamper progress. If a very cold spell is forecast, the building of walls and patios will have to wait, as frost can weaken new concrete and mortar; you should only do such construction work in temperatures above 3ºC.

Employing experts

If you need to install or move major services – gas, electricity or water pipes – then you must employ a qualified engineer to survey the site and undertake the job. They will see obstacles and also shortcuts that you may not have noticed, and ensure that any work done complies with all the relevant regulations.

New laws in force since 1 January 2005 impose much tighter restrictions on electrical work in homes and gardens in England and Wales. Before you begin any electrical work outdoors (other than minor repairs and replacements), you must now notify your Local Authority Building Control Department, which has responsibility for ensuring the work is inspected and tested. Failure to comply with the new law carries a heavy fine. You may also find it very difficult to sell a property where the electrical system has been adapted without Building Control consent and approval. See also page 373.

If you haven't the time or the skill to create a garden yourself, find a good landscaping company. Word of mouth is

always the best recommendation, so have a look around the area and, if a garden catches your eye, drop a note through the door asking who did the work; everyone likes to have their garden praised so people will rarely resent the intrusion. A good garden designer will ask lots of questions. Expect them to deter you from any outrageous or unworkable plans, and to explain any compromises that are required. They will help you develop your ideas, but don't allow them to impose their own upon you. Their job is to use their expertise to realise your vision and to make the space work for you.

create

Each of us has a dream of the perfect outdoor room – a unique space that reflects our tastes and lifestyles, changes through the seasons, and evolves year on year. Here we show you how you can fulfil those visions. There are projects and ideas for everyone and every garden. All of them were created expressly for this book in order to inspire and enable you to create the outdoor room of your dreams.

create the look

Cottage dreaming

Colour, perfume, texture; a profusion of plants crammed into every nook and cranny and spilling over onto paths and lawns – these are the joys of a cottage garden. Such delights are not exclusive to a thatched cottage in the depths of the countryside. You can create your own cottage garden (or even just a cottage corner) in a town, city or suburb.

A green oasis

Take a small derelict garden in the heart of a city and imagine a private space, isolated from the bustle of the metropolis, where you can take time to be regenerated and relax in a natural but well-organised outdoor room – this is a city oasis worth creating.

A garden for getting together

A big garden, if you are lucky enough to have one, is a wonderful opportunity to make a flexible space that is perfect for welcoming family and friends, for children's play, or for withdrawing to privacy and solitude. A grand water feature and deck provides a focal point and a talking point, drawing guests outdoors and encouraging them to linger on a warm summer's evening.

Family fun

Young children love to let off steam in the open air. Create a good-looking garden where they can play safely and happily – and you can relax in comfort too.

Get away from it all

Your garden can be a magical space, a private retreat from a busy world. Hot tubs provide year-round pleasure and therapy. If you have a sheltered garden or live in a warm region, match the look with tropical planting – you really will be able to escape to another world.

Up front

The front garden is a much neglected space that can easily be made to look good and enhance the value of your home. Practical and easy to maintain – we show you how.

Small spaces, big ideas

A bare balcony is instantly transformed into an inviting living space by plants in pots and containers that soften the hard outlines and bring colour and perfume. The comfort of a conservatory can be enhanced with handsome and exciting planting that brings the pleasures of an outdoor garden into the year-round shelter of your home.

Cottage garden

For centuries almost every rural cottage had a small plot of land that was used to grow fruit and vegetables, herbs and medicinal plants, scented flowers, leaves and seeds. So developed the cottage garden – utilitarian, but also ornamental. Today the cottage garden with its profusion of colours and scents can flourish with almost any style of home and create a traditional, relaxed and informal garden.

Planning a cottage garden

The secret of cottage-style planting is that it is not too contrived, so rough planning is all that's needed, taking account of the different light and conditions across the site. Don't have plants neatly graded from short at the front to tall at the back, but mix them up a bit to achieve a more random look. Plant plenty of perennials to cut down on maintenance in the long term. For the first year or two you can sow annuals between them to fill the spaces as they become established. This kind of garden is a perfect environment for wildlife. Encourage butterflies and bees by choosing plants that attract them, such as marigolds, foxgloves, salvia (sage), sedums, marigolds and lavender. Organic composts, fertilisers and pest-control methods will also help wildlife to flourish.

The design brief

The goal of this makeover was to turn the front garden of a sixteenth-century Cornish cottage into a traditional-style cottage plot, using plants that give colour and interest for as much of the year as possible. Along the southwest side of the house is a wide cobblestone path and then the garden itself, raised 500mm with a dry-stone retaining wall, covering an irregular area roughly 14m x 9m, much of which was previously covered with grass. This is enclosed by walls and other buildings, and a fence, making it secluded and sheltered. The area near the house is very sunny and dry, but further away it is shaded and damp. The soil is neutral to acid and has a good structure, neither too heavy nor too sandy.

The existing plot

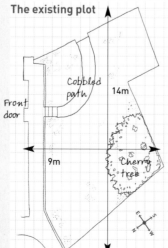

Cobbled path   14m

Front door

9m

Cherry tree

Wants

- All-year-round colour and interest.
- Wide range of traditional cottage garden plants.
- Generous flowerbeds.
- Plants to attract insects and birds.

Problems

- A blanket of brambles and Virginia creeper extends from the walls and has killed several shrubs; this will all need clearing first.
- Soil contains a lot of stones, broken pottery and glass.
- Lawn is full of moss and weeds.
- Pipes and cables for the gas, water, electricity, telephone or drainage services may run underground through the garden to the house.

Developing ideas

A cottage garden is all about plants. But even so, it needs paths
and walkways, and some seating where you can sit and enjoy
the space – a seat in a warm sunny corner is likely to become
a favourite spot for a tea break or sociable glass of wine.
Think about the views from inside the house as well as outside.
Sketch a plan of the garden, showing its shape and boundaries,
and try out different ideas. Keep the outlines simple and
informal; paths should meander and beds curve. This is
not a garden for symmetry or obvious straight lines.

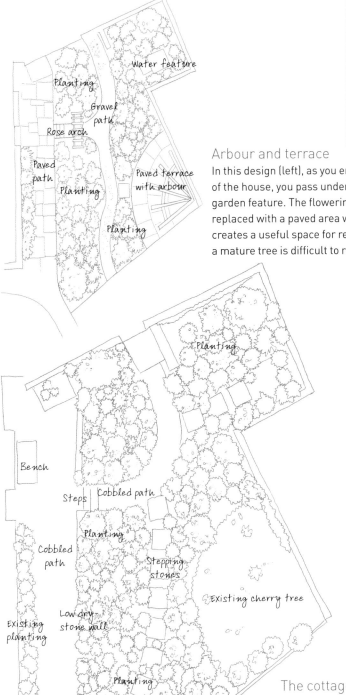

Arbour and terrace

In this design (left), as you enter the garden from the path in front
of the house, you pass under a rose arch, a quintessential cottage
garden feature. The flowering cherry tree has been removed and
replaced with a paved area with a wooden arbour and seat. This
creates a useful space for relaxing and entertaining outdoors, but
a mature tree is difficult to remove, and may also be protected.

Pergola walkway

In the version above, a wooden pergola runs the length of the
path in front of the house. This provides support for sun-loving
climbers. The cherry tree is preserved and the northern corner
of the garden is given over to a small paved area with seating.

The cottage dream

This design – true to the cottage garden tradition – gives maximum
space to planting, and so there are no new paved sitting areas.
Stepping stone paths lead across and through the planted areas,
adding to the country look, as well as providing all-important
access to the flowerbeds even when the ground is wet. This is the
plan that is to become the new garden (see pages 66–73).

Cottage
garden

A profusion of plants

A garden with conditions ranging from sunny and dry (nearer the house) to shaded and damp (by the next-door cottage and under the cherry tree) provides a wonderful opportunity to grow a wide variety of plants. It's a good idea to divide an outline plan of the plot into zones according to the light levels and soil conditions, then sketch in planting ideas. Shady areas are great for plants that prefer damp conditions, many of which have interesting foliage, such as hostas, heucheras and ferns. Dry, sunny conditions suit herbs and alpine plants like thyme, lavender, catmint and pinks.

This plan shows only a selection of what was actually planted in this garden. That's because, in typical cottage style, plants were crammed into every available space to create a dense mass of flowers and foliage. This is a garden style that doesn't need excessively detailed planning: but as always, take care to position plants in conditions where they will thrive (see below).

ideal plants for a cottage garden

Suitable for most conditions
Alchemilla mollis (Lady's mantle)
Geranium (Hardy geranium)

Damp, shady spots
Ajuga (Bugle)
Corydalis
Ferns
Helleborus (Christmas rose)
Heuchera
Hosta
Ligularia
Lobelia cardinalis
Lonicera (Honeysuckle)
Oxalis adenophylla
Viola

Warm, sheltered spots
Delphinium
Erysimum (Wallflower)
Euphorbia (Spurge)
Iris
Lavandula (Lavender)
Lily
Origanum (Marjoram)
Salvia (Sage)
Scabiosa (Pincushion flower)

Dry, warm, sunny spots
Alyssum
Anthemis (Chamomile)
Artemisia (Wormwood)
Convolvulus cneorum

Dianthus (Pinks)
Erigeron (Fleabane)
Eryngium (Sea holly)
Hyssopus (Hyssop)
Nepeta (Catmint)
Santolina (Cotton lavender)
Saxifrage
Sedum
Thymus (Thyme)
Veronica

Taller plants for sun or light shade
Achillea (Yarrow)
Alcea rosea (Hollyhock)
Campanula
Digitalis (Foxglove)
Echinacea (Coneflower)
Lupinus (Lupin)
Papaver orientale (Oriental poppy)
Rudbeckia (Coneflower)

Annuals as quick fillers
Calendula (Marigold)
Eschscholzia (California poppy)
Linaria (Toadflax)
Matthiola (Night-scented stock)
Nigella (Love-in-a-mist)
Papaver rhoeas (Shirley poppy)

Damp and shady corner

Warm and sheltered bed

Sunny and dry

Light shade

Colour in a cottage garden

Different colours of flowers can be happily mixed and matched in a cottage garden, but there are limits. Highly bred plants with very large flowers, such as dahlias, chrysanthemums and modern hybrid roses, can look out of place. Their big flowerheads and vivid colours look brash against the softer hues of traditional meadow flowers. Plants with lots of small or middle-sized flowers tend to blend together more easily, just as wild flowers do, even if their colours are contrasting.

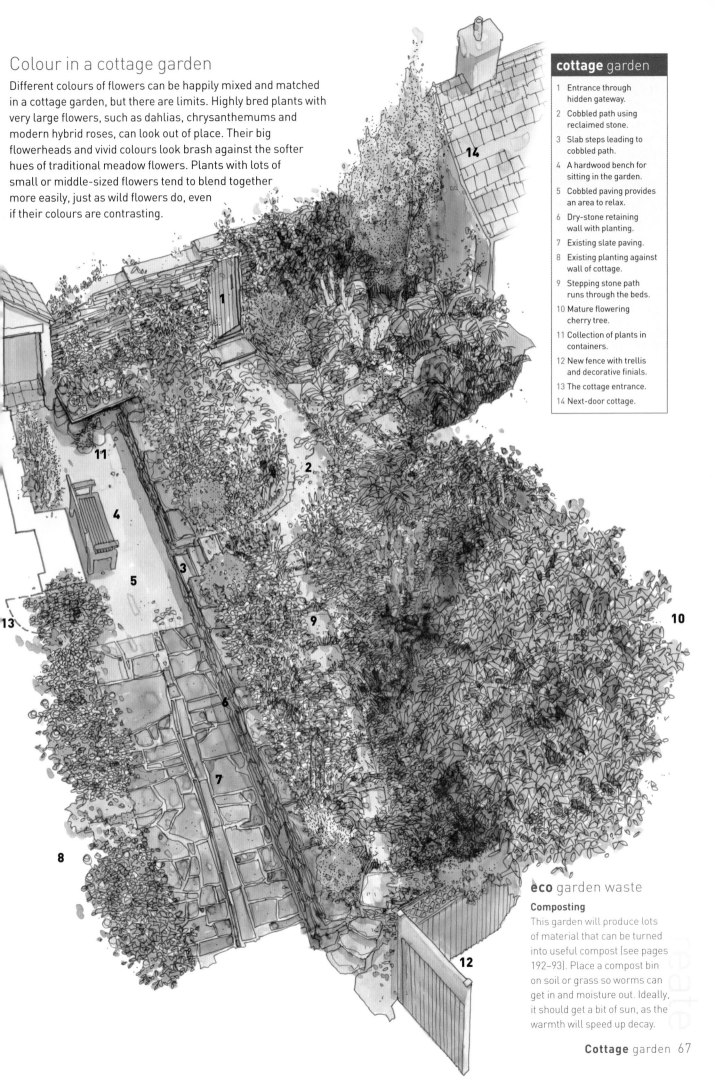

cottage garden

1. Entrance through hidden gateway.
2. Cobbled path using reclaimed stone.
3. Slab steps leading to cobbled path.
4. A hardwood bench for sitting in the garden.
5. Cobbled paving provides an area to relax.
6. Dry-stone retaining wall with planting.
7. Existing slate paving.
8. Existing planting against wall of cottage.
9. Stepping stone path runs through the beds.
10. Mature flowering cherry tree.
11. Collection of plants in containers.
12. New fence with trellis and decorative finials.
13. The cottage entrance.
14. Next-door cottage.

eco garden waste

Composting

This garden will produce lots of material that can be turned into useful compost (see pages 192–93). Place a compost bin on soil or grass so worms can get in and moisture out. Ideally, it should get a bit of sun, as the warmth will speed up decay.

Creating a new cottage border

Borders closely packed with drifts of flowers in glorious colours make up the dream image of a cottage garden – something that looks like the picture on a packet of seeds. Although a new border requires a fair amount of weeding at first, once the plants are established it can be easy to maintain, and wonderfully attractive.

Clearing the area

Clear any dead or overgrown shrubs and trees from the area and prune away dead or overhanging branches. Dig out the roots of larger weeds such as nettles and brambles. Work systematically over the whole area and complete each section before moving on to the next.

Removing turf

Removing turf is the quickest and cleanest method of converting a lawn to a border. Although you lose about 50mm of soil, this is barely noticeable once the area is dug over and prepared.

tools materials

- **edging tool**
- **spade**
- **garden fork**
- **rake**
- **wheelbarrow**
- **gardening gloves**

- garden or organic compost
- general-purpose fertiliser
- coarse horticultural grit

1 Cut the turf into 300–400mm squares using an edging tool. This size of turf square is easy to lift. Keep your work neat by cutting in straight rows.

2 Use a spade to cut through the roots and soil beneath the turf. The squares of turf should be around 50mm thick. Keep the handle of the spade near to the ground so that you cut an even thickness.

3 Move the turf squares in a wheelbarrow. Only load up as many as you can easily move: struggling with an overloaded barrow wastes time and may cause strain.

You can do it...

Turning turf to loam

Make use of the turf you remove from the old lawn by stacking it upside down and leaving it to rot. This makes garden loam, which is the basis of many potting composts.

B&Q

create

Preparing for planting

Traditional cottage gardens were well tended and the soil would be enriched with compost or farmyard manure. Soil that has been under a lawn for some time may be compacted and depleted of organic material and nutrients. Break it up thoroughly, then add compost and fertiliser to improve water retention and provide plant nutrients (see pages 190–91).

While an enriched soil suits most food crops, it is not ideal for all the plants in a cottage garden. Many herbs, such as lavender, rosemary, thyme, hyssop, catmint and sage, have adapted to life in dry, poor soil. You need to provide adequate drainage for them and they benefit from having some coarse grit dug into the soil before they are planted (see page 196).

1 Use a garden fork to turn the soil and break up all the lumps. Remove any large stones, roots and rubbish.

2 Spread a layer of compost over the soil, then turn it in with the garden fork.

3 For areas where you intend to grow Mediterranean plants, such as lavenders, santolina, hyssop, catmint, thyme and oregano, improve the drainage by digging in coarse grit.

4 Add fertiliser to enrich the soil (for quantities, follow the manufacturer's instructions). Always wear gloves and avoid breathing in the dust. Work the fertiliser into the soil with a rake.

Laying stepping stones

Stepping stones are an attractive way of making an informal path through a wide border so that you can reach the furthest parts without trampling on the plants and soil. Concrete stepping stones are fairly inexpensive and simple to lay, with lots of different types to choose from. Rustic-looking stone-effect concrete slabs look particularly good in a cottage garden.

tools materials

- **spade**
- **rake**
- **spirit level**
- **gardening gloves**

- sharp sand
- rustic stone-effect concrete slabs

1 Remove any stones and rake the area flat. Lay the slabs in place to get the spacing and arrangement right. A gentle curve adds more interest, and a little unevenness in spacing and alignment gives a more natural look.

2 Remove each slab in turn and spread a layer of sand about 25mm deep to bed it on. Use a spirit level to smooth the sand and check that it is level.

3 Gently lay the slab back in place and check with a spirit level to make sure it is quite level.

safety first

Level slabs

Set the slabs in the soil at intervals convenient for walking – you don't want to have to leap from slab to slab in wet weather. Make sure the slabs are securely supported in sand and completely level to avoid them becoming a tripping hazard.

Planting a new
cottage border

A traditional cottage garden was a working area in which vegetables were mixed with flowers. Borders were edged with hedges and stone walls where plants thrived. With a little careful planning and planting you can achieve a seemingly random look.

Positioning plants

A planting plan may look straightforward on paper, but it's easy to lose track of once you're in the garden, especially in a large bed that's packed with plants. To avoid this, divide the prepared beds and borders into zones for different plants and then mark out the zones with sand. This makes it much easier to group the plants in their correct planting position.

1 Level the prepared soil with a rake. Mark out the zones within the border with sand, following your planting plan.

tools materials
- **spade**
- **rake**
- **gardening gloves**

- sand
- plants

2 Sort the plants and arrange them in position in their pots on the bed.

Transferring from pots

Careful planting gets plants off to a good start and helps keep them healthy. Plant one at a time and make the hole deep enough to allow the plant to be at the same depth as it was in its pot. Be very gentle as you remove a plant from its pot. Once it is planted, make sure the surrounding soil is firm.

1 Use a spade to dig a hole slightly deeper than the depth of the pot in which the plant is growing and about twice the width.

2 Loosen the soil at the bottom of the hole. This will help the roots get a foothold.

3 Hold the plant around its base with one hand to support it and carefully ease it with its compost out of the pot. If it's stubborn, try pushing in the bottom of the pot with your thumb. Loosen congested roots, but try to avoid breaking them.

4 Stand the plant in the hole. Its compost should be level with the soil. Add or remove soil at the bottom of the hole until it's the right depth. Fill in around the plant and firm the soil with your hands, or for larger plants the heel of your boot, to get rid of air pockets. Water thoroughly.

create

Planting a dry-stone wall

A dry-stone wall has lots of crevices, which provide wonderful sites for alpine and rock-garden plants that will tumble down its surface. These include alpine pinks and alpine species of gypsophila such as *Gypsophila repens*, and *Saponaria ocymoides*, which has a profusion of bright pink flowers. If you're building a new dry-stone wall, you can plant as you build. For an existing wall, make sure you work in as much compost as possible. Water regularly to help the plant become established.

Asplenium trichomanes Maidenhair spleenwort

1 Find a suitable gap between the stones and work in as much compost as you can, leaving just enough space for the plant.

2 Ease the plant from its pot and remove any loose compost, but don't break the roots.

3 Carefully push the plant into position and work in more compost around it. Water the plant thoroughly; use a gentle spray to avoid washing the compost out. Water regularly until the plant is established.

You can do it...

Watering
Water all plants thoroughly when first planted. While they are becoming established they need to be watered every day. If there's no rain, use a sprinkler and leave it running for 30 minutes or so in each part of the garden. Use a gentle spray for plants in the dry-stone wall. Plants in containers need water every day and plant food through the summer.

Caring for a cottage garden

Staking Many taller cottage garden plants, such as hollyhocks, foxgloves, lupins and delphiniums, benefit from cane or wire supports. It's better to stake early, as supports will then be hidden by the growing plant and damage is prevented. Tie loosely with raffia or soft garden string to allow for growth and some movement.

Deadheading Regular removal of dead flowerheads not only keeps beds looking tidy, but can lead to more flowers.

Keeping on top of weeds It's a lot easier to remove weeds when they are small. Make sure you completely dig out the roots of perennial weeds such as buttercups, docks and dandelions or your garden will be visited by them again and again.

Pests Most cottage garden plants are fairly pest resistant, but slugs and snails can wreck all your hard work. There are many ways to reduce their population. Encourage birds, frogs and wildlife. Use deterrents like sharp sand, copper collars and crushed eggshells. You could even go out with a torch after dark and pick them off by hand. If you do resort to slug pellets, always use sparingly and look for ones formulated to cause least harm to other wildlife. See pages 254–59 for more advice on dealing with garden pests and diseases.

Autumn clearing Remove dead or dying stems and leaves and mulch thickly with compost, soil improver or manure (see pages 190–91) to give winter protection and improve the soil for next year.

Digitalis purpurea Foxglove

Cottage garden
planting

The irregular shape and varied conditions of this garden provide the opportunity to use a wide range of plants. These include many traditional cottage plants, but in modern varieties if these are easier to obtain. A number of less traditional plants extend the range of interest into autumn and winter, and provide ground cover that will help keep weeds at bay.

Summer flowers

The stepping stone path is bordered by bushes of lavender, santolina and hyssop. In the shade of the flowering cherry tree are taller rudbeckias, hollyhocks and yarrow, while in the sunnier, drier section near the main path are lupins, sedums, eryngiums and many small clump-forming plants which enjoy the warmth and drier soil. Gaps were interplanted with poppies, linaria, marigolds and other annuals grown from seed (see page 66).

1 *Sedum* 'Autumn Joy' (81)

2 *Sedum telephium* subsp. *ruprechtii* (81)

3 *Eryngium alpinum* Sea holly (83)

4 *Achillea filipendulina* 'Cloth of Gold' Yarrow (138)

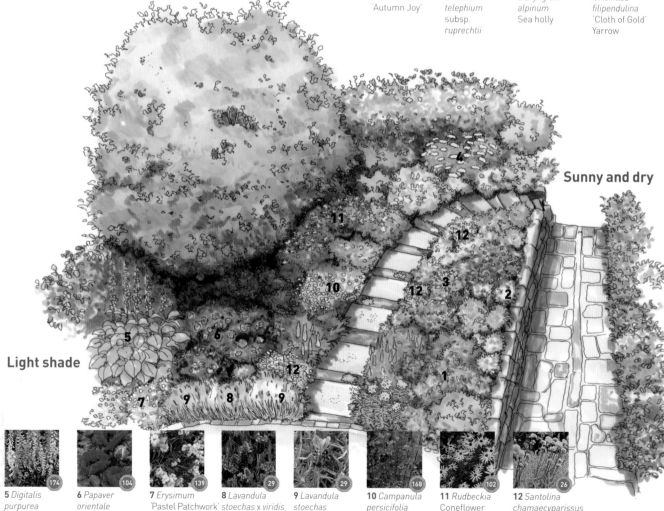

Sunny and dry

Light shade

5 *Digitalis purpurea* 'Excelsior Hybrids' (174)

6 *Papaver orientale* Oriental poppy (104)

7 *Erysimum* 'Pastel Patchwork' Perennial wallflower (139)

8 *Lavandula stoechas x viridis* 'Fathead' French lavender (29)

9 *Lavandula stoechas* 'Blue Star' French lavender (29)

10 *Campanula persicifolia* (168)

11 *Rudbeckia* Coneflower (102)

12 *Santolina chamaecyparissus* Cotton lavender (26)

A patchwork of foliage

What was a dull and neglected corner has been turned into a patchwork of contrasting foliage forms and colours, including ferns, hostas and ligularias. Honeysuckle, which thrives in partial shade, has been planted to screen the cement-rendered wall behind. The semi-shaded area to the right is planted with foxgloves. In front of them are clumps of heucheras, pulmonarias and variegated bugle: these are less conventional cottage garden plants, but their evergreen foliage will make interesting ground cover throughout the year.

Damp and shady corner

24 *Digitalis purpurea* 'Excelsior Hybrids' Foxglove

23 *Ajuga reptans* 'Arctic Fox' Bugle

22 *Hosta fortunei* 'Francee'

21 *Dryopteris filix-mas* Male fern

20 *Lonicera periclymenum* 'Serotina' Honeysuckle

13 *Heuchera micrantha* var. *diversifolia* 'Palace Purple' Coral flower

14 x *Heucherella* 'Sunspot'

15 *Hosta* 'Sum and Substance'

16 *Pulmonaria* 'Raspberry Splash' Lungwort

17 *Pulmonaria rubra* Lungwort

18 *Ligularia przewalskii*

19 *Ligularia dentata* 'Desdemona'

Colour and scent

The semi-circular area bordered by the dry-stone wall and cobbled path is the warmest and most sheltered part of the garden. Planted here are clumps of pink scabious, perennial wallflower (*Erysimum* 'Apricot Delight'), euphorbia, delphiniums and irises. Bushes of lavender and larger-growing thyme make a scented edging for the path and creeping thyme cascades down the edges of the steps.

33 *Thymus vulgaris* 'Silver Posie' Thyme

32 *Origanum* 'Country Cream' Oregano

31 *Erigeron* 'Rosa Juwel' Fleabane

30 *Iris* 'Black Swan'

Warm and sheltered bed

25 *Erysimum* 'Apricot Delight' Perennial wallflower

26 *Euphorbia characias* subsp. *wulfenii* Spurge

27 *Scabiosa* 'Pink Mist' Pincushion flower

28 *Delphinium* 'Pacific Giants Mixed'

29 *Thymus serpyllum* var. *albus* Thyme

plant chooser

Plants with a numbered rosette are featured in more detail in the Plant Chooser, pages 294–327.

Cottage garden planting 73

City **oasis** garden

In the centre of any city there are lots of people who live in flats that overlook small gardens or courtyards. Often these are neglected or empty. But with a neat design and imaginative planting, it's easy to transform a nondescript patch of ground into a magical outdoor living space.

Planning a city oasis garden

A garden that belongs to an upstairs flat will give double the pleasure if it looks as good when viewed from above as it does at ground level. A simple, symmetrical layout can be particularly effective. Choosing colours, styles and materials that echo those indoors can make the garden appear like an extension, and your property feel more spacious.

Finding inspiration

Think of the kind of garden that will suit your lifestyle and the style of your home. A cottage garden in the middle of the city, for instance, might look out of place, and may also need more work than many pressured city-dwellers have time to devote. With limited space, you will probably have to be ruthless about what you include and what you leave out: careful planning is even more important in a small garden than a big one. Draw up a wishlist of priorities. Maybe you want mostly planting, or a pond, somewhere for entertaining, or a quiet spot where you can sit and read.

The design brief

This garden belongs to an upstairs flat and is separated from the property by an alleyway. Measuring 6.5m by 5.5m, the garden started out as a derelict space, an empty site with a bit of earth, used mainly for storing bikes. A large sycamore tree in one corner casts shade in the morning, but most parts of the garden receive a good amount of sunlight through the day. The goal is to create an oasis of calm in a bustling area by using strong design features and stylish planting.

The existing plot

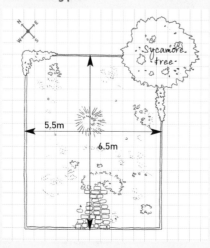

Wants

- Attractive entrance to the garden.
- Plenty of seating.
- Space for a table and chairs.
- A formal layout that will look good seen from the windows above.
- An interesting focal point to lead the eye right into the garden.
- Plenty of flowers, colour and interest all year round.
- Easy maintenance.

Problems

- The boundary fences are all of different types and colours, so there is no uniformity.
- Boundary fences belong to the neighbours, who are unwilling to replace them. (See page 48 for options in this situation.)

Developing ideas

Apart from its large sycamore tree, this garden has no particular features and no planting – it is a blank canvas on which to work. As always, the place to start is by drawing a simple plan showing the shape and boundaries of the plot, and then to try out different designs in order to work out what is to be included, such as grass, paving or areas of planting. Sketch in structures such as seating or a pond. Do discuss your plans with the neighbours, especially if anything you want to install will be visible over the top of the fence or overlook their garden.

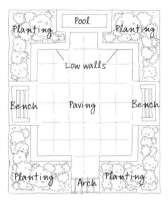

Paved courtyard

Here most of the garden is a terrace laid with square paving slabs. An archway leads straight on to this terrace, and a rectangular pool is positioned directly opposite the entrance. Two benches facing each other across the garden emphasise the symmetry. The walls around the terrace and pool are built to sitting height to provide seating. Planting is confined to L-shaped areas in the four corners.

A green space

A lawn replaces the paving, making this a less expensive but higher maintenance option. A small tree provides a focal point opposite the paved entrance to the garden. The planting to either side of the entrance and at the far end of the garden is flanked by four neat, formal blocks of yew hedging.

Lines and circles

This striking design centres on a circular area from which paths radiate outwards. Tightly clipped topiary, neat cobble edging, circular paving and planting, and a round bird bath create a symmetry that is quite formal. However, the mood is softened by the rest of the planting – a mass of foliage and flowers, dominated by white bush roses and underplanted with bulbs for spring and early summer. Roses, clematis, honeysuckle and other climbers scramble over fences, trellis, and the arched entrance, filling the garden with their fragrance. Paths are lined with low lavender hedging, which will release its scent as it is brushed past.

A wooden bench, a pergola corner seat and room for a table and chairs on the paving circle mean it's possible to sit, enjoy and admire the garden from any direction. This is the sketch that is chosen to become the new garden (see pages 76–87).

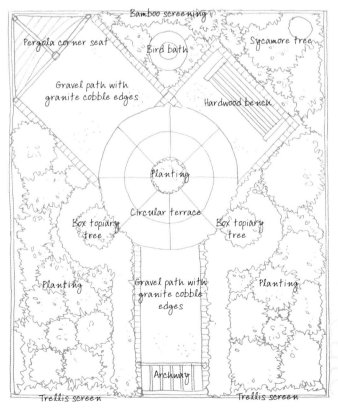

City oasis garden

With its strong sense of structure and abundance of colourful and fragrant planting, this pretty garden makes an inviting space in the heart of the city: a quiet haven for relaxing and reading, and a stylish area for outdoor entertaining.

Design for a perfect haven

The symmetry of this design and the careful balance of planting creates a garden that is quite formal, but at the same time extremely pretty. The new arched entrance frames the ornamental focal point at the end of the garden – the bird bath beyond the stone circle. Gravel paths edged with strips of granite cobble stones lead to the different areas of the garden. The central circle of stone paving is large enough to accommodate a temporary table and chairs for entertaining, and is an attractive feature in its own right, with its centre planted with creeping thyme (the table cannot be positioned over this permanently, however, or it will die). Other seating is provided by a pergola corner seat and a hardwood bench.

The hotch-potch of old fencing is hidden behind bamboo screening (see page 115). The pergola, arch and new trellis on either side of it are all painted a soft aqua green to complement the planting and enhance the prettiness of the garden.

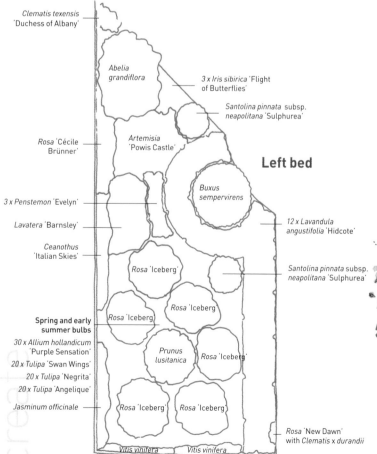

Clematis texensis 'Duchess of Albany'

Abelia grandiflora

3 x Iris sibirica 'Flight of Butterflies'

Santolina pinnata subsp. neapolitana 'Sulphurea'

Artemisia 'Powis Castle'

Left bed

Rosa 'Cécile Brünner'

Buxus sempervirens

3 x Penstemon 'Evelyn'

Lavatera 'Barnsley'

12 x Lavandula angustifolia 'Hidcote'

Ceanothus 'Italian Skies'

Rosa 'Iceberg'

Santolina pinnata subsp. neapolitana 'Sulphurea'

Rosa 'Iceberg'

Spring and early summer bulbs

Rosa 'Iceberg'

30 x Allium hollandicum 'Purple Sensation'

20 x Tulipa 'Swan Wings'

Prunus lusitanica

Rosa 'Iceberg'

20 x Tulipa 'Negrita'

20 x Tulipa 'Angelique'

Jasminum officinale

Rosa 'Iceberg'

Rosa 'Iceberg'

Rosa 'New Dawn' with Clematis x durandii

Vitis vinifera   Vitis vinifera

Focal point planting

Clematis viticella 'Purpurea Plena Elegans'

Lonicera periclymenum 'Graham Thomas'

Rosa 'Blush Noisette'

Hedera helix 'Glacier'

Prunus laurocerasus 'Otto Luyken'

3 x Heuchera micrantha var. diversifolia 'Palace Purple'

Roots of existing sycamore tree

7 x Anemone x hybrida

Spring bulbs
50 x Galanthus caucasicus

5 x Epimedium grandiflorum

Clematis 'Huldine'

3 x Iris sibirica 'Flight of Butterflies'

3 x Helichrysum italicum 'Korma'

3 x Digitalis x mertonensis

3 x Digitalis x mertonensis

5 x Dicentra spectabilis

Right bed

1 x Santolina pinnata subsp. neapolitana 'Sulphurea'

Hydrangea paniculata 'Floribunda'

Rosa 'Eglantyne'

5 x Hyssopus officinalis with underplanting of Nectaroscordum siculum

3 x Artemisia arborescens

Buxus sempervirens

12 x Lavandula angustifolia 'Hidcote'

Rosa 'Iceberg'

Santolina pinnata subsp. neapolitana 'Sulphurea'

Rosa 'Iceberg'

Chaenomeles japonica 'Nivalis'

Spring and early summer bulbs

30 x Allium hollandicum 'Purple Sensation'
20 x Tulipa 'Swan Wings'
20 x Tulipa 'Negrita'
20 x Tulipa 'Angelique'

Rosa 'Iceberg'

Rosa 'Iceberg'

Prunus lusitanica

Clematis viticella 'Etoile Violette'

Rosa 'New Dawn' with Clematis x durandii

Rosa 'Iceberg'

Rosa 'Iceberg'

Vitis vinifera

Vitis vinifera

city oasis garden

1 Pergola and its seat fits neatly into one corner of the garden.

2 Gravel paths edged with granite cobble stones link the different areas.

3 The centre of the garden is an easy-to-install circle of concrete stone paving.

4 The paved circle is big enough for a temporary dining table and chairs.

5 The hardwood bench provides extra seating.

6 Round bird bath makes an attractive focal point.

7 New climbing roses, honeysuckle and ivy clamber up and over the rear fence.

8 Existing sycamore tree provides welcome shade on hot summer days.

9 Rosebeds are underplanted with bulbs – tulips for spring, alliums for early summer.

10 Topiary box trees planted on either side of the garden enhance the formal layout.

11 More climbing plants cover the trellis on either side of the entrance to the garden.

12 A wooden archway covered in clematis and roses makes a pretty entrance.

13 Planting is echoed from one side of the garden to the other.

14 Bamboo screening covers the old fencing.

15 Soft colours for planting are visually gentle, creating an atmosphere of calm.

16 Low lavender hedging borders the paths.

City oasis garden
paths and paving

A paved circle provides the centrepiece and starting point for this symmetrical design. One gravel path leads from the entrance directly to the circle. Two more gravel paths radiate from it at 45° towards the outer corners. Flowerbeds and other structures are arranged around the circle.

Making a start

To make sure the design really is the same on both sides of the garden, take time to measure and set out carefully. Using long tape measures and spray paint, mark out all the features on the ground: the circular terrace, the gravel paths, the posts of the pergola corner seat, and the entrance arch.

1 Lay long tape measures down the centre and around the perimeter of the garden.

2 Use a builder's line, tape measure and spray marker paint to mark out the circle in the centre of the garden.

3 Mark out the paths with string lines and spray paint, checking all right angles with a builder's square. Measure the diagonals across the rectangular areas to make sure they are the same.

4 Measure and mark the positions of the posts for the pergola. Double check all the markings against your plan.

Checking for pipes and cables

The paving circle and the paths are laid on a base of compacted Type 1 granular sub-base stone to ensure they remain stable whatever the weather. Before you start excavating the area, use a hired cable avoidance tool (CAT) to check for any underground pipes or cables for gas, water, electricity, telephone or drainage services. Mark the position of any you locate using spray paint. Pipes and cables should be buried a minimum of 450mm below the surface, but you cannot be certain of that. You may have to revise your plans, or employ a professional to relocate service pipes, if they lie beneath areas you were intending to excavate.

Preparing the foundations

Remove any vegetation and the topsoil to a depth of 200mm for the paving circle. Dig the paths to a depth of 150mm. The post holes for the pergola should lie just outside the sub-base area.

tools materials
- **spade**
- **tape measure**
- **rake**
- **wheelbarrow**
- **plate compactor (hire)**

- wooden marker pegs
- Type 1 granular sub-base stone

1 Use marker pegs to mark the finished sub-base level of 100mm. Tip in a 150mm layer of Type 1 sub-base stone and rake it level.

2 Compact the Type 1 with a petrol-powered vibrating plate compactor.

Laying a stone circle

These concrete paving slabs are specially shaped to form a circle, so there is no need to cut them. The slabs are 35mm thick and are laid on a 20mm bed of concrete. The central stone is left out to create a planting area.

tools materials
- **tape measure**
- **metal dowel or stake**
- **builder's line and pegs**
- **cement mixer**
- **gloves**
- **rubber mallet**
- **spirit level**
- **bricklayer's trowel**
- **pointing trowel**
- **pointing iron (see page 267)**

- paving mix concrete (see page 376)
- circle slab kit
- mortar

1 Dry-lay the slabs for the inner stone circle. Drive a metal dowel or stake into the centre of the circle and stretch a level line from it to the outside edge at the finished ground level height – this is 50mm above the height of the sub-base (the same level as the gravel will eventually be).

2 Bed the first slab on a 20mm layer of paving mix concrete. Use a rubber mallet to tap it into the correct position level with the string line. Check the slab is completely level using a spirit level.

3 Continue laying slabs until the inner circle is complete. Keep checking that they are level with a spirit level.

4 Dry-lay the outer circle and then concrete the slabs in place in the same way.

5 Point the joints between the slabs with mortar and smooth with a pointing iron. Allow to dry for 24 hours; in wet weather, cover the slabs as they dry.

ideal tool

Cement mixer
A cement mixer will make short work of mixing concrete. Wash the drum thoroughly after use.

City oasis garden
paths and paving

Gravel paths blend well with paving, and their formal lines give structure and contrast to the densely planted beds. A row of stones or blocks forms a neat retaining edge and prevents the gravel spilling onto neighbouring areas.

Laying gravel paths

Once the paving is in place the paths can be spread with decorative gravel to a depth of 50mm. Gravel paths need an edging to stop the gravel spreading onto the flowerbeds. Here, the edging was created using granite cobble stones attached to a plastic mesh (known as carpet stones), which makes them particularly straightforward and quick to lay.

1 Cut single lines of granite cobble stones for the retaining edging, cutting through the mesh backing with pliers.

tools materials

- **pliers**
- **builder's line and pegs**
- **bricklayer's trowel**
- **spirit level**
- **pointing trowel**
- **rake**

- granite cobble stones on plastic mesh backing
- paving mix concrete (see page 376)
- decorative pearl grey gravel (20mm size)

2 Stretch a builder's line from one end of the path to the other at the finished height of the path (that is, the height once the gravel is in place). Bed the strips on paving mix concrete. Be careful to keep the tops of the stones at the height of the line. Use a spirit level to make sure the stones are level.

3 Haunch the concrete up against the edging on both sides to hold the stones in place. But take care to keep it lower than the level of the finished path so that it will be hidden by the gravel. Use a pointing trowel to fill the joints between the stones.

4 When the edging is dry, spread decorative gravel over the surface of the path to a depth of about 50mm, then rake it level.

create

Planting within paving

Flowerbeds either side of paths and within paving provide a colourful contrast to hard areas of gravel and stone. Low-growing, creeping thyme is ideal in an area created by leaving out a paving slab, such as at the centre of this paved circle. This fast-growing plant will quickly spread to fill the space, forming a springy mat. Its attractive green leaves have an aromatic scent when crushed and its violet flowers look pretty in summer. It's robust enough to cope with being trodden on occasionally, but don't position outdoor furniture over it permanently, or it will die.

tools materials

- **garden spade**
- **garden fork**
- **trowel**

- multi-purpose compost
- coarse horticultural grit
- decorative pearl grey gravel (20mm size)
- plants

1 Dig out the granular sub-base stone from the centre of the circle with a garden spade.

2 Fill the space with compost and a good spadeful of coarse horticultural grit.

3 Mix the compost and grit well together by turning over with a garden fork.

4 Using a trowel, dig holes slightly deeper than the depth of the pots in which the plants are growing and about twice the width. Gently remove each plant from its pot and stand it in a hole. Fill in around the plant with compost and firm with your hands. Scatter a top dressing of decorative gravel around the thyme plants. Water thoroughly.

Thymus praecox Creeping thyme

City oasis garden
pergola corner seat

In one corner of this garden, a pergola seat offers shelter and shade from the glare of the sun. Easy to assemble, it is painted with decorative wood preserver in soft aqua green to harmonise with the planting, and echo the colour of the arch that forms the entrance to the garden.

Pergola with a seat

All kinds of pergolas can be bought in kit-form, with their pieces ready cut and treated against rot. A corner pergola with a timber seat can fit into the smallest outdoor room, creating a secluded spot where you can sit and admire the garden.

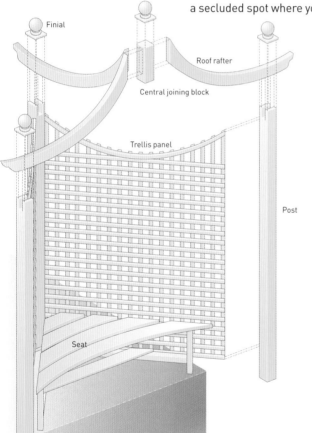

Finial

Roof rafter

Central joining block

Trellis panel

Post

Seat

tools materials

- **tape measure**
- **spade**
- **post hole borer**
- **gloves**
- **spirit level**
- **watering can**
- **hammer**
- **power drill**
- **step ladder**

- corner pergola with seat flatpack kit
- canes
- dry-mix post-fix concrete or footing mix concrete (see page 376)
- timber props and nails

Setting posts

The pergola posts are fixed in place with concrete. It's essential to position the post holes precisely, or you will have trouble fitting the pergola pieces together.

1 Mark the post positions by pushing a cane into what will be the centre of each hole. Dig each hole to a depth of 500mm.

2 Fit the back corner post into its hole. Ask a helper to hold it vertical. Pour dry-mix post-fix concrete into the hole around the post. Moisten the mix in the hole with a measured amount of water from a watering can. Nail temporary timber props to the post while the concrete dries. Repeat with the other two posts.

Fixing posts

All the posts here were secured with special rapid-set post-fix concrete – a mix of sand, cement and aggregate that is poured into the hole dry and then wet with a measured amount of water. It takes just 10–15 minutes to set.

You could equally use a conventional footing mix concrete (see page 376). The post will need to be securely cross-braced to hold it in position for 24 hours as the concrete sets.

create

Fitting the trellis and roof

Pretreated timbers can be left as they are, or painted. If you wish to paint this pergola, do so before you assemble it in position (see below right). The structure here is sited on gravel, so the trellis can sit right on the ground without danger of it rotting. On bare earth, it's better to position wooden trellis panels just above the ground.

1 Drill pilot holes and nail the first trellis panel in place. Nail the second panel, checking that it's level with the first one.

2 Screw the roof rafters to the central joining block, following the manufacturer's instructions.

3 Slot the ends of the roof rafters into the slots at the tops of the posts. Fit a finial to each of the posts and one at the top of the joining block in the centre.

Fitting the seat

The pergola seat section is made of curved slats, echoing the curves of the rafters and of the paving circle. These are screwed to a frame and then the whole unit is positioned in the pergola.

1 Make up the frame for the seat, following the manufacturer's instructions. Screw the smallest seat piece to the back corner of the frame.

ideal tool

Post hole borer
If you have lots of post holes to dig, a post hole borer will make the work easier. You can use it both to dig and remove soil from the hole.

2 Fit the frame's brace piece halfway between the back and the front of the frame.

3 Screw the other seat pieces in position on the frame, working from back to front.

4 Position the seat and use a spirit level to check it is level. Paint the rest of the structure.

City oasis garden
arch and trellis fencing

A simple timber arch makes an appealing entrance, framing the view of the interior and enticing you to walk through and into the space beyond. Its shape echoes the curves and circles that recur throughout this small space – in the paving, the pergola, the bird bath, and the topiary.

Making an entrance

Pre-shaped timber and iron arches are widely available and easy to install. If you plan to grow climbing roses over an arch, be sure it is wide enough and high enough that people won't snag their clothes on thorns as they pass. New trellis fencing on either side of this timber arch completes the transformation of the entrance to the garden.

The arch posts need to be securely fixed in concrete to make sure the structure is stable. Mark and dig the post holes as for the pergola to a depth of 500mm, pushing a cane in to mark the centre of each hole .

Assembling the roof

The posts and trellis sides are already assembled with the kit used in this garden. All the holes are pre-drilled, too, so it's a simple matter to assemble and fit the roof section.

tools materials

- **tape measure**
- **spade**
- **rubber mallet**
- **screwdriver, or power drill with screwdriver bit**
- **spirit level**

- timber arch flatpack kit
- canes
- dry-mix post-fix concrete or footing mix concrete (see page 376)
- timber props

1 Fix the cross members to one of the roof rafters, fitting the wooden dowels into the pre-drilled holes. Use a rubber mallet to tap them into place.

2 Fit the second rafter, again tapping the dowels home with the rubber mallet.

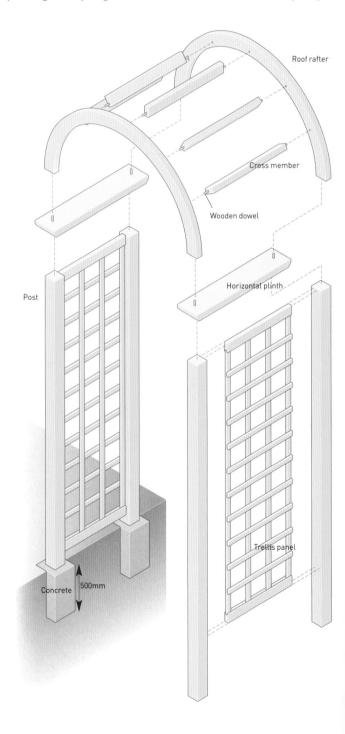

Roof rafter

Cross member

Wooden dowel

Horizontal plinth

Post

Trellis panel

Concrete | 500mm

Erecting the arch

Horizontal plinths are attached to the top of each side panel, then the roof section is fixed to the plinths. With the arch framework fully assembled, you are ready to secure the posts in the ground with rapid-set post-fix concrete, or a conventional footing mix concrete (see page 376).

(see page 376)

safety first

Two pairs of hands

Don't let the arch topple over and fall on you while you are stretching up to fit the roof rafters to the trellised sides. Get a helper to hold the structure steady while you screw the roof of the arch to the posts.

1 Secure a plinth to the top of each side panel with a screw either side of the dowel.

2 Fix the arched roof to the posts with long screws, following the manufacturer's instructions.

Putting up trellis fencing

When the arch is installed and the concrete dry, trellis fence panels are fitted either side of it to create a new boundary. The gap to be spanned is wider than one panel (but narrower than two), so a fence post must be erected mid-way and a trellis panel cut to fit. This second panel is fixed to a new post next to the side fence. Measure and mark the positions of the post holes, and dig them to a depth of 500mm. It's often easier to paint or treat trellis panels before you mount them; pay special attention to any cut ends, which are most liable to rot.

tools materials

- **power drill**
- **spade**
- **tape measure**
- **watering can**
- **panel saw**

- trellis panels
- fence posts
- galvanised screws
- dry-mix post-fix concrete or footing mix concrete
- timber props and nails

1 Screw a trellis fence panel to the first arch post. Ask a helper to hold the trellis level for you.

3 Stand the arch posts in the holes and use a spirit level to check the posts are vertical and the roof is level. Make sure the trellis panels for the fencing on either side of the arch will fit under the plinths; adjust the depth of the holes if necessary. Concrete the posts in position (see page 82). Support them with timber props while they dry.

(see page 82)

2 At the end of the trellis panel cement the post in place (see page 82). Support the post with temporary timber props until the concrete is fully dry, then attach the trellis.

(see page 82)

3 Concrete the second post in place next to the fence and support with timber props as it dries. Measure the distance between the two posts that the trellis will need to span, and cut a panel to fit. Then attach the trellis.

City oasis
planting

The planting of this pretty garden is abundantly floral. But at the same time strong elements of symmetry, and formal touches like clipped topiary shapes, preserve a sense of order and calm, making this a magical space in the midst of a busy urban setting.

Contained abundance

The beds to either side of the entrance are similar, but not identical. Both are densely planted with a profusion of cluster-flowered white roses behind a tidy row of lavender that defines the outline of the path. A mass of pretty climbers – rose, clematis, jasmine, even a vine that should produce tasty grapes – are planted to climb up and over all the vertical surfaces, including the arch through which the garden is entered. Multi-layered clipped box balls rise up at the end of the path on each side, striking a note of formality amid all this verdant growth. Their round shapes echo the circular theme that is repeated throughout the forms and layout of this garden.

ideal plant (62)

For clambering over fences and trellises
Jasmine is an easy-to-grow climber with delicate foliage which is covered in summer with white flowers that release a heavenly perfume at dusk.

Left bed

Entrance

15 *Prunus lusitanica* Portugal laurel (6)

14 *Vitis vinifera* Grape vine (71)

13 *Rosa* 'Iceberg' Bush rose (57)

12 *Jasminum officinale* Summer jasmine (62)

11 *Ceanothus* 'Italian Skies' California lilac (51)

10 *Lavatera* 'Barnsley' Tree mallow (32)

9 *Penstemon* 'Evelyn' (135)

1 *Buxus sempervirens* Box (19)

2 *Lavandula angustifolia* 'Hidcote' English lavender (29)

3 *Santolina pinnata* subsp. *neapolitana* 'Sulphurea' Cotton lavender (26)

4 *Iris sibirica* 'Flight of Butterfies' (123)

5 *Abelia grandiflora*

6 *Clematis texensis* 'Duchess of Albany' (73)

7 *Artemisia* 'Powis Castle' Wormwood (31)

8 *Rosa* 'Cécile Brünner' Climbing rose (72)

Focal point planting

Directly in line with the arched entrance, a stone bird bath forms the central focus of a small triangular bed against the rear fence. Planted either side of the bird bath is the dainty *Iris sibirica* 'Flight of Butterflies', with small blue flowers in June and very upright, slender blue-green foliage. In front is *Helichrysum italicum* 'Korma', or the curry plant – a dwarf shrub with felty, silvery grey leaves that release a pungent, curry-like scent when brushed. At the back of the bed, lots more climbers – ivy, clematis, honeysuckle – are positioned to grow up the fence and the trellis panels of the pergola corner seat.

plant chooser

Plants with a numbered rosette are featured in more detail in the Plant Chooser, pages 294–327.

16 *Helichrysum italicum* 'Korma' Curry plant

17 *Iris sibirica* 'Flight of Butterflies'

18 *Prunus laurocerasus* 'Otto Luyken' Cherry laurel

19 *Clematis viticella* 'Purpurea Plena Elegans'

20 *Rosa* 'Blush Noisette' Bush rose

21 *Lonicera periclymenum* 'Graham Thomas' Honeysuckle

22 *Hedera helix* 'Glacier' Ivy

---

ideal plant ㉙

For edging paths
Lavender is hard to beat for creating edges to paths and beds in sun. It doesn't need rich soil and has dense spikes of fragrant blue flowers, plus aromatic silvery foliage that releases its scent when brushed against.

Right bed

34 *Vitis vinifera* Grape vine

33 *Prunus lusitanica* Portugal laurel

32 *Rosa* 'Iceberg' Bush rose

Entrance

31 *Hyssopus officinalis* Hyssop

23 *Buxus sempervirens* Box

24 *Lavandula angustifolia* 'Hidcote' English lavender

25 *Santolina pinnata* subsp. *neapolitana* 'Sulphurea' Cotton lavender

26 *Hydrangea paniculata* 'Floribunda'

27 *Rosa* 'Eglantyne' Bush rose

28 *Artemisia arborescens* Wormwood

29 *Chaenomeles japonica* 'Nivalis' Japonica

30 *Clematis viticella* 'Etoile Violette'

Socialising garden

A socialising garden is fun and inviting. It's a space that's perfect for all kinds of get-togethers – from the kids' friends or neighbours popping in for an informal barbecue or drink, to leisurely Sunday lunches and summer parties.

Planning a socialising garden

A garden that's designed for people to meet and relax together needs to have places for cooking, sitting and playing, with lighting and heating to extend the hours of entertaining. All these elements can be blended with attractive planting to bring the practical and ornamental aspects of the garden into harmony with each other.

Finding inspiration

Think of all the different ways you like to entertain indoors and see if you can do the same outdoors. Do you enjoy barbecuing, candlelit meals, or casual drinks with a group of friends on the patio? Garden lighting and a patio heater can make evening entertaining much more comfortable. Do you want the garden divided into different areas with a place for a table and chairs, colourful flowerbeds, a secluded corner, or a play area? What kinds of plants and colour schemes do you like? And how about making a real statement with a grand focal point like a deck, garden building, or large water feature?

The design brief

This family garden is 19m long and 15.2m wide. At the start of the project it was mostly level, apart from a raised area at the back. The soil was dry and depleted, and the lawn mossy, weed-infested and uneven. The raised area was neglected, strewn with sand, stones and moss. The roots of an old apple tree had lifted the slabs on the York stone path on the left-hand side of the garden, leaving the surface uneven. This was a plot needing drastic changes to transform it into a sociable outdoor living space.

The existing plot

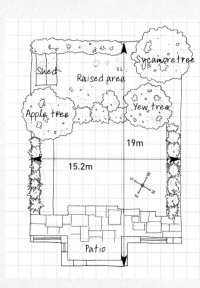

Wants

- A modern, social garden for all the family to enjoy.
- Dramatic focal feature of some kind.
- A mix of surfaces, including hard areas for all-weather use.
- A children's play area, preferably tucked away from the main garden.
- Larger patio, with more interesting shape.
- Summerhouse for relaxation and storage, and to double as a home office.
- More lighting, for security and to highlight features.
- Retain mature planting in side beds.

Problems

- Because of the change of level, the low retaining wall will need to stay.
- Need to find matching paving slabs for the patio extension.
- Need space to store garden tools that are currently in the shed.
- The old apple and sycamore trees can be removed, but the yew is subject to a tree preservation order.
- Grand plans in a big space can prove expensive, so budget must be closely monitored.

Developing ideas

A fair-sized conventional garden offers much potential as a space for socialising. Get some ideas down on paper so you can start to get a view of what will work, and decide on a budget.

Vine arbour

In this design a wide path runs down the centre of the garden. On each side at either end there are low squares of box with underlit mop-head bay trees planted in their centres. The path draws the eye along the length of the garden to an arbour covered with vines at the back of a raised deck. A new summerhouse is positioned on the deck and a play area is created behind the yew tree.

Relaxing water

This more minimal approach features a large raised pool with jets of water spurting from each end. The yew tree has been taken down, letting in more light, and a hedge planted at the end of the garden. Paths on either side of the lawn lead to a raised deck that has topiary trees in pots. However, there is no summerhouse or dedicated play area; and the mature yew tree is protected by law, so felling it is not permissible (see page 49).

A place to work, play and entertain

Here a water feature on several levels makes a big impact. It's situated on the raised area, most of which is covered with decking. The shed is replaced by a summerhouse that is large enough to double as a home office, while the area behind the yew tree becomes a play area. The patio by the house has been extended in an elegant curve towards the lawn. This design is chosen for the new garden (see pages 90–109).

Socialising garden

Designed for use day and night, this spectacular garden has a clean-cut contemporary look. It provides an ideal venue to have a good time, party and be with friends. And it's a great place for older children to play in safety.

A design for entertaining

This garden provides three distinct areas for socialising – patio, lawn and deck. The symmetry of the layout and some of the planting (the box and lavender hedging that skirts the patio, for example) creates a formal mood. But at the same time this is balanced by the mixed, more informal planting of the new central bed and the existing side beds. A deck runs across much of the raised area at the rear, with one corner given over to a children's area that includes a playframe standing on natural play bark (see page 116). New paths run either side of the lawn linking the deck and the patio. The ragged edge of the old patio has been straightened and reshaped with an elegant curved area that projects into the lawn and leads the eye towards the dramatic modern water feature at the back of the garden. The water falls from a large blockwork structure into a small pool, then runs under the deck to flow across stainless steel sheets before dropping into a lower pool.

Floodlights are fitted to the house. There are marker lights along each path, lights either side of the steel waterway and lighting on the deck. The spiral box trees on the deck are backlit and lights shine up into the yew tree from the bed.

Soft colour and shape

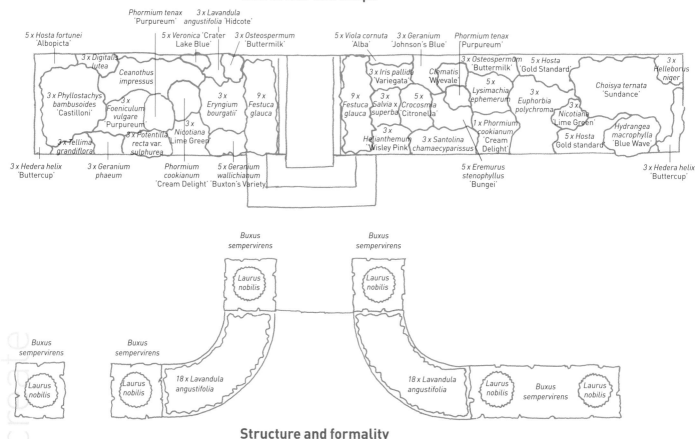

5 x Hosta fortunei 'Albopicta'

Phormium tenax 'Purpureum'

3 x Lavandula angustifolia 'Hidcote'

5 x Veronica 'Crater Lake Blue'

3 x Osteospermum 'Buttermilk'

5 x Viola cornuta 'Alba'

3 x Geranium 'Johnson's Blue'

Phormium tenax 'Purpureum'

3 x Digitalis lutea

Ceanothus impressus

3 x Iris pallida 'Variegata'

Clematis 'Wyevale'

3 x Osteospermum 'Buttermilk'

5 x Hosta 'Gold Standard'

3 x Helleborus niger

3 x Phyllostachys bambusoides 'Castilloni'

3 x Foeniculum vulgare 'Purpureum'

3 x Eryngium bourgatii

9 x Festuca glauca

9 x Festuca glauca

3 x Salvia x superba

5 x Crocosmia 'Citronella'

5 x Lysimachia ephemerum

3 x Euphorbia polychroma

Choisya ternata 'Sundance'

3 x Nicotiana 'Lime Green'

3 x Nicotiana 'Lime Green'

3 x Tellima grandiflora

3 x Potentilla recta var. sulphurea

3 x Helianthemum 'Wisley Pink'

3 x Santolina chamaecyparissus

1 x Phormium cookianum 'Cream Delight'

5 x Hosta 'Gold standard'

Hydrangea macrophylla 'Blue Wave'

3 x Hedera helix 'Buttercup'

3 x Geranium phaeum

Phormium cookianum 'Cream Delight'

5 x Geranium wallichianum 'Buxton's Variety'

5 x Eremurus stenophyllus 'Bungei'

3 x Hedera helix 'Buttercup'

Buxus sempervirens

Buxus sempervirens

Laurus nobilis

Laurus nobilis

Buxus sempervirens

Buxus sempervirens

Laurus nobilis

Laurus nobilis

18 x Lavandula angustifolia

18 x Lavandula angustifolia

Laurus nobilis

Buxus sempervirens

Laurus nobilis

Structure and formality

A family space

Although designed with socialising in mind, the garden is also laid out in a practical way for family life. The summerhouse makes a useful home office, allowing some peace and quiet away from indoor distractions. The play area allows the children and their friends to have fun under the watchful eye of adults relaxing on the deck. However, the open pools of water mean this is not a garden suitable for very young children (see page 100).

socialising garden

1 Sculptural water feature makes a dramatic centrepiece.
2 Spiral box topiary in pots.
3 Large deck for relaxing and socialising.
4 Patio heater for evening warmth.
5 Summerhouse doubling as home office, with separate storage area.
6 Playframe on play bark.
7 New paths and steps with outer edges lined with lights.
8 Water flows over stainless steel sheets into a lower pool.

9 New planting in central raised bed.
10 Deck built around trunk of yew tree.
11 New lawn (see pages 270–73).
12 Mop-head bay trees planted within square box hedging.
13 Enlarged patio makes a curved entrance to lawn.
14 Hardwood table and chairs with a parasol.
15 Barbecue.
16 Pot plants add colour to the patio.
17 Existing planting in side beds is retained.

Socialising garden
restyling a patio

The curved outline of the restyled patio gives a new elegance to this part of the garden, and leads the eye to the 2m-high water feature that adds such drama and style to this outdoor space.

New-look landscaping

The existing patio was rectangular in shape, with an uneven, ragged edge. Its smart new outline is created by lifting, cutting and relaying some of the stones along the lawn edge. New concrete slab paths are laid alongside the beds on either side of the garden. Concrete slabs are available in a variety of finishes, so it is usually possible to find a close match to existing slabs.

Reshaping a patio

Mark out the new shape of the paving using a straightedge, long tape measure, string and spray marker paint. New slabs must be laid on a properly prepared sub-base. This should consist of 100mm compacted Type 1 granular sub-base stone, followed by a thin layer of sharp sand or all-in ballast. The new slabs need to maintain the fall of the existing paving, so water runs away from the house. For more information on laying slabs, see pages 160–61, and also **You Can Do It: the Complete B&Q Step-by Step-Book of Home Improvement**.

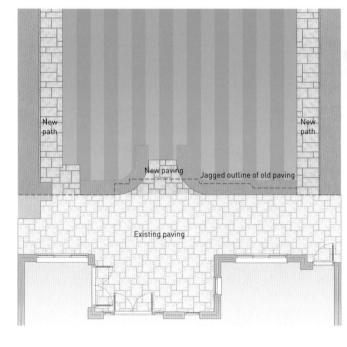

New path

New path

New paving

Jagged outline of old paving

Existing paving

1 Mark out the new outline of the paving with spray marker paint. Excavate the extended patio area to the correct depth: allow for a 100mm layer of compressed Type 1 sub-base stone, plus 20mm mortar, plus the depth of a slab. Lay the sub-base (see page 155).

2 Mark the slabs to be cut using string and a pencil or spray paint. Cut along the line with an angle grinder fitted with a stone-cutting disc. Always follow all safety instructions supplied with this tool, and wear safety goggles, ear defenders, a gauze dust mask and heavy-duty gloves. Use a rubber mallet to break away the surplus pieces. Smooth the cut line with the angle grinder.

3 Dry-lay the slabs and cut any small in-fill pieces. Bed them on mortar, using a spirit level to check the surface is flat and maintains the fall of the existing patio. Allow a gap between slabs for pointing; this should match the width of the existing pointing. Leave to set for 48 hours, then fill the joints (see page 161).

tools materials

- **straightedge**
- **long tape measure**
- **builder's line and pegs**
- **spade**
- **shovel**
- **wheelbarrow**
- **spirit level**
- **rake**
- **safety goggles**
- **dust mask**
- **ear defenders**
- **heavy-duty gloves**
- **plate compactor (hire)**
- **angle grinder with stone-cutting disc**
- **rubber mallet**
- **builder's trowel**
- **pointing trowel**

- spray marker paint
- pencil
- string
- Type 1 granular sub-base stone
- sharp sand or all-in ballast
- mortar

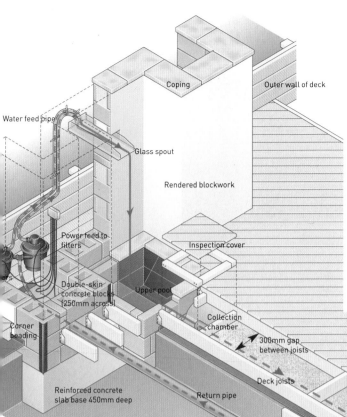

Coping

Outer wall of deck

Water feed pipe

Glass spout

Rendered blockwork

Power feed to filters

Inspection cover

Double-skin concrete blocks (250mm across)

Upper pool

Corner beading

Collection chamber

300mm gap between joists

Reinforced concrete slab base 450mm deep

Return pipe

Deck joists

Gravel over landscaping fabric

Decking

Coping stones

Water outlet

Stainless steel sheets laid on concrete paving slabs

Stone retaining wall

Deck post set in concrete

Pond liner over a concrete base

Lower pool

Pump

Single-skin concrete blocks (100mm across)

Reinforced concrete slab base 150mm deep

Integrated deck and water feature

This is an ambitious project. A professional landscaper could do some or all of the work for you, and also adapt the plan and dimensions to suit those of your garden. But the skilled and experienced home improver need not be put off. There are many stages of the job that will be made much easier by an extra pair of hands. Apart from the electrical connections (see page 373), there's nothing here that requires professional skills or hard-to-find specialist materials.

It is always sensible to approach the Planning Department of your local council before beginning any large-scale work in the garden. In many areas of the UK, this project would require planning permission (see page 373).

Laying the foundations

Water gushes out of a glass spout in the rendered concrete block structure, falling into a pool before flowing under the deck to a lower pool, from where it is pumped back up in a circuit. The upper and lower sections of the water feature are built first, and the decking is then laid around them. The blockwork structure is very heavy, so must be built on a double-reinforced concrete slab. The metal grille reinforcements can be cut to size using an angle grinder fitted with a metal-cutting disc.

1 Mark the area of the concrete base, first with sand or spray paint, then with builder's line and pegs. The water feature is 3m x 1m, and the base extends 100mm beyond it all around. The upper pool is 1m x 1m, and projects 450mm beyond the structure. If the feature is to be aligned to anything (here, the patio), then run string lines the whole length of the garden to ensure you position it correctly.

2 Excavate the marked area to a depth of 650mm. You will probably need a hired skip to take away the debris. Use a spirit level to make sure the sides and base of the trench are vertical and level. Hammer in pegs to mark the finished concrete height (450mm).

3 Pour the concrete in stages. When it is about 100mm deep, place the first reinforcing grille on top. Position the second at about 300mm. Then continue pouring until the concrete is level with the tops of the pegs. Leave to dry for 48 hours.

tools materials

- tape measure
- builder's line and pegs
- hammer
- spade
- heavy-duty gloves
- shovel
- spirit level
- wheelbarrow
- skip (hire)
- angle grinder with metal-cutting disc

- sand or spray marker paint
- wooden marker pegs
- 2m³ ready-mix concrete
- metal grille reinforcements

Socialising garden
building a water feature

This water feature makes an eye-catching focal point. Position it for maximum impact – in this garden it's directly in line with the curved extension to the patio.

Setting out

When working out where to begin construction of the water feature, precision is important. Such a simple, geometric structure will look awkward if not quite straight or slightly off-centre.

1 Run a line from the back of the concrete slab base all the way down the garden to find the exact centre for the water feature. Mark this centre point on the ground in a dollop of mortar, holding a spirit level against the line to ensure your mark is accurate.

2 Mark the centre position on the other side of the slab in the same way.

3 Join up the two marks on a thin layer of mortar. Score a line between them using the point of a trowel against a straightedge or long spirit level.

4 Lay a builder's square along this centre line and use it to mark out the line of the back of the feature in more mortar. Repeat on the other side.

5 Dry-lay the first course of double-skin blocks for the main structure, leaving 15mm gaps between them for mortar. Check the measurements again to ensure the outline of the structure is correct.

tools materials

- tape measure
- builder's line and pegs
- long spirit level
- builder's trowel
- builder's square
- heavy-duty gloves
- safety goggles
- dust mask
- angle grinder with stone-cutting disc
- rubber mallet
- mini scaffold tower (hire)

- mortar
- double-skin dense concrete blocks (215mm high x 440mm wide x 250mm deep)
- engineering bricks
- reinforced concrete lintel
- 300mm-wide coping stones
- single-skin dense concrete blocks (215mm high x 440mm wide x 100mm deep)
- two lengths of timber shuttering for water collection area
- water outlet pipe

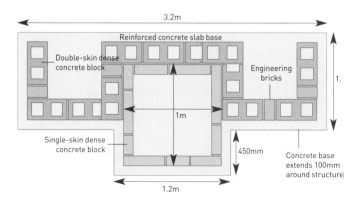

Reinforced concrete slab base

3.2m

Double-skin dense concrete block

Engineering bricks

Single-skin dense concrete block

1m

1.2m

450mm

Concrete base extends 100mm around structure

create

Laying the concrete blocks

Blocks can be cut with an angle grinder; but you can often avoid this by using frost-proof engineering bricks instead. Don't lay more than three courses (rows) of blocks in 24 hours, as their weight can displace the mortar between them.

1 Lay the first course on a 15mm bed of mortar. Tap each block with a rubber mallet to bed it in the mortar. Use a spirit level to ensure blocks are level.

2 Continue with the next course, staggering the joints. Apply mortar to the surfaces of the already laid blocks.

3 Position each block and tap it with a rubber mallet until level. Aim for 15mm-wide horizontal and vertical joints. If a block is too low or high, remove it and adjust the amount of mortar.

4 Keep checking the blocks are level as you scrape away excess mortar with the trowel edge.

5 Work from a mini scaffold tower as the blockwork grows taller. The water spout is at eye level. To avoid cutting a whole course of blocks, lay engineering bricks on top of the sixth course of blocks to make the wall up to the correct height.

6 Leave a 200mm-wide, 100mm-deep opening for the water spout. Lay a reinforced concrete lintel above the opening.

7 Continue laying blocks until the wall reaches approximately 2m. Finish it with coping stones, laid on a continuous bed of mortar. Wet the back of the slabs first.

The upper pool

Set into the indent at the foot of the blockwork structure is a 1m x 1m square pool. Water falls from the spout into this pool. As it fills, the water spills over into a collection area from where it is channelled into a pipe that carries it under the deck to the lower water feature.

Building the pool and collection area

The pool is 450mm deep and is made from two courses of single-skin concrete blocks. Once the mortar is dry, use an angle grinder to cut a notch, 25mm-deep and 150mm-wide, from its upper front edge. The notch will be hidden by coping stones that lie flush with the deck surface (see page 105). Place two lengths of temporary timber shuttering 300mm apart against the front of this pool, haunching the ground up each side to hold them. (Timber shuttering or formwork is used to hold wet concrete or mortar in shape as it dries.) Lay the water outlet pipe between the timbers. Mix a very strong mortar (see page 376) and mould it to channel water into the outlet pipe. The upper edge of the mortar and shuttering must be 100mm below the top of the blocks. When the mortar is dry, the shuttering is removed and replaced with deck joists (see page 101).

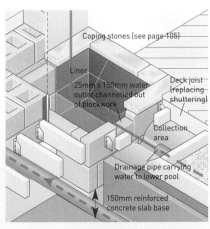

Coping stones (see page 105)

Liner

25mm x 150mm water outlet channelled out of blockwork

Deck joist (replacing shuttering)

Collection area

Drainage pipe carrying water to lower pool

150mm reinforced concrete slab base

Socialising garden
rendering concrete blocks

Standard concrete blocks are rather ugly – but they are transformed by a covering of render, which also gives a smooth surface for painting. This water feature is rendered and painted before the decking is laid, so that all parts of it can be reached.

Mixing render

Render is applied like a wall plaster. It is mixed from builder's sand with cement in a ratio of 3 parts sand to 1 part cement, and should be quite wet (see page 376). Don't apply too thick a coat (more than 3–5mm) or it will crack and fall off; instead, apply it in two layers. The first coat is scored to provide a key for the final coat to adhere to. Adding combined retarder, plasticiser and waterproofer will make the work easier (see opposite).

Applying the first coat

Metal corner beading is used to strengthen the outward-facing corners of the structure and ensure a crisp, clean edge. Cut lengths of beading with a hacksaw and seal the ends with metal primer. Choose a dry day for rendering.

1 Using a hose fitted with a nozzle, spray the block wall with water before you start rendering. This helps the render to stick.

tools materials

- **hose fitted with a spray nozzle**
- **heavy-duty gloves**
- **hacksaw**
- **builder's float**
- **spirit level**
- **pointing trowel**
- **plasterer's hawk**
- **plasterer's darby**

- metal corner beading
- metal primer
- render
- combined retarder, plasticiser and waterproofer
- polythene sheet

2 Apply patches of render on both sides of each corner, then press metal corner beading into position, allowing the render to squeeze through the mesh. Use a spirit level to make sure the beading is vertical.

3 Using a builder's float, spread a coat of render over the first section of wall, about 3mm deep, then roughly smooth it.

4 Before the render dries, score the surface in random curved and criss-cross lines about 50mm apart, using the side of a pointing trowel. Render the remaining surfaces in the same way. Leave to dry overnight, protected from rain with a polythene sheet.

Applying the top coat

When the first coat of render is completely dry, apply the second coat. This needs to be smoother than the first to give a good surface for painting.

The next day, apply the top coat of render in a thin layer 3–5mm thick, using a builder's float.

Smooth the render with a plasterer's darby, pulling off any excess.

Wet the builder's float and use it to smooth and polish the surface. Leave to dry overnight, protected from rain.

You can do it...

Easier rendering
You can make a basic render mix both easier to work with and more long-lasting by adding combined retarder, plasticiser and waterproofer. The retarder slows the drying process, enabling you to cover a bigger area in one application (or work more slowly if you are a beginner); plasticiser makes the render easier to apply; and waterproofer makes it more hardwearing.

B&Q

Painting the render

New render will harden within about 24 hours, but needs significantly longer to dry out fully ready for painting: in hot, dry weather, two weeks will be enough, but if the weather is wet allow at least four. Choose a day when the weather is fine for painting the render. It will be much quicker if you use a roller. However, a roller cannot reach all the way to the edges so you will need to use a brush for 'cutting in' (painting these areas). This is best done before you paint the main area. New render needs two coats of exterior masonry paint.

tools materials
- **paintbrush**
- **roller and paint tray**
- **gloves**
- **protective overalls**
- exterior masonry paint

Starting under the coping stones, use a brush to 'cut in' a neat line all the way along the top of one section of the rendered wall.

Switch to a roller to paint the main part of the wall. Repeat the process on each section of the wall. Leave to dry before giving the render a second coat of paint.

Socialising garden
making a water shoot

There are two parts to this spectacular water feature. Water runs beneath the deck to emerge over smooth stainless steel sheets and drop into another pool sunk into the lawn. From there it is pumped back up to the main structure.

Building the lower pool

The lower pool for the water feature in this garden measures 1.8m x 650mm. Excavate the area to a depth of 650mm and lay a 150mm-thick reinforced concrete slab base that extends 100mm beyond the pool. Like the upper pool (see page 95), this one is built from two courses of single-skin concrete blocks. However in this case the upper course of the back wall is laid not with blocks but with the stone of the retaining wall that runs across the garden at this point. In order to do this, the central portion of this wall is dismantled and rebuilt. The pool is lined before its stones are relaid (see opposite), so they are visible through the water. Remember to leave a suitable gap in the blocks of the upper course for an overflow pipe to a soakaway (see opposite, below).

Pipework and pump

Water flows from the upper pool through a hidden pipe to the front edge of the deck, where it spreads across metal sheets fixed to concrete slabs laid on a very slight downward gradient, and then spills off in a vertical sheet into the lower pool.

A submersible pump in the lower pool forces the water back into a second (return) pipe which carries it up and under the deck. It passes through two UV filters hidden behind the blockwork structure, which keep it algae-free, then up the back wall of the block feature, where it discharges into the back of the spout. A new cycle starts as water gushes out.

Return pipe

Lay the return pipe to carry the water pipe from the lower pool back to the upper water feature. It also carries the electric cable for the pump. You may need to cut the pipe to length with a hacksaw. Run the pipes and cables through the return pipe, and pull them to one side, away from the excavation area, to prevent them getting damaged (see below right). The IEE Wiring Regulations require that all exposed electrical cable is mechanically protected, for example by plastic conduit. If the cable supplied with your pump is not fully protected, you will need to run it in conduit until the point that it reaches the return pipe: check the pump manufacturer's instructions.

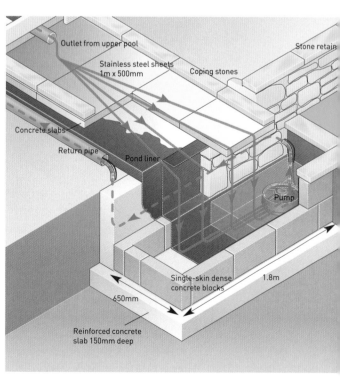

Outlet from upper pool
Stone retain
Stainless steel sheets 1m x 500mm
Coping stones
Concrete slabs
Return pipe
Pond liner
Pump
Single-skin dense concrete blocks
1.8m
650mm
Reinforced concrete slab 150mm deep

1 Before you lay the concrete base, line the lower pool with pond underlay (see page 105) and then pond liner. Pull a generous overlap of liner (up to a metre) over the back of the pool. Coping stones are used here to weight it down.

4 The shoot is 1m wide. You may need to cut slabs: remember to leave a 15mm pointing gap between them. Set each slab on four or five generous blobs of mortar and tap it with a rubber mallet to bed firmly. Use a spirit level to check the slabs are level and maintain a slight fall towards the pool. Cover with waterproof polythene sheeting and leave to dry for 24 hours.

Cover the end of the overflow pipe with a stone to hold it in place and prevent it being blocked while more cleanstone is filled in around it.

Building the water shoot

The stainless steel sheets of the water shoot are fixed to paving slabs which need a solid, level concrete base, approximately 100mm deep and extending 100mm beyond the shoot each side. Excavate the area for this base and mark the concrete height with pegs, allowing a slight downwards fall towards the pool.

2 Build up the stone wall on top of the pond liner at the back of the pool, to a total height of about 450mm. Keep checking the level of the wall: when the slabs and sheets are laid on top of it, their surface must still be slightly lower than the water outlet pipe.

5 Bond the stainless steel sheets to the slabs with clear silicone sealant. Butt sheets together and run a bead of sealant along the joins to ensure they are watertight. Build up the wall either side of the shoot.

3 Lay the concrete base for the slabs. Fold the pond liner forward while doing this. Once the concrete is dry, fold the pond liner back over it. Cover the concrete with another sheet of liner, overlapping the one that started from the pool.

6 Bed coping stones along the edges of the stainless steel sheets with silicone sealant. Apply the sealant to the underside of the stones. Leave a 15mm gap between the stones for pointing.

7 When the sealant has hardened, point the joints between the coping stones with mortar.

Soakaway

If the pump or power should fail, the lower pool could flood your lawn. So it's a good idea to install an overflow pipe draining into a soakaway (see page 197). Dig a hole 1.2m square and 1.2m deep and line it with geotextile landscaping fabric, overlapping it by 300mm where necessary. Run an underground drainage pipe from just under the coping stones in the pool (secured in place with mortar) to the soakaway; make sure that the pipe lies on a downward angle. Fill the hole with cleanstone (see page 375), allowing for a 300mm depth of topsoil. Spread a layer of landscaping fabric over the aggregate to stop the pipe being blocked with soil. Replace the soil and the lawn.

tools materials

- **spirit level**
- **builder's line and pegs**
- **shovel**
- **club hammer**
- **scissors**
- **craft knife**
- **tape measure**
- **builder's trowel**
- **rough length of timber**
- **angle grinder with stone-cutting disc**
- **rubber mallet**
- **pointing trowel**

- wooden marker pegs
- pond liner underlay
- pond liner
- mortar
- footing mix concrete (see page 376)
- polythene sheet
- timbers and bricks to support polythene sheet
- wall stones
- coping stones
- concrete slabs
- stainless steel sheets
- exterior clear silicone sealant

safety first

Steel sheets
Take great care laying the stainless steel sheets. They are slippery, so quite hard to handle. Protective gloves are essential, as the edges are extremely sharp.

You can do it...

Positioning a soakaway
Because damp can damage the foundations of a building, a soakaway must lie a minimum of 6m away from any built structure.

B&Q

Socialising garden
water spout and deck

The final element of the water feature is the glass shoot from which the water spills forth. Then you are ready to begin laying decking over and around it.

Assembling the water spout

The glass pieces are glued together with exterior silicone sealant. To hold them in place while they dry, make a simple mould from offcuts of ply and batten nailed or screwed together. The mould should be just wide enough to hold the base piece of glass. The battens stop the side sections falling outwards. When the back piece of the spout is pushed into position, it holds the other three sections in place.

Glass water spout

This is made from four pieces of 7mm safety glass – a base, back and two sides – which any glazier can cut for you. It measures 570mm at its longest point and is 194mm wide. The side pieces are 87mm high. The back is 180mm wide and 87mm high. These dimensions allow a tolerance of 3mm on all sides in a 200mm x 100mm hole; check the exact size of your hole before you order the glass, or it may not fit. The top edges are smoothed and angled slightly at the front: ask the glazier to do this for you.

tools materials

- **wooden mould made from ply and batten**
- 7mm safety glass pieces cut to size
- exterior silicone sealant

1 Assemble the glass pieces in the mould to check that they fit snugly.

2 Run sealant along all the joins, push the pieces together and leave the spout to dry.

3 At the back of the water feature check that the flexible return pipe is feeding directly into the back of the spout.

4 Secure the spout with a layer of silicone sealant to the underside of the base. This should be thicker at the rear, creating a very slight slope that will ensure the water flows forward and down.

safety first

Young children and water

Open pools of water mean this is not a garden suitable for young children. You could place rigid metal grilles over each pool, no more than a few millimetres below the water level. But these would have to be specially made.

Starting the deck

Decking is laid around the water feature on a sub-frame of outer and inner joists fixed to posts. The joists are laid 300mm apart to support diagonally laid boards. Lengths of timber are fitted between the joists at 1.8m intervals for added strength. For more information on building a deck, see **You Can Do It: the Complete B&Q Step-by-Step Book of Home Improvement**.

tools materials

- **spirit level**
- **builder's line and pegs**
- **protective gloves**
- **safety goggles**
- **dust mask**
- **spade**
- **post-hole borer**
- **craft knife**
- **scissors**
- **panel saw**
- **circular saw**
- **compound mitre saw**
- **jigsaw**
- **power drill**
- **socket set for coach screws and bolts**
- **paintbrush**

- deck posts
- footing mix concrete (see page 376) or dry-mix post-fix concrete (see page 82)
- landscaping fabric
- 20mm gravel
- 150mm deck joists
- 150mm coach bolts
- deck or galvanised screws
- abrasive paper
- deck boards
- end-grain preserver

Building the sub-frame

Start by clearing and roughly levelling the entire area. Mark out the outline of the deck with builder's lines and pegs, then run string lines across the site in each direction to accurately mark the position of the posts. These should be positioned at every corner, along all the outer edges, and a maximum of 1.8m apart beneath the body of the deck. Dig 600mm-deep post holes and bed the posts in concrete, leaving them standing about 300mm above the ground.

To deter weed growth, it's a good idea to spread permeable landscaping fabric over the ground beneath the deck. Lay this over the posts and make two diagonal cuts above each one. Push the fabric down over the posts and trim off the triangular flaps. Then spread a 40–50mm layer of gravel over the fabric.

Attach the outer sub-frame joists to the posts, and then assemble the inner joist framework. Use a spirit level to ensure that the sub-frame is level right across the site. The finished height of the deck should be 60mm higher than the concrete blockwork of the upper pool. Finally, saw off the tops of the posts level with the joists.

Laying deck boards

Once the sub-frame is complete, you are ready to lay the deck boards. Fix the boards down into each sub-frame joist they cross with two deck screws or galvanised screws. Lay deck boards with a 3mm gap between them to allow rainwater to drain through. Lengths of deck board should meet exactly halfway across a joist, so that both boards can be screwed into it. Stagger the joins, and remember to coat cut ends with end-grain preserver. Buying boards in longer lengths (4.8m) will reduce the number of joins on the surface of a larger deck. For a neat finish, allow boards to overlap the outer joists of the sub-frame, and then when they are all laid cut a clean edge with a circular saw, or a curved edge with a jigsaw.

You can do it...

Decking around a tree

It's easy to lay decking around a tree: just remember to leave enough room for the trunk to grow and sway in the wind. With a young tree install temporary deck boards.

B&Q

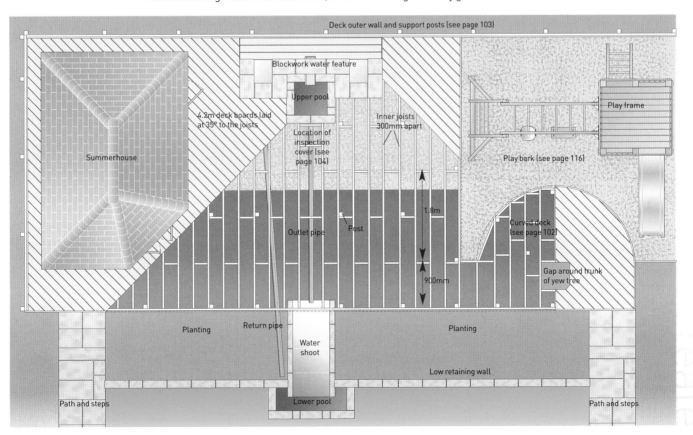

Deck outer wall and support posts (see page 103)

Blockwork water feature

Upper pool

4.8m deck boards laid at 35° to the joists

Location of inspection cover (see page 104)

Inner joists 300mm apart

Play frame

Play bark (see page 116)

Summerhouse

1.8m

Curved deck (see page 102)

Outlet pipe

Post

900mm

Gap around trunk of yew tree

Planting

Return pipe

Planting

Water shoot

Low retaining wall

Path and steps

Lower pool

Path and steps

Socialising garden
decking awkward areas

Decking laid over a large area may need to be fitted around an existing structure, attached to a wall or shaped on a curve. An outer deck wall is a practical and attractive addition to a big area of decking.

Attaching joists to a wall

Where decking runs right up to a built structure, such as the blockwork water feature in this garden, instead of posts you need to attach each joist to the surface with wall brackets.

Mark the position for each wall bracket in turn on the wall with a pencil. Use a spirit level to check that the marks are all at exactly the same level.

Screw each bracket to the wall with masonry screws and plugs.

Slot the end of the joist into the wall bracket and secure it with galvanised screws.

tools materials

- pencil
- spirit level
- power drill with hammer action

- wall brackets for 150mm joists
- masonry screws and plugs
- galvanised screws

Decking on a curve

When laying decking on a curve, the deck boards overlap the sub-frame slightly. Provided they are cut to a smooth, clean line, it doesn't matter if the sub-frame has a jagged outer edge, so long as it is solid and secure.

tools materials

- **power drill**
- **pencil**
- **string**
- **jigsaw**
- **panel saw**
- **hammer**

- deck boards
- deck or galvanised screws
- 6mm exterior-grade plywood
- 30mm x 10mm edge beading
- 30mm galvanised panel pins

Screw the boards to the sub-frame, letting them overhang the joists by at least 100mm. Measure and mark the curve using a string line and pencil.

Cut the boards along the line with a jigsaw and cover the saw cut with wooden beading attached with panel pins. Fix exterior-grade plywood to the sub-frame to prevent play bark spilling under the deck.

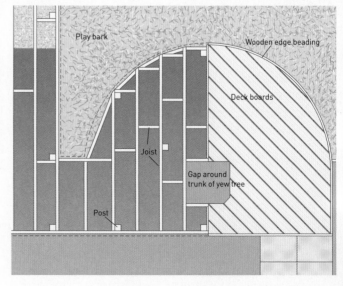

Play bark

Wooden edge beading

Deck boards

Joist

Gap around trunk of yew tree

Post

Building the deck outer wall

The low wall running around the outer edges of this deck has its own line of support posts. The posts are fixed once the sub-frame of the deck is assembled; the deck joists and boards that form the face of the wall are attached after the deck surface is laid. Dig the post holes to a depth of 600mm next to the outer joists of the sub-frame. Make the holes no more than 1.8m apart.

tools materials

- **spade**
- **post-hole borer**
- **spirit level**
- **bricklayer's trowel**
- **bucket**
- **gloves**
- **clamp**
- **socket set for coach screws**
- **power drill**
- **paint brush**
- **panel saw**

- deck posts
- footing mix concrete (see page 376) or dry-mix post-fix concrete (see page 82)
- offcut of timber
- 100mm coach screws
- deck joists
- deck boards
- 50mm deck or galvanised screws
- end-grain preserver

Place the first post in its hole and check it's vertical using a spirit level. The posts need to stand at least 100mm taller than the finished height of the wall.

Clamp the spirit level to the post and pour concrete into the hole. Tamp it down with an offcut of timber. Repeat the process with the rest of the posts.

Before the concrete sets, fix the posts to the outer frame with 100mm coach screws, making sure they remain vertical. The deck boards now need to be attached to the sub-frame before the wall can be finished.

Finishing the wall

When the deck boards are in place, you are ready to complete the outer wall. This has two layers: horizontal lengths of deck joist are attached to the posts; then deck boards are fixed to these joists. Do remember to paint all cut ends with end-grain preserver.

Working from the bottom to the top, screw lengths of deck joist to each post with two countersunk 100mm coach screws. Join lengths at the centre of a post. Unlike on the deck surface, there's no need to leave a 3mm drainage gap between these boards.

Continue attaching boards up to the required height: here the wall is 600mm (four deck joists) high. Then cut off the posts level with the top board, sawing them at a slight downwards angle so rainwater will run off away from the deck.

Attach deck boards to the joists using 50mm deck or galvanised screws. These are spaced 3mm apart to match the deck surface. They stand slightly taller than the joists, hiding the posts.

eco timber
Decking   FSC

When buying decking always check for the FSC symbol. This means you can be sure that the wood comes from a responsibly managed, sustainable source certified by the Forest Stewardship Council.

Socialising
garden
finishing deck and pool

It's important to be able to access all parts of this water feature – you don't want to have to take up half the deck should there be a problem or blockage. That's why it's necessary to construct an inspection hole over the outlet pipe from the upper pool. Then finally you are ready to line the upper pool and finish it with attractive coping stones.

Making an inspection hole

The inspection cover is simply a small, square section of the deck surface which is attached not to the joists of the sub-frame but to a removable square frame. This may be made from a deck joist cut lengthways, or 100mm x 50mm lengths of treated timber. The cover slots snugly in place, without being fixed down in any way. A finger-sized hole on one side enables it to be lifted.

tools materials

- **tape measure**
- **combination square**
- **power drill**
- **spirit level**
- **panel saw**
- **jigsaw**

- two short lengths of treated timber
- 100mm galvanised wood screws
- 150mm galvanised countersink wood screws
- deck boards

ideal tool

Combination square

A combination square can be used for measuring and for marking angles of 90° or 45°. It also has a small spirit bubble for levelling and a scribe for marking.

Check the width between the joists immediately in front of the pool, above the open end of the water outlet pipe.

Cut two short supporting timbers and screw them at right angles to these joists, 50mm below their top edges, to create a support for the square frame of the inspection cover. Check the supporting timbers are level using a spirit level.

Measure and cut a square frame that will sit inside the joists on the supporting timbers. Allow a minimum 5mm expansion gap on all sides. Check the right angles with a combination square. Fix with 150mm countersink screws through the corners.

Check that the frame fits and its upper edge lies flush with the joists, then leave it in position.

Fitting the deck board cover

Make the cover for the inspection chamber as you lay deck boards up and over that part of the deck. This way, it will be almost invisible in the finished structure.

tools materials
- **straightedge**
- **pencil**
- **panel saw or circular saw**
- **power drill**
- **32mm flat wood bit**
- **tape measure**

- deck or galvanised screws
- deck boards
- abrasive paper

1 Loose-lay deck boards over the inspection hole, maintaining a 3mm drainage gap between them. Draw a line marking the outer edge of the frame. Lift and cut the boards along this line.

2 Screw the sections of deckboard to the frame of the inspection cover, keeping them exactly in line with the boards forming the surface of the deck.

3 Drill a finger-sized hole right through the inspection hole cover using a 32mm flat wood bit. Position it centrally, to one side, making sure it is inside the frame. Smooth the edges of the hole with abrasive paper.

4 The cover can be lifted when necessary by hooking a finger through the hole.

Lining the pool

The pool below the water spout is lined with plastic pond liner on top of pond liner underlay. The underlay provides a layer of cushioning which helps to protect the liner from being punctured by sharp stones. The pond liner is pulled over the notch in the blockwork, which allows the water to overflow into the collection chamber. Coping stones are set on mortar on top of the liner, with their upper surface flush with the decking.

1 Measure and cut pond liner underlay to fit the base and sides of the pool. Cut it with a craft knife on an old board.

tools materials
- **tape measure**
- **craft knife**
- **scissors**
- **spirit level**
- **builder's trowel**
- **pointing trowel**

- pond liner underlay
- pond liner
- exterior silicone sealant
- coping stones
- mortar

2 Lay the liner on top of the underlay, smoothing it over the edges. Place some coping stones round the edges to hold the liner and stop it slipping. A little exterior silicone sealant will secure the liner over the notch.

3 Half-fill the pool with water to weight the liner down, then trim the excess and fix coping stones on top of the liner with mortar, using a spirit level to check they are level. Point the coping stones.

You can do it...

Pool lights

Fully waterproof outdoor pool lights can be simply dropped into the water. To avoid having cables on view, run them to an outdoor power point before you lay the deck boards.

B&Q

Socialising garden
summerhouse

A summerhouse can be an attractive and very useful addition to a garden, providing a space to sit, play, relax or work, and also storage for outdoor furniture and equipment.

An outdoor retreat

Summerhouses are available in a wide range of styles and sizes. They can be wired for light and heat by a professional electrician, and so double up as a useful home office. But be sure to fit secure door and window locks if you plan to keep valuable items inside, and don't leave them on view.

This summerhouse has two rooms, each with a door to the outside. The front part is an ideal seating area, one that can be used even when the weather is slightly chilly. The back, windowless area, is perfect for storing garden tools. The walls are built up from horizontal interlocking wooden boards.

When deciding where to position a summerhouse, take care not to block neighbours' views or sunlight. In many areas you would need planning permission for a garden building this size.

Assembling the base

The foundation joists sit directly on the decking. Leave a minimum 500mm gap on all sides of the summerhouse for window opening and to allow room to walk by. Many stages of this job will be made safer and easier by an extra pair of hands.

Plywood roof panels

Rafter bracket

Rafter

Door module

Metal support post and bracket

Window module

Door module

Intertlocking wall boards

Sheet flooring

Foundation joists

1 Assemble the foundation joists and door threshold according to the manufacturer's instructions, then slot in the first row of wall boards. Check the base is level with a spirit level.

2 Attach the remaining floor joists to the framework and fit the door seal according to the manufacturer's instructions.

3 Lay the flooring sheets. Mark the position of the joists beneath so you can screw into them at 500mm intervals.

tools materials

- **spirit level**
- **pencil**
- **tape measure**
- **panel saw**
- **power drill**
- **screwdriver**
- **tall stepladder or ladder**
- **hammer**
- **paint brush**
- **cutting-in brush**

- flatpacked summerhouse, including fixings
- wood preservative, if required
- outdoor paint or stain

Once four rows of interlocking wall boards are in place, slot in both door modules.

Building up the walls and roof

The summerhouse walls are assembled one row of interlocking boards at a time, leaving gaps for the doors and windows. These come as prehung modules that simply slide into place. The roof rafters sit in angled brackets on top of five metal corner posts, one at each corner and one either side of the double doors.

Assemble a further three rows of wall boards and then slot in the window modules.

Finish assembling the walls, then attach the metal corner posts.

Slide the rafters into the support brackets on the corner posts and the rafter brackets at the ridge. Secure them in the brackets with screws.

Nail the plywood roof panels to the rafters, starting from the front of the summerhouse and working towards the back.

Nail the felt tiles to the panels. Start at the bottom of the roof and work upwards, so the overlap gives a waterproof seal. Nail the felt ridge tiles along the ridge and angles of the roof.

Adding colour

Check the manufacturer's instructions to see if your summerhouse needs treating with wood preservative to weatherproof it before you paint or stain it; or you could use an all-in-one stain and preservative. You can paint or stain it all one colour or, as here, use different colours for the walls and window. Make your last brush strokes in the same direction as the grain of the wood, and pick up wet edges before they begin to dry and spoil the look of your handiwork.

ideal tool

Tool belt

A tool belt is an ideal and safe way of carrying nails, screws and a variety of tools you need to complete a task. It's helpful to have all your tools handy, especially if you are using a ladder.

Paint or stain the walls, taking care at the corners – don't let the paint or stain collect in crevices or it will create runs.

Use a cutting-in brush with specially angled bristles for painting the highlight colour on the windows.

Socialising
garden planting

This breathtaking garden design is brought together by a planting scheme that combines formality and informality, structure and colour, evergreen and seasonal elements.

Splendid symmetry

The grand centrepiece of this garden is the double water-feature, and much of the planting is designed to frame it and emphasise its dramatic presence. The reshaped patio deliberately points towards it, and the formal planting along the patio edge reinforces this effect: low box and lavender hedging follows the outline of the paving, while six mop-head topiary bay trees rise up at regular intervals. At the opposite end of the garden these are echoed by two box topiary trees in pots standing guard either side of the water feature, their crisp spiral outline and deep colour contrasting with the gleaming white-painted blockwork behind. Because it is fairly slow-growing, box topiary isn't too much of a chore to maintain. Trimming it into shape twice a year is normally enough (see page 246).

The beds running along the two outer edges of this garden contain mature shrub and evergreen planting that was left undisturbed; any brand-new planting will inevitably look a bit thin for a couple of years, so a new garden will often benefit in the short-term if you opt to keep some existing plants. This can be a useful way to keep your budget under control, too.

● plant chooser

Plants with a numbered rosette are featured in more detail in the Plant Chooser, pages 294–327.

1 *Buxus sempervirens* Box

2 *Laurus nobilis* Bay tree

3 *Lavandula angustifolia* English lavender

Structure and formality

Lifting the mood

Too much dark evergreen planting can make a garden feel dull and gloomy, so this central bed is filled with a mix of shrubs and perennials in yellows and blues to lift the mood. The two halves are similar but not identical, introducing a more relaxed feel to the planting. Flanking the steel sheets of the water feature is the ornamental blue grass, *Festuca glauca*. A pair of phormiums rise up either side: *Phormium cookianum* 'Cream Delight' has broad leaves with yellow centres; standing taller is *Phormium tenax* 'Purpureum', with brownish-purple leaves. A dense mix of lower-growing plants such as geraniums, nicotiana and viola bring colour and interest. The height of the planting increases towards the outer edges, with the green and yellow bamboo *Phyllostachys bambusoides* 'Castilloni' defining one edge, and the golden-yellow-leaved *Choisya ternata* 'Sundance' the other.

 4 *Phyllostachys bambusoides* 'Castilloni' **56**

 5 *Hosta fortunei* 'Albopicta' **141**

 6 *Digitalis lutea* Perennial foxglove **110**

 7 *Ceanothus impressus* California lilac **51**

 8 *Veronica* 'Crater Lake Blue' Speedwell **159**

 9 *Lavandula angustifolia* 'Hidcote' **29**

 10 *Osteospermum* 'Buttermilk' African daisy **109**

 11 *Phormium tenax* 'Purpureum' New Zealand flax **50**

 12 *Festuca glauca* Blue fescue **82**

 13 *Hedera helix* 'Buttercup' Ivy **60**

 14 *Tellima grandiflora* Fringecups

 15 *Geranium phaeum* Hardy geranium

 16 *Potentilla recta* var. *sulphurea* Cinquefoil **130**

 17 *Phormium cookianum* 'Cream Delight' Mountain flax **108**

 18 *Foeniculum vulgare* 'Purpureum' Fennel **50**

 19 *Eryngium bourgatii* Sea holly **119**

 20 *Nicotiana* 'Lime Green' Ornamental tobacco **83**

 21 *Geranium wallichianum* 'Buxton's Variety' Hardy geranium **176** **130**

Soft colour and shape

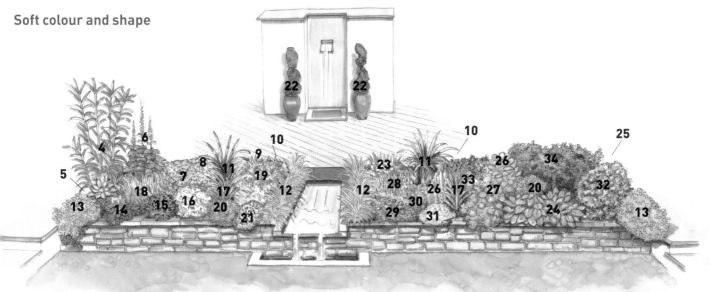

 22 *Buxus sempervirens* Box **19**

 23 *Iris pallida* 'Variegata' **123**

 24 *Hosta* 'Gold Standard' **141**

 25 *Helleborus niger* Christmas rose **134**

 26 *Eremurus stenophyllus* 'Bungei' Foxtail lily **107**

 27 *Euphorbia polychroma* Spurge **133**

 28 *Salvia* x *superba* Sage **47**

 29 *Helianthemum* 'Wisley Pink'

 30 *Crocosmia* 'Citronella' Montbretia **103**

 **31** *Santolina chamaecyparissus* Cotton lavender **26**

32 *Hydrangea macrophylla* 'Blue Wave' **58**

33 *Lysimachia ephemerum* Silver loosestrife **97**

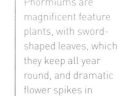 **34** *Choisya ternata* 'Sundance' Mexican orange blossom **36**

Family garden

A well-loved family garden is one that has something for everyone: areas for adults to relax or entertain, and plenty of space for boisterous children's activities. It's perfectly possible to incorporate all the different elements into one garden in a way that looks attractive and is easy to care for – it just takes a little careful planning.

Planning a family garden

Apart from good-looking planting, most adults want areas in a garden where they can enjoy a bit of peace, or alternatively eat and socialise. Children are more likely to want a playground equipped with things to climb up and slide down, and maybe somewhere to ride a bike. Younger ones will spend many happy hours in a sandpit. Children love sowing seeds and watching plants appear a few weeks later; if there is room, let them have their own patch of garden where they can grow flowers, fruit and vegetables.

Finding inspiration

A wishlist for a family garden might include: furniture, barbecue, patio heater, summerhouse, climbing frame, slide and swing. Ask the family – you may not have the space or budget to please them all, but something for everyone is a worthwhile goal. With much of the garden inevitably given over to lawn and sitting/play areas, the possibilities for planting will be restricted. Pots and containers are one answer; another is to make the most of the vertical surfaces with climbers growing up the wall and fences.

The design brief

This average family garden (9.8m x 10.6m) started out in a reasonable state, with a lawn, perfectly good patio and some planting. But it was full of clutter and badly in need of some order. The lawn tended to become very worn in summer beneath the children's play equipment. It is a very open plot so nowhere is particularly dark or shady.

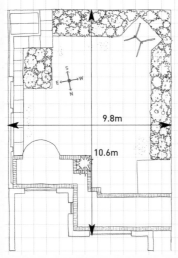

The existing plot

9.8m

10.6m

Wants

- Kids' play area with climbing frame, slide, swing and sandpit.
- Good-size lawn to play on.
- Area where the children can grow their own plants.
- To retain existing patio near the house for table, chairs and barbecue.
- Somewhere for adults to sit in the sun at the bottom of the garden while supervising the children.
- Storage place for outdoor toys.
- Replacement or screening of unattractive boundary wall and fences.

Problems

- Bottom end of garden is prone to poor drainage, so structures such as a climbing frame cannot be placed straight on the grass or they will sink.
- Shed takes up a significant chunk of the sunniest part of the garden.
- The boundary fences belong to the neighbours, who are unwilling to replace them.

Developing ideas

There is no better starting point than drawing a simple plan of the garden, showing its shape and boundaries, and trying out different schemes. It doesn't matter how rough the sketches are, they will still reveal the advantages and disadvantages of your ideas. Decide if anything has to go – such as prickly or poisonous plants – and draw in anything that is to stay or that needs hiding. Here it made sense to retain the planting in the right-hand bed: roses, shrubs and evergreens that had already matured over several years. Plan pathways to the various zones in the garden so the lawn doesn't take all the traffic. Do discuss your plans with the neighbours, especially if the top of a summerhouse or climbing frame will be visible over the boundary fence.

Playroom

Here the children's play area is at the end of the garden, behind a willow screen. A new deck in the bottom half of the garden gives the adults somewhere to sit and relax in the sunnier half of the garden. However, it offers little shelter, and nor can the children be seen from the house. The play area, patio and extra decking leave only a small space for the lawn.

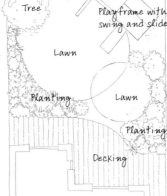

Circular lawns

The rounded shapes give this garden a softer feel. The new decked area just outside the house is big enough for a table and chairs. The lawn offers plenty of play space and there is room for planting around the edges, with an activity play area at the bottom of the garden. But so much planting will multiply the work of maintaining this garden, and it leaves no room for a summerhouse or children's planting area.

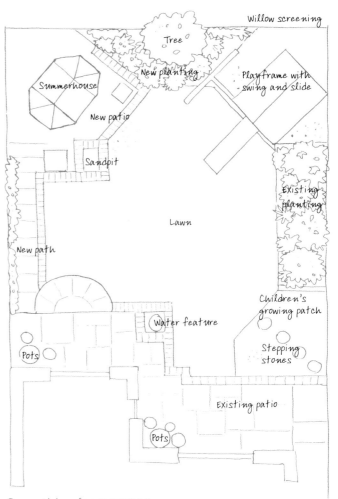

Something for everyone

Here the play area is at the end of the garden but is not screened from view. The shed is replaced by a summerhouse where the adults can sit and keep an eye on the kids. By keeping paths and structures to the outer edges, it is possible to retain a good-size lawn. Offering the best all-round solution, this is the sketch that is to become the new garden (see pages 112–21).

Family garden

With places to relax, places to play, and plants
that will give colour and interest year after year,
this garden is one that all the family will enjoy.

A design for all the family

This layout introduces a play area and summerhouse
at the bottom of the garden. The existing terrace
adjacent to the house has been retained and is large
enough for garden furniture, patio heater and a
barbecue for all the family and friends to enjoy.
A paved path at the left-hand side joins this terrace
with a new one at the end of the garden, which
provides a solid base for the summerhouse and
a seating area in front. A sandpit has been sunk
into the lawn on the edge of this new terrace.
Pots and hanging baskets add bright splashes
of colour to all the paved areas, and a small
water feature has been installed in a
previously planted section of the terrace.
Two Japanese maples (see page 296)
in pots either side of the
summerhouse help to soften the
building and integrate it into the
garden. Willow trellis screens the
ugly fence at the bottom and along
the right-hand side of
the garden.

**Hot and
sunny wall**

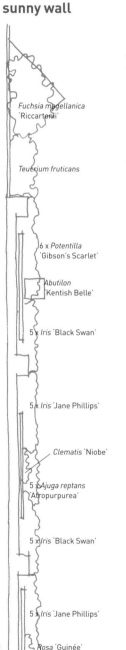

Fuchsia magellanica
'Riccartonii'

Teucrium fruticans

6 x *Potentilla*
'Gibson's Scarlet'

Abutilon
'Kentish Belle'

5 x *Iris* 'Black Swan'

5 x *Iris* 'Jane Phillips'

Clematis 'Niobe'

5 x *Ajuga reptans*
'Atropurpurea'

5 x *Iris* 'Black Swan'

5 x *Iris* 'Jane Phillips'

Rosa 'Guinée'
Clematis 'Jackmanii Superba'

5 x *Heuchera micrantha*
var. *diversifolia*
'Palace Purple'

You can do it...

Keep it tidy

Hide your dustbin in its
own little shed. This
flatpacked wheelie bin
tidy is easy to assemble,
and can be painted or
stained to match your
garden's colours.

B&Q

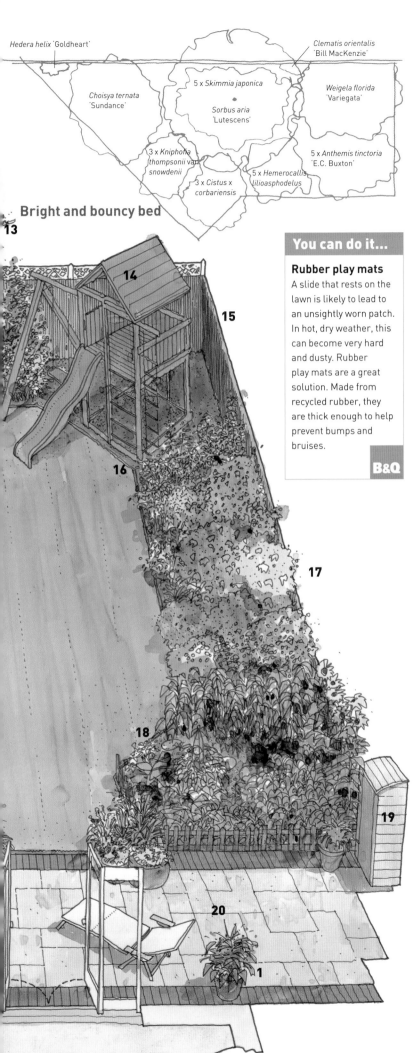

Hedera helix 'Goldheart'

Clematis orientalis 'Bill MacKenzie'

Choisya ternata 'Sundance'

5 x *Skimmia japonica*

Weigela florida 'Variegata'

Sorbus aria 'Lutescens'

3 x *Kniphofia thompsonii var. snowdenii*

5 x *Anthemis tinctoria* 'E.C. Buxton'

3 x *Cistus x corbariensis*

5 x *Hemerocallis lilioasphodelus*

Bright and bouncy bed

Planting a family garden

It's important to avoid spiky or poisonous plants, or anything too fragile, when deciding what to grow in an area where small children will play. The bed running beside the path along the left-hand edge of this garden (opposite) is only about 200mm wide, so the emphasis here is on climbing plants that will grow up new trellis panels and make the most of the vertical space. A new tree, *Sorbus aria* 'Lutescens', provides a central focus to the rear bed. Some existing mature shrub planting is retained along the right-hand side of the garden, with an area of 2.4 square metres near the patio enclosed by low picket fencing and turned into a children's plot. This is planted with easy-to-grow flowers, fruits and vegetables. For more detail on the planting of this garden, see pages 120–21.

You can do it...

Rubber play mats

A slide that rests on the lawn is likely to lead to an unsightly worn patch. In hot, dry weather, this can become very hard and dusty. Rubber play mats are a great solution. Made from recycled rubber, they are thick enough to help prevent bumps and bruises.

B&Q

family garden

1 Pots and hanging baskets add colour to paved areas.
2 Barbecue.
3 Small solar-powered water feature in a previously planted area of the patio.
4 Patio heater to make the garden more inviting when the temperature drops .
5 Outdoor dining table and chairs, with sun parasol.
6 Path connecting the two paved areas.
7 Brick lawn edging at ground level for easy mowing.
8 Timber and metal trellis panels that will soon be covered with climbing plants.
9 Sandpit incorporated into the terrace.
10 A pair of Japanese maples grow in pots either side of the summerhouse.
11 Storage box for outdoor toys.
12 Summerhouse positioned on a new extension to the paved terrace.
13 A new tree, *Sorbus aria* 'Lutescens', is the central focus of the newly planted end bed.
14 Children's climbing frame, slide and swing on an area of play bark.
15 Willow trellis screens the old fencing.
16 Timber lawn edging along the borders and play area.
17 Mature shrub planting, including lavender and roses, is retained.
18 Children's plot, surrounded by low picket fencing.
19 Wooden wheelie bin tidy, built from a flatpack kit.
20 Existing patio adjacent to the house is retained.

Children's plot

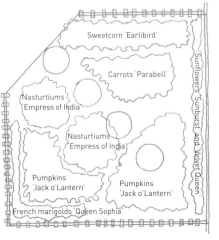

Sweetcorn 'Earlibird'

Carrots 'Parabell'

Nasturtiums 'Empress of India'

Nasturtiums 'Empress of India'

Sunflowers 'Sunburst' and 'Velvet Queen'

Pumpkins 'Jack o'Lantern'

Pumpkins 'Jack o'Lantern'

French marigolds 'Queen Sophia'

Family garden
lawns, fences and trellis

It's well worth installing a hard mowing strip around your lawn: in the long run you'll save hours of work cutting and trimming the edges. Willow screening and trellis panels to support climbers are two goodlooking and affordable solutions to the problem of ugly boundary walls and fences.

Installing wooden lawn edging

There's no getting away from it: it takes regular work to keep a lawn looking good. One way you can cut down on that work is by installing a lawn edging. This is a hard strip at ground level that can be mowed up to and over, meaning you won't have to hand-trim or recut the edges. You can use bricks, blocks or slabs for a lawn edging: any weatherproof material will work, so long as its top edge is level with the ground (ie just below the level of the cut grass). Even easier to install are wooden deck boards fixed to sharpened pegs. Be sure to use timbers that have been pressure-treated against rot, and paint all cut ends with end-grain preserver.

tools materials

- **builder's line and pegs**
- **club hammer**
- **spade**
- **spirit level, if required**
- **power drill**

- 50mm x 50mm treated sharpened wooden pegs, 400mm long
- deck boards
- end-grain preserver
- 50mm galvanised screws or deck screws

1 Mark the edge of the lawn with builder's line. Dig out a trench 150mm deep, keeping the soil for refilling later.

ideal material

Timber lawn edging

Deck boards make an ideal lawn edging. They are supplied pre-treated, so even buried in the ground they will last for years.

2 Using a wooden edging board check the level and depth of the trench. Only use a spirit level if the lawn itself is perfectly level. The deck board must be positioned level with the earth – not the grass – so that it won't be struck by the mower.

3 Use 50mm x 50mm treated wooden pegs, sharpened at one end, to hold the edging boards in position. Drive them in with a club hammer to below ground level: they should be invisible once the trench is refilled.

4 Drill pilot holes and attach the pegs to the boards using 50mm galvanised screws or deck screws. Position the pegs roughly 1m apart. Finally back-fill the trench with soil.

Drill pilot holes and fix battens to the fence at 500mm intervals with galvanised screws

tools materials

- **power drill**
- **hammer**

- 20mm x 40mm treated wooden battens
- galvanised screws
- willow trellis
- bricks or blocks (for temporary support)
- galvanised staples

Stand the trellis on bricks or blocks while you position it – you need a gap between the bottom of the trellis and the soil to prevent it rotting.

Attaching willow screening

With willow trellis the lengths of willow are closely packed together, making it the perfect screening for an ugly fence. If you also fix lengths of open-weave trellis to the fence-top, you will be able to train climbers along it as they reach this height.

Hammer three rows of galvanised staples through the trellis and into each batten, at the top, bottom and middle of the willow trellis.

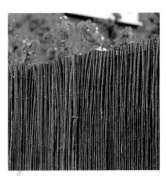

Join lengths of willow trellis at a batten. Place them side by side, without overlapping, and secure with more staples.

Fixing trellis panels to a wall

This curved trellis panel, coloured with blue wood stain, is a striking feature. It's important to position it exactly vertical and central on the wall – even slight errors will be noticeable. Having someone on hand to help will make this much easier. A panel this size – 1.8m high – needs six evenly spaced fixings; a smaller panel would need only four.

Measure the width of the wall you want to screen and find the centre point.

tools materials

- **tape measure**
- **spirit level**
- **power drill with hammer action**

- trellis
- bricks or blocks (for temporary support)
- 50mm galvanised screws and wallplugs

Stand the trellis on bricks or blocks while you position it – you need a gap between the bottom of the trellis and the soil to prevent it rotting.

Use a spirit level to check the panel is vertical and get a helper to hold it in position. Drill clearance holes through the trellis, then change from a wood to a masonry bit and drill into the wall.

Insert wallplugs and attach the trellis to the wall with galvanised screws.

Family garden
fun for kids

Children love a garden where they can be let loose to enjoy themselves. Special fun areas with things like a climbing frame, swing or slide, a sandpit, and their own growing patch will keep them entertained for hours.

Creating a family garden

Make sure the whole garden is properly enclosed, especially if the children are small. If you are introducing any structures that they could fall off – swing, slide or climbing frame – it's important to make sure that there is a soft surface beneath. Grass is an option, but heavy use will tend to turn it into a mud patch, and a hot, dry summer will bake it hard. Alternatives include rubber mats (see page 113), pellets made from recycled rubber, or natural play bark. It's important to allow enough space around a play frame so that, for example, a swing can be used safely, and it isn't possible to climb from the frame onto a fence or other structure. A space of 2m on all sides is advisable, but you should also check the manufacturer's guidelines.

Safe play

The playframe in this garden is positioned on an area of play bark retained by timber edging. The bark is 150mm deep; if you were laying it over concrete you would need double that.

tools materials

- **builder's line and pegs**
- **spade**
- **power drill**
- **club hammer**
- **rake**

- deck boards
- 50mm galvanised screws or deck screws
- 50mm x 50mm sharpened treated wooden pegs
- weed-control fabric
- play bark

You can do it...

Stable play

A playframe should be secured to the ground to stop it shifting or tilting. These ground anchors are twisted into the soil and bolted to the feet of the frame. On soft ground, with poor drainage, you should set the anchors in concrete pads, which will also support the weight of the structure. Lay one pad for every supporting post that stands on the ground.

1 Mark out the edges of the play area with builder's line and pegs. Remove the soil to a depth of 150mm. Install deck boards around the edge to form a retaining edge, just as for a wooden lawn edging (see page 114).

2 Lay weed-control fabric over the area to deter weed growth. Then tip in the play bark. You will need about two 100-litre bags for every square metre.

3 Rake the play bark level. The area is now ready for installing a playframe, swing or slide.

Making a sandpit

Flatpacked sandpits made from treated wood are simple to assemble. Attach permeable landscaping fabric to the bottom of the frame to stop earth getting mixed in with the sand and to deter weeds from growing up into the sandpit. A layer of gravel or crushed stone beneath the sheet assists drainage; on heavy soil with poor drainage, this should be at least 100mm deep. Paint or stain the timbers before you assemble the frame.

tools materials

- **screwdriver**
- **staple gun**
- **builder's line and pegs**
- **spade**
- **spirit level**

- flatpacked sandpit kit
- permeable landscaping fabric
- gravel or crushed stone
- play sand

1 Assemble the sandpit, following the manufacturer's instructions. Attach permeable landscaping fabric to the bottom of the frame using a staple gun. Mark out the area for the sandpit with builder's line and pegs and dig it to a depth of 400mm.

2 Spread a 100mm layer of gravel or crushed stone, then place the sandpit in the hole and use a spirit level to check it is level.

3 Finally, tip in the play sand. A sandpit cover (see right) will keep rain off the sand, and also prevent it being fouled by cats.

You can do it...

Sandpit cover

It's easy to make an attractive sandpit cover out of deck boards, cross-braced on the underside, and painted or stained.

B&Q

Creating a children's growing patch

Children love picking and eating produce straight from the garden, and it's even more fun when they've grown it themselves. Installing low picket fencing around their plot will mark it off and make children feel it is their own space. Choose picket fencing with rounded pales, rather than pointed ones. Concrete stepping stones laid across the area will allow them to walk back and forth without trampling the plants.

safety first

Garden tools
Garden forks, rakes and shears can be dangerous in tiny hands. Keep them well away from small children – look for child-size gardening tools which they can use safely.

tools materials

- **club hammer**
- **power drill**
- **spade**
- **rake**

- 300mm-high picket fencing
- timber offcut
- galvanised metal brackets and screws
- multi-purpose or organic compost
- concrete stepping stones
- seeds and plants

1 Place a timber offcut over the picket fencing and drive it into the ground with a club hammer, leaving a gap for the entrance.

2 Join the lengths of fencing with a metal bracket and screws on each horizontal rail. Fix these to the inside of the enclosure.

3 Dig over the top 150mm of soil and work in plenty of multi-purpose or organic compost. Lay concrete stepping stones across the area, one child's footstep apart.

4 The garden is ready for sowing seeds. See page 121 for planting ideas for a children's plot.

Family garden
summerhouse

A summerhouse is a great addition to a family garden, a place for adults to sit and keep an eye on the children during the day, or relax with a glass of wine in the evening. It offers shade from a hot summer sun and shelter on chilly days when the children are keeping warm by running around.

Creating a solid base

A summerhouse needs to sit on a level solid surface. Here a new terrace has been built using paving slabs, with a brick lawn edging laid just below the surface of the soil for easy mowing (see page 267). All paved areas must slope slightly to allow rainwater to drain away: this terrace slopes very slightly towards the lawn and adjacent bed. For more detail on laying paving see pages 154–61, and **You Can Do It: the Complete B&Q Step-by-Step Book of Home Improvement.**

Erecting the floor and walls

Positioning this octagonal summerhouse in a corner leaves a very handy space behind it – perfect for hiding a storage box for the kids' garden toys.

Don't try and erect a summerhouse single-handed – it's a two-person job. All models will differ slightly, so you should also follow the manufacturer's instructions.

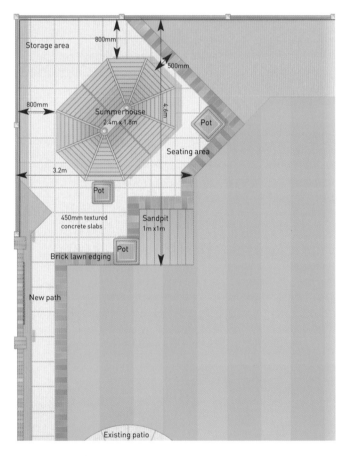

1 Lay out the summerhouse base and check it is level. Also check that it is in the right position: there must be a minimum 500mm gap all around the structure for the windows to open and to allow enough space to walk round the outside of it (essential for painting and maintenance).

2 Fit the wall panels together starting with the back, then the window and door panels. Drill pilot holes then screw the panels together with 50mm screws.

3 Once all the panels are joined and form an octagonal shape, attach the vertical panels to the floor joists with 70mm screws.

tools materials

- spirit level
- power drill
- hammer
- step ladder
- craft knife
- straightedge
- paintbrushes

- flatpacked summerhouse with fixings
- chalk
- exterior paint or stain

Assembling a summerhouse

The doors and windows are usually supplied installed in their frames in the wall panels, complete with catches and stays. Once all the wall panels are in place, the roof rafters can be assembled and plywood panels attached to them. These panels are covered with roofing felt and then finally with tongue-and-groove panels.

It's a good idea to arrange all the fixings, nails and screws by size on a tray so you can easily find what you need as you work.

Fitting the roof

The plywood roof panels act as a template/cutting guide for the roofing felt, so be sure to cut out the felt before fixing them in place.

Finial

Central roof support

Hip rafter

Plywood roof panel

Roofing felt

Tongue-and-groove outer roof panel

Window box

Corner trim

Base

1 Join the central roof support and hip rafters together with brackets and 35mm screws.

2 Gently turn the roof structure over and position the hip rafters on the eight corners of the summerhouse walls. Fix in place with 60mm screws. Using the plywood roof panels as a guide, mark cutting lines on the roofing felt in chalk and cut with a craft knife and straightedge.

4 Fix the roofing felt to the plywood panels with felt tacks. Each segment overlaps the next (follow the manufacturer's fitting guide). The tacks along the bottom edge go through the panel trim. Use 40mm nails to secure the felt down each rafter.

5 Fix the tongue-and-groove roof panels over the felt with 30mm screws.

3 Position the first roof panel so that it fits down the centreline of each hip rafter it touches. Nail the panels to the rafters with 30mm nails, spacing them evenly.

Finishing off

Nail the long upright corner trims in place over the joining edges of the main wall panels. To complete the roof, attach the finials to the central roof support. If you want to paint the structure, do so now, then finally fit the window boxes.

Family garden planting

The plants in this garden will provide colour and interest year after year. With a big lawn taking up much of the plot, the beds are fairly small, but lots of climbers will soon cover perimeter walls and fences.

Hot and sunny wall

Three trellis panels mounted on the left-hand boundary wall will support climbers grown in the long, narrow bed at its base. It's a warm, dry spot and the soil is quite shallow and poor – perfect for irises, of which there are two varieties here, the light blue *Iris* 'Jane Phillips' and the superb deep purple *Iris* 'Black Swan'. These provide necessary shade to the roots of purple *Clematis* 'Jackmanii Superba', which is planted at the foot of one trellis panel alongside *Rosa* 'Guinée', a climbing rose

with fragrant deep red flowers. These two will intertwine together and come into flower at the same time. *Rosa* 'Guinée', like *Heuchera* 'Palace Purple', prefers some shade, so both are positioned nearer the house. Trained up the other wooden trellis panel is *Abutilon* 'Kentish Belle', which will produce orange-yellow and red, bell-like flowers throughout the summer. The blues and purples that dominate the bed are echoed by the blue stain used to colour the trellis panels and the summerhouse.

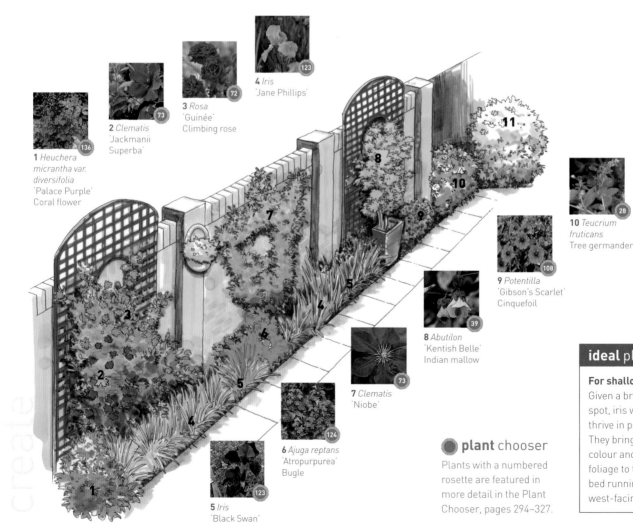

1 *Heuchera micrantha var. diversifolia* 'Palace Purple' Coral flower 136

2 *Clematis* 'Jackmanii Superba' 73

3 *Rosa* 'Guinée' Climbing rose 72

4 *Iris* 'Jane Phillips' 123

5 *Iris* 'Black Swan' 123

6 *Ajuga reptans* 'Atropurpurea' Bugle 124

7 *Clematis* 'Niobe' 73

8 *Abutilon* 'Kentish Belle' Indian mallow 39

9 *Potentilla* 'Gibson's Scarlet' Cinquefoil 108

10 *Teucrium fruticans* Tree germander 28

11 *Fuchsia magellanica* 'Riccartonii' 46

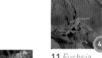
plant chooser

Plants with a numbered rosette are featured in more detail in the Plant Chooser, pages 294–327.

---

ideal plant 123

For shallow, dry soil
Given a bright, warm spot, iris will positively thrive in poor, dry soil. They bring brilliant colour and strap-like foliage to the narrow bed running along this west-facing wall.

Bright and bouncy bed

The planting between the summerhouse and playframe, at the end of the garden, is dominated by cheerful yellows and whites. Climbers will soon scramble up the fence and entwine themselves around the low trellis fixed along the top: yellow *Clematis orientalis* 'Bill MacKenzie', and the vigorous *Hedera helix* 'Goldheart', a variegated ivy with green and bright yellow foliage. The new tree, *Sorbus aria* 'Lutescens', will help draw the eye away from the houses behind as it matures and grows fuller and taller.

21 *Hedera helix* 'Goldheart' Ivy

20 *Choisya ternata* 'Sundance' Mexican orange blossom

19 *Skimmia japonica*

ideal plant ①

Tree for a small-to-medium garden
Sorbus aria 'Lutescens' has silvery leaves, white flowers, and small red fruits in early autumn. It grows quickly for the first couple of years, but then takes thirty years to reach its maximum 6m height.

12 *Sorbus aria* 'Lutescens' Whitebeam

13 *Clematis orientalis* 'Bill Mackenzie'

14 *Weigela florida* 'Variegata'

15 *Anthemis tinctoria* 'E.C. Buxton' Chamomile

16 *Hemerocallis lilioasphodelus* Daylily

17 *Cistus x corbariensis* Rock rose

18 *Kniphofia thomsonii* var. *snowdenii* Red-hot poker

Children's plot

The children's patch was planted with a mixture of flowers and tasty fruits and vegetables – all easy to care for and quick to grow. There are two different kinds of sunflowers, marigolds, sweetcorn, edible nasturtium flowers, pumpkins, and 'Parabell' carrots – a small, round variety grown from seed sown directly into the ground in April. To keep the kids interested, there is something ripening or flowering throughout the season. You may prefer to choose organic compost, soil improver and fertiliser when growing edible produce.

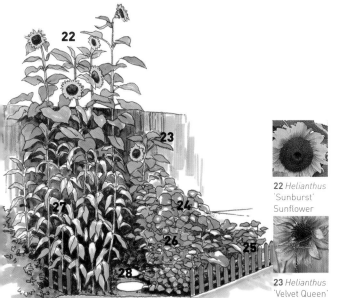

22 *Helianthus* 'Sunburst' Sunflower

23 *Helianthus* 'Velvet Queen' Sunflower

24 Pumpkin 'Jack o'Lantern'

25 French marigold 'Queen Sophia'

26 *Tropaeolum* 'Empress of India' Nasturtium

27 Sweetcorn 'Earlibird'

28 Carrot 'Parabell'

Contemplation
garden

We all need a place of sanctuary where we can wind down after a busy day. An enchanting, tranquil garden can be just that – somewhere to meditate, practise yoga or simply sit in peace and quiet, letting the delightful surroundings soothe the stresses and tensions of everyday life.

Planning a contemplation garden

A contemplation garden is a serene space that interweaves the kind of features that make you feel peaceful and rested, in mind and body. These might include the soothing ripple of flowing water, beautiful views of graceful plants, and being hidden from the sight and sound of the surrounding neighbourhood. Such a garden should be as secluded as possible, with hedges or trees, fencing, walls or trellis to create privacy. Watch the sun's progress in your garden – does it get morning sun or afternoon sun? – and then plan your seating areas according to the time of day you are most likely to use them. A pergola will add height and screening to a flat landscape. It might cover a walkway to a seat and a water feature where you can sit and be calmed by the sound of the water. The planting can reinforce this sense of calm: choose soft, harmonious colours, such as blues and grey with touches of pink, and grasses that will sway in the wind. If you can't transform your whole garden into a sanctuary, try making a relaxation zone in one area of a busy garden.

The design brief

The idea of this contemplation garden is that it should be a peaceful sanctuary with a minimal and contemporary look. The planting should complement the theme of escape and contemplation. The 11.5m x 17.4m garden is separated from the house – a converted barn – by a driveway and a hedge. The garden is very flat and started out completely empty apart from grass.

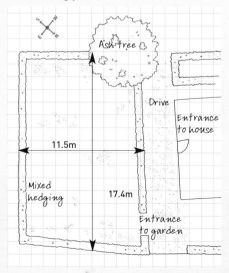

The existing plot

Ash tree

Drive

Entrance to house

11.5m

Mixed hedging

17.4m

Entrance to garden

Wants

- Privacy.
- Restful atmosphere.
- Water: a pool or a water feature.
- Attractive seating areas.
- A space for meditation and yoga practice
- Good-size lawn.
- Outdoor lighting.
- A minimal look.
- Planting that gives a sense of calm.

Problems

- Pipes and cables for the gas, water, electricity, telephone or drainage services may run underground through the garden to the house.
- Electric cable to power any lighting and water pumps will have to run a considerable distance to the house.

Seeking inspiration

A garden designed to bring peace of mind might borrow ideas from other cultures, particularly Eastern ones. The flow of yin and yang in Chinese philosophy is represented by a curved line rather than a rigid straight one, and yoga exercises are based on gentle, flowing movements. You might try and make the components of your contemplation garden interconnect in the same kind of unhurried way. Keep it simple and think about creating harmonious echoes between the various shapes, colours and materials of your design. Pick and mix aspects of these ancient philosophies with the push-button convenience of modern technology, which lets you, for instance, install cascading fountains of water wherever you want in the garden.

Draw a simple plan of your garden and draw in different ideas. Quick sketches like the ones below will help you get in tune with the space and give you an intuitive sense of what it requires to turn it into a sanctuary.

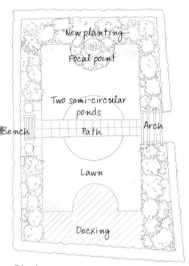

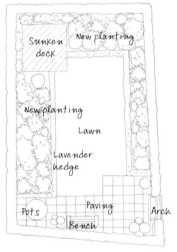

Circles

The simplicity and symmetry of this design are themselves contemplative. A short pergola walkway makes a stunning entrance onto the lawn and a path that leads between a pair of semi-circular ponds. Lots of planting, however, means that this will be a relatively high-maintenance garden. And the fact that the entrance lies directly opposite the front door of the house may reduce the sense of seclusion.

Rectangles

Instead of organic circles and curves, this design divides the garden into a series of squares and rectangles for a more minimalist look. The large paved terrace gives a generous seating area. A low lavender hedge fringing the beds will perfume the garden in summer. But again these are large beds, requiring significant levels of maintenance.

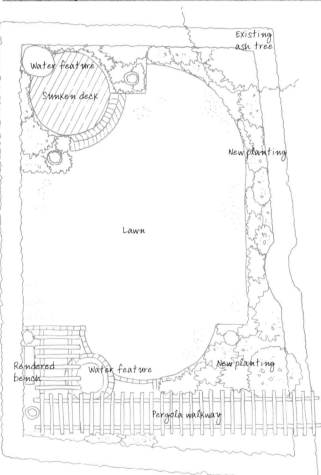

A calm and secluded retreat

The privacy of this enclosed garden is reinforced by the long walkway through which it is entered. Because the interior can't be seen from the driveway, it feels that the space withholds its secrets until you step right inside. A pair of matching water features introduce the soothing flow of water, gently audible from all parts of the garden. A sunken deck provides a sheltered spot dedicated to retreat and relaxation. This is the design that is to become the finished garden (see pages 124–39).

Contemplation garden 123

Contemplation garden

Soothing colours, textures, sounds and shapes make this garden a peaceful haven. The curved lines of the beds and deck feel inviting and organic. The carefully screened entrance keeps the world at bay. It's the perfect place to retreat and unwind.

A calm and secluded retreat

The 2.3m-high pergola over the walkway that leads into this garden adds instant height to the flat landscape, even before the climbers planted at its base have clambered their way up and over the structure. The soft crunch of footsteps on the gravel path complements the swish of the breeze through the grasses of the beds and borders. Beneath what will soon be the dappled shade of the pergola, a simple bench made of rendered blockwork and timber provides a point to sit and enjoy the view of the planting. Facing this is a contemporary water feature, against whose abstracted wave-form a sheet of water ripples onto the pebbled base. In the furthest corner from the entrance is a sunken circular deck surrounded by planting, with a matching water feature mounted on a plinth at its rear. As you step down into this space from the lawn, the sense of total immersion in the garden is complete.

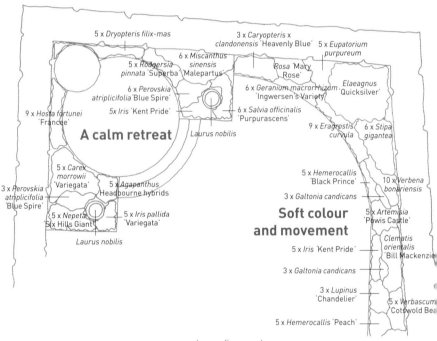

5 x *Dryopteris filix-mas*

3 x *Caryopteris x clandonensis* 'Heavenly Blue'

5 x *Eupatorium purpureum*

5 x *Rodgersia pinnata* 'Superba'

6 x *Miscanthus sinensis* 'Malepartus'

Rosa 'Mary Rose'

6 x *Perovskia atriplicifolia* 'Blue Spire'

6 x *Geranium macrorrhizum* 'Ingwersen's Variety'

Elaeagnus 'Quicksilver'

9 x *Hosta fortunei* 'Francee'

5x *Iris* 'Kent Pride'

6 x *Salvia officinalis* 'Purpurascens'

A calm retreat

Laurus nobilis

9 x *Eragrostis curvula*

6 x *Stipa gigantea*

5 x *Carex morrowii* 'Variegata'

5 x *Agapanthus* Headbourne hybrids

5 x *Hemerocallis* 'Black Prince'

10 x *Verbena bonariensis*

3 x *Perovskia atriplicifolia* 'Blue Spire'

3 x *Galtonia candicans*

5 x *Artemisia* 'Powis Castle'

Soft colour and movement

5 x *Nepeta* 'Six Hills Giant'

5 x *Iris pallida* 'Variegata'

5 x *Iris* 'Kent Pride'

Clematis orientalis 'Bill Mackenzie'

3 x *Galtonia candicans*

Laurus nobilis

3 x *Lupinus* 'Chandelier'

5 x *Verbascum* 'Cotswold Beauty'

5 x *Hemerocallis* 'Peach'

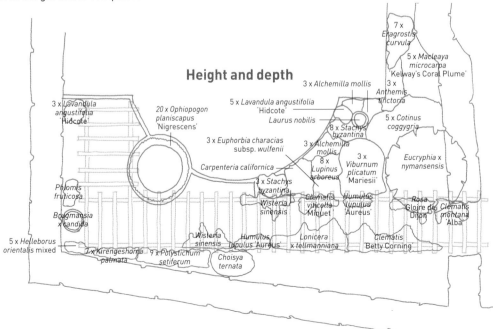

Height and depth

7 x *Eragrostis curvula*

5 x *Macleaya microcarpa* 'Kelway's Coral Plume'

3 x *Alchemilla mollis*

3 x *Anthemis tinctoria*

3 x *Lavandula angustifolia* 'Hidcote'

20 x *Ophiopogon planiscapus* 'Nigrescens'

5 x *Lavandula angustifolia* 'Hidcote'

Laurus nobilis

5 x *Cotinus coggygria*

8 x *Stachys byzantina*

3 x *Euphorbia characias* subsp. *wulfenii*

3 x *Alchemilla mollis*

3 x *Viburnum plicatum* 'Mariesii'

Eucryphia x nymansensis

Carpenteria californica

8 x *Lupinus arboreus*

Phlomis fruticosa

3 x *Stachys byzantina*

Clematis viticella 'Minuet'

Humulus lupulus 'Aureus'

Rosa 'Gloire de Dijon'

Clematis montana 'Alba'

Brugmansia x candida

Wisteria sinensis

5 x *Helleborus orientalis* mixed

7 x *Kirengeshoma palmata*

9 x *Polystichum setiferum*

Choisya ternata

Wisteria sinensis

Humulus lupulus 'Aureus'

Lonicera x tellmanniana

Clematis 'Betty Corning'

create

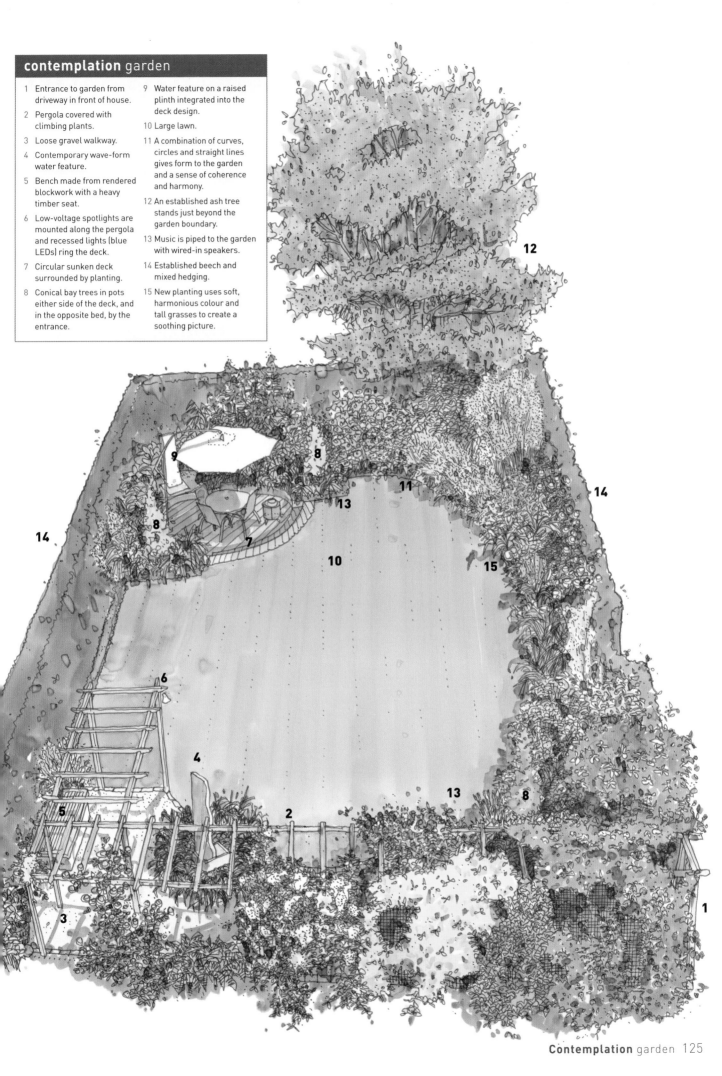

contemplation garden

1 Entrance to garden from driveway in front of house.

2 Pergola covered with climbing plants.

3 Loose gravel walkway.

4 Contemporary wave-form water feature.

5 Bench made from rendered blockwork with a heavy timber seat.

6 Low-voltage spotlights are mounted along the pergola and recessed lights (blue LEDs) ring the deck.

7 Circular sunken deck surrounded by planting.

8 Conical bay trees in pots either side of the deck, and in the opposite bed, by the entrance.

9 Water feature on a raised plinth integrated into the deck design.

10 Large lawn.

11 A combination of curves, circles and straight lines gives form to the garden and a sense of coherence and harmony.

12 An established ash tree stands just beyond the garden boundary.

13 Music is piped to the garden with wired-in speakers.

14 Established beech and mixed hedging.

15 New planting uses soft, harmonious colour and tall grasses to create a soothing picture.

Contemplation garden
pergola walkway

A pergola is an open roof mounted on posts. Trellis panels fixed between the posts will encourage climbing plants like wisteria, clematis and roses to clamber up the sides at great speed, providing welcome summer shade. Spotlights along the pergola roof are invitingly atmospheric after dark.

Marking out the site

The first task is to mark out the area for the walkway and cable runs with a marker line paint spray. Check for any hidden pipes or cables (drainage, gas, water, electricity or telephone) using a hired cable avoidance tool (CAT). Mark the position of any you find with a different coloured spray paint. If they lie directly beneath areas you wish to excavate, you must either change your plans or employ a professional to dig up and relocate them. Remove the topsoil within the walkway area to a depth of 150mm. You may need to dispose of the excavated rubble in a hired skip.

Running electrical cable

The water features and lights in this garden are powered by a new electrical circuit. This supplies two weatherproof sockets, one attached to the rear of the bench, the other to the plinth by the deck, as well as transformers which step down power to the low-voltage recessed LED lights that ring the deck and the spotlights fixed along the top of the pergola.

Laying electrical cable is the first task in a garden makeover. A circuit at mains voltage must be wired using three-core steel-wire-armoured cable (SWA) buried in a trench at least 450mm deep under a path or driveway and 750mm deep below unpaved areas that may be dug up at some point. Electrical route marker tape should be laid above it at a depth of about 150mm to show where it runs. Accidentally cutting through low-voltage cable will not injure or electrocute. Nonetheless, any loose cable is a trip hazard, so it is better to bury it about 450mm deep. If run in the same trenches as mains-voltage cable, it must be separated by plastic conduit, which will also protect it from vermin, corrosion or accidental damage. All outdoor fittings must be fully weatherproof and suitable for their location (see page 373).

If you decide to lay cables and install outdoor electrical fittings yourself, you must ensure that the work complies fully with the IEE Wiring Regulations and Building Regulations, and that when completed an electrical test certificate is issued (see page 373).

safety first
Remember the new rules
If you plan to install or make changes to a power or lighting circuit outdoors, you must inform your local authority's Building Control Department first (see page 373).

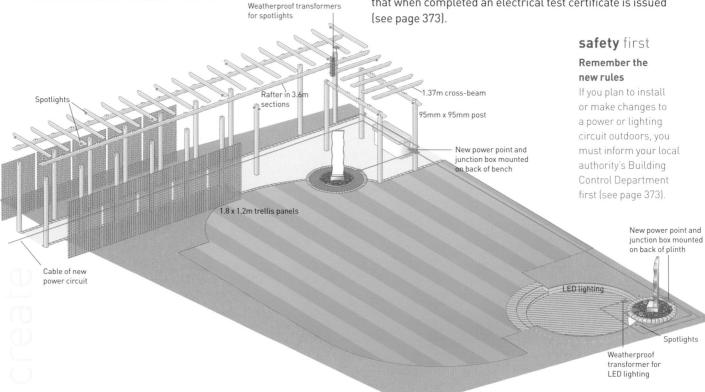

Weatherproof transformers for spotlights

Spotlights

Rafter in 3.6m sections

1.37m cross-beam

95mm x 95mm post

New power point and junction box mounted on back of bench

1.8 x 1.2m trellis panels

Cable of new power circuit

New power point and junction box mounted on back of plinth

LED lighting

Spotlights

Weatherproof transformer for LED lighting

create

Fitting vertical pergola posts

Pergolas are available in a flatpack kit containing vertical posts, rafters and cross-beams, so it's possible to construct a pergola whatever length you want using multiple kits. When digging lots of post holes it is well worth hiring a power post hole borer. Put in the two end posts along each row first, starting where the pergola turns the outer corner, and then followed by the furthest posts along the row in each direction. They should be spaced to allow post widths of 95mm and trellis panel widths of 1.8m.

Dig the post holes to a depth of 450mm. You could use a spade or a manual post hole borer (see page 83), but a power post hole borer will make easy work of this task.

Place the first corner post in the hole and check it is vertical using a spirit level.

Pour concrete into the hole around the post to hold it securely. Or you could use dry-mix post-fix concrete, which sets much more quickly (see page 82).

Hold the post level and tamp down the concrete with an offcut of timber.

Cross-brace the post with temporary timber props. Repeat the process at the opposite end of the row.

tools materials

- **spade**
- **post hole borer (hire)**
- **spirit level**
- **power drill**
- **builder's line**
- **long tape measure**
- **builder's square**
- **rake**
- **plate compactor (hire)**
- **bucket**
- **wheel barrow**

- pergola timbers and fixings
- footing mix concrete (see page 376) or dry-mix post-fix concrete (see page 82)
- offcut of timber
- timber props
- trellis panels

Run a string line between the tops of the two posts and use it to set the height of the rest of the posts. Double-check the measurements between the posts to make sure there is room for the trellis panels. Fix the intervening posts with concrete in the same way and allow to dry.

The second row of posts must be exactly level with the first. Before you concrete each post in, get a helper to hold it while you check it is level with the post on the other side using a spirit level on a cross-beam.

You can do it...

Accurate corners

A builder's square is useful for checking the corner of the pergola forms a true right angle. Made from stainless steel, it folds up for easy storage.

B&Q

Contemplation
garden
pergola walkway

With the pergola's vertical posts securely in place the roof timbers can be fitted, and finally the trellis panels. These will provide support for the climbers that are planted all along the foot of the structure, and will soon form a wall of foliage and flowers.

Fitting the roof beams

The open roof of this pergola consists of rafters that run lengthwise along the posts and horizontal cross-beams that are fixed onto the rafters. The cross-beams are secured with small timber rafter blocks. Finally the trellis panels are fixed to the vertical posts. Trellis is entirely optional on a pergola. It was added here on the opening section of the walkway to support climbers and partially screen the view of the garden as it is entered, enhancing the sense of mystery and seclusion.

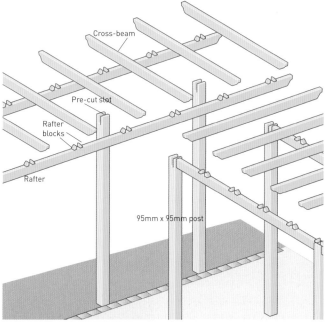

Cross-beam

Pre-cut slot

Rafter blocks

Rafter

95mm x 95mm post

1 Fit the rafters into the ready-made slots in the top of the posts. Lengths of rafter should meet halfway across a post. Drill pilot holes and screw them in place.

ideal tool

Spirit level

Keep checking as you work that the posts are level along the rows and across the width of the pergola. A long spirit level is ideal for this.

2 Measure and mark the position of pairs of rafter blocks so they will fit on the rafters either side of each cross-beam. Screw the rafter blocks to the rafters.

3 Lay each cross-beam across the rafters resting between two rafter blocks. Screw sideways through the rafter blocks into the cross-beams to secure them.

4 Screw the trellis panels in place, leaving a gap between the bottom of the trellis and the ground to prevent the timbers rotting.

Pergola pathway

The pergola pathway is surfaced with small decorative white chippings. These add a bright visual highlight, and will also crunch gently underfoot, bringing another pleasing sound element to the calm ambience of this garden. Stone chippings and aggregates need firm boundaries to stop them spreading onto the rest of the garden, so this path is edged on either side with small square granite-finish paving blocks known as setts. The rendered bench positioned at the end of this pergola walkway (see pages 130–31) was constructed before these chippings were laid.

tools materials

- spirit level
- builder's line and pegs
- builder's square
- tape measure
- bricklayer's trowel
- rubber mallet
- shovel
- rake
- plate compactor (hire)
- wheelbarrow

- paving mix concrete (see page 376)
- granite-finish setts
- wooden marker pegs
- Type 1 granular sub-base stone
- decorative chippings

1 Stretch a level line from one end of the path to the other, 150mm above the excavation level, to mark the finished height of the edging. Bed the setts in position along the path in paving mix concrete, haunched up either side to hold them.

2 Drive sharpened wooden pegs into the path to mark the height of the compacted Type 1 sub-base stone (100mm above the excavation level). Then spread Type 1 to a depth of 150mm and rake it level.

3 Compact the Type 1 stone with a vibrating plate compactor, taking particular care not to loosen the edging stones.

4 Add decorative chippings to a depth of about 25mm and rake them level. They should lie about 25mm below the top of the edging stones.

Atmosphere after dark

Lighting brings a different dimension to the garden at night: spotlights mounted on the pergola posts illuminate the walkway and the plants. Alternatively, you could use lights mounted on spikes that are pushed into the ground. These can be moved to highlight different plants through the summer. Only use fully weatherproof lights designed for outdoor use, and be sure not to allow your lights to interfere with your neighbours' right to privacy and darkness (see page 343).

Adding sound

Weatherproof outdoor speakers can be positioned permanently in the garden. Here there is one alongside the

pergola, another behind the deck. The cables connecting them to an amplifier inside the house are run in plastic conduit in the same trenches as the power cables. Always be considerate towards your neighbours with music and other noise in the garden.

Contemplation garden
rendered bench

At the end of the pergola walkway, positioned to face one of the garden's two water features, is a modern, minimal bench made from concrete blocks covered with white-painted render. Its seat is made from heavy timber sleepers.

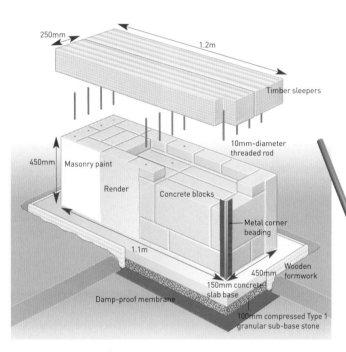

- 250mm
- 1.2m
- Timber sleepers
- 10mm-diameter threaded rod
- 450mm
- Masonry paint
- Render
- Concrete blocks
- Metal corner beading
- 1.1m
- 450mm
- Wooden formwork
- 150mm concrete slab base
- Damp-proof membrane
- 100mm compressed Type 1 granular sub-base stone

Foundations for the bench

The finished bench is heavy so needs a solid foundation of concrete on top of compressed Type 1 sub-base stone. Mark out an area about 150mm larger than the size of the bench on all sides using sand or spray marker paint. Excavate to a depth of 250mm then add a 150mm layer of Type 1. Rake this level and then compress it using a plate compactor or earth rammer.

Concrete needs to be supported by a frame (known as formwork) while it sets. Use treated timber planks about 25mm thick and 150mm deep to make this frame, nailed or screwed at the corners.

ideal tool

Earth rammer

An earth rammer – a heavy steel club on a long handle – is ideal for compacting small areas of earth or sub-base stone.

tools materials

- **spray marker paint**
- **spade**
- **shovel**
- **wheelbarrow**
- **plate compactor (hire) or earth rammer**
- **tape measure**
- **spirit level**
- **heavy-duty gloves**
- **workbench**
- **multi-purpose panel saw**
- **rake**
- **bricklayer's trowel**
- **hacksaw**
- **power drill**
- **9mm twist bit and 10mm masonry bit**
- **circular saw**
- **clamps**
- **hammer**

- Type 1 granular sub-base stone
- treated timber planks about 25mm x 150mm
- damp-proof membrane
- footing mix concrete (see page 376)
- two treated timber sleepers, 250mm x 130mm x 1.2m
- end-grain preserver
- 10mm threaded rod, cut into twelve 200mm lengths
- mortar
- metal corner beading
- render
- exterior masonry paint

You can do it...

Choosing concrete blocks

Lightweight concrete blocks are easy to work with and can be cut using a multi-purpose panel saw. But they are only suitable for outdoor use in very sheltered spots. Otherwise you would need to choose dense concrete blocks, which must be cut with an angle grinder; or avoid cutting by using engineering bricks to make up the dimensions.

1 Spread plastic damp-proof membrane over the compressed Type 1 sub-base stone and place the wooden formwork on top. Place a spirit level across the width of the frame all the way along it to check that it is level.

2 Pour in the concrete and spread it roughly with an old rake or shovel, leaving it about 20mm higher than the frame. Level it off and remove the excess using a spare length of timber.

Building the bench base

The body of the bench is built on top of the concrete slab base using lightweight concrete blocks. These are easy to lift and cut and quick to lay.

ideal tool
Bricklayer's trowel

A bricklayer's trowel is bigger than a pointing trowel, enabling it to pick up a good quantity of mortar at once. Its pointed shape is designed for scoring through the mortar before the bricks or blocks are laid.

1 Loose-lay the blocks on the concrete foundations to check the size of the bench. You may need to cut blocks into sections to reach the required height (see Step 2).

2 Cut blocks to size on a workbench using a multi-purpose panel saw.

3 Lay the blocks on a 15mm bed of mortar. Run the trowel point through the mortar to score it.

Fitting the wooden seat

Leave the blockwork to dry overnight. The timber sleepers are fixed to the base with 200mm-long threaded metal rods which go into the top of the base and the underside of the seat. Threaded rod is sold in long lengths and can be cut into shorter pieces with a hacksaw. The holes in the seat and the blocks are slightly different sizes – the thread will grip into the timber if the fit is tight, whereas in the blocks the holes are slightly bigger and the rod is bonded with a little render.

1 If you need to cut the sleepers for the seat to size, place them on top of the concrete blocks and mark where they need to be cut, allowing a 10mm gap between them for drainage, and a 30mm overhang beyond the base on all sides. Clamp a straightedge along each marked line and cut with a panel saw or circular saw. Paint the cut ends with end-grain preserver.

2 Turn the sleepers upside down and mark the positions of two fixing holes at either end and two holes in the centre of each timber (see diagram opposite). Drill the holes to a depth of 100mm using a 9mm bit, taking care to ensure the bit goes in vertically. Hammer a length of rod into each hole.

3 Measure and mark corresponding holes on the top of the concrete blocks (see above right). Drill vertically into the blocks using a 10mm masonry bit. Spread a thin layer of render on the blocks and position the sleepers on top, inserting the rods into the drilled holes.

You can do it...

Marking the holes
Once the rods are inserted in the sleepers, the easiest way to mark the positions of the corresponding holes in the blocks is as follows. Spread a thin layer of render on the blocks then, with a helper, turn the sleepers over and allow the rods to make indents in the render where the holes need to be drilled.

B&Q

4 Attach metal corner beading to the corners with render. Apply two coats of render (see pages 96–97). Finish with exterior masonry paint.

Contemplation
garden deck with
water feature

This sunken circular deck is built around a
rendered brick plinth, topped with granite
blocks and decorative pebbles, on which
stands a stylish contemporary water feature.

Excavating the site

The plinth for the water feature is 1.5m in diameter. This
is built first and the decking then laid alongside it. The
diameter of the deck is 3.5m. The top step and the top of
the curved outer wall are both level with the ground. The
two steps each measure 400mm from front to back. Using
a spray marker paint, draw the outline of the structure on
the ground, including the plinth and steps. Then extend
this area by an extra 300mm or so all around for access.

Excavate all vegetation and topsoil within the marked
area to a total depth of 560mm. A hired skip will almost
certainly be necessary to take away the removed earth and
rubble. If it's possible to reach the site with a mechanical
excavator, this will make the work much quicker and easier.

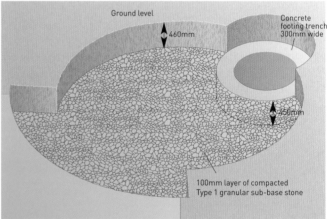

Ground level

460mm

Concrete
footing trench
300mm wide

450mm

100mm layer of compacted
Type 1 granular sub-base stone

tools materials

- **tape measure**
- **mechanical excavator
  (hire)**
- **shovel**
- **skip (hire)**
- **spirit level**
- **bricklayer's trowel**
- **paintbrush**
- **bucket**
- **metal float**
- **rake**
- **plate compactor (hire)**
- **earth rammer**

- spray marker paint
- length of metal dowel
- footing mix concrete
  (see page 376)
- engineering or frost-
  resistant bricks
- mortar
- liquid masonry waterproofer
- cleanstone
- granite-finish setts
- cement
- PVA
- render
- geotextile landscaping
  fabric
- Type 1 granular
  sub-base stone

1 Mark out the area for the
sunken deck with marker
line paint spray. Excavate
the area for the deck to a
depth of 560mm.

2 Drive a thin length of metal
dowel into the ground to mark
the centrepoint of the plinth.
Use a tape measure to double-
check the radius is the same
all round.

Laying foundations for the plinth

The plinth that supports the water feature needs a stronger foundation consisting of a concrete footing trench, 300mm wide, centred beneath its circular brick wall. Mark the outlines of the footing trench with spray marker paint and excavate it to a depth of 450mm. Fill with footing mix concrete (see page 376), and ensure it is level across the width. Allow to dry overnight.

Building the plinth

The circular plinth consists of a single-skin brick wall (the thickness of a single brick), built with engineering or frost-resistant bricks. It is topped with granite-finish setts that match the edges of the pergola pathway (see page 129). The interior is filled with cleanstone: grit- and dust-free aggregate that will allow water to drain freely. The brickwork is then rendered and eventually painted.

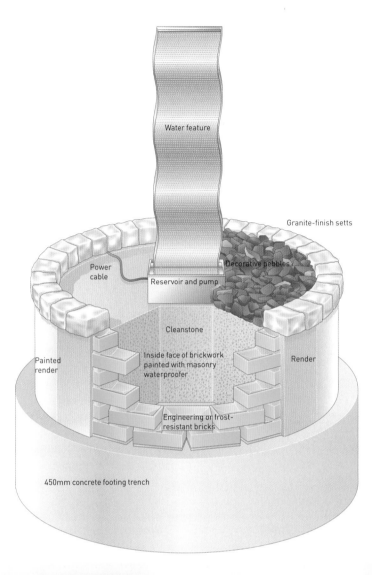

Water feature

Granite-finish setts

Power cable

Decorative pebbles

Reservoir and pump

Cleanstone

Painted render

Inside face of brickwork painted with masonry waterproofer

Render

Engineering or frost-resistant bricks

450mm concrete footing trench

1 Lay the first course of bricks on a 15mm bed of mortar. Keep checking the brickwork is level along each row and across the plinth as you lay all six courses.

Allow to dry for 48 hours, covered over if the weather is wet. Paint the inside of the brickwork with liquid masonry waterproofer. Then fill the plinth with cleanstone level with the top of the last course of bricks, leaving a dip in the middle for the water feature's reservoir. Pull out the metal dowel marking the centre.

2 Cap the brickwork with the granite-finish setts laid on a 15mm layer of mortar. Position them so that they overhang the brickwork by 15mm.

3 Mix a shovelful of cement and 250ml PVA with enough water to make a fairly thick solution. Coat the brickwork with this using a float. When dry, apply the render (see pages 96–97).

You can do it...

Paint-on waterproofer

A waterproof layer on the inside of the brickwork will protect the masonry and render from damp. You could line the structure with damp-proof plastic sheeting. Or paint the inside with liquid masonry waterproofer.

B&Q

ideal tool

Metal float
For a really fine finish on a rendered surface, use a metal float.

Completing the sub-base

Once the brickwork of the plinth is complete, you are ready to install the layer of Type 1 granular sub-base stone that provides a firm but porous foundation for the deck. First spread geotextile landscaping fabric over the excavated site; this will deter weed growth while allowing water to drain through. Then distribute the Type 1 stone over the area in an even layer, 150mm thick. This should be compacted down to 100mm using a hired plate compactor and an earth rammer.

Contemplation
garden deck with
water feature

Water adds a sense of freshness and calm to a garden, whether it is the still, cool water in a pool reflecting the sky and the planting around it, or a modern water feature arching water up into the air or cascading it down over rocks or stones.

Water in the garden

Including water features in a garden makeover enables you to integrate them into their surroundings so that they become like part of the landscape. This is the second of a pair of identical water features in this garden (see page 126). Its tall abstract wave-form creates an undulating wall of water that ripples gently down onto decorative stones at the base. Always follow the manufacturer's instructions when positioning and installing a water feature; this model should not be sited under a tree.

Installing the water feature

The water is pumped from a small reservoir surrounded by decorative stones that are laid over the cleanstone in the plinth. The feature is supplied with a length of weatherproof outdoor cable, which must be hard-wired to the mains electricity supply. Like any outdoor electrical installation, it must be protected by an RCD (residual current device), which will cut off the power in a split second if there is an earth leakage (see page 373).

tools materials

- **spirit level**
- **power drill with hammer action**
- **10mm masonry bit**

- water feature kit
- decorative pebbles

Water feature

Pipe

Power cable

Granite-finish setts

Reservoir and pump

Decorative pebbles

1 Place the water reservoir on the cleanstone in the plinth and use a long spirit level to make sure it is perfectly level, and that it is at the same height as the granite-finish setts.

2 Drill a hole through the brickwork at the back of the plinth, just below the setts, using a power drill fitted with a 10mm masonry bit. Feed the power cable through the hole.

3 Follow the manufacturer's instructions to assemble the water feature and connect the pump to the electricity. Fill the reservoir with water.

4 Cover the top of the reservoir and the surrounding area with decorative pebble stones.

Constructing a sunken deck

tools materials

- **long spirit level**
- **pencil**
- **tape measure**
- **workbench**
- **circular saw**
- **compound mitre saw**
- **panel saw**
- **socket set for coach screws**
- **combination square**
- **power drill**
- **jigsaw**
- **paintbrush**

- deck joists
- 150mm coach screws
- weatherproof transformer for LED lights
- deck boards
- deck or galvanised screws
- end-grain preserver

The decking is laid on a framework of joists which run at right angles to the deck boards. The joists are spaced 400mm centre to centre, and are joined together at staggered intervals with shorter lengths of joist. Be sure to paint cut timber ends with end-grain preserver. The weatherproof transformer for the LED lights (see page 137) is attached to the deck sub-frame before the deck boards are laid.

For more detailed advice on building decking, see page 101, and **You Can Do It: the Complete B&Q Step-by-Step Book of Home Improvement**.

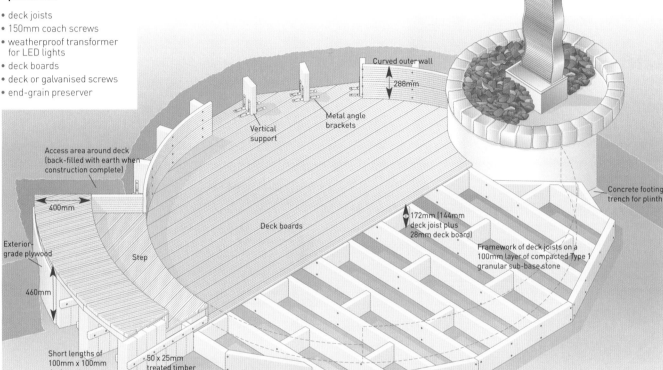

- Curved outer wall — 288mm
- Metal angle brackets
- Vertical support
- Access area around deck (back-filled with earth when construction complete)
- 400mm
- Exterior-grade plywood
- 460mm
- Step
- Deck boards
- 172mm (144mm deck joist plus 28mm deck board)
- Framework of deck joists on a 100mm layer of compacted Type 1 granular sub-base stone
- Concrete footing trench for plinth
- Short lengths of 100mm x 100mm deck post
- 50 x 25mm treated timber

Drill holes and assemble the joist framework with two countersunk coach screws into the ends of each joined section.

Angle both the inner and outer joists to follow the circular outlines of the plinth and deck.

Fix the deck boards to the joists, leaving a 3mm drainage gap between boards – a 3mm deck screw makes a good spacer. Position joins halfway across a joist so both boards can be screwed into it.

You can do it...

Rough edges

The outer wall of this circular deck forms a clean, curved edge that will hide the cut ends of the deck boards. So there's no need to waste time and effort profiling the boards; simply cut them roughly to extend just beyond the edges of the joist framework. But don't cut them in position or you risk sawing through a joist – saw them on a workbench.

B&Q

Contemplation
garden deck with water feature

The sunken deck is a peaceful spot in a corner of the garden well away from the house, so it can be quite dark in the evening. Discreet LED lights are set into the curved sides, creating a magical effect at night.

Making the curved outer wall

Once the deck boards have been attached to the joist sub-frame, the curved outer wall can be added and the steps constructed. The curved wall is made from a double row of deck boards. To allow them to bend without breaking, shallow cuts are made across their width. First draw the curve on the deck with pencil and string then fix 270mm sections of deck joist at right angles to the line as support posts, spaced about 300mm apart. These are fixed in place with galvanised screws and angle brackets.

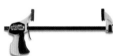

tools materials
- tape measure
- pencil
- string
- circular saw
- workbench
- power drill
- clamps
- filling knife
- 10mm flat wood bit
- jigsaw
- gloves
- sanding block

- deck joists
- galvanised metal angle brackets and screws
- deck or galvanised screws
- deck boards
- exterior wood filler
- deck posts
- 25mm x 50mm treated timbers
- low-voltage LED deck lights
- plastic cable conduit
- 6mm exterior-grade plywood
- end-grain preserver
- thick waterproof wood preservative
- damp-proof membrane
- galvanised felt tacks
- medium-grade abrasive paper

1 Hold the deck board in a workbench and make a series of cuts, about 30mm apart and 20mm deep, along the length with a circular saw.

2 Position the curved edge on the deck with the cuts to the outside and clamp it to the support posts. Attach it to the posts with deck or galvanised screws.

3 Fill the cuts along the top edge with a matching exterior wood filler to hide the saw marks.

Making the step framework

The step risers are made from curved deck boards; the lower riser is a continuation of the curved outer wall, and is fixed to upright sections of deck joist in the same way (see above). The remaining framework supporting the treads is created from short lengths of deck post, braced horizontally with 25mm x 50mm treated timbers. To form the treads, sections of deck joist are attached centre to centre across this post framework, then short lengths of deck board are laid on top. Fit LED deck lights (see opposite above) before laying the treads (opposite below).

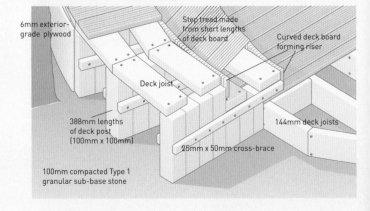

6mm exterior-grade plywood

Step tread made from short lengths of deck board

Curved deck board forming riser

Deck joist

388mm lengths of deck post (100mm x 100mm)

144mm deck joists

25mm x 50mm cross-brace

100mm compacted Type 1 granular sub-base stone

Fitting LED lighting

Low-voltage blue LED deck lights are set into the curved sides of this deck, about 300mm apart, spreading a gentle glow over the whole area. More lights are fitted to the curved riser of each step to prevent anyone tripping on them in the dark.

1 Drill holes in the side of the deck using a 10mm flat wood drill bit.

2 Feed the cable through the drilled holes and set the lights in position. Run the cable in plastic conduit to protect it from vermin and corrosion.

Completing the steps

With the LED lights installed, you are ready to finish the steps. Once the tread timbers are in place, thin exterior-grade plywood is attached to the outside of the tread framework. This is protected with preservative and a layer of damp-proof membrane so that the soil is not banked against the deck timbers, which would make them rot. For the same reason, it's a good idea to fix plastic damp-proof membrane all around the outer deck timbers before you back-fill with earth.

1 Place the deck boards for the treads on the frame, using a screw as a spacer to maintain a 3mm gap between the boards. Trace the profile of the riser in pencil on the underside of the boards.

2 Place the deck boards on a workbench and cut along the pencil line with a jigsaw. Treat the cut ends with end-grain preserver then attach the boards to the frame.

3 Fix exterior-grade plywood to the outside of the tread framework. Paint with thick waterproof preservative, then cover with a layer of damp-proof membrane, attached with galvanised felt tacks.

4 Sand any rough edges along the steps and retreat with end-grain preserver where necessary.

ideal tool

Jigsaw

The narrow blade of a jigsaw allows you to profile deck boards and timbers to a smooth curve.

Contemplation garden planting

Soft colour graduates through beds and borders. The gentle swish of grasses harmonises with the relaxing ripple of water. The planting is subtle and soothing, creating an ideal environment in which to unwind and forget your cares.

Relaxing with nature

Majestically tall grasses introduce gentle sound and movement to the borders of this garden: African lovegrass (*Eragrostis curvula*); *Miscanthus sinensis* 'Malepartus'; and golden oats (*Stipa gigantea*), which grow to a stately height of up to 2.5m and bear magnificent seedheads. Planting around the deck is dominated by cool, calm blues. Moving around to the bed opposite, colours gradually become warmer and livelier. The silver-grey foliage of *Elaeagnus* 'Quicksilver' is balanced by its clusters of pale yellow flowers. *Verbascum* 'Cotswold Beauty' produces tall spikes of smoky peach flowers with purple centres.

Closer to the garden's entrance, the peaches and yellows give way to the dusky pink of the fluffy blossoms borne by the smoke tree, *Cotinus coggygria*, whose leaves provide rich autumn colour. Touches of white from the flowers of *Viburnum plicatum* 'Mariesii' and *Carpenteria californica* lift and brighten the area closest to the entrance. The pergola is clothed with climbers: pale blue *Wisteria sinensis*; the yellow-flowered golden hop, *Humulus lupulus* 'Aureus'; and two intertwining clematis, *Clematis viticella* 'Minuet', with striking purple and white flowers, and the pale mauve *Clematis* 'Betty Corning'.

● **plant** chooser

Plants with a numbered rosette are featured in more detail in the Plant Chooser, pages 294–327.

1 *Iris* 'Kent Pride'	**2** *Laurus nobilis* Bay tree	**3** *Perovskia atriplicifolia* 'Blue Spire' Russian sage	**4** *Miscanthus sinensis* 'Malepartus'	**5** *Rodgersia pinnata* 'Superba'	**6** *Dryopteris filix-mas* Male fern

ideal plant

For a contemporary look

Grasses come in all shapes and sizes, from magnificent to minimal, and provide texture, delicacy and a sense of soothing movement as they sway in the breeze.

A calm retreat

7 *Hosta fortunei* 'Francee'	**8** *Carex morrowii* 'Variegata' Sedge	**9** *Nepeta* 'Six Hills Giant' Catmint	**10** *Salvia officinalis* 'Purpurascens' Purple sage	**11** *Iris pallida* 'Variegata'	**12** *Agapanthus* Headbourne hybrids African lily

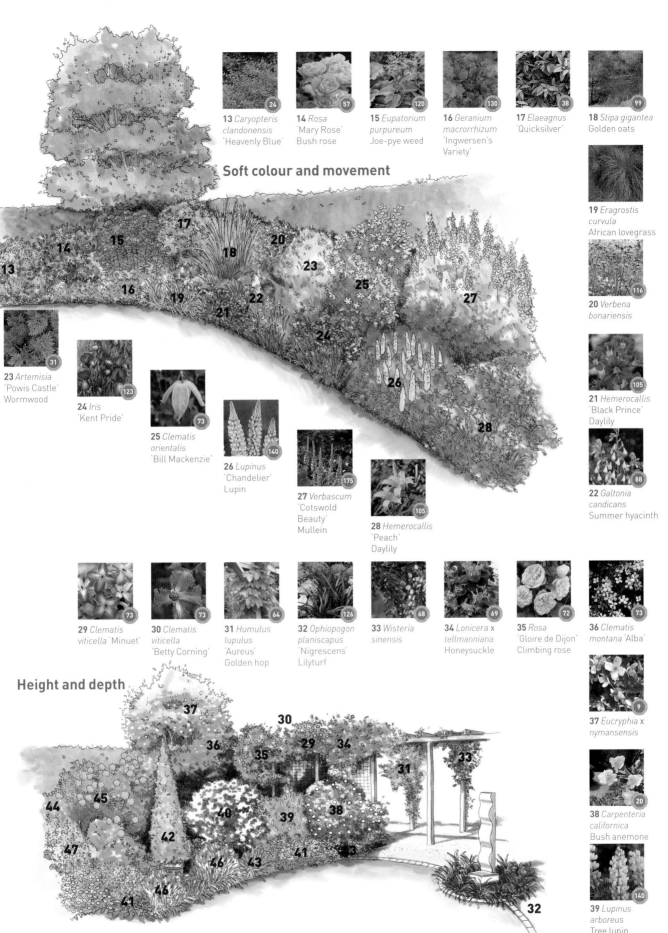

13 *Caryopteris clandonensis* 'Heavenly Blue' (24)

14 *Rosa* 'Mary Rose' Bush rose (57)

15 *Eupatorium purpureum* Joe-pye weed (120)

16 *Geranium macrorrhizum* 'Ingwersen's Variety' (130)

17 *Elaeagnus* 'Quicksilver' (38)

18 *Stipa gigantea* Golden oats (99)

19 *Eragrostis curvula* African lovegrass

20 *Verbena bonariensis* (116)

21 *Hemerocallis* 'Black Prince' Daylily (105)

22 *Galtonia candicans* Summer hyacinth (88)

Soft colour and movement

23 *Artemisia* 'Powis Castle' Wormwood (31)

24 *Iris* 'Kent Pride' (123)

25 *Clematis orientalis* 'Bill Mackenzie' (140)

26 *Lupinus* 'Chandelier' Lupin (175)

27 *Verbascum* 'Cotswold Beauty' Mullein (105)

28 *Hemerocallis* 'Peach' Daylily

29 *Clematis viticella* 'Minuet' (73)

30 *Clematis viticella* 'Betty Corning' (73)

31 *Humulus lupulus* 'Aureus' Golden hop (64)

32 *Ophiopogon planiscapus* 'Nigrescens' Lilyturf (126)

33 *Wisteria sinensis* (68)

34 *Lonicera* x *tellmanniana* Honeysuckle (69)

35 *Rosa* 'Gloire de Dijon' Climbing rose (72)

36 *Clematis montana* 'Alba' (73)

37 *Eucryphia* x *nymansensis* (9)

38 *Carpenteria californica* Bush anemone (20)

39 *Lupinus arboreus* Tree lupin (140)

Height and depth

47 *Anthemis tinctoria* Chamomile (95)

46 *Lavandula angustifolia* 'Hidcote' English lavender (29)

45 *Cotinus coggygria* Smoke tree (48)

44 *Macleaya microcarpa* 'Kelway's Coral Plume' Plume poppy (86)

43 *Stachys byzantina* Lamb's ears (85)

42 *Laurus nobilis* Bay tree (3)

41 *Alchemilla mollis* Lady's mantle (80)

40 *Viburnum plicatum* 'Mariesii' (44)

Exotic garden

There's a lot you can do with a garden that is really too small to have a conventional lawn and borders. An exotic jungle look is a great option, using dramatic plants such as palms, banana plants and tree ferns. These are tender plants that need a warm, sheltered garden, such as in London or the southwest; in other parts of the UK they will need to be brought indoors or wrapped in hessian over the winter.

Planning an exotic garden

Even in a tiny garden you can cook, eat and entertain, have lots of plants in pots and planters, squeeze in a tool store – even install a spa. Make the most of the garden's advantages: after all, a small garden means less maintenance if you have little time for mowing a lawn, digging, weeding and pruning. An uncluttered design and carefully chosen planting for maximum visual impact will enable you to make the most of the space you have.

Finding inspiration

Borrow ideas from books and television, and visit stores and gardens to see the kind of exotic plants that appeal to you. Then choose the ones that will thrive in your garden's conditions. Look at the existing layout and features in your garden and decide whether you want to incorporate any of them into your new design, or whether you want to get rid of them all and start from scratch.

The design brief

This town garden measures only 4.8m x 5.6m, plus a strip down the side of the house. It was mostly lawn with overgrown climbers all over the fencing and a good part of the garden. A brick plinth running around the edge supported wooden boards, creating a kind of built-in bench. Low-maintenance solutions were a priority, so that time outdoors in the garden could be spent relaxing rather than working.

The existing plot

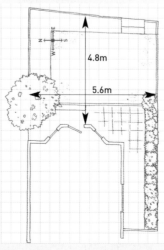

4.8m

5.6m

Wants

- All-weather surface.
- Plants that create a jungle effect with dramatic patterns and shapes.
- A spa for luxurious relaxation.
- Space to put a table and chairs for entertaining.
- A low-maintenance garden.
- Improve the drab fencing.
- More lighting so the garden can be used at night.
- Somewhere to keep garden tools.

Problems

- Limited space limits what can be included.
- Overgrown climbing plants on the fence leave little room for anything else.
- The wooden bench around the edge of the garden allows no room for growing plants.
- There is not enough space for a standard shed.

Developing ideas

Everything in a garden this size has to earn its place – there is no room for anything that doesn't look spectacular, add to the enjoyment of the garden or serve a useful purpose. Draw a plan of the site and sketch in various ideas. Make sure everything is to scale and try to visualise plants at their final size when they have finished growing – you don't want them to get too big for their allotted space.

Decking and paving

A spa sits on a raised terrace in one corner of the garden, flanked by raised planters. The terrace is shaped on a curve. Another raised planter runs along the path beside the house. Decking covers the rest of the space. A small tree provides shade in the summer.

Circular deck

This layout centres on a circular deck that extends back to the house and down the side passage. Everything beyond the circle is raised. Instead of a spa, there is a corner seat beneath a pergola mounted over a paved terrace.

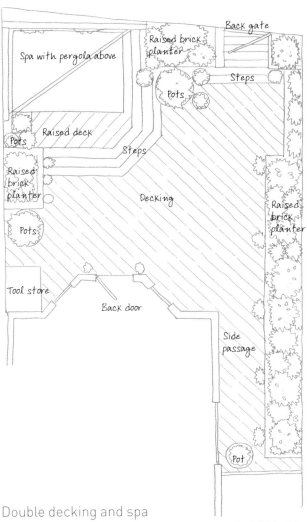

Double decking and spa

Here, most of the garden is covered with diagonally-laid decking that steps up to a raised decked platform at the end, with the spa situated on the platform, semi-screened by a pergola. Arranged in groups around the deck surface are lots of plants in pots, and the deck is almost entirely surrounded by raised brick planters. This is the chosen design for the new garden as it gives maximum open space and planting areas (see pages 142–49).

Exotic garden

Decking gives this garden a practical, all-weather surface. Structural exotic plants look equally impressive against it in winter and summer, and including a spa ensures that the garden may be enjoyed all year round.

An exotic design

By extending across the entire garden, the decking creates an impression of continuity that actually makes the space seem larger. The deck boards are laid diagonally to add extra interest, with the two levels following different directions. To complement the urban and modern style of the space, the boards are laid smooth side up, and stained a cedar wood colour, to match the steps and side panels of the spa. This is situated on a stepped, raised deck area in the northeast corner of the garden, where it will catch maximum sun but not be directly overlooked from the surrounding houses.

Container gardening

The hard lines of the deck boards are softened by a dense collection of plants, all of them grown in containers – brick planters around the edges, or large pots for exotic specimens like palms and tree ferns. The plants need little maintenance other than watering, feeding and maybe winter protection for the tenderest specimens if the weather is very cold.

Thinking vertically

The new fencing to the north side of the spa and the simple triangular pergola overhead are made from decking joists and deck support posts, stained to match the deck. Stainless steel plant training wires are attached to this fence and across the canopy of the pergola, encouraging climbers to grow up and over the spa and enhance the magic and privacy of this corner. Decking steps lead up to the back gate, which opens on to a footpath. The fence at the end of the garden has been replaced, and this and the fencing on the right-hand side are painted soft blue-green.

After dark

A network of low-voltage spotlights and recessed deck lights create drama by night. The deck lights outline the shape of the garden, while spotlights in the brick planters shine upwards through the foliage, creating spectacular patterns of shadow and colour.

Pots and planters against a south-facing wall

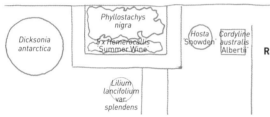

Containers for colour and fragrance

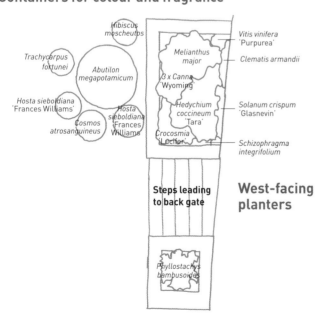

North-facing planter

Private spa therapy

Spas are freestanding pools – they are not plumbed in – and require only an electrical supply to operate the water heater and water jets. Relaxing in the warm swirling water reduces stress and is fabulous therapy for skin, muscles and joints. A spa can be a great refuge from the world – but also a fun experience to share with friends. This spa has a shell of tough plastic and acrylic, with an outer layer of cedar panelling. When not in use it has an insulated cover for retaining the heat, keeping the water free of debris, and preventing children or pets falling in. Planning permission is not usually required for a spa, but it is a good idea to check with your local planning office. You will need access for a spa to be rolled in on a trolley as it cannot be dismantled. The motor in a spa can create vibration and noise, especially when positioned on a deck: to reduce this, sit the spa on a weatherproof rubber mat.

exotic garden

1   Pergola-like timber framework supports climbers above spa.
2   Spa sits in the sunniest corner of the garden.
3   Raised decking built over reinforced concrete foundations supports weight of spa.
4   Deck boards laid diagonally and stained to match the cedar panels of the spa.
5   New fence constructed of deck joists.
6   Exotic foliage gives tropical style to garden.
7   Trellis is mounted along fence top to support climbers.
8   Plants in mixed containers add scent and splashes of vivid colour.
9   Brick planter runs the length of the right-hand side of the garden.
10 A small tool store is tucked beside the house.
11 Gate leading to passageway at rear of garden.
12 Lighting includes external low-voltage fairy lights strung over the pergola.

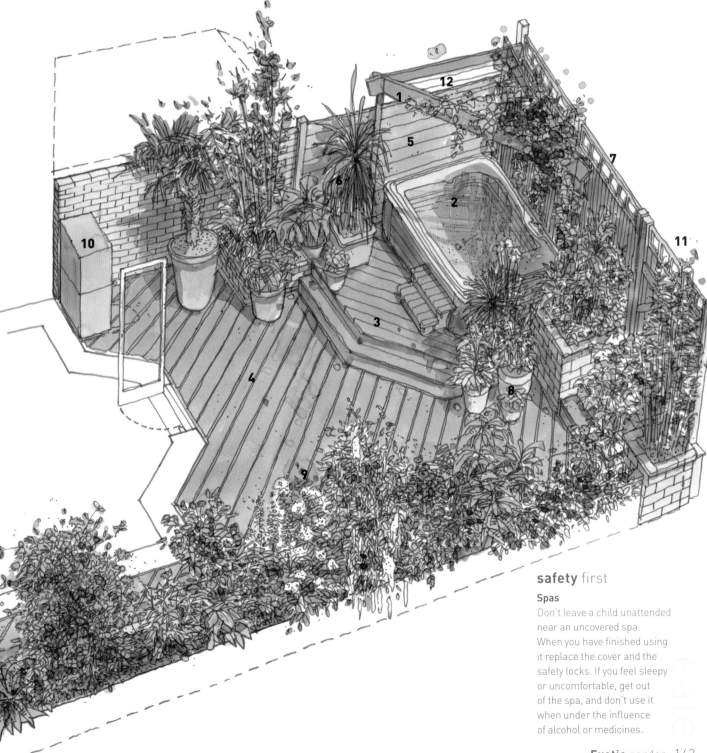

safety first

Spas

Don't leave a child unattended near an uncovered spa. When you have finished using it replace the cover and the safety locks. If you feel sleepy or uncomfortable, get out of the spa, and don't use it when under the influence of alcohol or medicines.

Exotic garden
building brick planters

By raising the plants above ground level, brick planters are an excellent way of adding variety to a flat garden and making the most of the vertical space in a small one.

Getting started

When creating a multi-level garden such as this, complete with decking at different heights, the first task is to establish the lowest fixed point and level the garden to it. Here, this was the height of the threshold at the back door. Some excavation was required, but not much – this was a mostly flat plot.

Then mark out all the new features on the ground – planters, decking, the double-reinforced concrete pad for the spa – using spray marker paint (see page 78). This will show you the relationship between the various elements (and is the time to make any adjustments, should anything seem awkward).

Constructing a brick planter

A brick planter is built the same way as a brick wall and it needs a solid foundation. Use spray paint to mark out a concrete slab base for each planter, which should extend 100mm beyond the brickwork at the front and to each side. Excavate this area to a depth of 150mm, fill it with footing mix concrete (see page 376), and level with a rough length of timber. Check the surface is level with a spirit level. Allow to dry for 24 hours.

A good height for a planter is about 600mm. Don't build it much higher or the amount of soil it will hold may push the walls out of shape when wet.

tools materials

- **spray marker paint**
- **spirit level**
- **tape measure**
- **builder's square**
- **spade**
- **shovel**
- **wheelbarrow**
- **rough length of timber**
- **scissors**
- **bricklayer's trowel**
- **power drill with hammer action**
- **spanner**
- **pointing tool**

- footing mix concrete (see page 376)
- damp-proof membrane
- stainless steel connectors and wall ties
- expanding masonry bolts
- frost-proof facing bricks
- mortar
- coping stones

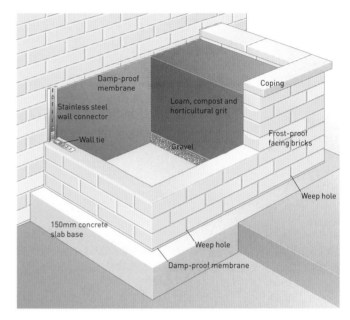

Damp-proof membrane
Coping
Stainless steel wall connector
Loam, compost and horticultural grit
Wall tie
Frost-proof facing bricks
Gravel
Weep hole
150mm concrete slab base
Weep hole
Damp-proof membrane

Building brick walls

Like any wall built at right angles to another, the side walls of the planter need to be attached using connectors and wall ties (see opposite above). It's not advisable to build a brick planter against the house wall – if the damp-proof membrane is damaged, moisture will penetrate the masonry.

For more detailed information on building a brick wall, see **You Can Do It: the Complete B&Q Step-by-Step Book of Home Improvement.**

1 Measure and cut a piece of damp-proof membrane to lay against the existing wall and extend beneath the base of the planter.

2 Use expanding masonry bolts to attach a stainless steel wall connector to the garden wall at the point where each of the planter's side walls will meet it. Lay the damp-proof membrane behind the wall connector.

3 Lay the bricks on a 15mm bed of mortar, using a spirit level to check that each course is level.

Leave a series of gaps or weep holes in the mortar in the first course of bricks in the wall – about two at the front and one in each side. These will allow excess water to drain out.

At every third course of bricks, hook a wall tie onto the wall connector and bed it into the mortar.

Lay coping stones over the top course of bricks, overhanging the wall. Smooth the mortar in the joints using a pointing tool. Allow to dry for a week before filling and planting.

Preparing for planting

The soil you put in a planter depends on what you want to plant in it. Some plants, such as bamboos, do not tolerate very dry conditions, so you would need to mix in a lot of moisture-retaining organic matter. Plants that thrive in free-draining conditions, such as lavender and Mediterranean herbs, need a greater proportion of grit. If you wish to grow lime-hating plants, use lime-free compost. As a general rule, use one part loam to one part multi-purpose compost (see page 208) to one part horticultural grit (about 2mm size), plus slow-release fertiliser (in a quantity advised by the manufacturer).

Sprinkle gravel or crushed stone to a depth of 40mm in the bottom of the planter to help drainage and prevent the plants becoming waterlogged.

tools materials

- **tape measure**
- **scissors**
- **bucket**
- **garden fork**

- gravel or crushed stone
- permeable landscaping fabric
- loam
- multi-purpose compost
- horticultural grit

Cut a sheet of permeable landscaping fabric and lay it over the gravel to stop it mixing with the soil.

Fill the planter with a mixture of soil and compost, according to the specific needs of the plants you choose.

Mix in horticultural grit with a garden fork, taking care not to puncture the landscaping fabric.

Exotic garden
raised deck for a spa

The most sheltered part of the garden is the best spot for a spa so that you can use it all year round and bring the garden into your life in the winter. Decking makes a good surface around a spa as it is warm and smooth underfoot.

Triangular pergola

To create a private space around the spa, a simple triangular pergola is erected using deck support posts and deck joists, stained the same cedar wood colour as the deck. Set the posts in concrete (see page 82), and fix the cross-beams to them with deck screws. Erect the posts and attach the first three deck joists forming the fence before laying the concrete pad (see below right). The fencing then serves as one side of the timber shuttering supporting the concrete as it sets.

When the structure is complete, stainless steel wires attached to vine eyes are strung between the overhead beams of the pergola to encourage the spread of climbing plants.

A firm footing

Spas weigh more than a tonne when full of water, and so must be positioned on a surface with very solid foundations. The part of the deck directly beneath this spa is supported by a 350mm double-reinforced concrete pad – that is, with two layers of steel mesh sandwiched within the concrete. This pad is laid on the ground, with the concrete held in place as it dries by pegged wooden timbers known as shuttering. Use footing mix concrete (see page 376). The deck sub-frame is laid directly on top of the concrete; the raised deck area beyond the pad is supported by posts set in concrete in the usual way (see page 82). It's a good idea to tack strips of damp-proof membrane to the underside of the deck joists that lie on the concrete pad, to protect them from rising moisture. For more information on laying concrete and building decking, see **You Can Do It: the Complete B&Q Step-by-Step Book of Home Improvement**.

Extra strength
Double-reinforce the concrete base for the spa by sandwiching two layers of steel mesh within the concrete.

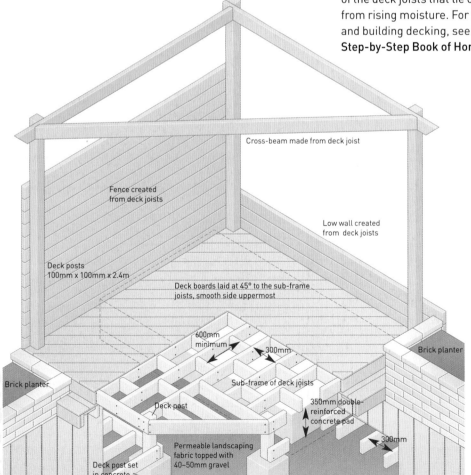

Cross-beam made from deck joist

Fence created from deck joists

Low wall created from deck joists

Deck posts 100mm x 100mm x 2.4m

Deck boards laid at 45° to the sub-frame joists, smooth side uppermost

600mm minimum

300mm

Brick planter

Brick planter

Deck post

Sub-frame of deck joists

350mm double-reinforced concrete pad

300mm

Permeable landscaping fabric topped with 40–50mm gravel

Deck post set in concrete

safety first
Electrical supply
The power supply for a spa must be a dedicated circuit with 30 milliamp RCD protection. You will need to ask a qualified electrician to do this work (see page 373).

Building the sub-frame

Apart from the raised section, the sub-frame of this deck lies directly on the ground. To deter weed growth and promote drainage, lay permeable landscaping fabric over the earth followed by a 40–50mm layer of gravel. The joists are spaced 300mm centre-to-centre and run lengthwise along the garden. It's a good idea to fix short cross-timbers between joists every 2.4m over long spans. To support the weight of the spa in the raised section, fit these joist cross-timbers at minimum 600mm intervals. The raised area has angled corners where steps lead down to the lower level. Mark and cut both the outer and inner joists of the sub-frame to the required angle to create this outline. Lay the deck boards diagonally across the joists, following one direction at the lower level, the opposite on the raised section.

Constructing angled steps

The step treads are made from two lengths of deck board joined side by side, both screwed down into a joist that runs beneath them. Two more lengths of joist form the upright risers, which are masked with deck boards when the step is in place.

tools materials

- **tape measure**
- **long spirit level**
- **pencil**
- **adjustable square**
- **compound mitre saw**
- **power drill**

- deck boards
- deck joists
- deck or galvanised screws

1 Hold a deck tread in position, allowing the joist sub-frame to overlap it by 25mm. You may need to ask a helper to hold the other end. Mark the point of the sub-frame corner in pencil.

2 Use an adjustable square to draw a line at a 22.5° angle, intersecting the pencil mark. Cut along the angled line with a compound mitre saw.

ideal tool

Compound mitre saw
This power mitre saw can be used with a variety of blades to cut hard and soft woods, plastic, alloys and non-ferrous metals. The blade can be adjusted to cut at an angle.

3 Cut a second deck board and a length of joist to the same angle. Screw the two boards side-by-side onto the deck joist, centring it beneath the join.

4 Cut two deck joists to the length of the step. Attach these to the underside of the tread by screwing through into the central anchor joist.

Fixing the steps in place

The steps are fixed in position once the deck boards are all laid. Secure them with angled screws. Finally screw deck boards along the length of the steps to form the face of the risers. Then stain the timbers.

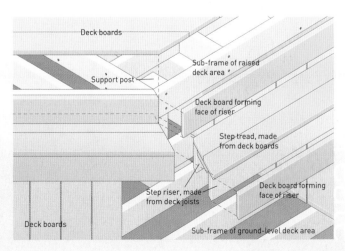

Deck boards
Sub-frame of raised deck area
Support post
Deck board forming face of riser
Step tread, made from deck boards
Step riser, made from deck joists
Deck board forming face of riser
Deck boards
Sub-frame of ground-level deck area

Exotic planting

When creating an all-season garden in a small space with hard surfaces all around, plant for drama – with strong shapes, lush tropical foliage and hot colours like reds and oranges.

Pots for easy outdoor living

The beds in this garden are small and shallow, and confined to brick planters, so planting space is limited. But freestanding containers of varying sizes, shapes and materials – from classic unglazed terracotta to modern metallics – provide the opportunity to introduce many more plants, as well as soften the hard outlines of the space. Really large pots are a dramatic addition to a garden in their own right. Here the stately upright shapes of a number of plants – including the New Zealand tree fern, *Dicksonia antarctica*, and *Cordyline australis* 'Albertii' – look magnificent in large terracotta pots.

Pots are easy to plant and arrange in a garden – but they do need watering regularly, particularly in summer or during a dry spell in spring or autumn. The easiest way to keep on top of watering is by installing an automatic watering system (see page 252) controlled by a timer.

● plant chooser
Plants with a numbered rosette are featured in more detail in the Plant Chooser, pages 294–327.

ideal plant ⑤⑥

For an exotic look
Bamboos are strikingly tall, upright plants with attractive foliage. Often fast growing, there are types to suit every kind of garden, including the black bamboo planted here, with its beautiful ebony canes.

1 *Dicksonia antarctica* Tree fern

2 *Hemerocallis* 'Summer Wine' Daylily

3 *Phyllostachys nigra* Black bamboo

4 *Hosta* 'Snowden'

5 *Lilium lancifolium* var. *splendens* Lily

6 *Cordyline australis* 'Albertii'

Containers for colour and fragrance

11

7

8

9

10

8

Pots and planters against a south-facing wall

3

2

4

5

6

1

Raised deck

7 *Trachycarpus fortunei* Chusan palm

8 *Hosta sieboldiana* 'Frances Williams'

9 *Abutilon megapotamicum* Indian mallow

10 *Cosmos astrosanguineus* Chocolate plant

11 *Hibiscus moscheutos*

12 *Clematis armandii*

13 *Vitis vinifera* 'Purpurea' Grape vine

14 *Melianthus major* Honey bush

15 *Solanum crispum* 'Glasnevin'

16 *Canna* 'Wyoming' Indian shot plant

West-facing planters

Steps leading to back gate

Creating a jungle effect

Start by building up a dominating framework of statuesque tropical plants with large, lush foliage. Bamboos, palms, tree ferns, banana, cannas and the honey bush are all ideal for this. In the background, soften fences and walls with a selection of climbers. Evergreen *Clematis armandii* is great for year-round coverage, while the vine, *Vitis vinifera*, trained up the pergola over the spa contributes not only a degree of privacy but also a teasing glimpse of edible grapes. Then think about adding low-growing elements with interesting leaf shapes and colours, for example *Brunnera*, *Rodgersia* and ferns such as *Polystichum setiferum* – these will provide lush ground cover and also help suppress weeds.

Hot jungle colours – reds and oranges – are contributed by *Canna* 'Wyoming', *Hedychium coccineum* 'Tara' (ginger lily), *Crocosmia* 'Lucifer' and *Hemerocallis* 'Summer Wine' (daylily). And don't forget to include some plants for fragrance – *Cosmos astrosanguineus* from Mexico is known as the chocolate plant because its flowers really do smell of chocolate.

21 *Polystichum setiferum* Soft shield fern

17 *Hedychium coccineum* 'Tara' Ginger lily

18 *Crocosmia* 'Lucifer' Montbretia

19 *Schizophragma integrifolium*

20 *Phyllostachys bambusoides* Bamboo

22 *Skimmia japonica* 'Rubella'

23 *Lonicera* x *brownii* 'Dropmore Scarlet' Honeysuckle

24 *Tricyrtis formosana* Toad lily

North-facing planter

25 *Hosta sieboldiana* 'Frances Williams'

34 *Tetrapanax papyriferus* Rice paper plant

33 *Matteuccia struthiopteris* Shuttlecock fern

32 *Musa basjoo* Banana

31 *Canna iridiflora* 'Ehemanii' Indian shot plant

30 *Foeniculum vulgare* 'Purpureum' Fennel

29 *Itea ilicifolia*

28 *Brunnera macrophylla* 'Jack Frost' Siberian bugloss

27 *Rodgersia podophylla*

26 *Schisandra rubriflora*

Exotic garden planting 149

Front garden

An attractive front garden makes a great first impression when people visit your home. Yet so many of us neglect our front gardens. With passing traffic and little privacy, they can seem not worth the bother. But with some simple ideas and clever planting it's possible to create a front garden that looks colourful and welcoming all year round.

Planning a front garden

To look good, the design of a front garden needs to be in harmony with the style of the house, the neighbours' houses and the street as a whole. Choose materials that are in keeping; brick or stone usually work well for the hard areas. If the garden is small keep the plan uncluttered. Everyone who enters your home passes through the front garden (including you), so you want it to look well-cared for even if you have little spare time. Paving and evergreen plants are low maintenance, but hedges and a lawn need regular attention.

Finding inspiration

Consider the materials you'd like to include – paving, edging, pots, and maybe some sort of feature or focal point, such as a sculpture, urn, bird bath or even a garden seat if there's enough space. Think about the planting. Scented plants such as roses look and smell enticing; herbs such as rosemary planted either side of a path will release their scent as you brush past. Evergreens will give all-year-round screening to hide the view of the road, but take care not to overdo them as too many can look dull and dark in a small garden. Deter weeds and keep work to a minimum with ground-cover plants.

The design brief

The front plot of this detached 1980s house was turfed by the developers and had remained unchanged since. The garden (6.1m x 10.8m) was totally open: passers-by looked straight into the living room window, and the view from inside was of the road. So screening was a priority. The most direct route to the front door was straight across the lawn, so the grass was always worn. When the car was parked in the driveway there was no room for a pushchair or wheelchair. The house faces south, so the front garden is in full sun for most of the day.

The existing plot

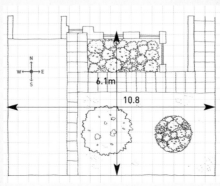

Wants

- A garden that looks inviting to visitors (but not thieves).
- Two entrances: one for the car, one for the pedestrians.
- Drive surface with more character than the existing dull concrete.
- Easy maintenance.
- Attractive views from the windows.
- More privacy and screening from the road.

Problems

- Slight slope downhill towards house, so rainwater must be channelled away.
- Existing drive has a poor surface and will have to be broken up and removed.
- All service pipes and cables to the house run underground through the front garden.
- Easy access makes the front vulnerable. Side passage to the back needs a secure gate.

Developing ideas

Draw a plan of the garden, showing its shape and boundaries, including the driveway to the garage, the front door, the windows that look out onto the garden and side access to the back. It's always a good idea to design the hard landscaping first before you think about the planting. Here the front garden has to allow adequate room for a wheelchair and a child's buggy as well as car parking.

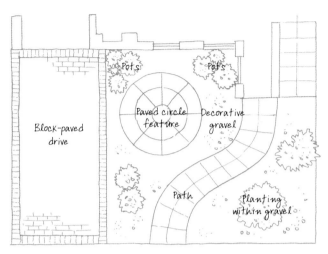

Easy care

Block paving for the drive is a much more attractive surface than concrete. A curved slab path with brick edging and a paving circle work well with gravelled areas, and make this a very low-maintenance space. Plants can be grown through the gravel surface, and pots can also add splashes of colour. Even so, the hard landscaping doesn't leave much scope for planting, and the lack of screening is not fully addressed.

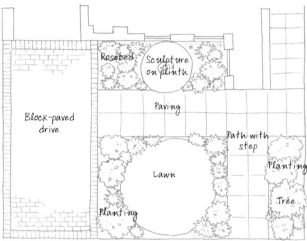

Making an entrance

A statue on a plinth at the centre of a formal rosebed gives this design a strong central focus and provides an attractive view from the windows. But the garden remains rather open. The paved path straight to the front door makes a practical entrance, but when the door is open the inside of the house is on full view.

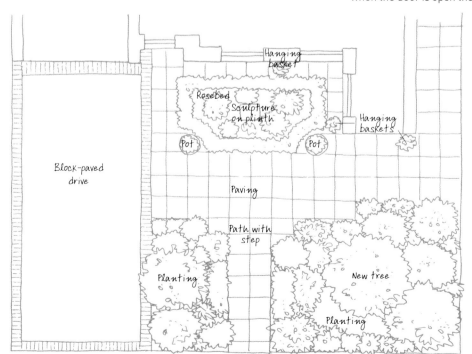

Colourful welcome

This design centres on a formal rosebed planted around a low brick plinth that serves as a stand for a contemporary sculpture. The rosebed provides a lovely view from the front window, and a focal point at the end of the path to draw visitors in. Mixed planting, including a new tree, screens the front door from the pavement. Pots and hanging baskets bring colour to the paved areas. This is the design that is to become the new garden (see pages 152–65).

Front garden

A well-planned front garden can add style, individuality and value to your home. Here, attractive planting and landscaping provides both privacy and a welcome to visitors.

A colourful welcome

The rosebed and plinth-mounted sculpture make a striking focal point at the end of the path. Higher planting to the left and right of this path, dropping down to lower levels either side, has the effect of drawing visitors in. The new tree (*Sorbus vilmorinii*) planted in line with the front door adds privacy, screening the house from the road. But at the same time its serrated, fern-like leaves allow light to reach the front door. Ground-cover planting helps to keep down weeds, and evergreens provide year-round interest. The garden is on a slope, so there is a step down from the path to the paved area in front of the house. The step is lit by two low-level outdoor lights.

The various hard landscaping materials have been carefully chosen to complement and balance one another. The paving blocks for the new drive surface are a random mixture of terracotta, grey and beige. These colours echo the red brick of the house, the grey-beige paving slabs of the paths, and the slate grey of the Victorian edging kerb – a modern copy of ceramic edging popular with the Victorians – that is laid around the planted areas to retain the soil and prevent it spreading over the paving in wet weather.

Colour and screening

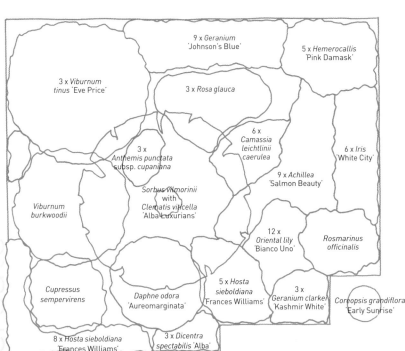

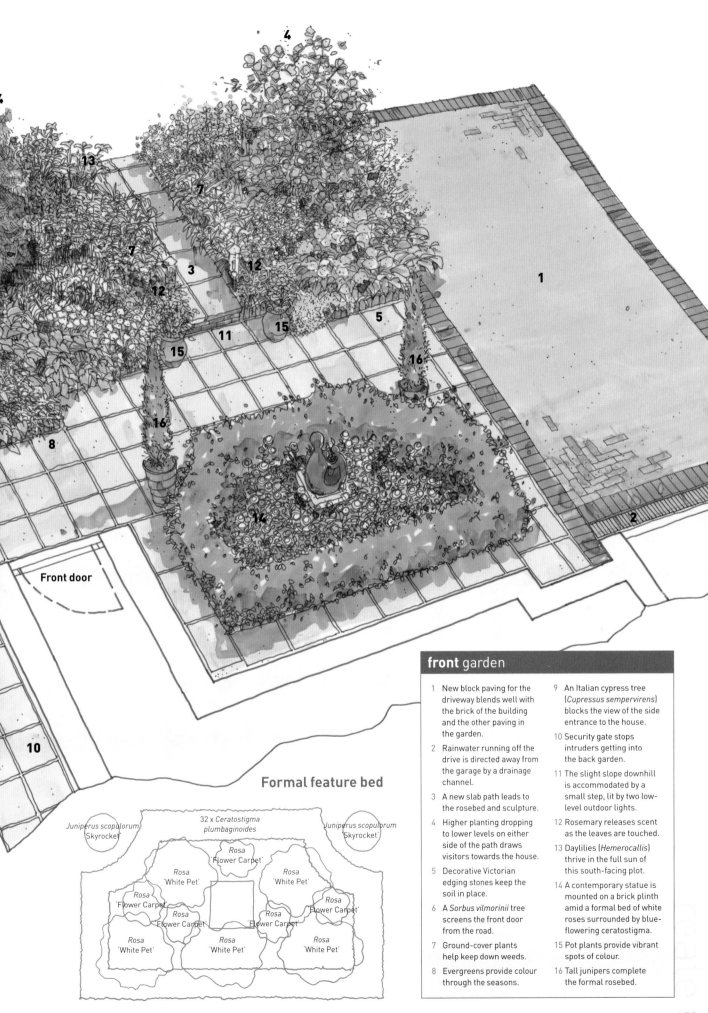

Front door

Formal feature bed

Juniperus scopulorum 'Skyrocket'

32 x Ceratostigma plumbaginoides

Juniperus scopulorum 'Skyrocket'

Rosa 'Flower Carpet'

Rosa 'White Pet'

Rosa 'White Pet'

Rosa 'Flower Carpet'

Rosa 'Flower Carpet'

Rosa 'Flower Carpet'

Rosa 'Flower Carpet'

Rosa 'White Pet'

Rosa 'White Pet'

Rosa 'White Pet'

front garden

1 New block paving for the driveway blends well with the brick of the building and the other paving in the garden.

2 Rainwater running off the drive is directed away from the garage by a drainage channel.

3 A new slab path leads to the rosebed and sculpture.

4 Higher planting dropping to lower levels on either side of the path draws visitors towards the house.

5 Decorative Victorian edging stones keep the soil in place.

6 A *Sorbus vilmorinii* tree screens the front door from the road.

7 Ground-cover plants help keep down weeds.

8 Evergreens provide colour through the seasons.

9 An Italian cypress tree (*Cupressus sempervirens*) blocks the view of the side entrance to the house.

10 Security gate stops intruders getting into the back garden.

11 The slight slope downhill is accommodated by a small step, lit by two low-level outdoor lights.

12 Rosemary releases scent as the leaves are touched.

13 Daylilies (*Hemerocallis*) thrive in the full sun of this south-facing plot.

14 A contemporary statue is mounted on a brick plinth amid a formal bed of white roses surrounded by blue-flowering ceratostigma.

15 Pot plants provide vibrant spots of colour.

16 Tall junipers complete the formal rosebed.

Front garden
sub-base for a drive

Replacing a drab concrete drive with rustic-looking paving blocks transforms the whole area. The blocks are available in a variety of colours, textured finishes and sizes. If the existing foundation is poor, a new sub-base is essential.

Setting out

A driveway has to bear the weight of one or more cars, so the paving blocks must sit on a solid foundation. In most cases it will be necessary to excavate the site to allow for a layer of Type 1 granular sub-base stone, which is then compacted and covered with a layer of sharp sand. Paving blocks are bedded into the sand with no need for mortar.

Mark out the precise area to be paved using builder's lines and timber profiles. Use a builder's square to check the corners form true right angles and measure the diagonals to make sure they are equal.

tools materials

- **builder's line and pegs**
- **long tape measure**
- **timber profiles**
- **builder's square**
- **safety goggles**
- **heavy-duty gloves**
- **dust mask**
- **ear defenders**
- **concrete breaker (hire)**
- **shovel**
- **wheelbarrow**
- **skip (hire)**
- **mini-digger (hire)**
- **spirit level**

- spray marker paint

safety first

Hidden pipes and cables
Before starting to excavate it is essential to locate underground service pipes and cables. If necessary, hire a cable avoidance tool or CAT (see page 78). Mark their positions on the ground with spray marker paint, and excavate those areas with extreme care: pipes and cables should be buried a minimum of 450mm below the surface, but you cannot be certain of that.

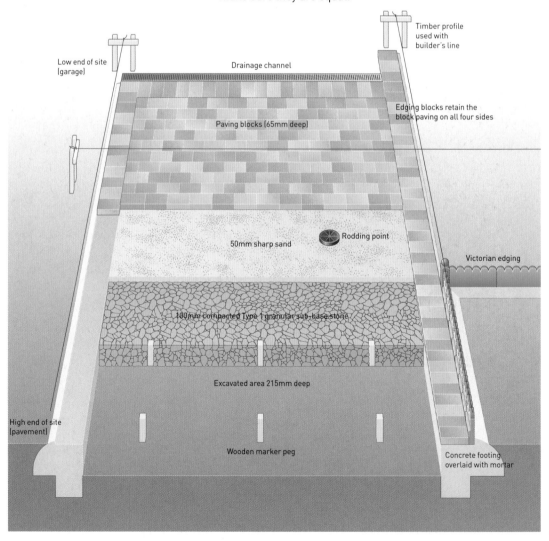

Timber profile used with builder's line

Low end of site (garage)

Drainage channel

Edging blocks retain the block paving on all four sides

Paving blocks (65mm deep)

50mm sharp sand

Rodding point

Victorian edging

100mm compacted Type 1 granular sub-base stone

Excavated area 215mm deep

High end of site (pavement)

Wooden marker peg

Concrete footing overlaid with mortar

Protective clothing
When using a concrete breaker, always protect yourself from the noise, dust and flying debris. Wear impact-resistant safety goggles to protect your eyes, a gauze face mask and heavy-duty gloves. Ear defenders will reduce the noise level, but do be extra vigilant while wearing them.

Creating a fall

Any paved area must have a consistent slight slope or fall, preferably going away from the house walls, so that surface water drains away. The ideal slope for a drive is about 1 in 40 (that is, a 25mm drop in level per metre). On a sloping site, you will need to measure the change in level across the site (see page 57) and divide that by the length (in metres).

Block paving on a slope

If your driveway slopes towards the house, you will also need to install a drainage channel to carry water away from the house or garage walls (see pages 156–57).

Laying the sub-base

With the area cleared to the correct depth, hammer sharpened wooden pegs in to mark the finished sub-base level. Set the fall using a spirit level, a 1m-long straightedge (a plank of wood) and a shim (a small piece of wood cut to the depth of the drop in level per metre; for a 1 in 40 fall, this would be 25mm). Start at the high side of the site, driving a row of pegs in to the desired level, and another row exactly a metre further down. Nail the shim to the underside of one end of the straightedge, then balance the straightedge between the first and second pegs, with the shim on the lower peg. Put a spirit level on top. Drive in the lower peg until the straightedge is level. Repeat at metre intervals all the way down the slope. Run string lines, also following the fall, to mark the finished height of the paving (115mm higher than the compressed sub-base stone).

Clearing the site

If clearing a new site, remove any vegetation and topsoil to a depth of 215mm. This is so you can lay a 100mm layer of compacted Type 1 granular sub-base stone, then a 50mm layer of compacted sharp sand, followed by the blocks (which in this case are 65mm deep). It may be possible to lay blocks over an existing concrete or asphalt surface provided this is intact and the finished level of the new drive will be 150mm below the house's damp-proof course. Otherwise you will need to break up the surface with a concrete breaker, which you can hire. You will need a skip for the debris. A hired mini-digger will make clearing this debris much quicker and easier. If you find the concrete has been laid over builders' rubble, such as broken kerb stones, remove this too.

Planning the work

A job on this scale can be seriously disruptive to daily life. Careful planning and timing of the work can help to minimise the inconvenience. In a front garden, it's also extremely important to protect the safety and right of way of pedestrians and road users. You should rope off the site, and make sure there is always safe access to the front door.

tools materials

- **heavy-duty gloves**
- **hammer**
- **shovel**
- **wheelbarrow**
- **spirit level**
- **1m-long straightedge**
- **builder's line and pegs**
- **long tape measure**
- **rake**
- **plate compactor (hire)**

- wooden marker pegs
- 25mm shim
- Type 1 granular sub-base stone

1 Tip in enough Type 1 sub-base stone to fill the excavated area to 50mm above the marker pegs. Rake it level.

2 Compact the Type 1 with a petrol-powered vibrating plate compactor.

3 Check the depth and fall against the builder's lines as you progress.

Front garden drainage for a block-paved drive

Paved areas such as drives and patios are always built on a slight slope so rainwater can drain into the surrounding soil. When the natural slope of the ground runs towards the property, you need to incorporate a drainage channel at the lowest point to direct water away from the building.

Surface-water drainage

Rainwater must be drained into a surface-water drain or into a soakaway, not into the main sewerage system. The water is channelled along plastic drainage pipes that must be buried a minimum of 600mm below ground level in fields and gardens; and 900mm below a light road or driveway. So that the water flows efficiently away, they need to lie on a minimum gradient of 1 in 100 towards the soakaway or drain. You may not find a convenient drain outlet point directly beneath the area where you wish to position a new drainage channel, in which case you could extend an existing pipe run. But installing a completely new drainage system is a major job, best undertaken by a professional.

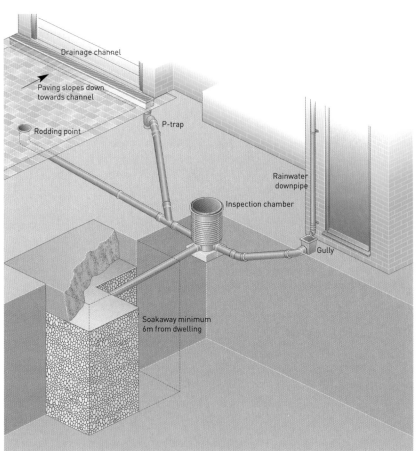

Rodding point

Modern drainage systems have rodding points or chambers so that you can access the drain to clear a blockage with drain rods. If this is embedded in concrete that is being broken up and removed, you will probably have to replace it before laying a new surface. This is straightforward, as drainage components are all designed to a standard fitting. Use a spirit level to check that the new point is set to the level of the finished paving. Take care when compacting the surrounding sub-base stone not to crack the new fitting.

Connecting to the drain

If there is an existing surface-water drain outlet in the area you wish to pave, you can install a drainage channel to direct water into it. Be very careful when digging around the drain that no loose debris falls into the pipe to cause a blockage: it's a good idea to stuff a rag into the pipe as you work. Install a drainage channel before you lay sharp sand and paving blocks over the compressed Type 1 sub-base stone (see pages 158–59). The top of the drainage channel should be level with the base of the garage and the finished height of the block paving.

Dig out the area around the existing drain to expose the drain connection, ensuring no debris falls down the pipe.

Measure the distance from the drain connection to the underside of the drainage channel, allowing for the pipe coupling (see Step 1, below).

tools materials

- **spade**
- **rag**
- **tape measure**
- **hacksaw**
- **gloves**
- **1m-long straightedge**
- **power drill fitted with a hole saw**

- 12.5mm shim
- drainage channel and stop-end outlets
- paving mix concrete (see page 376)
- plastic underground drainage pipe
- plastic drainage channel
- plastic drainage pipe coupling
- exterior silicone sealant
- metal grating

Cut a section of plastic underground drainage pipe to the measured length using a hacksaw.

Installing the drainage channel

A drainage channel should run at right angles to the slope of the paving, with a fall of 1 in 80 towards the drain. Use a 1m-long straightedge and shim of 12.5mm to set the fall in the same way as for the sub-base (see page 155). Excavate a channel 100mm deep and fill it with paving mix concrete (see page 376) for the drainage channel to be bedded onto.

Using a power drill fitted with a hole saw the size of the diameter of the drainage pipe, drill a hole in one section of the drainage channel. Use a plastic pipe coupling to fit the cut length of pipe onto the underside of the drainage channel. Turn it over and slot the pipe into the existing drain.

Use waterproof sealant to fill the recess in the end of each section of channel. Fit the next section and repeat the process until your drainage channel reaches the required length.

Secure the drainage channel in place with more concrete. Make sure that both the channel and the connection are firmly bedded in. Clip stop-end outlets over each end of the channel.

Fit metal grating over the top of the drainage channel to finish it.

Front garden
laying block paving

Paving blocks are bedded into a layer of sharp sand on top of compressed Type 1 sub-base stone. They aren't fixed with mortar, so there must be a retaining edge or kerb to stop them spreading. These edging blocks are securely bedded on mortar.

Laying a retaining edge

Excavate a strip around all four edges of the sub-base and lay 100mm-thick concrete footings for the edging blocks. The footings should project 75mm to the outside of the edging blocks and no more than 25mm to the inside.

1 When the concrete is dry, lay the edging blocks on a bed of mortar. Use a builder's line and spirit level to position the blocks and allow for the fall across their surface. Bed the blocks down firmly into the mortar with a rubber mallet.

2 Use a spirit level to keep checking that the blocks are level with the string line across their width.

3 To hold the edging blocks in place, build up the concrete against their outer edges to at least half the block height. Leave to harden for 3 days.

Sharp sand for bedding blocks

With the edgings in place you can cover the sub-base with sharp sand. This is levelled to the correct depth with a board supported at each end with carefully positioned timber offcuts.

1 Dampen the sharp sand slightly and spread it to a depth of about 65mm. Use the board to level the sand, pulling the excess towards you.

2 Compact the sand to 50mm using a vibrating plate compactor, then loosen the top 10–15mm with a rake.

3 Use a builder's float to smooth the sand down around any drainage point.

tools materials

- **spade**
- **shovel**
- **wheelbarrow**
- **long and short spirit levels**
- **builder's line and pegs**
- **builder's trowel**
- **rubber mallet**
- **safety goggles**
- **heavy-duty gloves**
- **dust mask**
- **ear defenders**
- **plate compactor (hire)**
- **rake**
- **builder's float**
- **knee pads**
- **pencil**
- **angle grinder with a particle diamond disc**
- **broom**

- footing mix concrete (see page 376)
- edging blocks
- mortar
- sharp sand
- paving blocks
- length of timber and offcuts
- fine kiln-dried sand

Laying paving blocks

Paving blocks can be laid in all sorts of different patterns, but when you are using them to make a drive the joints must be staggered to ensure the surface is strong enough to take the weight of a car. The pattern here is totally random, but you could lay different-sized blocks (small, medium and large) in regular sequences. Dry-lay a few rows first to check your design will work, especially at the corners and edges. Try a few different patterns to see which you prefer. It's a good idea to work from several packs of paving blocks at a time, mixing up the individual blocks, as colours may vary slightly from pack to pack.

1 Starting from one corner, lay the blocks on the compacted sand in the pattern of your choice. Butt the blocks tightly up against each other. Wear knee pads and kneel on a length of timber so that you spread your weight over several paving blocks.

2 If you have to pave around anything, such as a rodding point, loose-lay the blocks that will need to be cut to fit.

3 Use a straightedge to mark the cutting line in pencil on the blocks.

4 Place each block to be cut on a bed of sand to hold it firmly in place. Wearing protective clothing (see below), cut the blocks one by one using an angle grinder with a particle diamond disc.

The perfect result

The laid paving is finished by filling the joints with fine sand. Then the blocks are compacted down into the sand, bringing them level with the top of the retaining edge.

1 Once all the blocks are laid, fill in the gaps between them with fine kiln-dried sand, brushing it into the joints with a broom.

2 Press the paving blocks into the sand with the compactor. If they drop too low, or they won't compact enough, take them up and adjust the sand bed. Brush more kiln-dried sand into the joints, if necessary.

ideal tool
Angle grinder

An angle grinder is designed to cut stone, paving blocks and slabs, as well as cut and grind metal. Choose the right disc for the job. Use a particle diamond disc for cutting paving blocks, and a stone-cutting disc for slabs.

safety first
Using an angle grinder
Always read and follow the safety instructions when using an angle grinder. Wear safety goggles, ear defenders, a gauze face mask and heavy-duty gloves. An angle grinder continues to run for a few seconds after it has been switched off, so don't put it down until the blade has stopped turning.

Front garden
laying slab paving

Concrete paving slabs are an attractive and practical choice for a front garden, and their hard surface can be balanced by colourful planting.

Setting out

Before you start, check for any hidden pipes and cables beneath the area to be excavated, and mark their position with spray marker paint (see page 154). Then set out the area to be paved with builder's line and pegs. The fall of this patio (see page 155) is in two directions: towards a drain just beyond the garden by the side alley; and towards the central bed in front of the house. The path ends in a single step down to the patio.

Preparing the site

The level of the finished paved surface must be at least 150mm below the building's damp-proof course. Excavate the topsoil to a depth of another 150mm for the sub-base: this should consist of 100mm compacted Type 1 granular sub-base stone (see page 155), followed by a thin, even coat of sharp sand or all-in ballast.

Electrical cable supplying power to new garden lights should be buried before the paving slabs are laid (see page 163).

Paving choices

There is a wide choice of paving slabs. They come in many different shapes, sizes and materials to suit any budget – anything from hydraulically pressed concrete to expensive quarried and reclaimed natural stone. Concrete slabs are available in numerous smooth and textured finishes and lots of different colours, so you should be able to find the perfect match, or contrast, for your garden.

Creating a pattern

Laying slabs in a symmetrical pattern either side of an accurate centre line is often a successful option – but only if this won't require you to make many small or difficult cuts in the slabs. Once you have prepared the site, dry-lay the paving slabs to check the size of the area and make sure that your chosen pattern works. The first slab you lay – the key slab – serves as a guide for positioning and levelling all the others.

Run string lines across the site to mark the alignment and finished height of the slabs. Don't forget to allow for the fall across their surface.

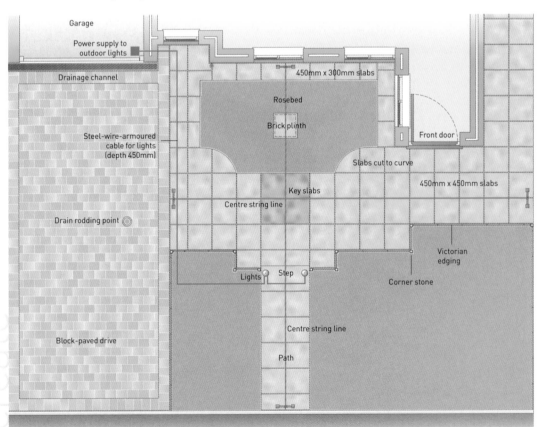

tools materials

- **builder's line and pegs**
- **tape measure**
- **shovel**
- **wheelbarrow**
- **heavy-duty gloves**
- **plate compactor** (hire)
- **safety goggles**
- **ear defenders**
- **dust mask**
- **builder's trowel**
- **spirit level**
- **pencil**
- **string**
- **angle grinder with stone-cutting disk**
- **rubber mallet**
- **hand brush**

- Type 1 granular sub-base stone
- sharp sand or all-in ballast
- slabs
- mortar
- Victorian edging and corner stones
- engineering bricks
- jointing compound

Labels in diagram: Garage / Power supply to outdoor lights / Drainage channel / 450mm x 300mm slabs / Rosebed / Brick plinth / Front door / Steel-wire-armoured cable for lights (depth 450mm) / Slabs cut to curve / 450mm x 450mm slabs / Key slabs / Centre string line / Drain rodding point / Victorian edging / Lights / Step / Corner stone / Block-paved drive / Centre string line / Path

Laying paving slabs

Bed the slabs on a 50mm bed of mortar, aligning them to your string lines. Wetting the back of each slab before you lay it will improve adhesion and make it more easy to slide into position. Use a spirit level to keep checking the slabs are level in one direction, and follow the required fall in the other. Allow a 20mm gap for pointing: to keep this gap consistent, it can help to cut small timber spacers to wedge between the slabs. Tap each slab into position with a rubber mallet. If you lay a slab and find it is not level, take it up and adjust the mortar underneath. Where Victorian edging kerb is to be laid alongside the paving, cut the mortar flush with the slabs before it dries. The edging is bedded in concrete, which is haunched up against the outside of the stones to hold them firm.

Leave the mortar to set for 48 hours before walking on the slabs. Then remove the spacers and point the joints with jointing compound or mortar (see below).

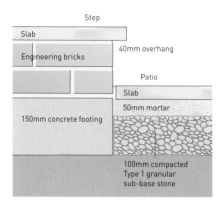

Step
Slab
Engineering bricks
40mm overhang
Patio
Slab
50mm mortar
150mm concrete footing
100mm compacted Type 1 granular sub-base stone

ideal tool
Builder's line and pins

This nylon line attached to hammer-in pins is an invaluable tool when setting out new paving, or for any kind of garden construction work.

Building a step

The gradient in this particular garden requires the construction of a step between the path and patio. A step riser (the vertical part) should be minimum 100mm and maximum 180mm. If a step would be lower than 100mm, you should set paving on a slight slope instead. The slabs forming the front edge of the step are laid on two courses of engineering bricks, which in turn need a 150mm concrete footing to support them. Excavate the ground for this footing before laying the slabs of the patio, but after you have positioned the key stones, so that you can use these to set the height of the step and path. The slabs forming the front edge of the step overhang the bricks by 40mm.

Cutting slabs on a curve

Modern power tools make it easy to cut slabs in a curve so you can create curved areas of paving. Wear safety goggles, ear defenders, a gauze dust mask and heavy-duty gloves while using an angle grinder.

Pointing using jointing compound

You can buy vacuum-packed sand jointing compound for pointing paving as an alternative to traditional mortar. It's chemically treated so that when the pack is opened and brushed into the joints it reacts with the air and begins to harden to a permanent, weed-resistant finish. It is designed for joints that are a minimum of 5mm wide and 25mm deep.

Mark a curve using a pencil tied to a length of string. Hold the other end of the string at the opposite corner of the slab and pull it taut.

Carefully cut along the marked line with an angle grinder fitted with a stone-cutting disc. Use a rubber mallet to break away the surplus piece, striking gently to avoid damage. Carefully smooth the cut line on the slab with the angle-grinder, working fairly slowly.

Open the vacuum pack and empty the compound on to a plastic sheet or a clean board. Lightly rake it over to let air get into it. Brush the compound into the joints and compact it with a jointing tool. The compound dries hard in 2–6 hours – protect it from rain until then. Any residue on the paving should be swept off immediately with a stiff brush.

You can do it...
V-pointing the slabs

V-pointing is a decorative finish in which a conventional wet mortar mix is moulded to form an upward point between the slabs. Or you could finish the joints with a jointing tool (see page 163).

B&Q

Front garden finishing touches

Sculptures and ornaments add interest to any outdoor space, and in a front garden they can be a striking focal point that draws the visitor towards the house. Lighting can enhance security, or pick out a potential hazard such as a step. It can also be purely decorative, highlighting a particular plant, tree or feature in the garden.

Building a brick plinth

A brick plinth makes an instant centrepiece of a statue or sculpture, raising it above the rest of the garden and putting it on display. Built out of the same bricks or materials as the house, it will blend in harmoniously.

A plinth sited in a planted area of the garden needs to be built on a solid concrete footing about 150mm wider than the finished structure and 150mm deep. This plinth has a single-skin outer wall (that is, the thickness of a single brick) and a hollow centre. Each side is one and three-quarter bricks long. It's necessary to cut the bricks so that the coping slab set on top of the plinth will overhang the brickwork by 25–30mm. Use engineering bricks for the first two courses (rows), which will lie below ground level once the bed is filled with topsoil, and frost-resistant facing bricks for the four courses above ground.

tools materials

- spade
- shovel
- wheelbarrow
- heavy-duty gloves
- bricklayer's trowel
- spirit level
- pencil
- ruler
- bolster
- club hammer
- safety goggles
- rubber mallet
- jointing tool
- hand brush

- wooden marker pegs
- footing-mix concrete (see page 376)
- engineering and frost-resistant facing bricks
- mortar
- coping slab

1 Dig out the footing to a total depth of 310mm to allow for 150mm concrete and two courses of engineering bricks, all below ground. Drive wooden marker pegs into the bottom of the trench as a guide to make sure the trench is filled to the correct level. Fill with footing-mix concrete and leave to set for 48 hours.

2 Cut and dry-lay the first course of engineering bricks, then remove them and lay a 15mm bed of mortar. Use your trowel point to outline the position of the bricks before bedding them into the mortar.

3 Check that the bricks are level using a spirit level as you build up the structure of the plinth.

ideal tools

Club hammer and bolster
To cut a brick, measure and mark the cutting line on all four sides in pencil. Score right along this line by tapping a bolster gently with a club hammer. Then lay the brick on grass or sand and hit the bolster firmly to cut all the way through. Always wear safety goggles when cutting bricks or blocks.

Laying the coping slab

The light colour of this coping slab enhances the visual impact of the sculpture mounted upon it. Coping also has an essential practical role: its overhang directs rainwater away from the brickwork. If security is a concern, an ornament can be bedded on mortar. Or you could drill through this resin sculpture and screw it to the coping slab using two expanding masonry bolts.

This roller tool makes it easy to create neat, regular pointed joints in brickwork. Its spike is also useful for raking out old mortar before repointing.

1 Lay a 15mm bed of mortar on the top bricks. Wet the back of the coping slab, as this helps it stick to the mortar, and place it in position.

2 Press the slab down with a rubber mallet, using a spirit level to check that it is level.

3 Leave the mortar until it is semi-dry, then scrape a concave recess into the brick joints, using a jointing tool.

4 Brush down the brickwork with a hand brush, then put the sculpture in position.

Lighting a front garden

Lighting in the front garden can improve your safety and security. An outdoor light mounted on the house wall helps you see your way to the front door and also shows you who is calling at night. A security light with movement sensors will detect visitors or intruders and switch itself on to illuminate them. Mains-powered lights in the garden away from the house, such as those used to light a step, need to be firmly secured. All fittings must be fully weatherproof and designed for outdoor use.

Mains-voltage lighting

Garden lights can be powered from a spur off an existing lighting or power circuit inside the house or garage. Any circuit used must be protected by a 30 milliamp RCD (residual current device), which will cut off power in an instant in the event of an earth leakage. Normal cable is not frost-resistant, so once outdoors steel-wire-armoured cable (SWA) must be used, and it must be buried in a trench at least 450mm deep under paving or 750mm below unpaved areas to avoid accidentally cutting through it. Lay electrical route marker tape above it at a depth of 150mm to warn of its presence. If laying new paving, the cable needs to be laid before the slabs.

Low-voltage lighting

A good alternative is low-voltage garden lighting, fed by a transformer that can be plugged into a convenient socket indoors or in a shed or garage where it will be protected from the weather. Because it carries only low-voltage electricity, the cable can be laid on or just below the surface of the ground, but it is usually better to run it in protective conduit and bury it to avoid anyone tripping over it, or cutting through it with a spade when digging – leaving you with the cost and inconvenience of replacement. Low-voltage lights are often on spikes that you simply push into the ground.

Be safe

Since 1 January 2005, new laws have been in place requiring anyone carrying out electrical work in a garden in England or Wales to inform their local authority's Building Control Department first. If you do decide to lay cables and install outdoor electrical fittings yourself, you must ensure that the work complies fully with the IEE Wiring Regulations and Building Regulations, and that when completed an electrical test certificate is issued (see page 373).

Front garden planting

The planting of this front garden provides privacy and attractive views from inside the house, while also being appealing and welcoming to the visitor.

Colour and screening

Parallel planting either side of the path is designed to draw the visitor in. From the pavement it frames the plinth-mounted statue that provides a striking focal point to the plot. It includes rosemary that will release its scent as it is brushed against, and white irises which, when in flower, will create a visual link with the white roses of the formal bed ahead. Even when not in flower, irises have upright strap-like leaves that help define the path.

Plenty of evergreens provide year-round screening from the road and the neighbouring house. The highly scented *Daphne odora* 'Aureomarginata' is positioned right before the front door, so that its fragrance can be enjoyed the moment the door is opened.

Early flowering *Brunnera macrophylla* is a good ground-cover plant that will help deter weeds, as will low-growing plants such as *Geranium* 'Johnson's Blue'. Given an annual application of mulch to these beds, weeds should not be a problem. The roses will need a prune each year and the shrubs will eventually need trimming to prevent them growing too big. Herbaceous perennials such as yarrow need cutting back in autumn. But otherwise this is a relatively low-maintenance garden that will give year-round interest and screening.

ideal plant

Hanging baskets
A mixture of colourful bedding and foliage plants fill the baskets:

Petunia 'Express Mixed'
Fuchsia 'Florabelle'
Tagetes patula 'Honeycomb' French marigold
Lobelia erinus Trailing lobelia
Pelargonium peltatum Ivy-leaved trailing geranium
Glechoma hederacea 'Variegata' Variegated ground ivy

● **plant** chooser

Plants with a numbered rosette are featured in more detail in the Plant Chooser, pages 294–327.

1 *Coreopsis grandiflora* 'Early Sunrise'

2 *Anthemis punctata* subsp. *cupaniana* Chamomile

3 *Rosmarinus officinalis* Rosemary

4 *Anemone x hybrida* 'Honorine Jobert' Japanese anemone

5 *Brunnera macrophylla* Siberian bugloss

6 *Magnolia x soulangeana*

7 *Iris* 'White City'

8 *Campanula persicifolia*

9 *Kolkwitzia amabilis* 'Pink Cloud'

10 *Hebe pinguifolia* 'Pagei'

Formal feature bed

In front of the window is a small formal bed containing elegant white roses that will grow high enough to be seen from inside the house, but not so high that they block the view of the planting beyond. This bed is edged with a small hedge of blue-flowering *Ceratostigma plumbaginoides* which will grow back to cover the bare soil behind the roses. Pots planted with tall, thin junipers are positioned in the semi-circular indents at the corners of the bed. These indents are a small touch, but they make all the difference to what would otherwise be a plain rectangular bed.

11 *Juniperus scopulorum* 'Skyrocket' Juniper

12 *Ceratostigma plumbaginoides* Plumbago

13 *Rosa* 'Flower Carpet' Bush rose

14 *Rosa* 'White Pet' Bush rose

15 *Hemerocallis* 'Pink Damask' Daylily

16 *Achillea* 'Salmon Beauty' Yarrow

17 *Camassia leichtlinii caerulea* 'Electric Blue' Quamash

18 *Rosa glauca* Bush rose

19 *Geranium* 'Johnson's Blue' Hardy geranium

Formal feature bed

28 *Lilium* 'Bianco Uno' Oriental lily

27 *Geranium clarkei* 'Kashmir White'

26 *Daphne odora* 'Aureomarginata'

25 *Cupressus sempervirens* Italian cypress

24 *Viburnum burkwoodii*

23 *Sorbus vilmorinii* Chinese rowan

22 *Clematis viticella* 'Alba Luxurians'

21 *Anthemis cupaniana* Chamomile

20 *Viburnum tinus* 'Eve Price' Laurustinus

Quick and easy
gardens
balcony

A collection of carefully chosen plants and pots added to a balcony, patio or tiny suburban yard can instantly transform it into an inviting space that will enhance the experience of your home.

Outdoor living in small spaces

Even the smallest balcony or patio can be part of your living space. If there's room for a couple of chairs and a small table, you can use it for dining and entertaining al fresco, for a relaxing breakfast in the morning sunshine, or maybe as a spill-over area for parties. Decking and all-weather stainless steel furniture complement the chic, modernist simplicity of this apartment. Subdued lighting will add to the ambience after dark. A compact barbecue with cover that can be left out all year round is ideal for small spaces with minimal storage.

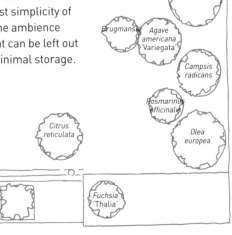
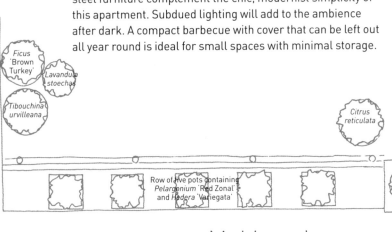

Vitis vinifera

Brugmansia   Agave americana 'Variegata'

Campsis radicans

Rosmarinus officinalis

Ficus 'Brown Turkey'   Lavandula stoechas

Tibouchina urvilleana

Citrus reticulata

Olea europea

Row of five pots containing Pelargonium 'Red Zonal' and Hedera 'Variegata'

Fuchsia 'Thalia'

Making plans

The direction a patio or balcony faces, and the amount of light it receives, will – as always – determine what plants will happily grow there. Shady, enclosed areas can be filled with lush foliage plants such as ferns and hostas. In a sunny spot you could grow salad crops, tomatoes and peas (see pages 276–89). This south-facing balcony, which gets lots of hot sunshine, is filled with Mediterranean plants with vivid colours, scents and flavours.

Balconies can be very exposed, so creating shelter for both you and your plants is an important consideration. Here, steel and toughened glass panels provide protection from wind without blocking light or interrupting the views. In particularly exposed sites you should choose your plants with care; a large-leaved banana (see page 325), for example, will love the bright sunlight but very quickly turn into a tatty, torn shadow of its former glory. And pots may need to be anchored to prevent potentially dangerous falls: you could bed them on mortar; fix them down with expanding masonry bolts; or secure them with heavy galvanised wire attached to vine eyes (see page 205).

create

Quick and easy gardens
balcony

Scent and flavour are combined with foliage and colour to make this a micro-garden to delight all the senses. Climbers will soon spread over the vertical surfaces, and a good mix of evergreens will keep it looking alive through the winter.

Planting in small spaces

You may be tucked up indoors during the winter months, but it's still far better to look out at pots with plants in them rather than empty ones or worse, last season's spent flowers. So allow for at least half of the plants to be evergreen; this way, there will still be some life left to carry the look through the winter (and you won't be ankle-deep in fallen leaves come autumn). If there is wall space, grow a climber; this not only softens the outlines but extends the planting upwards. Trellis panels can be attached to a balcony wall, or you can fix plant training wires to vine eyes for more unobtrusive support. If there isn't suitable wall space, you can train a climber up an obelisk or wigwam of canes placed in or over its pot.

Colour, flavour and style

The grape vine trained up the wall and along the underside of the awning will give shade to this south-facing balcony through the summer but in winter will drop its leaves, allowing natural light to reach the flat unhindered. It also brings the added bonus of edible fruits and vine leaves – vines can be really quite productive in a small space such as this.

The fig and satsuma are also excellent fruiting container plants. In fact with its roots constrained the fig is far more likely to fruit well and will be less vigorous (fig trees can become enormous). Its large leaves make a striking addition to the balcony's display of foliage. The satsuma may need to come inside for the winter but is well worth making a fuss of for its fresh green leaves and wonderful fruits.

Rosemary makes a good container plant when potted in a free-draining soil mix. It keeps its aromatic leaves all year round; these are always useful in the kitchen with roasted vegetables or meats. Rosemary also frequently flowers through the winter, adding to its charm. Apart from its wonderful scent, lavender produces blue flowers in summer that will contrast well with the reds and oranges of the pelargoniums, fuchsia, and *Campsis radicans*, a vigorous and exotic-looking climber that should quickly spread over the side wall with its fresh green leaves and brilliant orange trumpet-shaped flowers.

For summer colour, pelargoniums are hard to beat and will do well in the bright sun and sheltered conditions here. They are also highly drought-resistant. Ivy will produce a self-clinging mat of evergreen leaves trailing over edges and sprawling along the horizontal surfaces.

Agave americana makes a spectacular feature plant with its thick, glaucous, strap-shaped leaves arranged in a rosette and edged with vicious spines: beware brushing past this plant!

Caring for container plants

Regular feeding and watering are essential for all container-grown plants. Slow-release fertiliser sticks or granules added to the compost at the start of the growing season are the most efficient way to feed. An automatic watering system controlled by a timer (see page 252) will do the watering for you – especially useful for when you go away.

● **plant** chooser
Plants with a numbered rosette are featured in more detail in the Plant Chooser, pages 294–327.

1 *Ficus* 'Brown Turkey' Fig

2 *Lavandula stoechas* French lavender

3 *Tibouchina urvilleana*

4 *Pelargonium* 'Red Zonal' Tender geranium

5 *Hedera helix* 'Variegata' Ivy

6 *Citrus reticulata* Satsuma

7 *Fuchsia* 'Thalia'

Rosmarinus officinalis Rosemary
8

9 *Olea europea* Olive

10 *Vitis vinifera* Grape vine

11 *Agave americana* 'Variegata' Century plant

12 *Brugmansia* Angel's trumpets

13 *Campsis radicans* Trumpet creeper

create

Quick and easy gardens
conservatory

A conservatory filled with leafy, tropical foliage brings the pleasures of a garden into the comfort and shelter of your home. It's not only a wonderful space to relax, but a chance to grow plants that couldn't otherwise survive in our climate.

A room for plants and people

We are accustomed to centrally heated houses where the heat is very dry. Some plants like this – all the typical Mediterranean plants, such as geraniums, olive and citrus trees, and a multitude of succulents and cacti would thrive in a sunny, dry conservatory. However, many favourite conservatory plants, including those featured here, require a moist, humid environment. This is not ideal for the kinds of soft upholstered furnishings and carpets that you might put elsewhere in the house. So go for materials that will not be damaged by humidity: wood, wicker and metal furniture will all be fine under these conditions. Tiles are an ideal choice for the floor; if possible, install underfloor heating before you lay them. Add rugs in the sitting areas to make the space more cosy and comfortable.

Double-glazing and central heating will keep you and your plants warm in winter – especially important in a north-facing conservatory, which may get little or no sunlight for several months. Light-filtering roofing, blinds and ventilation (windows, roof vents and fans) will prevent you sweltering in the summer, as well as keeping condensation to a minimum. Purpose-built blinds may seem expensive; but you won't regret it, especially in a south-facing conservatory. You may decide to forgo them for the sides, but never resist installing them for the roof, even if the roof is of light-filtering panelling. Another option is to install an air-conditioning unit if summer temperatures become unbearably high inside your conservatory.

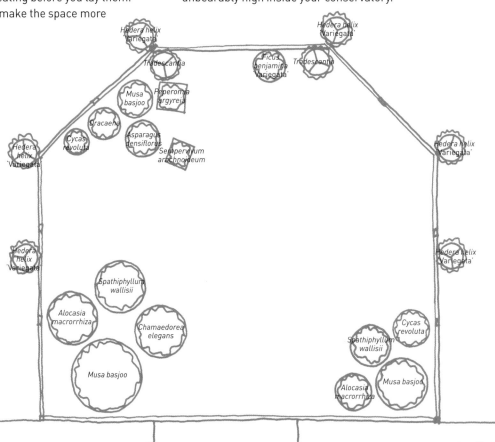

Quick and easy gardens

conservatory

Luxurious foliage fills this conservatory from floor to roof space, creating an interior like a miniature rainforest.

Moist and shady planting

Bananas (*Musa basjoo*) make wonderful conservatory plants, quickly producing massive leaves and a constant supply of new young plants (offsets) which can be separated, or left to grow with the parent to form an ever larger clump. They thrive in warm, humid conditions, in bright but diffused light. Another star plant in this collection is the *Alocasia macrorrhiza*, with massive, dark green leaves on long stalks. This will rapidly grow to the full height of the conservatory, adding to the tropical forest effect. The *Dracaena* will also become a striking feature plant as it grows larger, with exotic-looking, strap-shaped leaves rising gracefully from a single trunk. Very tough and adaptable, it prefers bright light, so position it against a sunny window. The *Ficus* (weeping fig) will quickly produce a mass of glossy, evergreen leaves, adding substance to the planting.

Cycas revoluta, the Japanese sago palm, makes a sturdy and handsome feature plant that may eventually grow to 2m, but only after many years. The elegant *Chamaedorea elegans* (parlour palm) can survive quite dense shade and, so long as is kept damp, will keep throwing up new leaf stems from the base, making a medium-sized, bushy plant which will survive well beneath taller-growing specimens. *Spathiphyllum wallis* (peace lily) will luxuriate in the warmth, damp, and diffused light of this conservatory, making a clump of rich green, pointed leaves above which rise flowers with a pure white hoo The feathery fronds of the asparagus fern provide a graceful contrast with the larger-leaved tropical foliage around it.

Evergreen *Tradescantia* is planted in baskets mounted on the roof beams. This will grow vigorously, forming a trailing mass of dense green foliage. Ivy in hanging containers fixed to the outside of the conservatory forms a matching trail of foliage, blurring the boundaries of this indoor/outdoor space.

Creating the right conditions

The plants grown here all require a warm humid atmosphere and most will grow in shade or partial shade – conditions that reflect a rainforest habitat. Many of them would suffer scorch to their leaves if exposed to prolonged direct sunlight. Light-filtering roof panelling is an option, but you could also train a sun-loving climber up into the roof space – passion flower or bougainvillea would be ideal – to create a living canopy. To rai humidity, group plants together and place them on shallow, pebble-filled trays that are kept constantly moist; it's best to use special porous 'expanded clay' pebbles that are sold for this purpose. Daily or twice-daily misting with a hand-held mister will be needed in summer when temperatures rise.

Fending off bugs and disease

Some pests prefer being indoors too: aphids, woolly aphids, red spider mite, whitefly, and scale insects are the main culpr All are easily eradicated with house plant insecticides, many of which are now organic (rather than chemically) based and long lasting, one application protecting plants for many week Check newly bought plants thoroughly before bringing them indoors – a few unseen pests can rapidly colonise an entire conservatory. As always, happy, healthy plants will better withstand any pest. But do be vigilant.

Feeding

Potting compost quickly becomes depleted of nutrients so regular feeding is a must. Liquid feed will provide a quick pick-me-up but will need repeat applications throughout the growing season; an easier option is to use slow-release fertiliser sticks pushed into the compost. Purpose-made fertiliser should always be used, not general garden fertiliser. Special formulas with a high nitrogen content are available for foliage plants. Wherever possible water with collected rainwater; leave it to stand in the conservatory for an hour or two to bring it up to room temperature.

1 *Musa basjoo* Banana

2 *Alocasia macrorrhiza*

3 *Chamaedorea elegans* Parlour palm

4 *Spathiphyllum wallisii* Peace lily

5 *Cycas revoluta* Sago palm

     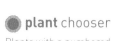

6 *Ficus benjamina* 'Variegata' Weeping fig

7 *Asparagus densiflorus* Asparagus fern

8 *Hedera helix* 'Variegata' Ivy

9 *Tradescantia*

10 *Dracaena*

11 *Peperomia argyreia*

12 *Sempervivum arachnoideum* House leek

● **plant** chooser

Plants with a numbered rosette are featured in more detail in the Plant Chooser, pages 294–327.

create

grow

What is gardening?

A garden is in fact a completely artificial environment. Left to the whims of climate, location and Mother Nature, it would soon be a vastly different landscape.

Plants from far and wide

When the rain is pouring down in July, it can be difficult to appreciate the gentle nature of the climate we enjoy in this country. But extreme weather conditions are really very rare, and because of that we are able to grow a vast array of plants from all corners of the globe. Few of the species sold here actually originate from these lands, yet they survive, indeed flourish in our gardens. That success is due to more than just luck and a plant's inherent desire to grow, however. It's due to cultivation.

What is cultivation?

All plants come with an in-built blueprint to grow, flower and reproduce. But their ability to do this is enhanced or hindered by the conditions they grow in. Cultivation is all about creating the conditions that will allow you to get the best out of your plants. Understanding the basics of how plants work is key to growing – or cultivating – plants successfully.

Primula vialii Vial's primrose

Agapanthus African lily

How do plants grow?

Plants need air, food, water and sunlight to live. They grow in much the same way as anything else, us included. They take in food – usually through their roots but they also produce their own food through sunlight (see opposite) – break it down, and convert it into energy. Unlike humans, though, plants – even carnivorous plants – have no teeth. All their nutrients are absorbed and transported in water, which is their most vital component.

Bread and butter

The basic elements of a plant's diet are nitrogen, phosphorus and potassium – known by their chemical symbols NPK. These are all present to a greater or lesser extent in ordinary garden soil, along with smaller (in some cases minute) amounts of minerals such as calcium, sulphur, iron, magnesium, copper and zinc (see below). All are needed by different plants for different purposes, in varying degrees, and plants will only take in the amount they require – so long as it is available. By topping up supplies of particular nutrients in the soil, we gardeners give a plant the chance to absorb the optimum amount.

plant nutrients
N: Nitrogen is the building block for leaves
P: Phosphorus is needed for healthy root growth
K: Potassium is needed for flowers and fruit

Other nutrients

Minerals such as magnesium and iron are usually in plentiful supply for the average plant, but there are some exceptions. Tomatoes in particular will suffer from a lack of magnesium; acid-loving plants planted in an alkaline soil will suffer from a lack of iron. See pages 190–91 for more in-depth information on adding nutrients to your soil.

Key ingredients

Plants have a special recipe for producing their own food. The key ingredients are sunlight, water and air, needed by all plants without exception. Understanding how plants use these to grow can help us look after them and create a healthy, thriving garden.

Light

Plants make, store and use food through a process called photosynthesis (see diagram), which is dependent on sunlight. Chlorophyll, the stuff that makes leaves green, is a substance that absorbs the energy of sunlight. This enables a chemical reaction to take place between the carbon dioxide taken in by the leaves and the water taken in by the roots, the product of which is sugar. Some of the sugar is used to make cellulose – the walls of a plant cell. Some is converted into starch. Starch is the plant's larder, a reserve of food to be used at a later date if need be, and usually stored in the roots – when we eat carrots and potatoes we are raiding that larder. A by-product of all this chemical wizardry is oxygen, which passes from the plant back into the atmosphere.

Dryopteris filix-mas Male fern

Water

Like humans, plants have a network of veins that transport food and air around their structure in fluid. When a plant is watered, the nutrients needed for growth are dissolved out of the soil, sucked up by the roots and circulated throughout the plant. The water evaporates out again through pores on the under-surface of the leaves. This process is called transpiration (see diagram). Because plants don't have the equivalent of a heart constantly recirculating that fluid, if they don't have access to enough water to replace evaporated fluid, they will quickly die. There is an emergency system within plants to try to ward this off: when water is in short supply, the cells surrounding the pores will shrink, closing them off and preventing further evaporation. If their water supply isn't restored quickly enough, more cells lose their pressure and shrink. This is what is happening when a plant visibly wilts. Eventually it will dry out and die.

Air

While humans breathe in oxygen and breathe out carbon dioxide, in daylight plants absorb carbon dioxide and give out oxygen. Without plants and trees on the planet, the supply of oxygen for us to breathe would very quickly become depleted. Plants enable us to survive; the very least we can do is give them every assistance to continue to do so, starting with cultivating our own gardens.

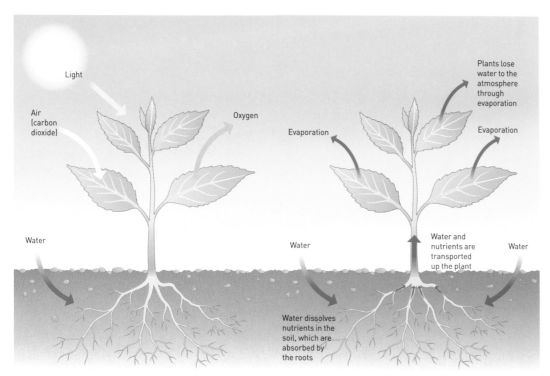

Photosynthesis

Transpiration

Every gardener needs a variety of tools to tend and maintain their outdoor space. Some tools will be used very often, such as secateurs or a spade. Others will be used less frequently but are still essential, such as a rake or wheelbarrow. Nowadays you can spend more time relaxing and entertaining in the garden than ever before thanks to a constantly developing selection of easy-to-use, efficient and labour-saving garden tools and equipment.

garden tools

Better and better

The choice of tools for the garden grows every year. Modern technology has made them more effective than ever, ranging from old designs such as spade handles in space-age, lightweight materials, to power tools newly available for home use such as shredders and power vacs. Special designs also make it simpler and more comfortable to tend your garden with a minimum of strain and effort.

Hand tools

Most of the hand tools we use in the garden today were invented before the industrial era and have survived the test of time – the spade, hoe and rake are examples. Today you can find many versions which improve on this old technology with new ideas that make them easier to use, such as gearing for better cutting, lever action to reduce effort, telescopic action for increased reach and longer handles to reduce back strain. Good-quality hand tools will make easy work of day-to-day tasks and often become timeworn personal favourites.

Power tools

Garden power tools are ideal for repetitive tasks, from mowing the lawn to cutting a hedge. New technologies make these tools easier and safer to use as well. Cordless power tools such as a lightweight trimmer often have powerful motors and long-lasting, rechargeable batteries.

Safety

Look after yourself and your tools. Select the tools that suit your strength and ability and always follow the manufacturer's instructions. Wear protective clothing such as gardening gloves and goggles when appropriate. All corded electrical garden tools must be protected by an RCD (residual current device), which will cut off the power in a split second if, for instance, a power cable is severed. These are inexpensive and easy to use: simple plug-in versions are available (see page 21). Sadly, garden tools are a popular target for petty thieves, so it's wise to secure them when not in use, preferably somewhere locked and out of sight such as a garage, workshop or shed.

Garden hand tools

Whether you are an everyday or occasional gardener, you will need a selection of simple hand tools. As with all tools, match the tool to the task for the best results. And don't forget the easy-to-use tool options, which blend modern technology with traditional design.

Everyday tools

For a compact garden without a lawn, some simple hand tools are probably all you need: secateurs, a garden knife, a hand fork and trowel, a hose pipe and a hand sprayer. A garden broom, dustpan and brush will help keep it tidy.

Larger gardens need a wider selection of hand tools. Some power tools will also come in handy (see pages 182–83).

Anvil secateurs

Bypass secateurs

Secateurs

An indispensable gardening companion, secateurs are used for cutting thin woody stems or soft shoots. Anvil secateurs have one sharp blade that cuts against a blunt anvil, and are best for thicker stems. Bypass secateurs have two cutting blades, similar to scissors, and are better suited to light tasks such as taking flower cuttings. If you need to use two hands to cut with your secateurs, they may need sharpening or replacing. Otherwise the stem you are cutting is too thick and you may need to use a long-handled pruner or lopper instead.

Telescopic hand shears

Shears with geared action

Shears

Ideal for shaping a hedge or clipping topiary, hand shears are extremely versatile. They are also useful for cutting small areas of grass or lawn as well as clearing beds in autumn or spring. For longer hedges, consider a lightweight, easy-to-use powered hedge trimmer (see page 183). Shears are available with long handles for trimming the edges of lawns and geared action to reduce effort and strain.

Sawing, cutting and chopping

Keep your garden in order with a selection of sharp-edged cutting tools for trimming, tending, pruning or shaping.

Telescopic loppers

Telescopic long-handled pruners

Loppers or pruners

Long-handled loppers or pruners are designed to cut through woody stems or branches. The long handles make for easier cutting while the longer reach is good for work on taller bushes and trees. Telescopic loppers are extra-long and are perfect for extending your reach even further – use them for pruning trees and woody climbers. To increase your cutting power, look for loppers that have geared action.

Folding saw

Retractable saw

Pruning saws

When a branch or stem is too thick to cut with secateurs or a lopper, a pruning saw is what you need. The blade has large, sharp teeth for cutting coarsely through green wood; retractable and folding versions can be stored more safely. For cutting hardwood or logs, a larger bow saw is effective, though you may need a chain saw for the bigger tasks (see page 183).

Comfort and protection

Gardening can be done all year round, so look for comfortable protective clothing and accessories for every season. Be prepared for rain or shine, whether with waterproofs and wellies for when it's grey and wet, or sunscreen and a floppy hat for when it's dry and sunny.

Thin cotton gloves

Thick leather gloves

Knee pads

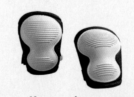

Gloves

Sometimes you need to feel what you are touching; at other times you need to be protected from nature. Choose your gloves for the task – whether thick leather or thin cotton, there are gloves to suit every need.

Kneeler

Knee pads or kneelers

If you're planning on doing intensive, detailed gardening for any amount of time, prepare to do some kneeling. Knee pads or a garden kneeler will help keep you comfortable.

grow

Digging, planting and weeding

When preparing, tending or improving your soil, the most effective digging and weeding tools are lightweight, strong, well made and easy to use. If you are clearing and improving a large area, consider hiring or buying a mechanical cultivator (see page 195).

Border spade   **Wide spade**   **Shovel**

Forks

These multi-purpose tools are essential for breaking up clumps of soil, turning over and preparing the ground for planting, moving compost and aerating lawns.

Border fork   **Large-size fork**

Spades and shovels

These tools come in a variety of sizes, which are suited to different tasks. A narrow border spade is ideal for planting, while a wider spade is better for heavy digging. When you have to shift a lot of loose material such as sand or soil, it's best to use a shovel.

Hand forks and trowels

Perfect for smaller gardens, a hand fork is ideal for cultivating the soil around plants and a trowel is indispensable for planting.

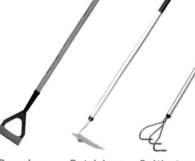

Draw hoe   **Dutch hoe**   **Cultivator**

Rakes

A traditional garden rake is used for final soil preparation before sowing or planting, as well as for levelling earth and collecting debris (see page 264 for lawn rakes).

Hoes

Use a draw hoe or long-handled cultivator to break up the surface of the soil and cut down low-growing weeds. A Dutch hoe is used with a sliding action just below the soil surface, whereas a draw hoe is designed for a downward chopping action to destroy weeds and break up the soil.

Tidying and carrying

Keeping your outdoor room tidy needn't be hard work. Some basic tools can make a world of difference.

Foldaway wheelbarrow

Wheelbarrows

For shifting material around the garden, a traditional wheelbarrow is a tried and tested design. It's also worth looking at the more modern, easy-to-store versions such as the foldaway wheelbarrow or garden buggy (see page 190).

Garden brush   **Adjustable broom**

Brooms

For clearing debris and leaves from hard surfaces, use a garden brush with strong bristles. Some brooms have an adjustable head, making light work of sweeping hard-to-reach corners.

Wheelbarrow

Garden power tools

Garden power tools make it easy to improve and maintain a garden, whatever its size. For the smaller garden there are lightweight, inexpensive tools such as electrical cordless trimmers, and for the larger garden you can choose from a range of more powerful petrol-engined models that have increased cutting power.

Power tools safety

Power tools can make maintaining a garden much less hard work – but they must always be treated with respect. Read the manufacturer's instructions before use and wear protective clothing if necessary. Store power tools in a safe place and, when working at a height, have someone help you secure the ladder or platform.

Clearing and cleaning

Power tools make light work of keeping a garden tidy. Use a shredder to break up vegetation, a blow vac to clear leaves, and a pressure washer to remove dirt, moss and algae from garden surfaces and furniture.

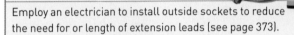

electric power tools
Safety
Always use an RCD (residual current device).
Employ an electrician to install outside sockets to reduce the need for or length of extension leads (see page 373).
Never use electrically powered garden tools in a wet garden or when it is raining.
Always disconnect the electrical supply before inspecting or maintaining a power tool.
Cordless tools prevent tripping over wires – rechargeable batteries are lighter and more long-lasting than ever before.

Shredders

These reduce branches, twigs and leaves to small chips and shreds, which can easily be disposed of, used as mulch or added to your compost heap. The more powerful the engine, the faster the shredding action and the thicker the branches it can take. There are two kinds of electric shredder: impact shredders, which have a high-speed revolving disc or blade, and quiet shredders, which have a revolving spiral or drum mechanism that cuts and crushes material. Petrol shredders are also available: noisier than electric shredders, these mobile tools have the advantage of being extra-powerful.

Shredder

Petrol blow vac

Blow vacs

For clearing the garden of leaves, clippings and other light debris, blow vacs are the ideal tool. They can be switched between blowing and vacuuming, and are also equipped with a shredding facility to reduce the volume of debris collected before being stored away in a bag. The shredding ratio describes the reduction power of the machine: 7 to 1 means that seven bags of leaves will be reduced to one bag of shredded material. Electric blow vacs are quiet and great for smaller gardens. Petrol versions are powerful and provide maximum mobility so are best for larger areas and frequent use.

Pressure washers

About fifty times more powerful than a standard garden hose, a pressure washer is extremely useful for removing moss, algae and heavy dirt deposits from garden furniture, patios, wooden decking, brickwork, conservatories, fences and walls, as well as bicycles, cars, trailers and caravans. Pressure washers use the power of water to clean, and most machines have an option for adding cleaning fluids or wash and wax detergents. For greatest flexibility choose one with a variable pressure rating: high pressure for tough tasks such as cleaning a patio, and lower pressure for more delicate jobs such as rinsing down a conservatory. Also look for a washer that is compatible with a wide variety of accessories, such as cleaning chemicals, brushes and lances.

Pressure washer

Electric blow vac

Cutting

Trimmers are ideal for cutting back areas of grass that a regular mower cannot reach such as the ground around trees, along fence panels or walls. The cutting is done by a line of nylon, which is flexible and allows you to get to overgrown plants right up to the edge of an obstruction. Be careful around saplings and young trees, though – the nylon line will cut into the bark and disfigure the trunk. The nylon line will wear down as you cut, so for frequent use select an autofeed model, which allows you to extend the nylon line as you work.

Petrol trimmer

Petrol trimmers and brush cutters

The most powerful trimmers run on petrol and will cut and trim larger areas with ease. A petrol trimmer is long-lasting, cordless and portable, and its heavy-duty cutting power is ideal for longer, thicker grass and brush. For clearing very dense vegetation and brush, use a brush cutter fitted with a solid metal blade. If you are working over a large area you may find that a trimmer equipped with handles and a harness will be more comfortable to use.

Cordless trimmer

Electric trimmers

Lightweight, quiet and inexpensive, electric trimmers start at the flick of a switch and come in very portable cordless models. If you want to trim the edge of the lawn with accuracy, then select a trimmer with an edger facility. Electric trimmers are ideal for shorter, thinner and smaller areas of grass.

Electric trimmer

Petrol hedge trimmer

Hedge trimmers

For pruning thin-stemmed hedges, topiary and shrubs, hedge trimmers will achieve a well-manicured look. The cutting blades are either single-sided – easier to handle for the novice – or double-sided for faster cutting action. Longer blades will reach across the top or width of a hedge and are ideal for cutting and shaping a simple hedge shape. Shorter, more manoeuvrable blades are better for topiary work.

Electric hedge trimmer

Electric or petrol hedge trimmers

Quiet and lightweight, electric hedge trimmers come in cordless portable models. Petrol hedge trimmers give you mobility and increased power for the bigger tasks, but are heavier and noisier too.

Cordless hedge trimmer

Chain saws

Tasks such as cutting firewood, pruning large branches and cutting down trees are made easy by a chain saw. Electric ones are lightweight, easy to start and require only minor periodic maintenance, but they have to be used close to an electrical outlet. Petrol chain saws are more powerful and better suited for heavy-duty tasks. Before you fell or prune a tree, check it is not subject to a Tree Preservation Order (see page 49).

Electric chain saw

Petrol chain saw

Storing, cleaning
and maintaining tools

Garden tools will last a long time and continue to perform well if you clean and maintain them regularly. For security as well as safety, always store them in a dry, lockable place, whether a tool tidy, shed or garage.

Caring for your tools

Garden tools will bear the brunt of all your gardening activities, whether it's light work such as keeping your garden in shape or a major landscaping project. It pays to see your garden tools as an investment: choose your tools carefully, always use the right tool for the task and look after tools by cleaning and storing them with care.

Hand tools are simple to maintain. Always wipe or wash off any soil, clippings or other plant material from the blade or tool surface. Dry and then wipe all metal parts with an oily rag, minding the sharp edges, or spray them with lubricant. Cutting tools will need sharpening from time to time (see below).

Power tools, and petrol-engined tools in particular, require more attention. Follow the manufacturer's recommendations for everyday care and make maintenance part of your regular routine – it's best not to wait until something goes wrong.

Sharpening cutting blades

Keep your secateurs, pruners and loppers sharp – you will find they are much easier to use. What's more, a clean cut is much better for plants. Sharpening kits are simple to use and will quickly restore the cutting edge of your blade.

tools materials
- **secateurs, pruner or lopper**
- **screwdriver**
- **sharpener kit**

1 Fit the sharpening guide onto the back edge of the blade and tighten the retaining screw. Select the appropriate hole in the guide for the cutting angle of the blade.

2 Place the sharpening arm in the guide hole and move it up and down over the blade. The abrasive stone will restore the edge in minutes.

Cleaning steel tools

More often than not, your digging tools will be coated with damp soil, mud or dirt after use. Try not to leave dirt to harden as it will make the tools more difficult to clean later on. Instead, wash or wipe tools down at the end of the day, dry them off then wipe the metal with an oily rag to keep the steel from rusting. (Stainless steel tools won't rust and so do not need oiling.)

Cutting tools will also benefit from regular oiling – not just the blades, but the joints and levers too.

Tool rack

Garden tools are best stored in a dry and secure place. A tool rack is ideal: since garden tools come in various sizes and shapes, instead of piling them up in a jumble you can keep them sorted by storing them on a universal tool rack attached to the wall of a shed or garage.

1 Find a suitable space on a shed or garage wall that will not be in the way and that is preferably not visible through any windows. Use a spirit level to ensure that the rack is level.

4 Put the rack into position and then fix it in place with screws. Tighten the screws securely.

2 Hold the rack in position and mark the drilling holes on the wall surface with a pencil.

5 Position the tools on the rack. You may need to experiment so as to make the best and safest use of the space.

tools materials

- **spirit level**
- **power drill with hammer action**
- **masonry bit**
- **pencil**
- **screwdriver**

- tool rack
- screws
- wall plugs

3 Use a hammer drill with a masonry bit to drill the fixing holes. Push wall plugs into the holes.

safety first

Safe storage

Store your tools securely – not only from thieves, but also from children. Small hand tools should be kept out of reach and out of sight. Lock up sharp or pointed tools as well as all power tools.

Your soil is the lifeblood of your garden. Plants depend on it for vital nutrients, and any garden will benefit from having its soil enriched in one way or another. The thinner and poorer the soil, the more organic matter you should add. The best time to do this is right at the beginning, before planting a bed, but keeping your soil in good condition is an ongoing process. Recognising the type of soil you have and taking steps to improve its structure will make a world of difference to the health of your plants.

your earth

What is it made of?

Soil is made from crumbled rock particles enriched by decayed organic matter, both plant and animal. The decaying process is aided and abetted by millions of bacteria and fungi – the more the better. A high count of worms and insects living within the soil is a clear indication of healthy fertility.

Soil is formed and laid down in three distinct layers – topsoil, subsoil and bedrock. Topsoil is the stuff gardeners concern themselves with most. This is the layer whose structure and depth we influence by digging in or mulching with organic matter. It is also the most fertile. However, it is within the lower two layers that the soil's all-important drainage abilities and acidity or alkalinity are determined.

Beneath the earth

Over millions of years rock is weathered and eroded into tiny particles. Different types of rock have different chemical compositions, and these define the nature of the topsoil they eventually produce. Soils formed from and sitting upon a bedrock of chalk will be alkaline; a bedrock of granite will result in an acidic soil. Limestone will give a more alkaline topsoil than sandstone. Older houses, built with local stone, can give some clues as to the type of soil you might expect to find in an area – but not always. Topsoil is often imported into gardens, especially those of new houses. It may have come from miles away and bear no relation to the local soil. So soil testing, as discussed in the following pages, is a must.

Keep it separate

If you were to dig a fairly deep hole, say a metre deep, the two distinct layers of topsoil and subsoil would be clearly evident. There is a marked contrast both in colour and structure, the top being dark and crumbly, the subsoil paler and denser. Every care should be taken when digging, cultivating or doing any excavations to keep the two separate. Plants do not like subsoil – it has very little nutrient content and is far too dense to contain enough air for them to grow successfully.

Know your soil

Soil is the most important raw material for creating a beautiful garden. Whether your soil is fertile and free-draining or needs a bit of extra help, once you know what you have to work with you can take steps to improve it.

Which kind is yours?

There are many different kinds of garden soil – chalk, clay, sand, peat and, the best of all, loam. Loam is ideal: neither too light nor too heavy, too moisture-retentive nor too free-draining. Improving your soil is all about achieving just that balanced combination of qualities.

To find out what kind of soil you have, you'll need to do a bit of detective work. By looking out for some basic clues, you should be able to tell a lot about what kind of soil you'll be working with.

Clues from your garden

Step back and look at what's growing in your garden. Lots of weeds, headache though they may be, are an indication of fertility. On the other hand, a lack of vegetation will mean that your soil may need some extra help.

Take a closer look

On a day when your soil isn't either soaking wet or bone dry, grab a handful and squeeze it. What colour is it? Does it feel light or heavy, crumbly or smooth? To find out what type of soil you have, compare what's in your hand with the table below, which will also tell you more about it.

different types of soil

	Appearance	Fertility	Drainage	When to work it	Improving it	Acid or alkaline
Sand	Gritty and unwilling to stick together	Not very fertile	Drains freely and is not prone to water-logging	Spring	Fertilise regularly and work in plenty of organic matter	Can be either – soil needs testing (see opposite)
Clay	Dense and smooth: holds together without crumbling	Fairly fertile	Slow-draining; hard and prone to cracking when dry; turns muddy after rain	Autumn	Dig in horticultural grit and plenty of organic matter	Can be either – soil needs testing (see opposite)
Chalk	Pale in colour; often contains white chunks of chalk	Not at all fertile	Very free-draining	Any season	Add lots of soil improver; try green manures, e.g. red clover (see page 191)	Alkaline
Peat	Rich, dark and moist	Not very fertile	Prone to water-logging, but will not re-absorb moisture easily if allowed to get too dry	Any season	Feed regularly and work in plenty of grit; consider raised beds if water-logging severe	Acid
Loam	Rich, dark and crumbly	Highly fertile	Holds moisture yet drains easily	Any season	Add plenty of organic matter	Can be either – soil needs testing (see opposite)

grow

Acid or alkaline?

The importance of finding out whether your soil is acid or alkaline cannot be underestimated, as it will determine what you can and cannot grow. Soil alkalinity or acidity is measured against the pH scale, which runs from 1 to 14. Neutral soil, neither one nor the other, has a pH value of 7; anything below is acid; above is alkaline. Some plants prefer ericaceous (acid) soil, while others prefer lime (alkaline) soil.

Testing your soil's pH

The surest way to assess the pH value of your soil is to do a test. Testing kits are inexpensive and simple to use. You can choose between the electronic probe kind (pictured) and the more traditional test tube kits. To use a probe test, make a shallow hole, add a few drops of water to dissolve the soil slightly, place the probes in, and the reading is displayed on the dial. To use a test tube kit, simply shake a soil sample with water in the test tube, and measure the resulting colour against the chart.

It's worth doing a soil test in several areas of your garden as they may not all be exactly the same.

Soil tests

Traditional test tube soil tests use a chemical solution that changes colour when mixed with soil. Take care to avoid getting small stones in the soil sample, as this can produce a misleading result.

| pH 8.0 Alkaline |
| pH 7.0 Neutral |
| pH 6.0 Acid |
| pH 5.0 Very Acid |

Changing soil acidity

Most garden soils are either slightly acid or alkaline with a pH of between 6 and 8, which is fine for the majority of plants. But some plants, including cabbages and lettuces, are alkaline lovers, while others such as rhododendrons and heathers prefer acid soils. Altering the pH value of an entire garden is virtually impossible, but you can still grow lime-hating plants in an alkaline environment, or the reverse.

Acid lovers

If you really want to grow rhododendrons (above) or other acid-loving plants in a garden with alkaline soil, then either plant them in pots filled with ericaceous compost, or make an acid bed: excavate an area to a depth of 30–40cm, line with a permeable weed-control fabric, and then refill it with acid soil.

Alkaline lovers

It's best to grow lime-loving plants such as cabbages and lettuces (below) in alkaline conditions. Powdered lime, which can be bought in packets, will make your soil more alkaline if added to a plot. Always follow the dosage instructions, and never add lime and manure at the same time – it's much better to add one in autumn and the other in spring. Although people sometimes add lime to plots annually, in fact this is seldom necessary. Always do a soil test first.

Soil improver,
mulch and fertiliser

Improving, mulching and fertilising the soil are essential for any long-term success in the garden. They will all help to improve the condition of your soil, and will work wonders for the health and well-being of your plants.

What is soil improver?

Soil improver enhances soil structure, helps retain moisture and encourages beneficial organisms such as earthworms, whose activities help plants grow strong and healthy. It's also filled with the nutrients plants love. It is not used 'neat' for growing anything in, but as a soil conditioner, and should be worked into the soil before planting. Afterwards it can be added annually – spread it upon the soil's surface between the plants and work it into the top few centimetres of earth with a fork.

Soil improver works by adding humus to the soil – dead and decayed organic matter that is vital for healthy plant growth. Organic mulches (see opposite) do the same as they rot down.

The name 'compost' refers to any bulky, organic decayed matter. Various types of compost (including garden compost) can be used as soil improvers. But they are not to be confused with the potting compost you buy in stores, which is enriched to make it suitable as a growing medium for plants.

Composted bark

Ideal for enriching the soil, composted bark can also be used as a mulch (opposite).

Farmyard manure

Ready-to-use manure can be bought in stores and applied directly to your garden.

Choosing soil improvers

Soil improvers will help you get the most out of your soil, but with so many choices out there, how do you decide which one to go for? Well-rotted garden compost is certainly the cheapest option and also one of the best (see pages 192–93), but it's possible to buy soil improvers ready-made. Knowing a bit about the different kinds of product available will help you decide what's right for you and your garden.

ideal tool

Garden buggy

For shifting bags of compost or a mix of garden waste, a garden buggy is handy and adaptable. The large bag is designed to be lifted out and is tough, washable and resistant to tears. The entire buggy folds neatly away too.

choosing soil improver	
Garden compost	Well-rotted, home-made garden compost (see pages 192–93) is the favourite option of most gardeners. It is an excellent and wallet-friendly soil conditioner, as it is rich in nutrients and costs nothing to make.
Manure	Animal manure is widely available in the countryside and cheap to buy. If bought fresh, it needs to be stacked for six months so it has time to rot down before being used in the garden.
Leafmould	Dark, crumbly leafmould is made from leaves that have been left to rot for at least a year. An excellent compost, but one you will have to make for yourself from collected leaves.
Composted bark	The next best thing to leafmould is composted bark, which can be bought by the bag.
Mushroom compost	In addition to its peat base, mushroom compost contains bits of chalk, which is alkaline. It should not be used for acid beds or lime-hating plants, but can be useful if you want to grow alkaline-loving plants in acid soils.
Peat	There are no nutrients in peat, so it should be avoided in favour of other composts. Extracting peat from wetlands is also harmful to the environment.
Peat alternatives	Environmentally conscious gardeners should look out for organic or peat-free composts, and soil improvers made from recycled green waste.

grow

What is mulch?

Mulch is any material, organic or inorganic, that is spread on the surface of the soil to seal in moisture and deter weeds. Organic mulches include chipped bark, garden compost and cocoa shells. They eventually rot down so are also good for conditioning the soil, but this does mean you have to top them up from time to time. Inorganic mulches include gravel, slate chips and recycled glass, which all work particularly well in modern garden designs.

Organic mulches
These add nutrients to the soil as they break down.

Inorganic mulches
Long-lasting inorganic mulches look good in modern gardens.

Mulching

The last stage after planting is mulching – this extra step will keep weeds at bay in the long run. For shrub beds and other permanent planting areas, consider laying a permeable weed-control fabric (see page 33) and planting through it, then spreading the mulch on top. This will allow you to reduce the mulch depth to around 7cm. Otherwise a deeper layer of 15cm will be needed. The most important thing to remember when applying any mulch is that the soil needs to be damp to begin with. Mulching an already dried-out bed merely makes it more difficult for rain to penetrate, so always give planted areas a good water first.

What is fertiliser?

Fertiliser or plant food can be liquid or solid (powdered, granular, pelleted), organic or inorganic. There are many kinds of fertiliser available, but they all contain varying amounts of three elements that are vital for plants: nitrogen, phosphorus (usually in the form of phosphate) and potassium (often as potash). Nitrogen encourages leaves to grow, phosphorus promotes root growth, while potassium is essential for producing flowers and fruits (see page 176).

Liquid or solid?

Liquid fertiliser works almost instantly because plants absorb their nutrients in liquid form (see page 177). It does need to be applied regularly, though, as it does not remain in the soil for very long. Solid fertiliser is much better for the garden in general as it releases nutrients more slowly and so remains effective for longer.

When to apply fertiliser

General-purpose fertiliser should be applied in the spring, at the start of the growing season. Some kinds, such as bonemeal which encourages root growth, should be worked into the soil when planting. Avoid using long-acting fertilisers, particularly ones high in nitrogen, after mid-summer. Nitrogen promotes leaf growth; a fresh flush of growth in late summer will not give shrubs long enough to toughen up and withstand frost.

Green manures

A green manure is a crop that is dug straight back into the soil to fertilise it. Usually from the legume family (especially bean or pea plants), these have the ability to 'fix' nitrogen in the soil. This is not the case with most plants: grass clippings or weeds, for example, require copious amounts of nitrogen in order to rot down, and will take this from the soil if they are dug in. Many plants used as green manures store nitrogen in nodules on their roots, so they already contain all the nitrogen they need for decomposition and add it to the soil instead.

choosing fertiliser	
General-purpose fertiliser	This contains similar amounts of the three main plant nutrients and often includes trace elements (see page 176). It is ideal for preparing soil for planting as well as general feeding. Growmore (inorganic) and blood, fish and bone (organic) are two which are often used.
Straight fertiliser	These target specific nutrient deficiencies, such as a lack of magnesium in tomatoes.

Granular fertiliser

Granular or powdered fertiliser is good for preparing soil for planting and for topping up available nutrients in spring, right before growth starts. You can also give vegetables a boost in summer by digging this into the soil around plants.

Making your own
compost

A compost bin isn't just the easiest and cheapest way of disposing of garden waste; it also produces the best possible soil conditioner. Garden compost can be made from any organic matter that will rot down. As well as plant material, you can compost paper, cardboard, raw vegetable trimmings and natural fibres such as cotton.

What's it for?

Garden compost not only contains many enriching nutrients, but its bulky organic quality improves the structure of the soil, increasing water-retention in a dry chalk or sandy soil, and aiding drainage in a heavy peat or clay one.

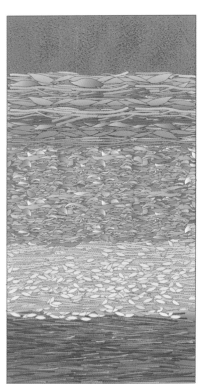

A layer of manure or compost accelerator will make the heap break down more quickly

Grass cuttings or annual weeds should be in shallow layers, with layers of woodier material in between

Each layer of material shouldn't be too deep, or too tightly packed; woody prunings should be shredded first

A fibrous bottom layer – hedge clippings, straw, nothing too dense – will allow air to circulate

Building up the layers

What's the secret ingredient?

It may come as a surprise, but there is no special ingredient for making good compost. You'll find everything you need in your garden and at home. So long as you take care to leave out the bad stuff (see table, below), what matters more is the way you put the different elements together.

Friendly bacteria are responsible for breaking down organic matter in your compost bin, and to do this they need air, moisture, nitrogen and warmth. Layering is the key to encouraging them. Start with a layer of fibrous, woody material – this will keep air circulating in your compost bin. Follow this with different layers of shredded material, making sure that no layer is too deep or tightly packed.

A compost bin will go anywhere in the garden, though it's best kept out of sight. It's worth having more than one compost bin if you can possibly find the room: one to fill up and one that is already full and rotting down.

What to aim for

Rotting down can take anything from three to six months, depending on ingredients, climate and layering technique. Once ready, garden compost will have reduced to about 70% of its original size. It should be dark in colour and crumbly in texture, a bit like coffee grounds. What you don't want is large, un-rotted chunks in otherwise soil-like compost. Shredding or cutting up hard, woody materials before you add them to your bin will prevent this.

ideal tool

Shredder

Forget chopping – the fastest way to get rid of bulky garden waste is to use a shredder. Hedge clippings, twigs and even small branches can be added to your compost bin once cut down to size. Some shredders can deal with branches up to 3cm thick.

what to include, what to leave out

What to include	What to leave out
• Uncooked kitchen waste: vegetable trimmings, tea bags, coffee grounds and eggshells	• Cooked kitchen waste
• Annual weeds (before seedheads form)	• Animal products and bones
• Spent bedding plants and flowers	• Bread
• Soft hedge clippings	• Diseased plant materials
• Soft prunings	• Soil pests
• Lawn clippings	• Weed seedheads
• Shredded natural fibre materials such as newspapers, paper, cotton and wool fabrics	• Synthetic fabrics
• Shredded woody stems	• Non-biodegradable materials
• Cardboard	• Dog or cat waste
• Sawdust	• Unshredded woody material
• Straw	

grow

Avoiding problems

Most problems with compost bins can be easily avoided and are simple enough to fix. Some people swear by 'turning' the compost – taking it out, mixing it up and putting it back in again. In fact this shouldn't be necessary if it is layered properly in the first place. However, you might want to speed up the rotting process by using an activator (see table, right).

successful composting	
Keep layers shallow	Deep layers of any one material, particularly lawn clippings, will slow down the rotting process and lead to smelly, slimy compost. Keep layers shallow and mix cut grass in with other materials.
Shred it	Thick, woody stems will take longer to rot down than soft, fleshy plant matter, so will slow down the decomposition of material in your compost bin. Cut them up finely or shred them.
Just enough moisture	Garden compost needs to be damp, not sodden but not dry either. Watering during the summer months may be necessary, but you might also need to protect the heap with a waterproof lid during wetter weather.
Speed it up	You can buy compost activators which will speed up the rotting process. Or a layer of garden soil, animal manure or a sprinkling of pelleted chicken manure every 30cm or so will have a similar effect.

Constructing a compost bin

A compost bin isn't essential for making garden compost, but it is much neater and easier to manage than a sprawling pile. It will also be warmer, meaning the contents rot more quickly, and more evenly moist. You can buy a flat-packed wooden bin like the one assembled here, which comes pretreated with wood preservative.

tools materials

- **hammer**
- **screwdriver or power drill-driver**
- **spade**
- compost bin kit

ideal tool

Plastic compost bin

For smaller gardens, custom-made plastic compost bins are a good option – these look a bit like a plastic dustbin with a hatch at the bottom.

1 Join the four side panels with three 65mm screws at each corner.

2 Attach the first metal catch that holds the access hatch in the open position. A plastic spacer ensures it is at the correct distance from the bin.

3 Attach the second catch and open the hatch to check that the catches are working properly.

4 At the front of the bin, the semi-transparent plastic cover hooks over a screw that is not fully screwed home. Fit this screw and secure the cover over it.

5 Pull the cover back and nail it to the back of the bin through the batten attached to the plastic.

6 Begin loading the bin with garden waste. The bottom layer should not be too dense so that air can circulate freely.

You can do it...

Uninvited guests

An active compost heap should generate enough heat to keep rodents and other pests at bay. The most important thing to remember is never to add any cooked food, meat or dairy products to it. Bury fruit and vegetable trimmings well within the other ingredients. You can also cover your bin with a lid and line the bottom with wire mesh.

B&Q

Preparing the ground

If you get this bit of gardening right, it will make life easier for you in the long run. You might have to do a bit of digging to begin with, but it will definitely be worth it.

Getting rid of lawn

If time isn't a priority, you may choose not to peel off your lawn, and instead let it die off naturally. To do this, place a thick covering on the ground to exclude all light – this will take at least six months to be effective.

A quicker method is spraying or watering the area with weedkiller. A glyphosate-based treatment (see page 284) is absorbed by the foliage and carried down to the roots, so though it starts to work immediately, it will take two to four weeks to be fully effective. But because it doesn't enter plants through their roots, or remain active in the ground, it won't kill any new planting in the cleared area. Be careful, though – it will destroy any plant it comes into contact with, so never spray it on a windy day. If in doubt, shield the surrounding area with pieces of board, or protect individual plants by covering them with bin bags, leaving these in place until the spray has fully dried.

Creating a new bed

Preparing the ground will often involve creating a new bed in an area already filled with vegetation, such as a lawn. In this case, the bed will first need to be marked out and any existing plants removed and composted – stacked turfs, grass-side down, will rot down and can be re-used as soil (see page 68). Or if it's in good enough condition, turf can be saved and used elsewhere in the garden.

Bamboo canes can be used to mark the corners of a square or rectangular bed. Check the shape is accurate by using string to make sure the diagonals are the same length. Or you could use a length of hose or rope, drizzled sand or special spray paint to show the outline.

Clearing weeds

Now is the best time to tackle weeds – prevention is the key to keeping them at bay, and it's much easier to clear the ground when it's empty. Some weeds are a bigger problem than others. Annual weeds such as shepherd's purse are easy to pull out; so long as they haven't set seed they can be added to your compost bin or simply dug back into the soil.

Perennial weeds are trickier to deal with. Bindweed, couch grass, docks, creeping thistle, dandelion and ground elder all spread through their roots, so be extra careful – leaving even the tiniest piece behind can create a whole new plant. Consider fighting them with two or three treatments of a glyphosate-based weedkiller.

tools materials
• edging iron
• spade

eco beds

Weed-control fabric
Instead of using chemical preparations to kill your weeds, consider using special weed-control fabrics that block out light and kill weeds naturally. But be prepared to wait up to six months before the area is ready for planting.

With a spade or an edging iron cut down 5cm into the turf, dividing it into squares of about 30–40cm so that it is easy to lift. Cutting in straight rows will help keep your work neat.

Work the spade underneath the turf to slice through its roots, maintaining an equal depth of 5cm. Peel back the cut sections and dispose or use elsewhere.

Preparing the soil

Before planting, it's a good idea to give the soil your undivided attention; a little effort at this stage will really pay off in the future. While the ground is still clear of plants, the first thing to do is test the pH levels of the soil in the areas you plan to use for planting (see page 189).

Next, work as much soil improver into it as possible, together with horticultural grit and fertiliser; this is your best chance of doing this properly, and if you do it now you will reap the benefits later on. If you've planted the area before, digging to a spade's depth may be all that's needed (see below).

Adding topsoil

Many new houses have a garden that is little more than a hastily tidied-up building site with hardly any topsoil. Before planting such areas, they will first need clearing of rubble, then an added layer of imported topsoil that has been screened to remove weeds and debris, and sterilised to kill any bacteria or pests. Ideally topsoil should be 30cm thick for a bed or 15cm thick for a lawn.

Calculating how much topsoil you need is easy. Just measure the area in metres and then multiply the length by the width and the depth – this will give you the volume in cubic metres. You can buy smaller quantities in bags or larger quantities by the tonne; one cubic metre weighs about 1.4 tonnes. Do bear in mind that even the best topsoil will still need enriching with soil improver and fertiliser.

ideal tool

Mechanical cultivator
When you want to break up and prepare a large area of topsoil, a petrol-powered cultivator will save you a lot of effort. It's best suited to areas of open, level ground, and should not be used on established beds.

Digging deeper

For areas such as footpaths where the soil is densely packed, a deeper style of digging might be called for: trench digging (to over a spade's depth), shown here. Although it can be hard work, it is no more strenuous than going to the gym – plus it has the added bonus of being free and in the fresh air. As with all digging, autumn is the best season for this because the soil is moist but not waterlogged. Still, it can be done at any time of year if weather and soil conditions allow.

tools materials

- **spade**
- **wheelbarrow**
- **garden fork**
- well-rotted garden compost or soil improver

1 Dig a trench two spades wide. Remove the soil and transport it to the end of the plot with the help of a wheelbarrow.

2 Break up the bottom of the trench using a garden fork, making sure not to mix the topsoil with the subsoil (see page 186). Fill the trench with well-rotted garden compost or soil improver.

3 Dig another trench immediately behind the first, placing the soil from this on top of the compost in the first trench. Continue over the entire plot.

You can do it...

Take your time
To make things a bit easier for yourself, spread digging over a season – it doesn't have to be done all in one go. If you start digging in autumn you won't have to start planting until spring, which will leave you with nearly six months to stop and start when you feel like it.

B&Q

Drainage in the garden

In ideal conditions, rainwater soaks away into the soil, the surface of the ground dries out after a shower, and plants flourish. Unfortunately, some gardens suffer from poor drainage. Pools of water form in wet weather and take ages to drain away, and there are areas where only wet-loving plants such as rushes and mosses will grow.

Drainage problems and solutions

Most plant roots cannot live in permanently waterlogged soil. The water fills the air pockets that hold the oxygen their roots require. It also leads to lower levels of nitrogen and other vital nutrients. Cold, wet soil takes longer to warm up in spring, so plant growth gets off to a slow start. If water lies on the lawn after wet weather, the area will quickly turn to mud when walked on and the grass will be damaged. In addition, some plant diseases flourish in wet soil. So it is well worth checking for any drainage problems and fixing them before you plant an area of the garden. That may mean waiting for up to a year before going ahead with landscaping plans for a new garden, as drainage problems may only be apparent in the wetter months.

Aerating a lawn

Lawns have a tendency to become 'panned' or compacted because of constant traffic. Water cannot seep through the solid soil to drain away, so it forms pools on the surface. You can improve the drainage by spiking a lawn to aerate it: include this in your annual cycle of lawn maintenance (see pages 262–63).

Digging

House-building sites have often had heavy machinery moving over them, compacting the soil of the new gardens. Water cannot drain through it to reach plant roots. Digging over the soil thoroughly and breaking up clumps with a fork or spade may be enough to solve the problem.

Dumped clay

In the garden of a new house, builders may have dumped clay on the topsoil. If so, the clay needs to be dug out and possibly more topsoil added (see page 195).

Adding grit

An easy way to improve the surface drainage in flowerbeds and borders is to work horticultural grit into the topsoil. It's important only to use grit specifically sold for this purpose, not limestone grit, which will affect your soil's pH levels (see page 189). Adding grit will benefit all soil types except the most sandy, but it is especially useful in heavy clay soils. Grit can also be scattered on the surface of the soil as a decorative mulch. It looks particularly attractive around low-growing alpine plants. When preparing new beds, don't forget the importance of adding soil improver such as composted bark or garden compost as well (see page 190).

tools materials
- **garden fork**
- horticultural grit
- soil improver

1 Distribute a couple of shovelfuls of grit per square metre – more on heavy clay soil or if you are preparing the area for planting bearded irises, lavender and other plants from the Mediterranean that prefer dry, stony soil.

2 Work the grit into the soil with a garden fork. For new beds, work in soil improver at the same time.

Piping water away

A persistent drainage problem in a garden may need more drastic intervention. Surface water can sometimes be drained away from parts of the garden by simply shaping the ground into drainage ditches that will carry the excess water away. However, in areas where the natural level of ground water (the water table) is high, standing water may need to be drained away by a system of pipes into a surface-water drain or into a soakaway. Rainwater should not be diverted into the main sewerage system.

Digging up the garden to install underground drainage pipes will inevitably cause significant disruption and damage, so if possible this should be done before planting or building a new garden.

Laying a perforated drainage pipe

Dig a trench, about 1m deep and 350mm wide, angled downwards to a surface-water drain or soakaway (see right). If removing turf, cut it into neat sections with a spade and reserve it for replacing later. Line the trench with permeable geotextile fabric and spread a 75mm layer of cleanstone (20–40mm) along the bottom of the trench, following the slope or fall. Then place a 100mm perforated plastic drainage pipe on top. Lengths of pipe can be easily joined with specially made push-fit connectors. Then cover the pipe with more cleanstone to within 200–300mm of ground level, making sure the pipe is in the centre of the trench. Wrap the geotextile fabric over the top and cover with topsoil or the reserved turf.

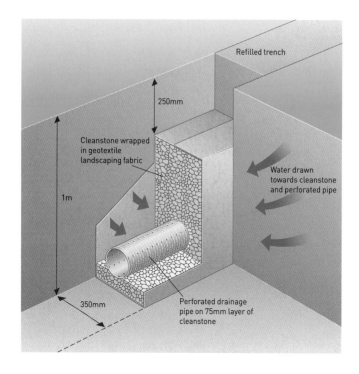

Refilled trench
250mm
Cleanstone wrapped in geotextile landscaping fabric
1m
Water drawn towards cleanstone and perforated pipe
350mm
Perforated drainage pipe on 75mm layer of cleanstone

Tackling a widespread drainage problem

An extensive drainage problem may require a series of these buried drainage pipes running across the whole garden, or a large part of it. They should be laid out in a herringbone pattern with a central trench and side trenches leading into it at a steep angle. The spacing of these trenches depends on the severity of the problem; they may be anything from 3m apart in clay soil to about 6m apart in loam. They should run from the highest point of the garden to the lowest and then into a soakaway.

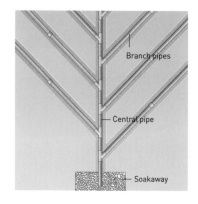

Branch pipes
Central pipe
Soakaway

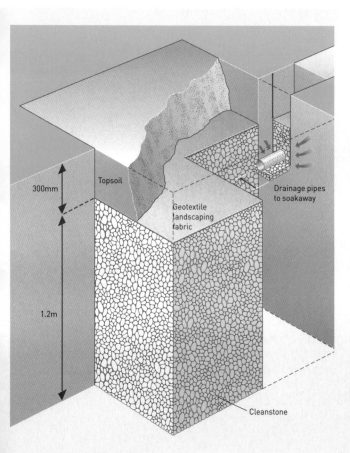

300mm
Topsoil
Geotextile landscaping fabric
Drainage pipes to soakaway
1.2m
Cleanstone

Constructing a soakaway

A soakaway is a deep hole lined with geotextile landscaping fabric and filled with cleanstone. Water is channelled from other parts of the garden into the soakaway, from where it seeps slowly away into the surrounding soil.

To construct a soakaway dig a hole about 1.2m square and 1.2m deep. Before going ahead with the construction, you should check that water will actually drain away from this spot. Fill the hole with water and see how quickly it drains; if it takes hours to clear, your soakaway isn't going to work and you will need to find a different location.

Assuming the water does clear, then line the hole with geotextile fabric; overlap it by 300mm where necessary. Underground drainage pipes should be about 600mm below ground by the time they reach the soakaway. Fill the hole with cleanstone (40mm or larger) allowing for a 300mm layer of topsoil above. Spread a layer of geotextile fabric over the aggregate and replace the topsoil and turf.

Choosing new plants for your outdoor room is an exciting challenge. Whether your garden is completely new – a blank canvas – or is filled with established vegetation, adding the plants of your choice will make it truly your own. Just as any interior decoration always looks better on a well-prepared surface, so careful soil preparation is much more likely to lead your plants to flourish.

planting your garden

Different plants for different gardens

Selecting, buying and growing plants is one of gardening's great pleasures. But it's worth thinking first about which plants will grow best in your outdoor room. Being familiar with the soil, light and drainage conditions of your garden will go far in helping you choose plants that will thrive without needing constant care and attention from you.

Know your soil

Not all soil is the same. But there are all kinds of plants that will suit your particular soil type, whether it's acid or alkaline, sandy or clay. And don't despair if the plants you want to grow aren't quite right for your soil – you can always provide a different soil for them in a container, or take measures to alter the soil conditions of a bed.

Local climate

Your local climate will affect the plants you grow. For instance, the growing conditions in a seaside garden will be totally different from those of a garden in the heart of Britain. There are also differences between city and country – usually a city will provide a warmer, more sheltered environment than the countryside. Do have a look at what flourishes in your neighbourhood, and take advantage of local knowledge where possible – gardeners everywhere love to share their experiences.

Sun and shade

Each part of a garden has its own climate too, known as a micro-climate. As the sun moves in the sky from day to day and season to season, so your garden receives ever-changing levels of sunlight and shade. Some parts of it may be in the shade all year round, perhaps because of a tree, hedge or building – shade-tolerant plants with strong shapes such as ferns, hostas and foxgloves are ideal for these areas. By contrast some plants positively thrive in full sun, such as roses, lavender and wisteria.

Easy-care gardens

Choosing your plants carefully can make your garden easier to maintain. You can find plants that need no deadheading, pruning, dividing or spraying to succeed; summer-flowering shrubs such as hebe, choisya and potentilla are examples. Remember too that you can cut down on weeding by suppressing weeds in your borders: cover the soil with weed-control fabric and mulch with bark or stone chips.

Buying plants

Filling a garden or patio with plants, containers and hanging baskets is a big investment. So how can you tell if the plant you're buying is a healthy one, especially in the dormant season when it appears to be little more than a pot of roots?

Choosing a healthy plant

A healthy plant is easy to spot in full growth: check that it is free from aphids and other pests, as well as signs of disease (see below and pages 256–59). Don't be put off by deteriorating top growth in perennials, as it may only mean that it's the end of the plant's growing season. Also resist choosing a plant just because it happens to be in flower; instead, look at it for overall signs of health, including the number of buds it has and a healthy root system.

Pests and diseases

A tell-tale sign that a plant has a pest is oddly shaped patches in the leaves. Also keep an eye out on leaves and stems for diseases such as black spot, shown here (see pages 256–57 for advice on how to treat them).

What's in a name?

Latin plant names can be daunting, but they are useful to gardeners because they help them identify different breeds of the same kind of plant (see page 292). Common names might seem more user-friendly, but they can be a real minefield. It's not unusual for a single plant to have several different common names, and usage may change from one county to the next. Don't let Latin names put you off growing a plant. Provided you can give it the right care and conditions, chances are you'll have no problems growing it – whether or not you can pronounce its name.

Phyllostachys bambusoides 'Castilloni' Bamboo

Inspecting the compost and roots

A plant that has been properly cared for will have no weeds or moss growing on the surface of the compost. Carefully tip the pot sideways. If the roots are spilling out of the bottom as shown below, think twice as the plant may be pot-bound, which means that it has been grown in the same pot for far too long. To be absolutely certain, knock it gently from its container: if the roots wind densely around the soil, that means the plant is definitely pot-bound. A pot-bound plant won't be as healthy as one that has been repotted regularly (see page 209).

A pot-bound plant

Checking the label

Ideally, a plant will come with a label telling you its name and giving instructions on how to grow it and the conditions that will suit it best. However, it's a good idea always to check that the flower and leaf pictured on the label actually match those of the plant: even in the best maintained stores, labels do sometimes get accidentally switched.

Matteuccia struthiopteris Shuttlecock fern

Buying for different seasons

Any shrub, tree or herbaceous perennial grown in a pot can be bought and planted at any time of year. But different seasons have their pros and cons.

Summer

Plants bought in summer will have large top-growth, creating instant impact in your garden. But their root system may be comparatively small; fewer roots mean less support, so a plant might have trouble staying upright. What's more, it will need lots of watering throughout the summer.

Autumn or spring

Plants will have a better chance of developing their root system if planted in autumn or spring, when they are going into dormancy or coming out of it. A bigger root system will provide better support for a larger plant, and because it rains more during these seasons, you won't need to worry about watering after the initial watering in.

Winter

Pot-grown plants bought in the dormant season may be little more than a clump of roots, but you should still check carefully that they are not pot-bound (see opposite).

Bare-root plants (below) are simply twigs with roots that come without a pot or soil. They are sold and planted in the dormant season, the period when plants are not in active growth. Roses are the plants most commonly sold like this, but you can also find bare-root trees and fruit bushes.

Special cases

Some plants are only available at certain times of year. Spring-flowering bulbs are sold in late summer, ready for planting in autumn. Annuals and most bedding are available in late spring to early summer because they are purely summer plants, though winter bedding can only be bought in autumn and winter.

Types of plants

The following categories cover most types of garden plant. You might also come across bog and pond plants, but these have very specific uses (see pages 216–17).

different kinds of plants	
Trees	Woody, with a permanent structure of branches growing from one central trunk (see page 220 for basic shapes).
Shrubs	Woody, with many stems and a permanent or semi-permanent structure. Unlike trees, these have no central trunk.
Annuals	Germinate, grow, flower and set seed in one season. Some survive in seedling form through the winter months: these are known as hardy annuals.
Biennials	Germinate and grow in the first year, then flower, set seed and die in the second. Some, such as carrots, develop swollen roots to store food to last through the winter.
Perennials	Live for three seasons or more, including all trees and shrubs.
Herbaceous perennials	Non-woody perennials that emerge in the spring, grow through the summer months, and then die back and stay dormant throughout the winter. The top-growth will usually die, but the roots will live on and put up new growth the following year.
Climbers	Grow vertically and require support on which to 'climb'. Some seek out and cling to whatever they can find; others need tying to a support system of wires or trellis (see pages 204–5).
Bulbs	A bulb is an energy source for the plant that emerges from it. Whether it flowers in spring, summer or autumn, bulbs will do so only once a year before dying down to re-emerge the following year.

Bare-root beech plants

Planting shrubs and perennials

Rosa 'Clair Matin' Bush rose

Planting your garden can be incredibly satisfying. Often when designing a garden it's all too easy to get lost in details, which means it's hard to visualise the bigger picture. Planting makes the gardener's dream a reality – this is where your ideas come to life, and you finally get to see what your original plan looks like in practice.

Planning

Even if you can't wait to get started with buying and planting for your outdoor room, don't forget to do a little planning – it will make a huge difference to the end result. Your plan doesn't have to be set in stone; it just needs to be thought through.

Think about the eventual size of each plant you choose. If you don't give your plants enough space to grow, they will very quickly crowd each other; you can fill big gaps in between plants with temporary annual plants. Also remember changes in season. A balance of deciduous and evergreen plants will avoid leaving your garden bare and empty between seasons.

Traditional plant beds were arranged so that the tallest plants were at the back, sloping down to shortest ones at the front. While this approach allows all plants to be fully viewed, it can end up looking artificial and uninteresting. Consider adding vertical 'accents' – taller plants – towards the front to break up the monotony.

Experimenting

Before planting anything, it's worth playing musical chairs with your plants (see page 70). Don't remove them from their pots just yet. Instead, place them where you think they should go in your garden, then stand back and have a look. It's much easier to see how different colours and textures will work with one another once you have them all in front of you. What's more, the light in every garden is unique and can have a strong effect on the way colours look. Even professional gardeners won't stick to their plans once they see plants on site. In fact, changing your mind can be part of the fun.

Group all of the plants together and give them a thorough watering, leave for half an hour or so to drain. Once planting has started, stand back regularly to look and move any which you are unhappy with. Once all the plants are in, give the whole area a thorough soaking.

Planting in the ground

Almost all plants should be planted at the same depth as they were in their original container. There are two exceptions: roses and clematis.

Roses

Roses are generally 'grafted' – their roots and top growth come from two different species of rose, grown together to form a single plant. If you look at a rose bush, it's easy to see where the two plants have been joined at the base of the stem. Plant this point a few centimetres below ground, as shown below. This will allow the cultivated top part of the plant to shoot from the lowest point possible, encouraging more top-growth and giving the plant extra protection and stability at the grafting point.

1 Dig a hole larger than the root ball of the rose plant. Fork over the bottom, adding a handful of bonemeal and rose compost.

2 Place the plant in the hole so that the grafting point is a few centimetres below ground.

Clematis

Like other climbers such as sweet peas, clematis will need to be planted with a support system in place (see page 205). Clematis prefer their roots in the shade but their 'head' in the sun – that is, they thrive in sunny spots, but their roots should be kept cool and moist. Plant them fairly deeply, with the base of the stem 5–8cm below ground level. This will help prevent a fungal infection called clematis wilt, as the plants will re-shoot from below the ground even if wilt kills the top part.

3 Fill the hole with the removed soil mixed with compost and bonemeal. Firm in, water well and rake the area level.

tools materials
- **gloves**
- **spade**
- **hand trowel**
- **rake**

- bonemeal
- rose compost
- rose plant

Planting in gravel

Gravelled areas can end up looking like a car park; but it's easy to soften the look by planting through the gravel. Small trees and shrubs are ideal. Choose plants to suit the situation, and prepare the ground according to their needs: lavender, planted here, prefers a sunny spot and free-draining soil.

1 Scrape back the gravel and dig in sharp sand and/or horticultural grit to ensure adequate drainage.

2 Plant lavender or similar lovers of free-draining soil, firm in and water well.

tools materials
- **fork**
- **rake**

- gravel
- horticultural grit or sand
- plants of your choice

3 Replace the gravel, dribbling more in between the plants to cover the soil entirely.

4 Rake the gravel smooth around the plants.

Planting shrubs and perennials 203

Climbers and support systems

Climbers will add a whole new dimension to your outdoor room. They can help disguise any less attractive aspects such as a wall or fence, and are ideal for smaller spaces, easily fitting at the back of a flower bed or in front of your house, where you might not have room for a larger plant.

Wall plants or climbers?

Two kinds of plants can be used as 'climbers'. True climbers will naturally trail on any surface, vertical or horizontal. Wall plants, on the other hand, will survive perfectly well freestanding but adapt very well to being trained on a wall or vertical surface. Ivy, clematis and virginia creeper are all examples of true, self-supporting climbers. Traditional wall plants include roses and fruit trees such as cherries, peaches and apricots (see pages 244–45), though almost any small shrub or tree can be used. Both types will need to be trained to a support (see below and opposite).

Planning your vertical garden

Although climbers are easy to grow, to get the most out of them it's worth putting some thought into which you choose to grow and where.

Choosing a site
A wall, fence, the side of your house or even an old tree could provide the perfect site for growing a beautiful climbing plant. If using a wall make sure the masonry is sound and the mortar is not crumbling. Bear in mind too that climbers tend to be hungry and will grow much faster in earth that has been enriched with well-rotted compost or soil improver; the soil should drain well and be in a good, crumbly state (see page 188).

Choosing a climber
First and foremost, a climber should be chosen for the site. Very vigorous climbers such as *Clematis montana* or crimson glory vine might engulf and spoil a smaller area. On the other hand, too small and delicate a climber will look lost and lonely on a huge wall. Conditions are important too: cool, shaded sites are good for ivy, while hot, dry south-facing walls are ideal for wisteria.

Think of climbers for the different seasons. Evergreen climbers come into their own in colder months, when other plants are bare or disappear below ground. The many forms of ivy are easily overlooked in the summer, but all of a sudden they emerge as beautiful vines in their own right. Many honeysuckles are evergreen, as are some clematis. The wonderful *Clematis armandii* flowers between February and March, while passion flowers retain their leaves throughout the year if grown in sheltered spots.

You can do it...

Climbers for all seasons
When selecting climbers, be sure to blend different kinds for an extended season. If you plant *Clematis cirrhosa* for the winter, for instance, have a summer-flowering climber such as jasmine nearby. For a quick mid-summer colour boost, try planting annual climbers such as nasturtium, canary creeper, sweet pea or morning glory.

Wisteria

Training climbers

Climbers will take a couple of seasons to develop after planting. At first a climber may be unable to reach the intended support (see opposite), so temporarily direct it there by tying it to a cane using soft twine or plastic-coated wire. Tie the plant to the main support once reached, and train stems horizontally to achieve a layered covering. Let some stems grow vertically to the desired height then prune the tip to a bud facing the direction required for the new shoot. Gaps within the framework can be filled in by leaving side-shoots unpruned; these are then tied in and tip-pruned as before.

Growing climbers against a support

Climbers and wall plants need to be trained on some kind of support – left to their own devices they will sprawl and become a nuisance. Training is neither difficult nor hard work. Most people begin by tying their plants to nails or screws hammered into a wall. Though this is the simplest method, it is also the least satisfactory as it limits the directions in which the plant can grow and may even cause it to be strangled. The best system is one in which some kind of framework is put in place to which plants can be fixed as they grow, such as wire or plastic mesh attached to a wall, or a ready-made trellis panel.

Walls

Strong wire, attached to a wall horizontally along lines of vine eyes (illustrated), is especially good for roses, whose stems can be tied to it individually using soft twine or mesh support clips. Set vine eyes roughly 2m apart, with 45cm between lines, and aim for the wire to be 2.5–4cm from the wall so it's easy to tie plants to it. Tension bolts will keep wire taut. Always plant climbers about a metre away from the base of a wall to prevent excess dryness at the roots and give them room to grow.

Trellis

Trellis panels work well for most climbers and are an attractive alternative to wire. A trellis can be freestanding or attached to a solid surface of a wall or fence. Be sure to fix it firmly as large climbers can get very heavy. Bear in mind, too, that a wall or fence may one day require maintenance – if possible attach the trellis with hooks at the top and hinges at the bottom so you can swing it away when necessary. The climber can be tied to the trellis using soft twine or, better still, special trellis ties.

plant supports

Hammer-in vine eyes
Secure wire supports to walls. Can be hammered directly into mortar.

Screw-in vine eyes
Secure wire supports to wooden fences, stakes and posts.

Mesh support clips
Fix plastic mesh to walls, brickwork and fences.

Trellis, wire and lap ties
Train plants up a trellis, wires or lap fencing.

Growing climbers in a border

Climbers can be grown in beds, borders or containers using a freestanding support such as a wire obelisk as shown, or a wigwam made of bamboo canes tied together on one end. Plant clematis deep and keep their roots cool with a thick mulch. If planting in a sunny position, lay some flat stones or decorative gravel over the roots – taking care not to damage the stems – or allow leafy ground-cover plants to spread around the spot.

tools materials
- **wire obelisk**
- **garden twine**
- **garden clips**
- **flat stones, decorative gravel or other mulch**
- clematis, or other climbing plant

1 Place the obelisk over the climber and push it into the ground to firm it in.

2 Tie the shoots of the climber to the obelisk using soft twine or garden clips.

3 Water in and place flat stones or decorative gravel around the base of a clematis plant.

Bulbs for all seasons

Bulbs provide more colour, for the space they occupy, than almost any garden plant. They can be used in almost every style of planting area, whether with formal bedding, informal mixed borders, a rock garden or a wild garden. Easy to grow and widely available, bulbs will cheer up your garden for years to come.

Tulipa 'Queen of the Night' Tulip

When to find them

Mention bulbs to people and they will probably think of daffodils and tulips, which we normally associate with spring. But there are many excellent and widely available bulbs that flower in summer and autumn. In fact, from the first snowdrops in spring through to the last crocuses in autumn, you can find bulbs to flower in every month of the growing season. Almost all of them are simple to grow.

What to look for

Bulbs, along with tubers, corms and rhizomes, are storage cells from which plants grow. They differ in size, shape and the time of year when we can expect them to flower, and the way in which they are planted, but to all intents and purposes, they are the same thing. When selecting bulbs, make sure they are as fresh as possible – the smaller the bulb, the fresher it should be. In general, look for firm, hard flesh with a dry skin. If the bulb is beginning to sprout, check that the young shoots have not been knocked off. Tiny bulbs dry out quickly, so plant them as soon as you can after purchase. If you must store them for a short while, keep them somewhere cool.

Mixed border with tulips

Borders

Bulbs are ideal for filling gaps in beds and borders and are also wonderful plants in their own right. Alliums are perfect for that empty space between the last tulips of spring and the first blooms of summer – their sculptural seedheads stay intact throughout the summer months and provide a refreshing contrast to softer perennials. Galtonia flowers later and will add elegance and a welcome splash of colour just when the border is beginning to look past its best. Other examples include crocosmia, *Gladiolus byzantinus*, dahlias and flag irises.

Fritillaria meleagris Snakeshead fritillary

Lawns and meadows

You can grow many types of bulbs in a lawn or meadow, but for the best overall effect go for ones that are closest to their natural form or species. Fritillaria work well, as do smaller-flowering crocuses and daffodils. Bulbs with larger flowers such as tulips look less at home in a natural setting as they tend to appear too top-heavy.

For a natural-looking spread of flowers, take a handful of bulbs and gently scatter them, then plant them where they have fallen. Once the bulbs have flowered, let the leaves die down as naturally as possible as they will provide food for the bulb to flower the following year. Try not to mow the grass at this time, or else only mow around the areas with bulbs.

Planting bulbs

Most bulbs are planted while dormant, usually in autumn. But some, including snowdrops, are better planted or transplanted in full leaf (see page 230) – just take care not to damage their stems or leaves. The most important thing to remember is that most bulbs like to be planted deep (see below).

tools materials

- **bulb planter, trowel or dibber**
- bulbs of your choice

Tulipa 'West Point' Tulip

1 Press the bulb planter into the ground to the correct depth.

2 Remove soil from the hole and place the bulb inside, making sure it is the right way up.

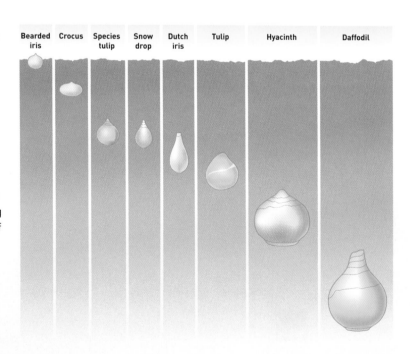

3 Break away some of the soil from the bottom of the soil core. Replace the rest of the core into the hole and firm it down level.

You can do it...

Irises
These colourful blooms grow from bulbs or rhizomes, depending on the species. Bulbs such as Dutch irises need to be planted quite deep, but rhizomes such as bearded irises will only flower if their skin is baked in the sun. Plant these on the surface of the soil with just the roots buried, and try to grow them away from too much shade.

B&Q

Where did they go?

Most bulbs pop up to flower again year after year, gradually bulking up their numbers. But sometimes people complain that their bulbs disappear, never to be seen again. This is usually caused by problems that are easy enough to avoid.

Planting at the wrong depth
It's tempting to dig a shallow hole, but in fact most bulbs need to be planted quite deep if you want them to grow year after year. As a rule of thumb, plant them at three times the depth of the bulb (see right). For instance, a daffodil's average size is 7cm, so plant it in a hole that is 21cm deep.

Too much moisture
Don't leave your bulbs sitting in waterlogged ground as this leads to rot. If your soil drains poorly, dig a planting hole that's a few extra centimetres deep and fill the bottom with grit.

Removing leaves too soon
Bulbs need their foliage for photosynthesis (see page 177), which is their only means of creating and storing energy. Without leaves, bulbs will have little chance of flowering the following year. Bulbs also need feeding after flowering, as their leaves are dying back.

Other common problems
Bulbs may also disappear if they are overcrowded, undersized or have fallen prey to pests or diseases (see pages 254–59).

Bearded iris	Crocus	Species tulip	Snow drop	Dutch iris	Tulip	Hyacinth	Daffodil

Laurus nobilis Bay tree

Pots, planters and containers

Every home, large or small, has space for a few pots. Even if your outdoor space is a tiny balcony, you can completely transform it with the help of a few plants in containers.

Why bother with pots?

Whether or not you have a garden, plants in pots are a handy addition to any outdoor space. Pots can be moved from place to place – they are perfect for protecting tender plants from harsh winters as they can be kept outside for the summer and simply moved indoors in the autumn. They allow you to add variety to your garden; for instance, if your garden is neutral or alkaline, you'll be able to grow plants that thrive in acidic soil. What's more, pots are ideal for borders. In early summer they can fill in gaps left by early-flowering perennials, or in late summer they can instantly refresh tired borders. In fact container plants can be interesting at all times of year, from winter-flowering pansies and heathers through to summer bedding and autumn-flowering bulbs.

Choosing a container

Any container can be used as a pot as long as it is big enough for the plant and provides holes for drainage. Containers come in a huge variety of shapes and styles, from sleek stainless steel to charming terracotta and rustic wood. The most important thing is for the container to be in proportion to the size of the plant: large, tall plants need bigger, heavier pots to prevent them from being blown over by the wind. Plants that require very good drainage such as *Agave americana* or echeveria are better in containers made from porous material such as terracotta. Moisture-loving plants such as hostas, however, will benefit from being grown in plastic or fibreglass containers, which require less watering than terracotta and are less susceptible to frost damage.

Which growing compost?

Commercially available composts all contain a balanced mix of chemical nutrients, except for organic products whose nutrients come from composted bark or plant residues. Wherever possible, choose peat-free composts and soil improvers (see page 190), which are now widely available: the extraction of peat is very damaging to wildlife and the environment. This table is a guide to some of the different composts available, though you will also find many more specialised formulations to suit the needs of different plants and situations.

You can do it...

Soaking it up

Terracotta pots should be soaked in a bucket of water for at least fifteen minutes before filling and planting. This is because terracotta is porous – if you leave it dry, the material will soak up every last drop of water in the compost, leaving your plants parched and thirsty from day one.

B&Q

choosing growing compost

Multi-purpose compost	Light and fluffy, with a peat base and added composted bark. Suitable for sowing and raising most plants.
Potting compost	Similar to multi-purpose compost but with added nutrients and water-holding capacity. Suitable for larger plants.
Seed-and-cutting compost	Fine-textured and very free-draining to allow fragile roots a freer run and prevent rot.
Loam-based compost	Often called John Innes, as it is produced to standard recipes drawn up by the John Innes Horticultural Institute. Based on loam or soil, with nutrients added to suit various uses, such as sowing, potting on or repotting larger plants. Heavier than non-loam composts, so can weight containers in windy areas.
Organic compost	Often based on composted bark and green waste. Usually contains a small but balanced mix of nutrients. Excellent for encouraging growth but needs supplementing with fertiliser more often than other composts. Suitable for most uses.
Hanging basket compost	Specially formulated to enhance moisture-retention and aeration.
Growing bags	Can be filled with any of the composts listed above. Crops are grown directly in the bag, rather than in a bed or container.

Planting in containers

Always leave a gap between the compost and the top of the container when planting – this will prevent compost being washed out during watering. Pot feet will raise the container off the floor, protect it from frost damage and allow water to drain freely from the bottom. When re-using a container, all old compost should be removed and the container thoroughly cleaned to avoid any pest or disease problems. Water-retaining granules and slow-release fertiliser may be added to the compost at this stage.

tools materials

- **broken crocks**
- **pot, planter or container**
- **watering can**

- container plant
- multi-purpose or potting compost
- slow-release fertiliser
- water-retaining granules

1 Place broken crocks in the bottom of the pot to ensure that the potting compost does not spill out of the hole in the bottom and to maintain good drainage.

2 If planting in spring, mix the compost with water-retaining granules and slow-release fertiliser, which will last for up to six months.

3 Place the plant in the pot and add compost around the root ball. Firm and water in.

Creating a display of summer-flowering annuals

A display of flowering annuals will look great all summer long; water it regularly, deadhead flowers once they die off and remove any weeds. Start by planting the tallest plant, followed by smaller plants around it. The leaves of trailing plants such as the ivy shown here are great for disguising the hard edge of the rim.

tools materials

- **prepared pot, planter or container**
- **trowel**
- **watering can**

- summer-flowering annuals of your choice

1 Starting with the middle of the pot and the tallest plant, make a hole using a trowel and place the plant inside, then firm in.

2 Plant more plants around the edges, starting with the largest ones first.

3 Continue to fill the spaces with more plants until all the gaps are filled.

4 Water thoroughly and place the container in a sheltered, lightly shaded position for a week or two until it becomes established. Do not allow it to dry out.

Plant supports

Some container plants such as sweet peas and clematis are climbers. These will need to be planted with a support in place (see page 205).

Hanging
baskets

Hanging baskets will brighten up any outdoor space. You can use all sorts of plants, so it's easy to create interesting and colourful displays.

When to plant

Late spring is the best time to plant summer bedding in baskets and planters. This gives plants a few weeks to establish, so they will give you instant impact when you hang them up outdoors. Keep your plants somewhere frost-free until it's safe to move them outdoors; if this isn't possible, then wait until all risk of frost has passed before planting. If the plants are not tender, then it should be fine to plant them mid-spring, when they will start to grow properly. Winter displays should be planted in autumn, at the same time as spring-flowering bulbs.

Baskets

Hanging baskets come in many styles. Traditional plastic-coated wire will need to be lined, as will wicker. Solid-sided baskets in terracotta, ceramic or even polished steel have built-in water reservoirs and are ideal for hot, exposed conditions.

Making up a hanging basket

Regular watering and feeding is the key to successful hanging baskets. You can either buy specially formulated compost or improve on multi-purpose compost by adding water-retaining granules and slow-release fertiliser, which will help keep the plants moist and nourished (see Caring for hanging baskets, opposite). Make sure the plants you are using are well watered when planting.

tools materials

- **wire basket**
- **gloves**
- **watering can**

- liner
- multi-purpose or hanging basket compost
- water-retaining granules
- slow-release fertiliser
- plants of your choice

Ivy-leaved geranium, trailing petunia and trailing lobelia

1 Place the liner (see Liners, opposite) in the basket and half-fill it with compost.

2 For the sides of the basket, gently push the roots of trailing plants through the liner and firm them into the compost. Do this all the way around the outside of the basket.

3 Plant the middle and top of the basket with the other plants and firm more compost around the root balls, keeping the level a few centimetres below the top of the basket to allow room for watering. Water in.

You can do it...

Nice and steady

To stop a hanging basket from rolling about while you're planting it, stand it on a bucket, pot or even a small saucepan.

B&Q

Hanging a basket from a wall

A fully planted basket, and especially one that has just been watered, is surprisingly heavy to support, so make extra sure that the bracket holding up your hanging basket is securely attached to the wall. Hang baskets well above head height to avoid accidents, and consider installing a pulley system to raise and lower them – this will make baskets easier to care for.

tools materials
- **bracket**
- **pencil**
- **spirit level**
- **power drill with hammer action**
- **wall plugs**
- **screws**

- hanging basket, fully prepared

1 Mark the fixing holes in pencil and check they are vertical with a spirit level. Drill into the brick, not the mortar.

2 Insert the right-sized wall plugs for the hole and screws. Fix the bracket to the wall and check that it is firmly attached.

3 Hang the basket to the bracket using the chains.

ideal tool

Watering wand
This long-reach hose attachment with a shower-head sprayer is an ideal tool for watering hard-to-reach areas such as hanging baskets.

Plants for hanging baskets

Almost any small plant can be used for a hanging basket, provided it doesn't outgrow its container.
- **Spring and summer bedding plants** The most common plants used for hanging baskets (see pages 212–13). They can also be interplanted with bulbs.
- **Young, small shrubs** Grow these temporarily. For instance, place evergreen hebes in hanging baskets to provide colour throughout the winter, and then pot them out into the garden in the spring.
- **Herbs** Keep herbs such as basil and thyme handy for cooking by hanging them just by the kitchen door.
- **Tomatoes** Trailing varieties are perfect for hanging baskets (see page 284).
- **Strawberries** Like tomatoes, an interesting edible addition to a hanging garden.

Mixed herbs

Liners

Liners retain moisture and keep compost from falling out of container holes. Until recently, most wire hanging baskets were lined with moss; this was often collected from the wild, which harmed the environment by stripping naturally occurring varieties of moss from their local habitat. Nowadays gathering moss from the wild is illegal and many gardeners are turning to alternative materials such as coconut fibre and wool fleece. Purpose-made options include thick, felt-like liners made from recycled fibres, and solid liners, which with care should last for several seasons. If you opt for the solid kind, check that it's deep enough for your chosen basket.

Caring for hanging baskets

Hanging baskets need water, water and more water (see pages 250–52). Even with the help of water-retaining granules in the compost, they dry out incredibly quickly. You will need to water them at least daily, and often twice a day at the height of summer. Feeding is also extremely important – the average planter or basket contains only a small amount of compost relative to the amount of plant growth it supports, and nutrients will quickly become depleted. Slow-release fertiliser comes in granules, sticks and nuggets that you can easily push into the compost – these are fantastic in the long-term, as opposed to liquid feeds which give plants an instant lift but need to be dosed regularly. As with all annuals and perennials, regular deadheading will prolong flowering and should be done weekly.

Bedding plants

Planting out bedding is as near as you can get to instant gardening. Easy to grow, bright and cheerful for most of the year, bedding plants will transform your garden into a glorious colourful display, whatever its size or style.

Impatiens 'New Guinea' Busy lizzie

What is bedding for?

Bedding plants will give your garden an instant lift. They let you update your outdoor room year after year, and are great for adding colour to permanent planting including shrubs, grasses and heathers. Plant them in groups or drifts in between perennials and shrubs, rather than as individuals.

Great fun can be had with bedding – even children can join in. Bedding plants can be arranged together in any way imaginable, so you can use them to create a living painting in a way that isn't really possible with any other form of planting.

What is bedding?

Technically, 'bedding' simply means setting plants out in beds. In terms of garden design, this is as close as you get to decorating surfaces, though instead of wallpapers or fabrics you use plants. Most bedding plants are annuals and therefore short-term, planted and removed within a single season. They are bought as small, established plants grown from seed and sold in trays.

Buying bedding

First decide which plants are most likely to thrive in the conditions of your garden so that your display does not let you down (see page 198). When choosing which plants to buy, look for healthy plants that are not showing too much flower and have plenty of roots so that they are firm in their pots or strips, without being too pot-bound (see page 200). Also resist the temptation to buy tender material too early, as you may risk losing all to frost.

Planting bedding

Always add extra soil improver to a plot when preparing a site for bedding. Summer bedding (see table below) is tender and should be planted out after all risk of frost has passed. Spring bedding can be planted either in autumn or very early spring.

tools materials

- **trowel**
- **watering can with rose**

- bedding plants
- soil improver
- general-purpose fertiliser

1 Water the bedding plants well while still in their original tray or container.

2 Lift each plant from its tray and plant it out into a plot that has been prepared with fertiliser and soil improver.

All year round

Bedding can provide colour in any season. Plants followed by an asterisk (*) are especially long-flowering.

Caring for bedding displays

Bedding plants generally germinate, grow and flower all in one year. If your soil is in good condition and has been enriched with soil improver and fertiliser before planting, bedding will thrive with minimal feeding. However, plants in containers will need to be fed frequently. Because of the lush, soft texture of most bedding, it is particularly susceptible to slug damage. This can be controlled in many ways (see page 255).

Keep bedding plants well watered throughout the summer. To make watering easier, you might want to install an automatic watering system controlled by a timer (see pages 251–52). When summer is over (usually after the first frost), bedding can be taken up and composted. It's best to clear and dig over the ground while it is still warm and before it becomes too wet. If you are planning to follow up with spring bedding, strip out summer plants by late September to early October. Spring bedding should need little or no fertiliser as there should be plenty left over from the summer.

bedding for different seasons			
Season		**What is it?**	**Recommended**
Spring		Almost as universal as summer bedding, this is set out in autumn and will slowly develop during winter to provide a dazzling climax in spring. Bulbs such as tulips are perfect for spring bedding, especially if accompanied by wallflowers.	Arabis Bellis daisies Forget-me-nots Polyanthus Primroses Primulas Spring-flowering bulbs (e.g. tulips) Wallflowers
Summer		The most popular and familiar kind of bedding, this may be a single flower bed or an entire garden given over to massed plants. Often with very strong colours, summer bedding will provide a beautiful display from early June until the first frost if properly maintained.	African and French marigolds Alyssums Antirrhinums Begonias Busy lizzies* Lobelias* Nasturtiums* Nicotiana* Pelargoniums* Petunias* Salvia
Autumn and winter		Though naturally a quiet time in the garden, you can ensure a little colour and plenty of greenery with a small collection of winter bulbs and other flowers.	Early-flowering bulbs (e.g. scilla, winter aconite, crocuses, snowdrops) Heathers Ivies Ivy-leaved cyclamens Winter-flowering pansies*

House plants

House plants are beautiful living ornaments that will add colour and interest to any interior, whether in a traditional country cottage or a chic, modern apartment. There are plant species that have adapted to survive in almost any environment, so you can find a plant for every room. And it's not nearly as difficult to keep them happy and healthy as many people think.

The value of house plants

Greenery and flowers make any indoor space feel more natural and welcoming, especially if a little thought has gone into how they are arranged. There are plenty of plant species that require only a minimum of attention to thrive. What's more, house plants can act as a natural air purifier for your home or office: in the process of photosynthesis (see page 177) plants gently cleanse the air around us, absorbing carbon dioxide and releasing oxygen during daylight hours.

Saintpaulia African violet

Aloe vera Medicinal aloe

Choosing house plants

Do you want to spend time tending your plants or would you prefer varieties that will largely take care of themselves? The bird-of-paradise plant, for instance, will provide a wonderfully exotic splash of colour but does require a bit of looking after. Less demanding but equally dramatic are orchids: the choice is vast and they will flower for weeks, and often months, on end – watering once or twice a week, feeding every three weeks during active growth and occasional misting will help them thrive. For easy-care but stylish options, consider succulents such as aloes, cacti or mother-in-law's tongue.

When selecting plants to buy, look for well-balanced, even growth and reject lopsided plants. Check that the leaves and stems are healthy and undamaged; remember also to look for signs of disease on the undersides of the leaves.

Sansevieria trifasciata Mother-in-law's tongue

Where to put them

There are some general guidelines to follow when choosing a spot for your house plants.

- Never put a plant directly above a radiator as the heat will quickly dry out the leaves and flowers.
- Place plants away from draughts – most plants prefer constant temperatures.
- Avoid direct sunlight. Most foliage plants thrive in bright but filtered light; strong sun will scorch the leaves. The exception to this is succulents such as aloe vera, which come from hotter climates than ours, and flowering house plants, which require more light than leafier plants.
- If there is only one light source, remember to rotate plants regularly or they will become lopsided.
- Do not leave plants on window sills behind curtains at night – it gets too cold.

Plants for the bathroom

The bathroom not only tends to be quite a shady room in many houses, but it is also prone to extremes in temperature, swinging between hot and steamy and cold and draughty. Surprisingly, however, there are many plants that thrive in these conditions. India rubber plants, ferns and aspidistras all provide lush, tropical foliage and will happily survive in most bathrooms.

Outdoors for the summer

Your house plants will be fine spending the summer months outside, provided they are in a sheltered spot away from too much direct sunlight. Just remember to bring them inside again before the first frost. It can be a good idea to water in a dose of vine weevil control to prevent these pests infesting the roots. Other pests including aphids, woolly aphids, scale insects and red spider mite (see page 258) can also attack house plants, so keep a careful eye on them; you may need to spray them with specially formulated house-plant insecticide if they succumb.

Caring for house plants

Making house plants thrive doesn't require a vast reserve of skill or knowledge, just a grasp of a few basic principles.

Watering

The larger the leaves and flowers, the more water a plant will usually need. But different species require different amounts of water, so make sure you have this information when you buy. Bear in mind that plants' watering requirements also vary depending on the season: cut back watering by half during the winter, when growth slows right down or stops. Rather than water from above it is better to place the plant in a shallow tray of water for half an hour or so and allow the compost to draw up the moisture it needs (but don't leave the pot permanently standing in water). As with outdoor plants, a thorough soaking once in a while is better than a regular dribble (see pages 250–51). To avoid overwatering, wait until the compost is nearly dry; it will turn a lighter brown as it dries out. Try not to wet the leaves of furry-leaved plants or succulents such as cacti because this will encourage rot.

Feeding

Most house plants never truly stop growing and still need at least some feeding. Avoid general-purpose fertiliser. Instead, use specially formulated house-plant fertiliser, either as a liquid or slow-release solid inserted into the potting compost. Feeding should begin in the spring and continue through the summer months before cutting down to allow for the plant's natural slowdown in growth over the winter.

Raising humidity

Many large-leaved house plants originate from lush tropical forests, and you will need to reproduce that environment if they are to thrive. The first step is to raise humidity levels around them; placing the plants upon a shallow dish or tray filled with either gravel or clay pebbles and always keeping this moist will be more than adequate. Occasional misting, particularly for plants such as maidenhair fern, is also vital. Don't, however, spray cacti or plants with hairy leaves, as this may lead to rot.

Adiantum capillus-veneris Maidenhair fern

Trimming, cleaning and repotting

Removing dead leaves and flowers will not only keep your plants looking tidy, it will also help ward off pests and disease. You should also not allow house dust and grime to build up on the leaves, as this will block the tiny pores through which moisture needs to pass (see page 177). Use a soft brush to dust foliage, or gently wipe big leaves with a damp, lint-free cloth.

Most house plants will eventually outgrow their pots and will need to be repotted if their roots are not to become constricted and pot-bound (see page 200). Resist the urge to do this too often, though, as this may encourage them to outgrow your home! Always repot in the spring, using a house-plant (not general-purpose) potting compost, and replant into a container that is one or at most two sizes bigger than the existing one. For plants that produce offsets – that is, small baby plants that develop around the base of a plant – these can be cut away and planted in a separate pot.

Tools for house plants

Caring for house plants doesn't require specialist tools, but it can still be very convenient to keep a few to hand.

Small watering can

A small-sized can, with a long, slender spout, is ideal for watering indoors. Store this with your plants and you are much less likely to forget to water.

Hand-held sprayer

Tropical plants love a humid environment, which you can create at home using a hand-held sprayer. Hanging or trailing house plants that are exposed to drying air from all sides will also benefit from being misted with a sprayer.

Trowels, secateurs and fork

Smaller versions of garden tools are handy for repotting and trimming house plants.

Pond plants
and bog plants

A pond is a lot more than a pool of water. It can attract a wonderful variety of wildlife that will benefit the garden, and also lets you grow a completely different group of plants.

Planting for a healthy pond

As well as giving us something to look at, plants are vital for a pond's health. A pond is a self-contained unit and has no flow of fresh water, so it can very quickly become stagnant and smelly. This is caused by algae and a lack of oxygen. Large-leaved plants such as waterlilies will discourage algae growth by blocking sunlight. Oxygenating weeds will encourage fish and other pond-life to thrive; usually sold as pre-tied bunches, these plants can either be dropped into the pond as they are or attached to a blunt weight that will not damage the liner.

Different types – what grows in and out of the water?

Water or aquatic plants are divided into three categories. These relate to the depth of water at which they can be planted:

- **Marginal plants**, as their name suggests, are planted at the edge of a pond where the water is usually no more than a few centimetres deep.
- **Submerged plants** can either be oxygenators such as *Lagarosiphon major* (also known as *Elodea crispa*) which are merely dropped into the pond, or plants in pots which are placed deeper within the pond.
- **Deepwater aquatics** are planted deeper still. These include Cape pondweed (*Aponogeton distachyos*), which has fragrant white flowers which float on the surface.

All water plants should have guidelines attached when you buy them. Read these to find out their ideal planting depth.

Planting at different depths

All one depth?

Even if the pond is all one depth, this doesn't limit what plants you can grow – you can bring plants up to the required level with the help of plinths to stand them on. These can be as simple as an upside-down plant pot or a stack of bricks; anything sturdy will do as long as it won't puncture the liner, although if in doubt you might want to lay a piece of pond underlay or surplus liner underneath. Just make sure the plant is stable enough to withstand being rocked by the wind.

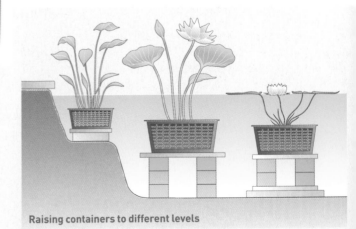

Raising containers to different levels

Not quite pond plants

Bog plants are often grouped in with pond plants because they too love moisture. But even though some of the smaller species can be planted as marginals, it's best to keep them apart – bog plants are rather aggressive and can quickly take over a pond. To give the area around your pond a natural look, dig it down to 40cm or so, line it with either surplus pond liner or polythene (old compost bags will do), puncture holes in the liner and refill it with soil enriched with garden compost or soil improver. This will be your bog garden; located right by your pond, it will retain moisture while avoiding the problems linked with planting in the pond itself.

Carex elata 'Aurea' Sedge

Repotting pond plants

Unlike other containers, pond plant baskets are open and sided with mesh to allow the roots to spread out into the water. As with all plants, pond plants will need repotting and/or dividing to maintain optimum growth and to prevent the pond becoming congested. This is best done in early spring. Clumps of waterlilies can be cut directly from the pond, while plants in baskets will normally have to be cut away from their containers. Always use a sharp knife when cutting and take care not to puncture the pond liner or cut through any growth buds.

tools materials

- **sharp knife**
- **rubber gloves**

- bucket of fresh water
- pond plant baskets
- aquatic compost
- galvanised wire
- horticultural grit

1 For waterlilies, cut a clump directly from the pond. Remove other kinds of pond plant from their basket – either cut them away or if possible tip them out.

2 Split the clump into smaller pieces, ensuring that each piece has a growth bud or leaves.

3 Dunk the plant sections into a bucket of water and give them a good wash so that you can see what you are working with.

4 Repot the clumps into new baskets using aquatic compost.

5 To prevent a plant from being loosened from the basket by the water, take a short length of galvanised wire and bend it into a hoop, then secure the plant by pushing the wire into the aquatic compost.

6 Cover the surface of the compost with horticultural grit to stop the compost from floating in the water and deter fish from rooting out the plants.

7 Gently lower the basket back into the pond.

eco planting

Aquatic compost
Always use aquatic compost for pond plants, never ordinary potting compost or garden soil. Aquatic compost is special soil-based compost with no added fertilisers or pesticides, which could pollute the pond water.

Leigustrum ovalifolium Privet

Choosing and planting a hedge

Hedges are normally used as a boundary between gardens, but they can do much more. A well chosen hedging plant can define the style of your garden. Hedges can also create a sense of different areas within a larger space, and be used to surround beds and borders.

Why a hedge?

As a boundary, hedges will absorb surrounding noise and pollution. They will outlive a fence by many years if well looked after, and can also be a habitat for wildlife. What's more, hedges can improve security – it's easy enough to scale a fence, but a lot trickier to get past a large, spiny bush.

Which plants?

In theory any plant can be used as a 'hedge', which just means a row of plants (usually all the same species) that is used to break up or define a space. Even so, some plants make better hedges than others. It all depends on where you plant them and what role you want them to play in your outdoor room.

Maintenance

Consider how much time you are willing to spend maintaining a hedge. Yew is perfect for bringing formal structure to a garden, but can take many years to establish; *Thuja plicata* gives much the same feel but will establish more quickly. Both require only one yearly trim, unlike the notorious Leyland cypress which needs almost constant attention – as many as three cuts a year – to keep it within the bounds of the average garden.

Size

Low hedges such as lavender will emphasise the design of a formal outdoor space such as a knot or ornamental flower garden. For screening purposes, taller hedges are needed – they must grow to at least 1.5–2m to give privacy.

Containers or bare roots?

Common hedging plants such as hornbeam, yew and beech can be bought both bare-root and containerised. Others such as lavender and box are more commonly found in pots.

Bare-root plants are grown in a nursery's ground, then dug up and sold as they are. This means they are only available during the dormant season. Because they are relatively cheap to grow, they tend to be less expensive than their pot-grown counterparts. Don't be fooled by their low price, though – it isn't a reflection of lower quality. You will actually be getting larger, older plants for your money, and this makes bare-root hedges a particularly smart choice if you're planting a particularly long hedge or want an instant 'hedge effect'.

When to plant them

Because a hedge defines the structure and layout of a garden, it is best to plant it before any other plants. However, this is really only possible for a completely new garden. To plant a hedge in an established garden, clear as much space around the proposed site as possible – this makes working much easier and minimises potential damage to other plants. It is best to plant during the dormant season; this reduces both stress to the plants and the amount of immediate care they require. Even so, containerised plants can be planted at any time of the year, though remember that they will need regular watering if planted during the growing period.

Beech hedge in summer

Beech hedge in winter

Screening

The level of privacy you can achieve with a hedge will depend on your choice of plant. Evergreens such as yew, holly and *Thuja plicata* will provide year-round screening as they retain their leaves through every season. Most deciduous plants, on the other hand, lose their leaves in winter – though in the case of beech, they turn brown but don't fall. The changing appearance of a deciduous hedge from season to season can be very attractive, from energetic budding in spring to lush summer growth and autumn colour, and finally the patterns of bare twigs and branches.

Preparing to plant a new hedge

A hedge is a permanent feature so give it the best chance of flourishing by planting it in really well-prepared soil. It's crucial to mark out its position before planting – this will allow you to change your mind before committing yourself, and will also ensure your hedge is straight.

tools materials
- **builder's line**
- **spade**
- **garden fork**
- **turfing iron**
- **wheelbarrow**

- canes
- soil improver
- general-purpose fertiliser

1 With two string lines spaced 60cm apart, mark and stake out the position for the hedge.

2 Slice the turf into manageable-sized pieces with a turfing iron and remove with a spade.

3 Beginning with a small section, break up the bottom of the trench using a garden fork. Put a good layer of soil improver in the bottom of the trench.

4 Dig the next section of the trench but place the soil upon the top of the first section. Repeat this for the rest of the trench.

5 Once you've reached the end of the trench, tip the soil removed from the first section on top of the last one.

6 Fork in a generous amount of general-purpose fertiliser.

Planting a bare-root hedge

Stretch a string line down the centre of the trench to mark the planting line. Position hedge plants about 50cm apart. You can save time measuring out the distance between plants by marking it on a cane and using this to show the space needed between each plant.

tools materials
- **builder's line and pegs**
- **spade**
- **wheelbarrow**

- cane
- bare-root hedge plants
- mulch

1 Plant the first hedge plant about 25cm in from the beginning of the line. Position the remaining plants 50cm apart along the line.

2 Give the soil a thorough soak and then mulch. Take care not to mulch right up to the stems.

You can do it...

Heeling in

If bad weather forces you to delay planting out bare-root plants, you can temporarily 'heel' them into a spare patch of ground. Dig a shallow trench, lay the plants in and cover their roots with soil. This will protect the roots from frost and prevent them drying out.

B&Q

Choosing trees
for your garden

Trees have a special charm and character of their own. They add a dimension to a garden that cannot be achieved with anything else. Whether they're evergreen or deciduous, ornamental or fruiting, full-size or dwarf, trees will give your outdoor room a fantastic focal point.

Size

Many gardens aren't large enough for more than one or two mature trees; and choosing from the many hundreds of species available can be a tricky task. It's often easier to start by eliminating those that aren't suitable. The starting point for most people is size: trees that will eventually become very large shouldn't be planted in an average-sized garden. They may be fine for twenty or thirty years, but one of the best things about trees is their long lifespan. It would be a shame to destroy a tree after a couple of decades simply because it has grown too big – it's much better to grow a smaller tree to maturity.

Purpose

Do you want a tree to screen a neighbouring house? To provide shade during the summer months? Or fruit? Or to add to the style of your garden? If your aim is to hide an unsightly view or provide privacy, a conifer will do that all year round. But there are other evergreen trees and shrubs that offer greater year-round interest, such as the strawberry tree (*Arbutus unedo*, see page 294) – although it may need a bit of protection from cold winds for a couple of years, thereafter it will be fully hardy.

Shape

No matter what type or size of garden you have, there is a tree that will fit and complement the style. To choose a tree perfectly suited to your needs, you need to consider not only the height; the width and shape are important too.

- **Fastigiate** means the branches grow vertically, almost in line with the trunk, so the tree takes up very little sideways room.
- **Pyramidal** or **conical** trees are wider at the bottom, tapering to a pointed top.
- **Round** or **spreading** is what we often think of as the typical, normal tree shape. All the large native trees, such as beech, ash and oak, are this shape. Many ornamentals are this shape too, though nowhere near as large.
- **Upright** or **columnar** trees are tall and thin. They are often used by garden designers to provide a living exclamation mark, particularly in Italian-style gardens.
- **Weeping** trees have long branches that drape to the ground. The weeping willow is the most familiar, though most varieties of this are much too large for the average garden. A better choice is an ornamental variety such as the weeping willow-leaved pear (*Pyrus salicifolia* 'Pendula', see page 295).

see page 294

You can do it...

A safe distance
Don't plant trees that will grow tall too close to your house. Their roots will undermine the foundations and cause structural problems. As a general rule, the diameter of a tree's roots are equal to its height – a tree 3m tall will have a 3m root run all round.

B&Q

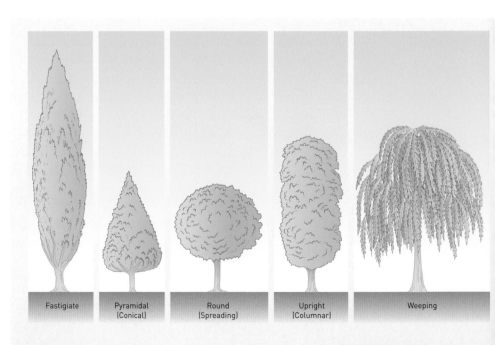

Fastigiate Pyramidal (Conical) Round (Spreading) Upright (Columnar) Weeping

What trees bring to a garden

The various characteristics of trees act as accent points in gardens and planting schemes. The texture and colour of foliage, blossom, bark, berries or fruit can all serve as a seasonal focus.

Blossom

No trees announce spring more exuberantly than ornamental cherries. Amelanchiers have more subtle spring blossom, plus glorious autumn colour. In winter, the sweetly scented yellow flowers of mimosa (*Acacia dealbata*) are unrivalled.

Berries and fruit

Fruit and berries add colours and shapes. No need to restrict your choice – why not plant a quince, mulberry or medlar?

Bark

Silver birch has an iridescent glow in winter. Paper-bark and snake-bark maples add a touch of interest when little else is present in the garden. The strawberry tree and many eucalyptuses have wonderful peeling bark.

Screening

Deciduous trees can give cover for sunbathing but let in winter light. For year-round privacy, plant holly, yew or conifers.

Buying a new tree

Container-grown trees are available for buying and planting all year round. The cost of the largest ones, found at specialist nurseries, may cause a deep intake of breath. But, although they are pricey, the balance between cost and waiting for quite a few years for a smaller, cheaper one to catch up is a fine one; large specimens give an instant sense of maturity to even the newest of gardens.

If you do decide to go for a big tree, getting it home shouldn't be a problem, as most nurseries will deliver – but getting it into the garden and planted may be more problematic. Before ordering, make sure your garden has adequate access, bearing in mind the size of the tree. Bare-root or field-grown trees are often larger and cheaper than trees grown in containers, and you may be able to pick one out and have it dug up specially for you. However, these can only be planted during the dormant season, from October/November to February/March.

Understanding nursery terminology

- **Whip** A year-old tree. Quite literally just a single upright whip-like growth, with no side shoots or branches. If you are planting a large area, such as a copse, this is the most economical type of tree to buy.
- **Feathered whip** As above, but a little older and with lateral shoots, giving the beginnings of a structured, recognisable tree shape.
- **Bush** A tree with little or no trunk, with branches growing most of the way down to the ground. Not the best shape to plant in a lawn, as mowing beneath the branches is difficult.
- **Standard/half-standard** A tree with the lower branches removed, to form a 'head' of branches with a bare trunk below it. A standard is taller than a half-standard.

What to look for

As when buying other plants, always go for the healthy one, even if it's smaller. Reject any that are sickly-looking or pot-bound (see page 200), or infected with pests or disease (see pages 256–59). As with other plants, it's vital to check that the tree's preferred site and soil conditions match those of its intended position. If you're buying a large tree, take a good look at the shape. If the one that appeals to you needs a little snipped off here and there, no problem – but if entire branches need lopping in order to make it right for your garden, then it is the wrong tree.

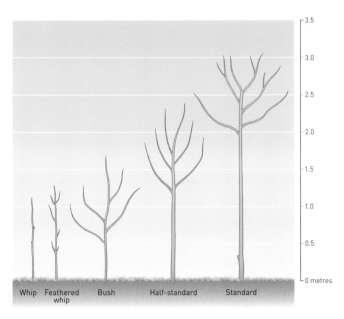

Whip Feathered whip Bush Half-standard Standard

3.5
3.0
2.5
2.0
1.5
1.0
0.5
0 metres

Juglans regia Walnut tree

Planting trees

There is something very satisfying about planting a tree. Not least is the knowledge that it will be enjoyed by future generations and that you're investing in the planet. Making sure the tree is planted properly is well worth the effort, so it gets off to the best possible start.

Marking the site

Although planting a tree varies little from any other planting, it's vital to get the position right as moving a semi-established tree is difficult and could even kill it.

Once you've decided where to plant the tree, the next step is to mark out the site. For the first few years, a new tree should stand in an area of bare or mulched soil about 1m across – in effect its own small bed.

Deciding where to plant

Before planting, place the tree – still in its container – in your chosen spot. Then stand back and try to visualise it as a fully grown tree. Will it block views you want to retain? How much shade will it cast and where? Will its roots interfere with drains or the foundations of buildings? Avoid planting beneath power or telephone cables; if the tree damages them, you may have to pay for repairs.

Improving the soil

Any drainage problems need to be dealt with before you plant the tree, either by working in grit and soil improver or in more severe cases by piping excess water away (see page 197). During winter months, avoid planting in waterlogged soil.

To get a tree off to a good start, enrich the ground with soil improver and bonemeal fertiliser – plus grit if needed.

1 Having decided where to plant the tree, cut a 50cm length of string and tie a strong cane at one end and a shorter stick at the other. Insert the cane firmly into the ground, then pull the string taut and mark a circle with the other stick.

2 Use a sharp edging iron to cut round the circle. To get a neat edge, cut with a see-saw action and push the iron round the circle without ever removing it entirely from the ground.

1 Remove the turf with a spade. To avoid damaging the edge of the circle, start at the centre and work outwards. If you want to re-use the turf, maintain an even thickness of 5cm as you slice it off.

2 Dig out soil from the centre of the circle, leaving a 10–15cm ring of undug soil around the hole. Place the removed soil in a wheelbarrow.

3 Mix in soil improver and a good handful of bonemeal to promote strong root growth.

tools materials
- **gloves**
- **strong cane**
- **short stick**
- **string**
- **edging iron**
- **garden fork**
- **spade**
- **wheelbarrow**

- bonemeal
- soil improver
- horticultural grit, if required

1 Firmly hammer in a stake, positioning it so that it will be beside the root ball.

5 Water thoroughly, then mulch to conserve water and suppress weed growth. Keep the area around the trunk clear of weeds and grass for at least three years after planting, as they will rob the soil of nutrients vital for the tree's development.

Planting and staking

Young trees need supporting – not only to ensure they don't break or get damaged in high winds, but also to keep the trunk growing straight. If unsupported, they will bend and grow at the angle of the prevailing wind.

2 Inspect the tree and, using sharp secateurs, trim away any shoots that are dead or facing towards the stake or crossing.

3 Remove the tree from its container, then gently tease out the edges of the root ball. This encourages the roots to grow out into the soil.

tools materials

- **gloves**
- **club hammer**
- **secateurs**
- **cane**
- **spade**
- **wheelbarrow**
- **watering can or garden hose**

- new tree
- stake
- tree ties
- mulch

4 Position the tree in the hole, placing a cane across the hole to act as a depth guide. Fill with soil from the wheelbarrow and firm in, making sure the top of the root ball is level with the ground. Attach the tree to the stake with tree ties.

Staking on windy sites

Some form of support is vital for young trees – without support, they quickly blow over and snap. Instead of using a single vertical stake, some gardeners prefer to use a shorter angled one. This allows the trunk to bend slightly with the breeze, rather than staying totally rigid. Swaying can actually promote trunk growth, making for a stronger, faster-growing tree.

In particularly windy or exposed areas, it's safer to use a double stake. This consists of two stakes hammered side by side into the ground. One or two horizontal braces are then screwed to the posts, and the tree is tied to the braces.

You can do it...

Minimising damage

Fit a mesh or fibre guard around the lower part of the trunk of a young tree to protect it from squirrels and rabbits, who love chewing off the bark. A guard will also deter cats from using your tree as a scratching post.

B&Q

Angled stake

Double stake

Growing from seed

Small acorns grow into mighty oaks, or so the saying goes. The fact that a tiny seed can produce a full-sized plant is just part of the fascination of raising plants from seed. Seeds can also save you money and extend the range of plants you are able to grow.

Why bother?

With good-quality plants so readily and cheaply available, it's a wonder anyone takes the trouble to grow plants from seed. Yet year after year hundreds of thousands of seeds are bought and grown. What makes it worthwhile?

- **Budget** Planting a large area with annual bedding is bound to be costly. A few packets of seeds, plus some bags of compost and a little patience, can lead to big savings.
- **Variety** Plant suppliers tend to stock plants with mass appeal, whereas seed catalogues feature a much greater range of species. Many of these are rarely available elsewhere – including a large selection of interesting vegetables.
- **Satisfaction** Watching a tiny seedling emerge from a dry wrinkled seed then transform itself into a mature plant, and knowing you have nurtured it at every stage, gives a feeling of satisfaction that is hard to beat.

How many?

Sow seeds sparingly. More seeds die from being overcrowded than for any other reason. Even if they all germinate, competition from densely crowded neighbours will keep them from growing properly, and they will either die or become leggy as they struggle to grow taller than the others. What's more, seeds sown too thickly are vulnerable to 'damping off' (see page 259), a fungal disease caused by lack of air circulation, too much water and not paying attention to hygiene – using dirty containers or re-using old compost are common mistakes.

Timing

Always look at the instructions on the packet to find out when to plant your seeds. As a general rule, sow annuals in late winter or early spring, depending on how and where you plan to grow them. A heated greenhouse or propagator is best for early sowing. Otherwise, wait until the middle or end of March, as a seed planted in cold, damp conditions will rot in the compost before it even has a chance to germinate.

Hardy annuals

Some annuals – 'hardy annuals' – can be sown directly into the ground outdoors. With these you can time sowing to make the most of your garden. For instance, if your border tends to look a bit sparse in August, simply sow seeds for a plant that normally flowers in June a few weeks later than it says on the packet.

For earlier blooms, sow hardy annuals outdoors in late summer the previous year. They'll remain dormant over the winter but produce bigger, stronger plants the following year. Better still, they will flower as much as a month earlier than if you had waited until spring to sow them.

How deep?

Sowing depth depends on seed size. The bigger the seed, the deeper you should sow it – but avoid covering it with compost deeper than its own size. Some of the smallest seeds need to be scattered on the surface of the compost and not covered at all.

Many seeds require light in order to germinate. Either sow these directly on the surface or cover them lightly with vermiculite – sponge-like granules that let light in but prevent the seeds from drying out or floating off during watering.

Watering

Seeds need to absorb moisture to sprout. Presoaking the larger and harder ones overnight before planting may speed up the process. When watering seeds, whether for the first time or as they begin to grow, don't water with a watering can as this may cause them to be washed away. Either use a fine spray from a multi-function gun (see page 250) or soak them by placing their tray in water, which will also draw the seeds into the compost.

ideal tool

Dibber

Whether wood, steel or plastic, a dibber is ideal for making holes for small to medium-sized seedlings and bulbs. Push it into the soil, work it around to make a conical hole, drop in the seedling or bulb, and cover.

Sowing

Small seeds are prone to drying out and can float away during watering, so take care when planting and wetting them. It's always best to use compost specially formulated for sowing seeds, as this is designed to provide just the right balance of nutrients for seedlings in their first few weeks of life.

tools materials
- **seed tray**
- **tamper**
- **folded piece of paper**
- **sieve**
- **shallow tray of water**

- seeds of your choice
- seed-and-cutting compost

1 Fill a seed tray with compost, then level the surface by running a piece of wood over it to scrape off the excess.

2 Using a tamper (see right), gently tamp down the compost to level the surface.

3 Place smaller seeds inside a folded piece of paper and sprinkle them evenly over the compost. Larger seeds can be planted individually.

4 Sieve compost over the seeds so they lie at the correct depth below the surface.

5 Stand the seed tray in a shallow tray of water. This draws the seeds down into the compost, instead of washing them out, which a watering can may do.

B&Q

Where to grow seeds

Keeping them warm

A heated greenhouse is the ideal place for sowing seeds, but not everyone has one. The next best thing is a rigid plastic propagator, large enough to accommodate one or two seed trays; some come with a heater at the bottom that plugs into mains electricity. A sunny window sill will also do – but take care to turn pots regularly, or the seedlings will grow towards the light and become weak and spindly. If the weather is warm enough, a coldframe – a wooden frame with a glass top (see page 284) – or a cloche (transparent cover), placed over a spare patch of ground, will often provide sufficient protection for seeds to grow outside.

Hardening off

Unless seeds are sown outdoors, they will need to get used to being outside before being planted there. Otherwise, the sudden change in temperature may kill them. If you have grown them indoors or in a greenhouse, either place the seedlings outside in a sunny spot for part of the day or transfer them to a coldframe. If they are in a coldframe, open the top a little at a time, for a bit longer each day.

Gradually increase the time the seedlings spend in the open, and finally plant them out after the last frost.

Fuchsia 'Tom Thumb' Fuchsia

Growing
from cuttings

Growing new plants from other plants is one of the most satisfying bits of gardening. We all like getting something for nothing, and this is exactly what cuttings provide – free plants. Here are some of the many different ways of doing this.

Softwood cuttings

Also known as tip or stem-tip cuttings, softwood cuttings are an easy and highly successful way to grow new plants from shrubs, house plants and herbaceous perennials. Cuttings are taken from soft shoot tips below a leaf node – where new growth starts from an existing stem. These then grow roots when planted.

It's generally best to take softwood cuttings in mid-summer, before the current year's growth hardens off. Tuberous plants are an exception to this – dahlias, for example, start into growth in late February or early March and you need to take cuttings two to four weeks later, when the shoots are 5–10cm long.

tools materials

- **garden knife or secateurs**
- **trowel**
- **small flower pot**
- **dibber or pencil**
- **garden wire**
- **plastic bag**
- **elastic band**

- hormone rooting gel or powder
- seed-and-cutting compost
- horticultural grit or perlite

1 Use a sharp knife to remove two or three strong, healthy non-flowering shoots.

2 Cut each shoot just below a leaf node, leaving a cutting about 10–15cm long.

3 Remove all the lower leaves with a garden knife or secateurs, taking care not to damage the stem.

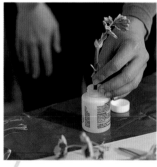

4 Dip the base of the cuttings in hormone rooting compound, either gel or powder.

5 Make a hole in the compost to one side of the pot with a dibber or pencil. Insert the first cutting and gently firm the compost around it. Repeat with the other cuttings and then water in.

6 Make two hoops with garden wire large enough to stand 15cm over the top of the cuttings. Push the ends securely into the compost. Cover the pot with a plastic bag secured with an elastic band.

ideal material

Seed-and-cutting compost
Cuttings are best grown in seed-and-cutting compost, as it is very free-draining. For best results, mix it with an equal amount of a draining aid such as horticultural grit or perlite. This will keep the compost open, allowing fragile roots a freer run and preventing stem rot as a result of soggy compost.

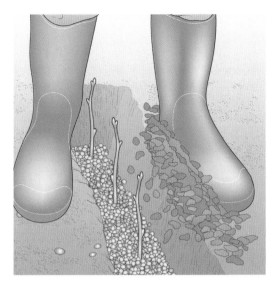

Hardwood cuttings

In contrast to softwood cuttings taken from soft fleshy growth, hardwood cuttings are taken when stem tips are hard and woody. Ideal for plants such as roses, box hedges and philadelphus, hardwood cuttings are best taken in mid-autumn, just after the leaves have fallen from deciduous trees. They are also planted differently from softwood cuttings.

Use secateurs to take 10–20cm cuttings from the parent plant. Remove any leaves from each cutting and, with a knife, make a nick just below a leaf node. Insert a spade in the soil and wiggle it back and forwards to make a slit trench. Fill the bottom with a few centimetres of grit. Place the cuttings in the trench, leaving only the top few centimetres poking out. Use your feet to scrape soil back into the trench, firm the shoots in and water (unless the ground is very wet). The shoots will be budding the following spring, when you can dig them up and replant them.

Division

Division produces new plants by splitting an old one. It is mainly used for clump-forming herbaceous perennials, many of which will weaken and produce fewer flowers if left undivided year after year. This weakening begins at the centre of the plant, the oldest part, as new growth spreads outwards. Division should be done in early spring or autumn.

1 Using a garden fork, dig around and under an established clump (take care not to damage the roots) and lift the whole clump out. This is *Iris sibirica*.

2 Insert two forks, back to back, into the clump and prise apart. You may need to sever thick fleshy roots with a knife.

3 Take each section and, using the same method, divide it into smaller pieces. Discard the old central part of the clump, and replant the new sections.

Layering

Another method of growing new plants from old is layering. This allows a new plant to grow from an established one without needing to be tended – the parent plant will provide all the nurturing needed until the new plant is ready to be cut away.

You do have to be patient with layering, as it may take as long as eighteen months before the new plant is ready to be cut away from its parent and transplanted. Because it takes such a long time, layering is best reserved for shrubs such as rhododendrons and viburnums that are difficult to propagate by cuttings or division.

Choose a shoot at the base of the shrub, long enough to extend easily down to the ground. Fork in some soil improver or compost and scoop out a shallow hole, 8–10cm deep. To aid rooting, make a nick on the underside of the shoot at a point that will be in contact with the soil. Secure the nicked part of the shoot in the hole with a U-shaped metal peg pushed into the ground. Cover with soil, then water.

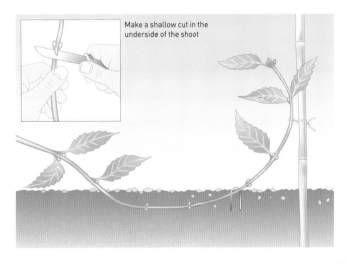

Make a shallow cut in the underside of the shoot

People new to gardening sometimes think caring for a garden has to mean endless hours of backbreaking toil. Nothing could be further from the truth. Caring for your garden doesn't have to be a chore. A few modern conveniences can make all the difference – and there's nothing wrong with making life easier for yourself.

caring for your garden

Plants and climate

To care for your garden, it helps to know what makes it tick. Most of us are aware of the effect that the different seasons have on plants: spring sparks fresh growth, summer produces an abundance of flowers and fruit, autumn is a time of falling leaves, and winter brings a lull in activity. But how do plants know when it's time to grow and time to take a break? There are two main factors: light and temperature. Growth is triggered by longer spells of sunshine and warmer air, and then slows down as the days get shorter and the temperature drops.

Planning ahead

Understanding how and why plants grow can help us make the most of our gardens by planning ahead. By anticipating what is coming, you can prevent potential problems – for instance, mulching borders early on saves a lot of weeding later in the year – and also learn to distinguish between tasks that can and cannot wait.

Being flexible

Nothing here has to be to followed to the letter. It's important to be flexible – as the best time for doing different jobs varies from place to place and from year to year, depending on the weather and other conditions. An unusually cold or wet spring may keep you indoors, but it's not the end of the world if your roses are sitting out there unpruned at the end of April. They will still bear flowers, even if the flowers appear a bit later than usual. Nothing in life is set in stone, least of all gardening, and an untended garden will still be there when you get back to it.

Enjoying the seasons

The gardener's calendar is not a fixed routine but a general guide to the principles of working with nature's annual cycle. It is fascinating to observe the sometimes subtle, sometimes dramatic shifts in weather and the effect the changing seasons have on your garden.

A gardener's calendar
Spring: February to April

This is the time when the garden begins to wake up after its winter rest. Although the skies may still be wintry, plants are beginning to show signs of growth. Aim to get out into your garden whenever weather permits. Every five minutes spent now will save ten minutes catching up if tasks are left undone.

Early spring: February to March

The earliest of the spring-flowering bulbs, such as snowdrops, will be coming to an end now. Crocuses will be in full flower and the promise of the daffodil display yet to come will be evident with their swelling flower buds.

Beds and borders

- Cut back old growth, so it won't get tangled with growth from the current year.
- Get rid of weeds. Spot-treat perennial ones with weedkiller.
- If necessary, divide and transplant perennials (see page 227). Deciduous shrubs in wrong places can be dug up and moved.
- Feed and prepare beds for the coming season – sprinkle general-purpose fertiliser and carefully fork it into the top few centimetres of soil.
- Give borders a good soak if weather has been unusually dry.
- Mulch flowerbeds – but don't mulch beds when they're dry or frosty, as that will make it harder for water to penetrate.
- If you want to install a watering system such as a soaker hose (see page 252), do so now while the ground is relatively clear.

You can do it...
Buy now, plant later In most areas the soil outdoors will still be too wet and cold for planting herbaceous perennials. But If you can't resist buying them now, don't worry. Just keep them in their pots in a sheltered spot for another few weeks. Remember, the summer is on its way! **B&Q**

Pruning

- Prune winter-flowering shrubs, including viburnum, once the flowers have faded.
- Late-flowering clematis, such as 'Jackmanii', *C. viticella* and *C. orientalis*, should be hard-pruned – but not too early, as frosts can kill them. Cut back all stems to a healthy bud about 75cm above soil level (see page 241).
- Hardy evergreen trees can be cut back to reduce their size.
- Deciduous trees can be shaped and any crossing branches removed (see page 245).
- Roses (see pages 242–43) can be pruned early in March in the south of the UK, and later in the month if you live further north.
- Cut back overgrown or untidy hedges to boost new bushy growth (see page 240).
- Resist pruning the more tender shrubs such as lavender and sage for a few weeks yet, to avoid frosts burning pruned tips.

Lifting and dividing

Some bulbs such as snowdrops and winter aconites prefer to be transplanted while still growing, so now is the time to dig up and divide congested clumps. Once replanted, they will quickly bulk up and flower well the following year.

1 Dig up any congested clumps and gently tease the individual bulbs apart.

2 Using a dibber, replant the bulbs separately at a distance of about 3–5cm apart.

Late spring: March and April

The days are lengthening, hawthorn is bursting into life, and daffodils are now in full swing. The first flush of bright-green leaves is full of the promise of summer. This is the time of year when gardeners get twitchy with anticipation – full of dreams of the wonderful displays to be created.

Beds and borders

- Apply a good dose of general-purpose fertiliser to any beds or borders that have not yet been fed this year.
- Transplant evergreen shrubs that need moving – don't forget to keep them well watered throughout the summer.
- Divide and replant late-flowering perennials.

Bulbs

- Deadhead spring-flowering bulbs such as daffodils when their flowers fade – but leave behind the foliage, which will provide the plants with energy to flower next year.
- Now is the time to plant summer-flowering bulbs such as lilies, galtonia and eucomis.
- Any bulbs, such as hyacinths and dwarf irises, that have been 'forced' into early flowering by being kept warm indoors can now be planted outdoors.

Seeds

- Continue sowing seeds for vegetables such as lettuce every six weeks, so you will have something to harvest throughout the summer.
- Hardy annuals such as sweet peas and calendula can now be sown outside.
- If you have a heated greenhouse, sow summer bedding. If not, wait until the second half of April before sowing.

Plant supports

Put supports in place for herbaceous perennials before they grow too large. Also, place obelisks or 'wigwams' (made by tying garden canes together at the top) in the border ready for annual climbers such as morning glory and sweet peas.

Plants such as phlox should be propped up as soon as possible – once they've flopped, they tend to look nipped in at the waist. Delphiniums, with their tall spires of flowers, should have each stem tied into a separate bamboo cane.

Low-growing hardy geraniums – traditionally supported by twigs – can be propped up by placing an upturned wire hanging basket over them before they grow too tall.

Hyacinthoides non-scripta English bluebell

Pots and containers

Check plants grown in pots to make sure they haven't become pot-bound or too large for their containers.

Either repot plants that have outgrown their pots or plant them in the ground. If you are going to plant them in the ground permanently, work soil improver and fertiliser into the soil first.

Lawns

Start paying attention to your lawn. Provided the weather is fairly dry and warm, you can begin to mow, feed and aerate it, and rake out or scarify any moss or thatch (see pages 264–68).

If you've decided to create a new lawn, now is a good time to seed it or lay down turf (see pages 270–73).

Ponds

- Remove netting laid over the pond in autumn, if not taken off already, before marginal plants start growing through it.
- Get rid of any dead growth from pond plants.
- Check pumps and filters, and give them a thorough clean (see page 249). Replace lights and pumps if not working efficiently.
- Feed fish, which will be hungry after the winter.
- Remove any overgrown oxygenating weeds (see page 216). Simply pull them out of the pond gently – but leave them at the edge for a few days, so creatures living in it can make their way back into the water.

Spring cleaning

- Clean patios, decking, paths and garden furniture. A pressure washer will make cleaning them much easier.
- Once clean and dry, all wooden furniture should be treated with a wood preservative or oiled.
- Examine any furniture that has been stored in the shed over the winter. Repair and repaint if necessary.

A **gardener's** calendar
Early summer: May and June

Garden activity goes into overdrive during early summer as plants burst with energy to grow, flower and bear fruit, before they are slowed down by the scorching heat of the later summer months.

Papaver orientale 'Saffron' Oriental poppy

Signs of the season

Bluebells and the first flush of roses are among the most obvious signs of this time of year. Plants are rushing to flower and produce seeds. The garden is now at its freshest and most lush – and brimming with activity, with plants, birds and insects alike buzzing with vigour.

Routine maintenance

- Feed the lawn in early summer. Mow it weekly, gradually lowering the cutting height.
- Water recently transplanted shrubs, newly divided perennials, and pots and planters.
- Deadhead faded flowers.
- Spot-treat perennial weeds such as bindweed and couch grass with a translocated weedkiller as soon as they make an appearance in flowerbeds and borders. Where possible, use a hoe to remove annual weed seedlings when they are still small (see page 254).

You can do it...

Lifting tulips
Some tulips, including the delightful *T. greigii* and *T. kauffmanniana*, will grow happily for years if they're left in the ground undisturbed. Others are best 'lifted' (dug up) annually and stored. Wait until the foliage has dried and turned brown, then dig up the bulbs with a fork, taking care not to damage them. Store the bulbs somewhere cool and airy for the summer, ready for planting in the autumn. Never put them in a plastic bag – it's best to hang them up in old tights or mesh bags.

B&Q

Pruning shrubs and hedges

Shrubs that flower in late spring or early summer, such as philadelphus and deutzia, should be pruned as soon as their flowers have faded. The new growth made after pruning will bear flowers the following spring.

Lightly trim topiary, box hedges and other formal hedging; this will keep them tidy through most of the summer, until they are pruned properly later in the season. Give Leyland cypress hedges their first trim of the year.

Clip fast-growing hedges, such as hawthorn, lonicera and privet, in early summer. Remember to water and mulch newly planted hedges.

Watch the weather forecast

Don't plant frost-tender annuals and summer bedding outside until all risk of frosts has passed. In some areas, they can occur as late as May.

If a frost is forecast, you can protect plants by covering them overnight with horticultural fleece, which acts as a sort of plant blanket (see page 288). Always remove it the next morning – as leaving it on for days on end generates too much warmth, making the plants vulnerable to pests and diseases.

Beds, borders and baskets

- Clear away spring bedding plants such as forget-me-nots and wallflowers, which will now be finished, and add them to your compost bin.
- Gradually harden off summer bedding plants sown indoors, before you plant them in the garden (see page 225).
- Plant up hanging baskets – but, like bedding plants, don't put them out until risk of frost has passed (see page 210).

Taking cuttings and dividing perennials

Start taking softwood cuttings (see page 226), remembering to use only non-flowering shoots.

Divide pulmonaria, early primulas, doronicum and other perennials that have already flowered.

Pests and diseases

Now is the time to start dealing with garden pests.
- Keep an eye open for slugs, snails and aphids on new shoots.
- Spray roses if necessary.
- If using nematodes (see page 255) to control slugs and vine weevils, water them on once the soil is warm enough.

Staking

Continue to stake herbaceous perennials, paying particular attention to the taller ones, such as delphiniums.

Some hardy annuals sown previously will now need support. Tie plants such as sunflowers to garden canes before they grow too tall and bend or break.

Bulbs

Remove any dead foliage from early spring-flowering bulbs. If lifting tulips (see opposite) and hyacinths, choose a dry day to do so, then store them in a cool, airy place.

Ponds

- Feed your pond plants using purpose-made pond-plant fertiliser – don't use any other kind.
- Remove any blanketweed or duckweed. You can do a lot of this by hand.
- If the water looks green or murky, give your pond a dose of algae treatment (see page 248).

Greenhouses

Temperatures rise quickly in greenhouses, so let in some fresh air and install shading before the intensity of the summer sun reaches its peak. You have two options for shading:
- Paint for greenhouse glass, which is inexpensive and easy to wash off at the end of the summer.
- Purpose-made greenhouse shading material, which is similar to curtains. This is more expensive than paint but will last for many years.

A gardener's calendar
Late summer: July and August

For many plants, the annual cycle is nearing completion: they have produced and stored food, and have reproduced through their seeds. Now is a good time to take a look at your garden, to see what might be changed or improved, and plan ahead.

Lavandula stoechas French lavender

Signs of the season

The glories of early summer are now over – many plants have flowered and are gone, and many more are looking tired. This is the time when dahlias and chrysanthemums, the late-summer show stoppers, step forward and take centre stage.

Routine maintenance

- To encourage plants to produce more flowers, continue with deadheading (see page 241).
- Support large dahlia flower heads with individual canes – without adequate support, they will flop and snap when wet.
- Mow the lawn regularly and feed it to keep the grass healthy (see page 266).
- Keep beds free from weeds by persevering with weeding.
- Water your garden as weather and soil conditions dictate (see pages 250–51).
- In August, prune summer-fruiting raspberries. Untie all of the canes and cut out any that have borne fruit. Select the strongest 8–10 new shoots and tie them to the wire supports.

Hedges

It's time to get out the hedge-trimming tools again. If your hedges are yew or laurel, this may be the first and only time you trim them this year; if you have Leyland cypress hedging, it could well be the third time.

To make it easier to keep the height of the hedge level, you can create a visual guide with a straight length of twine tied to a cane, inserted into the ground, at each end of the hedge.

Large-leaved hedges such as laurel can look a bit untidy if trimmed with a hedge trimmer or shears – secateurs, though more tedious to use, produce a much neater finish.

Trimming hedges

When using a hedge trimmer (whether electric or petrol-driven), work from the top of the hedge downwards, so gravity and the action of the trimmer are working with you. Hold the trimmer well away from your body, but no higher than your shoulders.

You can do it...

Making wasp traps
In late summer wasps become drunk, and dangerous, as they eat overripe fruit. Clearing fallen fruit from the ground helps, and you can buy wasp traps and hang them near your fruit trees. To make your own, put a teaspoonful of jam or honey in the bottom of a jam jar and add water until the jar is three quarters full.

B&Q

safety first

Hedge trimmers
- Wear gloves and safety goggles.
- Make sure the blade isn't blunt, otherwise it could snag – have your trimmer professionally serviced and sharpened.
- Never work with the trimmer held above shoulder height.
- If the hedge is tall, build a sturdy platform to work from, instead of using a ladder or steps.
- When using an electric trimmer, work away from the socket – not towards it – so the lead will trail behind you. Drape the flex over your shoulder, so it's less likely to get tangled or cut. Always use an RCD (residual current device, see page 21).

You can do it...

Saving for next year
On a warm dry day, snip off some ripe seedheads from annuals and store them in a paper bag in a cool dry place. With poppies and nigella, hang the head upside down with a paper bag tied round it; when the seeds are dry, they will fall into the bag.

B&Q

Mixed herbaceous border

Beds and borders

By late summer any gaps in borders or groups of plants that don't work so well together will have become apparent – so now is a good time to take notes and photographs to help you decide which seeds and bulbs to order for next year.

Vegetables

Look at your vegetable beds to see what you have too much of and what you would like more of next year.

- There's still time to sow more salad crops, to provide for the table until the first frosts.
- Remove any flowers that are still forming on tomato plants – they won't have time to mature and will simply drain energy from the plant.

Bulbs, corms and rhizomes

- Plant hardy cyclamen. These are corms which, unlike bulbs, do not like to be buried – the top of the corm should be peeking through the soil.
- Divide congested clumps of bearded irises, using a sharp knife. Discard any rhizomes that have flowered previously and those bearing this year's spent flowers. Replant the others in a sunny well-drained position – they need to be baked by the sun to flower (see page 207).
- Winter-flowering crocuses and other winter bulbs such as colchicum can be planted now.

Seeds

- In early July, sow spring bedding plants such as wallflowers and forget-me-nots, as well as biennials such as foxgloves and hollyhocks.
- Towards the end of August, sow hardy annuals that are being grown for flowering the following year, such as cornflowers, larkspur and calendula.

Slow down

As the end of summer draws near, try to avoid promoting growth outdoors. Nothing in the garden should be fed after the end of August.

Besides being a waste of time, it can even harm the plants. Feeding herbaceous perennials has the effect of kick-starting an effort to produce flowers – but these may not have time to bloom before the dormant season, so they will be using up energy unnecessarily.

Worse still, feeding shrubs will produce a surge of lush new growth that may not have time to harden off before winter arrives, leaving it vulnerable to being burnt by frost.

A gardener's calendar
Autumn: September and October

As the days shorten and a chill fills the air, the garden slows down for a well-earned rest. But there's still plenty to do out there – and some well-directed tending now will help your plants wake up healthy and strong in the spring.

Signs of the season

The gardening year is now beginning to wind down, with the season of harvest and the slow decline into the long sleep to come. The plants' job is done, yet many in their declining growth reward us with the rich jewel-like colours of their autumn leaves. Time for gardeners to give themselves a pat on the back for the glories created during the year.

Feeding and watering

At this point in the year, stop feeding plants entirely – and only water if the weather is very dry.

Beds and borders

- Cut down and clear all spent foliage and flowers. Compost everything that isn't diseased.
- Dig up and split overgrown clumps of perennials.
- Plant spring-flowering bulbs and spring bedding plants. If they have been sown and grown elsewhere in the garden, dig them up now and plant them in their final positions.
- Lift gladioli and dahlia tubers, and store them over the winter in a dry, frost-free place.
- Top up any bare or thin patches of mulch, to prevent weeds invading the beds.

Pruning
Climbing roses, such as 'Gloire de Dijon' and 'New Dawn', can be pruned from November. Remove aging wood and reduce flowering side shoots before retraining the stems (see pages 204–5) and tying them back to prevent wind damage.

Cuttings
Now is the time to take hardwood cuttings from shrubs and roses (see page 227).

Planting
Bare-root trees, shrubs and fruit bushes are available to buy from the end of October. You can plant them any time between now and March as long as the ground isn't frozen or waterlogged, but the sooner you get them in the better. Autumn is the ideal time because the soil is still warm enough for the plants to put on some root growth before the dormant season.

Ponds

- Clear the surface of the pond of dead or dying foliage.
- If oxygenating plants seem to be congesting the water, gently pull some out.
- Cover the pond with netting to catch falling leaves and debris.
- Gradually stop feeding the fish – they are almost dormant during winter, and uneaten food will simply rot in the water.
- Float a plastic ball on the surface, or several if your pond is large, so the butyl liner won't get damaged if the pond freezes over (see page 249).

Bring in the autumn harvest

- Harvest tree fruits as they ripen. To find out if apples and pears are ready to be picked, gently twist a fruit growing on the tree. If the fruit comes away easily, it is ready.
- Discard any blemished or diseased fruit before storing.
- Keep fruit in a dry, dark place that is cool but frost-free.
- Store fruit in single layers, leaving space around each fruit. This keeps rot from spreading from one fruit to the next.
- Pick up windfalls and compost any that are not diseased.

Clearing fallen leaves

Don't delay clearing leaves until the end of autumn – if left on your lawn for long periods, they will reduce the amount of light that reaches the grass and make it turn yellow.

It's best to clear the leaves frequently, a little at a time. A lawn rake is fine for large, flat areas of lawn but impractical for borders, so consider investing in a garden vacuum. If you use it on shredder mode, the leaves will rot down much more quickly when composted – add them to your compost bin in thin layers along with other organic matter.

Lawns

- Lawns should be scarified, aerated and treated with autumn lawn feed, and any worn patches reseeded. If it doesn't rain within three days of applying granular feed water the lawn.
- September is a good time to seed a new lawn. Wait a few weeks longer for the optimum time for laying turfing.

Preparing for winter

Some tender plants can stay outside during the winter months but need protection in order to survive. Here are some tips:

- Pack straw around the crowns of tree ferns (see page 148) to protect the sensitive growing point, then wrap them with several layers of horticultural fleece and tie them up securely. To prevent rot ruining banana plants (see page 325) grown outdoors, strip them of their leaves before wrapping.
- Wrap a couple of layers of bubble wrap around the containers of tender plants to help keep their roots warm.
- Alpines (see pages 319–20) are vulnerable to too much moisture – they don't need to be covered up, but need to be sheltered from rain.

Conifers

Tie any loose side branches into the main trunk using wire – otherwise high winds, heavy rain and snowfall will bend them out of shape. Make sure the wire won't cut into the branch. If you think it may do so, thread an old piece of hose over the wire to help cushion the branch. Dispose of conifer leaves separately – don't add them to the compost bin.

Pots and containers

- Bring in any house plants that have been kept outside during the summer months.
- If any trees, shrubs, spring-flowering bulbs or spring bedding plants in containers need repotting, either transplant them into larger pots or plant them in the ground.

Greenhouses

Before moving plants inside, clean the greenhouse, giving the glass a good wash, and remove any shading used during the summer.

ideal tool
Garden vacuums

A garden vacuum makes light work of clearing leaves. It has three main functions:

Blow lets you blow leaves into manageable piles ready for collection.

Vacuum sucks leaves directly into a collection bag. The higher the wattage of the model, the greater the suction power.

Shred chops up leaves finely with an internal shredder blade.

A gardener's calendar
Winter: November to January

Before hanging up your tools for the winter and retreating indoors to relax, do a final clear-up and make sure everything is ready for next spring – putting the garden to bed for the winter is an important part of the gardening year.

Signs of the season

The garden still has its surprises and pleasures even in the dreariest of months. Plants such as holly, viburnum and witch hazel come into their own at this time of year – their subtlety brought out by the quieter winter landscape.

Clearing leaves and debris

To prevent rot, continue clearing fallen leaves from beds and from the crowns of plants. Once all the leaves have dropped from the trees, pond netting can be removed and any debris cleared from the water to leave it clean for the winter.

Large pots outside

Any pots containing tender plants that are too large or heavy to move indoors can be wrapped up for insulation, in a couple of layers of bubble wrap tied round the pot. Use horticultural fleece if you want to cover the plants themselves, or cover them with hessian stuffed with straw (see also page 237).

Winter care of trees and shrubs

Some fruit trees can be pruned once all the leaves have fallen and they are completely dormant (see page 245). To kill insect eggs, spray them with a wash that has a vegetable-oil base (not tar oil, which is no longer licensed for use). These washes kill all insects, including beneficial ones – so to protect them, cover up any plants around the tree.

Burn or dispose of prunings. Never compost them, as they may harbour pests and disease that will survive composting.

Planting bare-root trees and shrubs
Bare-root trees, shrubs and roses can be planted now. If they were not freshly dug from the ground when you bought them, remove all the wrapping and plunge the roots in a bucket of water for 24 hours before planting. Never plant them with dry roots.

Roses often come with a wax coating to protect their roots. There is no need to remove this – it's biodegradable and will rot off in the ground.

Hardwood cuttings
These can be taken from trees and shrubs now (see page 227).

Preparing for spring

Beat the spring rush – book mowers and hedge trimmers in for a service now. Waiting until spring may leave you without them for a few weeks, as service centres always experience a sudden increase in demand as soon as the sun starts shining again.

Watering systems
Clean and descale watering systems (see page 252).
• Dismantle supply pipes and clean them by soaking them in diluted disinfectant. Rinse thoroughly.
• In hard-water areas, follow cleaning with a soak in a solution of descaler. Again, rinse thoroughly.

Tools
Give all your garden tools a good wash to clean off soil, and check them for damage.
• Stainless steel tools can simply be dried after washing; all other metal tools should be oiled to prevent rusting.
• Give bare wood handles a coat of linseed oil.
• The movable parts of shears, loppers and secateurs will benefit from a little light oiling to prevent them rusting and seizing up during the winter.
• Wash flower pots and seed trays in a dilute disinfectant solution. Never re-use pots without washing them first.

Unheated greenhouses
You can raise the temperature of an unheated greenhouse significantly by covering the inside of the glass with a layer of bubble wrap. In mild districts this is often enough to protect overwintering plants.

Cleaning your greenhouse
Pests and diseases loiter in the warmth of greenhouses, ready to prey on newly grown plants in the spring. If you haven't given your greenhouse an end-of-season clean-up already, now is the time to do so. Wearing rubber gloves, wash every surface with dilute disinfectant – paying special attention to nooks and crannies. If your greenhouse stands on bare earth and the ground is hard, scrub the disinfectant in with a stiff broom, and then use a pressure washer to prevent algae building up.

Rhododendron Dwarf rhododendron

Laurus nobilis Bay tree

Pruning
and deadheading

Regular pruning helps maintain healthy, vigorous shrubs and keeps them within bounds. Deadheading also brings its own rewards – a little time spent with a sharp pair of secateurs can prolong flowering. The result? A garden with more flowers.

Pruning

Why do it?

Pruning is used for a variety of purposes: to remove dead, diseased or damaged shoots, to encourage flowering or fruiting, to shape plants attractively, and to restrict the size of trees and shrubs, whether planted in the ground or grown in containers. Topiary – shrubs or trees that are clipped into unnatural shapes – is simply an extreme form of pruning. Similarly, the art of cultivating bonsai trees is completely reliant on pruning. With bonsai, roots are pruned as well as top-growth.

Pruning shrubs

Start by removing all dead or diseased wood. Then, if you aren't reducing the overall size of the shrub, concentrate on cutting out shoots that have flowered. Cut back to healthy outward-facing buds. The direction in which the bud is facing dictates the direction of the shoot – and the aim is to have shoots growing outwards, not towards the centre of the shrub.

To rejuvenate old shrubs or contain fast-growing ones such as buddleia that have become too big, cut them back almost to ground level. A pruning saw or loppers will probably be needed.

What can be pruned?

Almost anything can be pruned, though correct timing is vital for success. Some shrubs flower on wood made the previous season, others on the current season's growth. Pruning at the correct time ensures that future flowers aren't lost.

When to prune

As a general rule, shrubs that flower in spring or early summer should be pruned immediately after flowering; and those that flower later in the summer should be pruned during the winter. Most roses should be pruned in spring (see pages 242–43). In addition, tall rose bushes can have their height reduced the previous autumn – to prevent them being blown around in the wind, which loosens their roots and may lead to water freezing around the roots or the base of the stem.

Cornus (dogwood) and other shrubs grown for their stem or bark colour should be pruned back almost to ground level in late winter or early spring.

ideal tool

Secateurs

For cutting stems that are not too thick, secateurs are the ideal tool; for thick or dense branches, loppers or a pruning saw are needed (see page 180). Always use sharp pruning tools – blunt ones damage the plant and encourage disease or result in dieback of shoots.

Buddleia

Renovating a vigorous shrub

Fast-growing shrubs such as buddleia need renovating every two years or so. Prune off any diseased, dead or congested branches, especially at the base, always leaving two or three growth buds above the plant's main framework.

Cornus

Pruning for new growth

To encourage new, bushy growth on shrubs such as cornus, perovskia and caryopteris, cut them back to quite low down on the plant. Try to avoid cutting into older, darker wood.

Cotinus

Pruning for shape

Some large shrubs such as cotinus, viburnum and choisya need little pruning. Keep them in shape by removing smaller branches.

Pruning clematis

Clematis is one of those peculiar plants that comes in different varieties that require different pruning at differing times. There are three main types: spring-flowering, summer-flowering and early summer-flowering. Spring-flowering clematis such as *C. armandii* should be pruned immediately after flowering; they will then make new growth, which will flower in the spring of the following year. Most summer-flowering clematis, including *C. viticella* and 'Jackmanii', need hard pruning in spring at the first sign of shooting, leaving them at just under 1m in height – the new shoots usually flower later in the summer. Early summer-flowering varieties such as *C.* 'Niobe' flower both in early spring and summer; these need only light pruning in spring to keep flowering well.

Clematis 'Jackmanii Superba'

Seedheads of angelica

When not to deadhead

Plants grown for their spectacular seedheads should not be deadheaded. Alliums are a prime example, and so are echinops (globe thistles).

Seedheads or spent flowers are left on some plants to give protection to emerging shoots during the winter. Hydrangeas, for example, are particularly susceptible to frost burn, and leaving the old flower heads helps protect the tender new shoots.

Deadheading

What is it?

Deadheading involves cutting off dead flowering growth from a plant. How far down you cut – just the flowerhead and stalk, down to the next bud or two, or almost down to the ground – depends on the type of plant.

Why do it?

Plants produce flowers to make seed, so they can reproduce themselves. Removing flowerheads interrupts or prevents the production of seed, so the plant produces more flowers in order to complete its reproductive cycle.

Some plants go on flowering all summer long, while others – some roses, for example – have a rest and then start flowering again (known as a first and second flush). Some plants, which use other methods to reproduce, will flower only once in the season, regardless of whether or not you deadhead them.

Deadheading bulbs

Plants that grow from bulbs flower only once every year. They reproduce by forming bulblets (baby bulbs) below ground, so removing spent flower stems will not result in continued flowering. However, deadheading does give them more energy, which helps conserve the strength of of the bulb, leading to more vigorous flowering the following year.

The same applies to plants such as crocosmia, which grow from corms (not bulbs) and produce offsets underground.

Caring for roses

Rosa 'Buff Beauty' Shrub rose

Roses are a staple of cottage gardens and formal gardens alike; their sweet-smelling blooms are loved by gardeners everywhere.

Different types of roses

Roses are divided into categories according to their growing and flowering habits. The main groups are large-flowered bush roses (hybrid teas), cluster-flowered bush roses (floribundas), shrub roses, climbers and ramblers. Some, such as ramblers and many of the old shrub roses, flower only once in a season. Others, including climbers, hybrid teas and modern shrub roses, have a main flowering period early in the summer and then, if deadheaded, produce another flush later in the season or flower sporadically throughout the summer.

All roses are prone to pests and diseases, so take special care to treat any problems as soon as you spot them. You can prevent them by keeping your roses strong and healthy: pruning, deadheading and feeding will help. To keep pests at bay, you might also want to spray plants with a rose pesticide.

Large-flowered bush roses (hybrid teas)
Hybrid teas are the most severely pruned of all roses. Any diseased stems should be removed entirely. With mature or overlarge bushes, remove one-third of all stems, along with any stems less than a pencil's thickness in diameter. In general, stems should be pruned to between 15–35cm. The more vigorous the species, the lighter the pruning should be. Cut back to just above an outward-facing healthy bud, angling the cut so it slopes slightly downwards – then rain will run off, instead of sitting on the surface of the cut, which induces rot and disease.

Shrub roses
Generally these require little or no pruning. Left to their own devices, they develop into large, graceful shrubs.

If deadheading, along with the spent flowers remove a few centimetres of stem, down to just above a leaf with a healthy bud nestling at its base. But first, check that yours is a species that repeat flowers; many shrub roses flower only once a year but produce attractive hips in the autumn, so deadheading would deprive you of the hips without stimulating more flowers.

Old shrub roses can be rejuvenated by cutting out a few stems each year to promote fresh growth from below ground.

Climbing roses
Most climbing roses have a permanent framework of stems that produce flowering side shoots each year. To promote greater flower production, the framework stems should be trained by tying them to wire supports as close to horizontal as possible (see pages 204–5). Each spring, prune all side shoots back to within 5–10cm of their main stem, cutting to a healthy outward-facing bud.

Rambling roses
More vigorous than climbing roses, rambling roses grow in a haphazard, untidy fashion, and will happily develop into a larger bush, hedge or tree. They flower only once in a season, on short shoots from last season's growth. Prune established ramblers after flowering, cutting out up to one-third of main stems that have produced flowers in previous years – this encourages new shoots from the base, which will flower next year. In the spring, prune side shoots that have flowered to within 10cm of their main stem.

Standard roses
Most standard roses are hybrid teas grown on an elongated stem, so pruning is the same as for ordinary hybrid teas.

Cluster-flowered bush roses (floribunda)
Floribundas are pruned in much the same way as hybrid teas – but any stems that aren't to be removed entirely should be pruned back to about two thirds their length.

Rosa 'Guinée' Climbing rose

When to prune

The main pruning period for all roses is spring, depending on location in the UK – usually early in March in the south, and around the end of March in the north. If you prune too early in the season, there's a risk that the first flush of growth prompted by pruning may be burnt by frost – so don't be too eager.

tools materials
- **gardening gloves**
- **secateurs**
- **for dense thick stems, pruning knife or pruning saw**

1 Remove all dead or diseased growth and any stems that are rubbing against one another or pointing towards the centre of the bush. Also cut out all stems that are thinner than a pencil.

2 Cut cleanly at an angle, and prune to an outward-facing bud wherever possible.

'Double' pruning

In addition to the main spring pruning, light pruning in late autumn is beneficial for some roses. Climbers that produce long whippy shoots should have them reduced. Standards, shrub roses and hybrid teas can be lightly pruned again too.

Large rose bushes and climbers may rock around in winter winds and rains. Standards are also prone to this and may snap in two. Rocking loosens the roots and allows water and frost to penetrate around the stem, damaging the roots. Reducing the size of the plant minimises the risk of this happening.

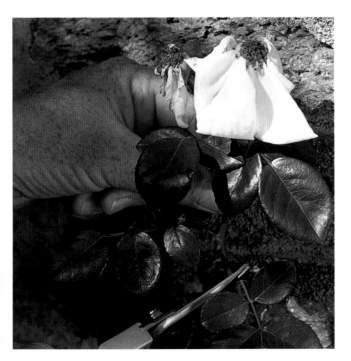

Rosa 'Charles de Mills' Shrub rose

3 The pruned bush should be balanced in shape and even in height, with an open centre and the stems pointing outwards.

Removing suckers

Many roses are in effect two plants in one – consisting of the species rose, which produces the flowers, and the rootstock upon which it has been grafted. Roses that have been grafted tend to put out suckers – shoots from the rootstock, below ground. These are usually lighter in colour than the other shoots and the leaves look more like those of a wild rose.

Suckers should be removed, or they will quickly overtake the weaker species rose. Wearing strong gloves, scrape the soil from around the stem with your hands and then gently tear the sucker from the base of the plant. Cutting suckers off above ground merely encourages them to grow more vigorously, so it is essential to remove them at the point from which they grow.

Deadheading roses

As with other plants, the purpose of deadheading is to persuade the plant to go on flowering. With roses, it is not only the flowers that are removed – the stem below a spent flowerhead should be cut back to a leaf with a strong healthy bud at its base.

In the case of floribundas and other roses that produce a 'head' of flowers, you can snip off individual spent blooms and then remove the whole head once it has finished flowering.

Fruit trees

You don't need an orchard to grow fruit trees. Nowadays fruit trees come in shapes and sizes to suit even the smallest garden and you can buy them for growing in tubs or pots on patios – so there's no need to deny yourself the pleasures of picking and eating your own fruit.

Tree size

Like roses, most fruit trees are grafted upon the rootstock of another plant. Which rootstock it is will dictate the eventual height of the tree and how early it can be expected to crop. With apple trees, the variation in height between the tallest and shortest is 6m or more; and there may be a five-year difference in how soon you can expect to be picking your own crop.

Fruit trees are generally labelled with a code such as M9 or M27, which tells you the rootstock used. The label should also tell you the eventual size. If it doesn't, or the information is unclear, ask the nursery staff.

Pollination

With most types of fruit, you can buy trees that are self-fertile, so there is no need for another variety of the same species to be planted close by. But for varieties that are not self-fertile, to pollinate and fruit they must be planted near another variety of the same species that flowers at the same time.

Different varieties flower at different times (this is particularly true of pears). If you live in the north, choose one that flowers later. This will reduce the chance of the blossom being burnt and killed by frost. No flowers? No fruit!

Tree shapes

Fruit trees come in many shapes – some of the most common ones being bush, standard, half-standard, fan-trained, cordon and espalier, shown here.

Bush

The most popular choice, it is grown on dwarf rootstock and has little or no trunk. Its size makes it easy to maintain and harvest but a nightmare to mow under, so it's not a good choice for growing on a lawn.

Standard

These are the biggies, grown with about 2m of bare trunk. Difficult to maintain due to their size, they are prolific croppers and will keep the entire neighbourhood in fruit pies for months. Not recommended for average-size gardens.

Half-standard

Similar to standards but slightly smaller – though they are still sizable trees, with 1m or so of bare trunk. They are only really suitable for growing in large gardens.

Fan-trained

Frequently used for apricots, peaches and nectarines, grown against a south-facing wall to give protection from frost and help ripening. Training begins when the tree is one year old, the branches being splayed out like the ribs of a fan. Although they don't protrude far from the wall, fan-trained trees need a spread of at least 3m.

Cordon

Single-stem dwarf-rootstock trees grown at an angle of 45°, cordons can be planted against a wall or, if supported by wires and posts initially, as freestanding trees. Mostly used for apples or pears. A straight row of cordons makes a productive and elegant hedge.

Espalier

The branches are splayed out horizontally in equal pairs, to form a tiered structure. Dwarf rootstock is used. Most often wall-trained, but if supported initially can be freestanding.

Pruning

It is useful to know when to prune, and why. You might want to prune a fruit tree to increase your harvest, for instance – an essential skill if you own an orchard or intend to sell your own produce. Fruit trees may also be pruned to improve their health and shape. Pruning can benefit fruit trees by:

- Rejuvenating old, neglected trees (see below)
- Removing dead or diseased wood
- Clearing and preventing crossing branches which, once they rub together and create a wound, will become vulnerable to pests and diseases
- Reducing, changing or maintaining a tree's shape

Pruning newly planted fruit trees

A new fruit tree needs only a light prune at first, then pruning to shape in subsequent years. During the first couple of years after planting, cut stems back to a bud to encourage the formation of more bushy growth.

Fig tree with fruit

When to prune

Some trees, such as bush trees and other fruit trees grown on dwarf rootstock, need little or no pruning. But when pruning is necessary, it must be done in the right season to avoid disease and promote fruiting. Pruning at the best time will also prevent the tree from 'bleeding' or oozing sap which, though not harmful, can be very messy.

Pruning neglected fruit trees

Never reduce overgrown or neglected trees by more than a third in any one season. If you prune them more severely, that will provoke a surge of non-fruiting new growth – so stagger the work over two years or more.

Before removing large limbs, step back and take a good look at the tree, as it's easy to lose the shape and balance. When using a saw, make a cut on the underside of the limb first and then cut from the upper side – this prevents tearing the bark on the tree as the branch comes away.

the best time	to prune
Winter	Apple trees
	Pear trees
Early spring	Young apricot trees
	Young nectarine trees
	Young peach trees
Early summer	Cherry trees
	Greengage trees
	Mature apricot trees
	Mature peach trees
	Mature nectarine trees
	Plum trees
Mid- to late summer	Trained trees

tools materials

- **loppers**
- **secateurs**
- **pruning saw**

First, remove any dead or diseased wood, using loppers, secateurs and, if need be, a pruning saw. Cut out as much of the infected branch as need be. Make a sloping cut, not less than 15cm below the diseased area. Don't cut absolutely flush – if you leave a centimetre or two, the wound will heal better.

Next, cut out branches that cross or rub one another, to avoid wounds that can become infected. Make each cut above a healthy outward-facing bud, slanting it downwards so rain will run off.

Use long-handled loppers to cut branches high on the tree that are within easy reach from the ground and not too thick.

safety first

Too high? Too thick?

If you can't reach a tree's branches from the ground, work from a well-secured stepladder or ladder. If you're dealing with very thick branches, always use the right tools: long-handled loppers for extra reach and a chain saw for added cutting power. Remember, though, that often the safest option is to leave the task to a qualified tree surgeon.

You can do it...

Worth saving

Gnarled old fruit trees add character to a garden. Rejuvenating an old neglected tree so that it will fruit again needs perseverance and can't be hurried. It will take two years or more, but is worth the effort. If the tree isn't capable of cropping any more, give it a graceful old age by growing a climbing rose or clematis through it.

B&Q

Topiary
and hedging

Clipped evergreen topiary will bring year-round structure and style to any outdoor space. Hedges are the most natural and wildlife-friendly way to define the shape and boundaries of your garden.

Topiary and ornamental hedging

Topiary is the artistic shaping of plants by training and clipping, to achieve fanciful, stylised or geometric forms. These can vary from simple clipped ball shapes through to spirals, pyramids, birds and animals.

Ornamental hedging is grown not merely as a means of enclosing or dividing a garden but as a decorative feature in its own right. Low-growing box or lavender hedging used as an edging for beds and paths is a familiar sight – more unusual are pleached trees or stilt hedging (see opposite).

Buxus sempervirens Box

Creating your own topiary

Topiary frames over which plants such as ivy can clamber may be bought preshaped from garden centres, or you can shape your own from galvanised mesh or chicken wire. Place the frame over potted ivy and as the plant grows tie the stems into the framework until it is entirely covered.

Clipping

The key to creating and maintaining any topiary shape is to take your time. As you clip, stand back frequently and look at the shape. Maintaining it is simplicity itself – simply snip off any protruding shoots. You can clip balls, spirals and other shapes from plants such as box, holly or yew. Whichever you choose, sharp shears and secateurs will be required.

When to clip

Clipping can be done any time from the end of April onwards. Generally, a light trim early in the summer followed by a final one in August is all that's required. However, if you are a particularly tidy-minded person and straggly bits annoy you, snip them off as often as you like. Clipping after the end of August isn't recommended – pruning of any type prompts new growth and if the plant doesn't have time to harden off, then it will be damaged by winter frosts.

Restoring the shape

If topiary shapes have been neglected for a year or two, all is not lost. Restoring them to shape may not be possible in one go, but within a season or two even the most overgrown can be saved. Cut back to the original shape as far as is possible; where this is not obvious, remove a little at a time until you are happy.

Clip away

Clipping should be done with sharp shears and secateurs. If yours are getting blunt, use a sharpening kit to restore their cutting power (see page 184).

Pruning overgrown hedges

If a hedge is particularly large and you can get to both sides, it will respond better if hard-pruned over two seasons. Prune one side severely one year and leave the other side until the next. This leaves plenty of old growth to feed the new – and will produce a better hedge more quickly, with less shock to the plants. A garden vacuum (see page 237) will make quick work of cleaning the trimmings.

(see page 237)

tools materials

- **hand shears and/or power hedge trimmer (plus eye protection)**
- **loppers**
- **secateurs**
- **gloves**

If you're pruning an overgrown old hedge, like this lonicera, use loppers to cut through the thicker branches.

Use hand shears to trim the lighter growth – or an electric hedge trimmer if tackling a large hedge.

Cut back hard – you'll find that a lonicera hedge, unlike some others, rejuvenates in response to severe pruning.

ideal tool

Pruning saw
Don't try to cut thicker branches with a pair of secateurs or a lopper – use a pruning saw instead. This cuts on the 'pull' and its coarse teeth will make it easy to cut through green wood.

How hard?

Some hedges – such as yew, laurel, privet and lonicera – respond well to severe pruning and readily generate new growth from old wood, which not all hedging plants do. Lavender, for example, resents harsh treatment – so don't cut into the old wood. When cutting back into old woody stems, a pruning saw and loppers make the job easier and produce a neater finish.

Pleached trees and stilt hedging

These are really one and the same thing: a hedge made from a row of trees that have a bare trunk at the bottom and tiers of interwoven branches further up. Lime trees are the traditional choice – but other trees, such as beech and hornbeam, work equally well. Pleached trees are perfect for screening areas without blocking all the light and for maintaining privacy when space is restricted.

To create a pleached hedge, plant young trees with flexible limbs, spacing them 1.5–2m apart. Decide on the height for the bare trunks and remove all limbs below that level. Next, space the tiers of branches that are to be trained and tie them to a support. The easiest method is to erect two stout poles – one at each end of the hedge – and extend wires between them, to which the branches are then tied. If the hedge is a long one, posts may be needed in between to ensure that the tautness of the wires is maintained. As the trees grow, continue to train and wire new tiers until the desired height for the hedge is reached; then prune out the central growing tip of each trunk.

Trimming and pruning thereafter is the same as for any other hedge. Continue to support the framework of horizontal branches until eventually, after a few years, they are strong enough to support themselves.

Pleached trees in winter

Pleached trees in summer

Preventing problems

New ponds will take a bit of time to settle in before a natural balance is established – it's common for the water to turn green due to a build-up of algae, but this should eventually clear up.

If the water stays murky for more than a few weeks, action will be needed. A filter with a built-in UV (ultraviolet) clarifier is the most effective means of algae control. UV light destroys the cell structure of algae, causing them to stick together in clumps large enough to be removed by a foam filter. Alternatively, you can grow waterlilies to block out sunlight, which algae and blanketweed rely on. You could also add a chemical treatment to the water, after checking that it won't harm fish or pond life.

Adding an algae treatment

To clear algae from the surface, mix a chemical treatment with some of the pond water and add it to the pond, using a bucket or watering can – distribute it evenly and avoid splashing your pond plants. There's usually no need to turn off filters or fountains, but always follow the instructions on the label.

tools materials
• **bucket or watering can**
• **rubber gloves**

• algae treatment

1 Take a bucket and scoop some water from the pond. Wearing rubber gloves, measure the correct dose of algae treatment and pour it into the bucket. Stir thoroughly, so it is completely mixed with the water.

2 Pour the contents of the bucket into the pond, distributing it evenly, or use a watering can.

Pond care

It doesn't take a lot of effort to keep a pond healthy – but the quality of the water and control of pond plants can make a great difference to fish and wildlife.

Clearing leaves and debris

In the autumn clear the water of as much decaying matter as possible and, before the leaves start to fall, cover the pond with netting to prevent fallen leaves fouling the water. Gather blanketweed by hand or use a pond net – carefully, as it's easy to puncture the pond liner. Plants and debris cleared from the water should be left on the side of the pond for a day or two; this gives any creatures lurking in it a chance to crawl back into the pond.

Deadheading flowers growing near or around the pond will help reduce the amount of debris.

Controlling pond plants

Planting pond plants in baskets inhibits their growth, so they don't spread so extensively or so quickly. Oxygenating plants (see page 216) are essential for the health of fish and help keep the water clear – but they will eventually need reducing to stop them taking over the pond.

Filters and pumps

Pumps and filters vary greatly in maintenance requirements so refer to the instruction manual for details. Regardless of type, they should have a check-over at the end of the summer.

Cleaning filters

Before cleaning your filter, always disconnect the electricity supply to the pump first. Lift the filter out of the water if necessary and then disconnect the pipes. Never clean your filter with tap water as the traces of chlorine will kill beneficial bacteria. Instead, use pond water in a bucket to rinse any sediment from the bottom of the filter and from the filter material itself.

Repairing holes

If your pond develops a leak, in order to locate it you should allow the water level to go down until it stops falling. The hole will then be at some point around the pond, at the final water level. Try to avoid emptying the pond completely, as it takes some time to re-establish bacteria living at the very bottom.

Holes in flexible pond liners can be fixed using a repair kit. Concrete ponds will need to have any cracks chipped out and then made good with waterproof render. Once this has set, seal the concrete surface with paint-on pond sealer.

Fish and wildlife

Regardless of the location of your garden, wildlife will appear within weeks of a pond being dug and take up residence. Frogs and toads have a marvellous ability to detect the presence of a new pond and will soon make themselves at home.

Fish and wildlife can live quite happily alongside each other, but large goldfish have a tendency to eat tadpoles – so if a truly natural wildlife pond is what you want, then it may be best to not include fish. If you do want fish, the time to introduce them is the spring.

Herons are notorious for decimating pond fish. They may be put off by a plastic heron standing guard, but the most effective deterrent is to run wire, about 15–30cm high, around the edge of the pond. This prevents them wading into the water – which is effective as they don't swoop and scoop but land and watch for fish, either from the bank or after walking into the shallows.

Cats may be attracted by fish, too. Dense marginal planting helps keep cats away from the water. But if they're determined, netting over the pond may be the only effective option.

Keeping kids safe

No one can keep an eye on their children every minute of the day – and children can and do drown, year after year, in just a few centimetres of water. The only reliable safety advice is if you have children don't have a pond.

There are plenty of other garden features that provide the tranquillity of water. Water running up and down an obelisk or over or through cobbles, for example, doesn't present the same danger – as there's no pool of water into which a child can fall.

If you have children and move into a house that has a pond, without delay either fill it in or ensure it is made safe. One option is to place galvanised mesh just under the surface, making sure it is securely fixed and that it's of a strong enough gauge to support the weight of a child. Another is to erect a padlocked fence around the perimeter of the pond. It needn't be 2m high or consist of solid panels – but it does need to be childproof.

Watering
the garden

Water is the earth's most precious resource. Like all living things, plants need it to survive. Fortunately watering wisely – in the right amounts and in the right places – will keep your garden healthy while minimising waste.

Conserving water

As recent hot summers have proven, water is not the infinite resource we once presumed it to be. Conserving the water we have and using it wisely within a garden makes sense on many levels. It will reduce costs if you have a water meter. You can also collect your own – not only is this free to do, but it's better for the environment (see page 253).

When to water

It's best not to water as a matter of routine. Only water plants when they show signs of needing a drink or if they are newly planted. If a border really does need watering then it should be done either early morning or preferably late evening; this minimises the water lost to evaporation and prevents scorching. When you do water, it is vital that the plants are given a thorough drenching, or else you will simply moisten the top few centimetres of soil and the roots will grow upwards in search of it. This creates a vicious circle: shallow-rooted plants require regular watering, whereas deep-rooted ones are capable of seeking out their own supply further down. Mulching beds will also greatly reduce the watering requirements as it seals in moisture, preventing evaporation.

How much to water

The amount of water plants need varies widely: those that thrive in full sun and free-draining soil require very little; large-leaved, luscious ones a great deal more. When first planted they all need a good soak; after that will depend upon plant and weather. Plants put in the ground in autumn will require no further watering unless the weather is unusually dry; by the time summer comes around their roots will be more than adequate to draw in water from the ground in all but the driest of weather. Plants put in either in spring or early summer will need watering throughout their first summer.

You can do it...

Thirsty plants
Wilting, drooping leaves are a sign of a thirsty plant. But you don't have to wait until this stage before watering. You can check the soil – it should feel moist but not soggy. If it is dry and quite pale, your plants definitely need watering. For plants in terracotta pots, you can also give the side of the container a gentle knock – if the pot sounds hollow and empty, it means the plant in it needs water.

B&Q

ideal tool
Multi-function gun

This hose gun provides a useful selection of spray and jet patterns. A standard spray can be used for established gardens, while a mist or perlator spray is ideal for watering delicate seedlings or newly seeded lawns.

Watering cans

A traditional and effective way to water plants on a small scale is with a watering can. New designs, which include angled rose attachments, help prevent spilling when full and enable more accurate watering.

Watering tools

If you can manage it, watering with a hose or watering can is best – this way you can keep a close eye on your plants, not only to see if they're thirsty but also to check for any problems such as pests or diseases. However, many people simply don't have the time for this. If that sounds like you, then consider a sprinkler, soaker hose or other automatic watering system (see page 252).

Hoses

A good garden hose will last season after season if stored carefully. Make sure the hose pipe is long enough to reach the areas you need to water. A long-reach watering wand will be handy for delivering water to hanging baskets and pots. For even more control when applying water, use a trigger pistol or multi-function gun, which provide a selection of spray patterns. Hose guides protect plants from damage by guiding the hose around obstructions as you unwind it.

Hose storage

Hose reels can be mounted on a wall or floor, or transported on a cart. An auto-rewind model (pictured) will let you wind your hose automatically.

Watering wand

Long-reach hose attachment – perfect for watering hanging baskets and pots.

Trigger pistol

For spraying or jetting water.

Effort-free watering

Sprinklers are useful for covering lawns or watering newly planted beds; traditional ones spray in a circular pattern, while newer models can be set to spray in a specific shape to suit your garden. Oscillating sprinklers rotate from side to side to cover a wider area. Some models have a choice of spray patterns: a standard spray suits established lawns and borders, while a mist spray is for newly seeded lawns. For delivering water exactly when and where it's needed, an automatic watering system is ideal. It can be fitted with a timer that will switch your water source on and off at specified times – great for when you're out or on holiday. In-line feeders make it possible to feed and water your plants at the same time.

The majority of water companies in England and Wales now require customers who use sprinklers or any unattended garden watering device to have a water meter installed. Contact your water supplier for details.

Sprinkler

Ideal for watering large areas of lawn or border.

Oscillating sprinkler

The width and length of the spray can be adjusted for your garden.

Water timer

For setting specific watering times.

How to water

The aim of watering is to raise the moisture content of the soil around a plant's roots, and not to wet the foliage or the surrounding ground. This will ensure the plant receives water where it is needed, without promoting weeds nearby. Bearing this in mind, here are a few tips:

- Aim to water at the base of the stem, beneath the foliage.
- Fine droplets are preferable to heavy watering, which will damage the soil structure.
- It's most important to water plants that are newly planted, young, shallow-rooted, in containers, annuals or edible.
- Established lawns, shrubs and trees need very little watering.
- Vegetables will benefit from extra watering in the two weeks prior to harvest, especially leaf crops such as lettuces.
- Avoid watering at the hottest time of the day or in full sun.
- Damp plants are vulnerable to fungal infection (see page 259). In dull weather, watering in the morning will give them a chance to dry out before it gets dark.

Watering systems
and storage

Watering can be made more efficient by use of modern watering systems and by the storage and recycling of rainwater and also some domestic waste water, known as grey water.

Water where it's needed

A good watering system will deliver water only to the plants that need it and at the most appropriate time. Normal sprinklers, though popular, tend to waste water as they often miss their target. Soaker hose or dripper systems are much more accurate ways of applying water as they deliver it exactly where you want them to. They are easy to install and, once fitted, will save you hours of time and effort. What's more, you can control the flow manually or with the help of a timer.

Which system to choose

A soaker hose watering system is made up of a porous hose that allows water to seep out all the way along its length. Once connected to a tap and woven in between plants as needed, the hose can be hidden under a few centimetres of soil or mulch. This system is best for raising moisture levels over a large area such as a border or bed.

A dripper system waters each plant or container using tiny water outlets or drippers connected to a supply hose. It can be assembled to fit any garden layout and is ideal for pots and hanging baskets as well as flowerbeds.

tools materials

- **watering dripper kit**
- **craft knife**

- mulch
- water timer

1 Unravel the supply hose and run it around the area you want to water. You may need to work between established plants or around the edge of the beds.

2 Once the supply hose is in place, close off the end by bending it back on itself and through the end plug provided.

3 Punch a hole into the supply hose wherever you plan to insert a subsidiary hose.

4 Position drippers as needed. Cut sections of subsidiary hose to length and use them to connect the drippers to the supply hose.

5 Once you have finished putting together your dripper network, peg the supply hose into place and hide it under a layer of soil or mulch.

6 Fit a water timer to your water tap. Connect the supply hose to the tap using a length of standard hose. Set the timer.

7 Test the system and adjust the drippers if necessary.

eco timing

Night water

Water at night with the help of a timer – it is good for the plants and the environment. You will lose less water by evaporation in the cool of the evening or night. Turn the timer off during wet periods, but remember that pots in the rain shadow of a house will always need watering.

grow

Collecting and storing water

You can do a favour to your plants, the environment and even your wallet by collecting, storing and recycling rainwater.

Rainwater

Not only is rainwater free, but it is better for plants than tap water as it contains more nutrients. What's more, unlike hard mains water, rainwater will not leave limescale deposits or increase the alkalinity of the soil. The best way to collect rainwater is in a water butt connected to a downpipe.

1 Choose a suitable and convenient downpipe for the water butt and place the stand beneath it. The butt needs to be raised high enough off the ground for a watering can to fit under the tap.

2 Place the water butt on the stand and mark its height on the downpipe. Cut the downpipe 3cm below this point with a hacksaw.

tools materials

- **power drill fitted with a hole saw**
- **hacksaw**

- water butt and stand
- rain diverter kit

3 Attach the rain diverter fitting to the downpipe; the cut section of downpipe fits onto the bottom of the diverter.

4 Measure 8cm down from the top of the water butt and drill a hole through which the water butt connector is fitted.

5 Attach the water butt connector to the water butt by pushing through the drilled hole and screwing fittings into place.

6 Attach the water butt connector to the rainwater diverter with the supplied fittings. Place the lid on the butt and lock it into place. A lid also prevents mosquitoes laying eggs in the water.

Grey water

Much of the waste water you produce at home can safely be used in the garden. This kind of domestic waste water is called grey water – completely different from black water, which is sewage. Every home produces large quantities of grey water, which is fine for plants as long as it is not contaminated by an excess of detergents, soaps or cooking residues.

- Never use grey water that contains bleach, disinfectants or strong cleaning products.
- Don't use grey water on edible plants or for filling ponds.
- Alternate the use of grey water with rain- or mains water.
- Never use grey water on container-grown, newly propagated, or conservatory or greenhouse-grown plants.

- Do not use grey water from dishwashers or washing machines.
- Use grey water as soon as it is cool – do not store it.
- Apply grey water to soil and not to the foliage.
- Never apply grey water with a sprinkler or a watering system.

Weeds, pests and diseases

Part of caring for your garden is dealing with weeds, pests and diseases. All of these will affect the health of your plants; keeping a close eye on your garden will help you nip these problems in the bud.

What are weeds?

Weeds are plants in the wrong place – they take space, water sunlight and nutrients from the plants we really want to grow. Some are more aggressive than others. Annual weeds such as shepherd's purse can grow and set seed in as little as a month in summer, but are easy to get rid of – simply remove them before they develop seedheads. Perennial weeds such as bindweed are trickier to control. They will survive the winter and often spread invasively through their roots – even the tiniest section of root left in the soil can produce a whole new plant. For help with identifying common weeds, see pages 256–57.

Can weeds be avoided?

Few gardens are completely clear of weeds, and some are more prone to them than others – those in the country, for instance, or located next to an unkempt neighbouring garden. However, weeds can be kept at bay, and doing this will save you a lot of work in your garden.

Prevention

You can reduce the likelihood of weeds taking hold by mulching beds and borders in spring or after planting (see page 191), but always clear the ground of weeds first. If creating a new bed, you could plant through weed-control fabric (see page 33).

Taking action

If weeds do set in, you can take control by weeding little and often – this is much better than blitzing a garden every few weeks or months, as the weeds won't get too big. Hoeing is an effective means of clearing annual weed seedlings from flower and vegetable beds, and is best done on dry days as the weeds will shrivel and die more quickly.

ideal tool
Hoe
A hoe is in effect a flat knife attached to a long stick. The best tool for tackling weeds in beds and borders, especially if your soil is crumbly, a hoe slices through the weeds just below soil level. Left on the surface of the soil, they will soon shrivel and die.

Chemical weedkillers

Trying to remove deeply rooted or dense weeds by hand is hard work. Chemical treatment is not as toxic as it may sound. Translocated (or systemic) weedkillers such as glyphosate are absorbed by the foliage and carried down to the roots. They are non-residual – they don't pollute the ground – so can be used to clear an area for planting. Be patient: they may take up to two weeks to work. And apply carefully – they are non-selective, so will kill any plant they touch.

safety first
Using weedkillers safely
- Always follow instructions exactly, and dilute and apply as directed.
- Don't leave weedkillers within reach of children.
- Never store weedkillers in unmarked containers.
- If weedkiller gets onto your skin, wash it off immediately.

You can do it...

Tackling bindweed
Stick a garden cane into the ground for the bindweed to climb up. Once it has climbed above other plants, paint or spray its leaves with glyphosate.

B&Q

Pests – natural defences

The first line of defence against pests is to grow strong, healthy plants that can withstand a bit of chomping here and there. Secondly, each pest has a natural predator which, if allowed to do so, is capable of controlling the problem for you – so welcome into your garden insects and other forms of wildlife that are the gardener's friends. Ladybirds, lacewings and hoverflies, for example, will devour copious quantities of aphids. Lure them with nectar-producing plants and flowering herbs such as santolina, lavender, sage or rosemary.

Birds can play an active role in reducing the population of caterpillars that eat your vegetables and other plants. The most virulent infestations occur when there are nests full of hungry mouths to feed. A well-stocked bird table is one way to increase the number of birds that visit your garden.

Every garden will eventually develop its own balance. In the meantime, here are suggestions for fighting the worst offenders.

Fighting pests

Manual collection
Pick off and dispose of slugs, snails, caterpillars and adult vine weevils (see page 258).

Barrier methods
- Lay horticultural fleece over crops susceptible to cabbage white caterpillars (see page 288).
- Sprinkle sharp sand, horticultural grit or even eggshells around plants susceptible to slug damage.
- Wrap copper-impregnated tape around pots. When slugs or snails try to cross the tape, they are zapped by a small electrical charge.

Traps
- In greenhouses, hang sticky yellow traps that attract aphids and whitefly.
- Hang pheromone traps from fruit trees. They attract the adult males, which become caught on the sticky inside.
- To decrease the wasp population, hang wasp traps close to fruit trees before the fruit becomes fully ripe (see page 234).
- Both beer traps sunk in the ground and upturned grapefruit skins attract slugs and snails, which can then be disposed of.

Slug pellets

Copper-impregnated tape

Companion planting
Many insects, particularly aphids, detest strong-scented plants.
- Marigolds planted next to susceptible plants serve a double purpose. They keep away a variety of insect pests and attract hoverflies, which feast on aphids.
- In vegetable plots, plant alternate rows of vegetables and flowers. The scent of the flowers will disguise the smell of the vegetables and will attract predators, too.

Slug pellets
Use slug pellets with caution as they can be poisonous to other wildlife if eaten in large quantities. Choose pellets formulated to cause least harm to other creatures. Scatter them thinly and always follow the instructions on the packet.

Pesticides
Those based on soft soap, insecticidal soap or quassia are non-residual. They can be used against aphids, caterpillars, red spider mites, sawflies and woodlice. However, they are not selective and kill all insects, good and bad. Lots of people swear by spraying dilute washing-up liquid onto affected plants, though its effectiveness has not been officially proven.

Nematodes
These are microscopic natural predators, resembling tiny worms. Some destroy insects, and all of them are species specific. They're most effective within greenhouses; less so in the open, as they need warmth to survive. They are usually sold in powder form, for mixing with water before watering onto plants and soil.

Keeping out other animals

- **Cats** If the toilet habits of neighbourhood cats are a problem, try placing moth balls or lemon or orange peel in their favourite spot, or spray it with cat-repellent.
- **Badgers** Remarkably strong and protected by law, badgers are very difficult to keep out. If they are destroying your fence, install a large drainage pipe beneath it as a tunnel for them.
- **Deer** These beautiful creatures will munch their way through a garden overnight, rose bushes being a favourite food. Deer-proof fencing needs to be at least 2.5m tall to keep them out.
- **Sonic deterrents** Designed to deter animals by emitting a noise unpleasant to their ears, but inaudible to ours. There are various types on the market, either battery- or mains-powered – the frequency and pitch of the sound is adjusted to repel particular animals, for example squirrels.

Identifying weeds, pests and diseases

In order to get rid of weeds, pests and diseases, you need to be able to recognise which ones are invading your garden or attacking your plants. Identifying the culprits enables you to decide what measures are most likely to be effective.

Unwelcome visitors

In any garden, as well as the many things that delight, there are others that are less welcome. Weeds, pests and diseases, if left unchecked, can quickly overwhelm, disfigure or kill your much-prized plants, rapidly undoing all that hard work. Knowing how to spot and manage problems will help protect your garden.

Bindweed

A fast-growing climber, with an extensive root system that can smother everything in its path. Digging it up works to some extent – but repeat applications of chemical treatment are needed to stop it growing back again, as each bit of root left in the soil will grow a new plant.

Japanese knotweed

Originally imported from Japan as a garden plant, this leafy perennial, 1–2m high, has now become an invasive weed. The roots grow deep into the ground – a metre or more down – so use repeat applications of chemical weedkiller as soon as you spot it.

Horsetail

A moisture-loving perennial with jointed stems and small scale-like leaves. It's rarely found in cultivated ground, but the roots are too deep to dig out – so if it does appear, apply repeat chemical treatments. In lawns, regular mowing will eventually kill it off.

Docks

Nature's cure for stinging nettle rashes. A tough perennial; two forms, curly-leaved and broad-leaved, are common. You can dig out the deep tap root using a sharp tool such as a garden knife, but chemical treatment is likely to be necessary. Try to prevent seedheads developing.

Nettles

Spring up quickly in vacant spaces. Roots are fairly shallow and can be pulled out by hand (wear tough gloves for the stinging kind), but a dense mat of roots will need treating with a translocated weedkiller.

Couch grass

Impossible to remove if it grows through the roots of plants, so deal with it quickly before it takes hold. Chemical treatment is effective – but try digging out all roots first, as each bit left in the soil will sprout again.

Dandelion

Don't let dandelions get to the seedhead stage, as the fluffy 'clocks' blow everywhere. The long tap root can be dug out, or selective weedkiller can be used in lawns. Young dandelion leaves are tasty in salads.

Shepherd's purse

An annual weed that doesn't pose a real problem – though it grows and sets seed so quickly that forests of them seem to spring up almost overnight. Either pull them out, hoe them, or dig them in.

Ragwort

On farmland it's illegal to allow ragwort to flourish, as the leaves are poisonous to grazing animals. Easy to pull or dig out, but clear away the plants and burn – as even dried-up dying leaves carry the same risk.

Creeping thistle

Has two means of reproducing itself – fluffy seeds that blow off with the slightest breeze and creeping underground roots. Chemical treatment is the most effective way of dealing with it.

Coltsfoot

A creeping plant that thrives in poor soil, especially clay (in the wild, it grows on wasteland and dry banks). The yellow flowers appear before the leaves. Can be dug out or treated with an appropriate weedkiller.

Groundsel

Looks a bit like ragwort and acts as a secondary host to many fungal rusts. Its light-weight downy seedheads enable it to spread very rapidly. Like shepherd's purse, either pull or hoe out, or dig in.

Creeping buttercup

Easy to dig out, as the roots are fairly shallow. The big problem is its ability to spread in all directions by sending out runners – just as strawberry plants do. If left unchecked, it can rapidly ruin a lawn; a selective lawn weedkiller can be used to prevent this.

Lesser celandine

Pretty golden-yellow harbinger of spring. Loves moist shade (makes an ideal groundcover plant for difficult spots). Almost evergreen, its leaves stop most other plants growing through. If unwanted, remove promptly – either dig it out or use repeat chemical treatments.

Deadly nightshade

So deadly a few berries can kill an adult human – and they're the least poisonous part of the plant. The roots are even more toxic. Tall, with large leaves, it has purplish flowers from June to August, then glossy black berries. Chemical treatment is really the only option.

Giant hogweed

Looks like a huge coarse form of cow parsley. It is illegal to let this grow as its sap, which reacts with sunlight, causes severe blistering. Chemical treatment when the plant is young is most effective. When removing, wear gloves, long sleeves and goggles.

Brambles

A real menace, as any stem touching the ground will root. Small ones are easy to pull or dig out. Cut back mature plants with loppers and thick gloves (burn or shred trimmings); then apply translocated weedkiller.

Ground elder

Highly invasive. Unless wanted as ground cover, try digging out – but any bits of root left behind will regenerate. Constantly removing top growth weakens it dramatically. If need be, treat with translocated weedkiller.

Himalayan balsam

A statuesque member of the 'Busy Lizzie' family, with large pink flowers. An annual weed that is easy to pull out, although each plant produces a vast number of seedlings.

Daisy

Delightful in the wild, but the subject of controversy among gardeners – either it's a weed or a pretty little white-flowered plant that looks good in lawns. For treatment in lawns, see pages 268–69.

Weeds, pests and diseases 257

Slugs and snails

Snails and slugs love cool wet weather and like eating tender plants such as hostas. Sweep up garden rubbish, so they can't hide under it. For traps and deterrents, see page 255.

Aphids and whitefly

Greenfly, whitefly and blackfly are all sapsucking insects that can severely disfigure flowers and growing tips. The honey-dew they deposit on leaves attracts a sooty mould.

Vine weevils

Grey long-snouted beetles, the adults just nibble leaf edges. But when the large, fat, brown-headed maggot-like grubs hatch in the soil, where they are laid, they eat every root in sight.

Caterpillars

Cabbage white and mullein moth caterpillars tend to be the biggest problem. The former attack nasturtiums as well as brassicas; the latter devastate verbascums.

Squirrels

They're notorious for causing damage to young trees – so protect the trunk with a tree guard (see page 223) when planting. To prevent squirrels digging up newly planted bulbs, fix chicken wire over them.

Leatherjackets

Looking like fat brownish, legless caterpillars, these are in fact daddy-longlegs' larvae. They live in the soil and feed on the roots of almost anything. Can be especially problematic in lawns, because they eat the roots of the grass (for dealing with lawn pests, see page 269).

Red spider mites

Tiny, almost invisible, spiders that betray their presence by spinning webs between leaves. More likely to be a problem in a greenhouse than in the garden, but will move out in warm dry conditions. Being sapsuckers, they cause mottling on leaves. Bad infestations can kill plants.

Millipedes

Shiny black many-legged creatures that like to eat roots. They are rarely a serious problem unless they occur in large numbers. Sweeping up garden rubbish regularly helps keep numbers in check.

Scale insects

Flat brownish sapsuckers that cling to stems, like barnacles to a boat. They secrete honeydew (the sugars from inside a plant), which encourages sooty mould to develop. Bad infestations can kill plants.

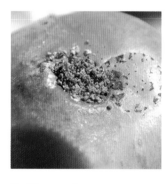

Codling moths

The moths lay their eggs on young apples. As the maggot-like grubs hatch, they burrow their way into the apples. Often there are no external signs, and their presence is revealed only when the apple is bitten into.

Sawflies

Like small caterpillars, their spotted grubs can defoliate a whole currant or gooseberry bush in days. Apple-sawfly grubs leave long scars on the fruit, which will drop when the pests burrow into its core.

Wasps

These feast on soft-skinned or damaged fruit so harvesting plums or picking up fallen pears may mean risking a sting or two. Wasp traps (see page 234) placed near fruit trees can help reduce their numbers.

Rose black spot

Disease causing black spots on leaves. Some rose varieties are more resistant to it. Burn the fallen leaves; cut off spotted stems when pruning. Repeated anti-fungal spraying helps.

Powdery mildew

Grey powdery coating on the leaves of roses and other plants. Mulching, balanced feeding and regular watering help. Some rose varieties are more resistant than others.

Grey mould

Mainly found on pelargoniums and other plants overwintering in humid greenhouses. Improve ventilation, and pick off and burn mouldy leaves. Also rots strawberries in wet summers.

Canker

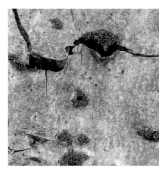

Often attacks apple and pear trees. Starts as discoloured sunken patches, followed by white then red pustules. Cut out and burn smaller branches and diseased parts of big ones.

Damping off

This affects seedlings and cuttings, especially in greenhouses – the base turns black, then they collapse and die. Poor hygiene and ventilation and overwatering are the main causes. To reduce risk, sow seed sparsely and drench soil around seeds and cuttings with a copper-based fungicide.

Rust

So called because it forms rust-like orange pustules. Mint, roses and hollyhocks are among the plants prone to forms of this species-specific fungal infection. Spraying with anti-fungal treatment does work – so long as it's done regularly throughout the summer.

Coral spot

Red pustular fungal spots that invade and eventually kill limbs or whole plants. Woody plants are particularly susceptible. Avoid letting it get a foothold by pruning out dead wood and making clean cuts above a healthy bud. On affected plants, prune back hard into healthy wood and burn all clippings.

Silver leaf

An airborne tree disease that enters through open wounds. Leaves develop a silver bloom, then turn brown and drop. To prevent it killing the tree, cut out and burn infected branches. Plum trees are particularly vulnerable, so should be pruned in summer only, when the cuts will heal more quickly.

Clematis wilt

May only be apparent when the plant dies. To protect clematis, plant it with the base of the stems 5–10cm below ground so the roots will re-shoot if the top of the plant dies. Keep roots moist and cool; mulch will help.

Brown rot

Quickly turns fruit brown, ringed with white spots. It spreads by contact, so pick off any affected fruits and burn. Those that drop to the ground will spread the disease unless collected and burned.

Fireblight

Enters trees through damaged tips and cuts, especially in fruit trees, quickly turning leaves brown and killing the tree. The entire tree has to be removed and burned, to stop the disease spreading to other trees.

Honey fungus

Spreads from decaying wood, which gradually dies from the tips down. Peeling back bark at the base reveals a white fungal growth that has a mushroom smell. Remove and burn all affected material.

A grassed area has been a feature in gardens since time immemorial. In bygone times it was often included for practical purposes, such as the grazing of animals. Nowadays a lawn of any size is a welcome luxury, ideal for relaxing and entertaining and as a safe play surface for children. In design terms, a lawn can play a key role, providing simplicity and open space and, particularly in city gardens, a refreshing splash of green.

the perfect lawn

Why have a lawn?

In many gardens, the lawn is a vital balancing element, the perfect backdrop to the more colourful flowering parts of the garden. Without it, mixed borders can seem messy and overwhelming, and subtle planting combinations just get lost in the crowd. Big or small, an expanse of green has a unifying effect, providing a visual link between the different elements of a garden.

Gardeners and non-gardeners unite

Even the least green-fingered people like to have a lawn. In fact, many who aren't much drawn to gardening will happily spend a considerable amount of time looking after the lawn. Why is this? Well, grass provides an ideal surface and space for children to play on, and for adults to laze around or entertain. It's also green all year round – and when mown in spring it has an amazing aroma, awaking thoughts of summer days ahead.

Why grass?

Because it is the perfect plant for the job. How many other plants could withstand being trampled on daily? Grass can tolerate long periods of drought and yet regenerate with the first drops of rain, and it is quite happy having its head cut off on a weekly basis. Plants other than grass are occasionally used to make a lawn. Chamomile, for example, makes wonderfully soft and fragrant groundcover, but it will not survive anything like the heavy use that grass will tolerate, and you also need to keep an alert eye open for weeds. It's therefore more suitable as a decorative detail than as a large-scale practical surface.

Go wild

If lying hidden while watching butterflies flit from flower to flower is your idea of paradise, then a wildflower meadow is the answer. Even in the heart of suburbia or amid inner city sprawl, it's possible to create a little bit of the countryside, complete with a wealth of wildlife. Unlike conventional grass, meadow grasses are left to grow and flower, creating a haven for ladybirds, bumblebees and other beneficial insects.

Lawn calendar

The job of looking after a lawn varies with the seasons, location and type of lawn. Grass that's bowling-green perfect demands a lot of regular maintenance, whereas a more informal lawn needs little more than mowing and edging, plus the occasional seasonal treatment with an appropriate fertiliser to maintain healthy growth.

Maintaining a lawn

If you have an established lawn (rather than one that's just been sown or laid), your priority will be to maintain the health of the grass and keep it looking good all year round, especially during warm dry weather. The best results will come from following a simple regular programme of maintenance throughout the year, rather than occasional bursts of activity and attention.

Early spring

February, March

This is the time when most remedial work is done. But only when the weather is mild and dry: if it's frosty or the ground is waterlogged, do nothing at all – treading on grass in these conditions will do more harm than good.
- Edges can be repaired or patched in early spring.
- If turf has been lifted by frost, go over it with a roller.
- In dry weather, brush worm casts away with a broom.
- If need be, apply moss killer. Spike and scarify now (see page 268) if you didn't do so in autumn.
- Start mowing as soon as the grass begins to grow, raising mower blades to the highest setting.

Late spring

April, May
- If gaps have appeared between the turfs of a new lawn, they can be top-dressed now (see page 266).
- Lawns that are patchy can have bare patches reseeded. Keep newly sown areas watered during dry spells.
- Apply fertiliser and weedkiller, using the correct feed for this time of year (one with a high nitrogen content: see page 191).
- Mow regularly, gradually lowering the blades – bearing in mind that the shorter the grass, the less resistant it is to wear and tear, and the more likely it is to suffer from water shortage.

Summer

June, July, August
- Continue to mow regularly. In dry spells, although the lawn is hardly growing, it's still worth doing this, as it removes the tall leggy sprouts that appear and cuts off weed seedheads.
- If after a long dry spell your lawn is looking a bit brown, don't panic – unless it is a new lawn, it will recover quickly.
- If you do decide to water, give the lawn a thorough soaking, leaving the sprinkler on for at least half an hour. A drop of water does more harm than none at all, as the roots of the grass turn upwards to seek it out – which makes them even more susceptible to drought damage.
- Don't feed your lawn or apply weedkillers in dry conditions – they will burn the grass.
- If a cool spell occurs, patchy areas can still be reseeded.
- Raise the mower cutting height in dry weather - if you cut the grass short, it will go brown very quickly.

Change your mowing pattern

Always mowing in the same direction compacts the soil and causes the grass to lean in the direction it is mowed. Changing your mowing pattern every few weeks will keep the grass healthier and more upright, and enable you to achieve a cleaner cut. It can be fun making different patterns on the lawn.

Whether you prefer neat contrasting stripes or concentric circles, every change of direction will contribute to a healthier, greener lawn. For a traditional striped effect, use a mower that has a roller.

Autumn

September, October

- Remove fallen leaves from your lawn regularly. If allowed to build up, they will kill the grass beneath.
- Continue to mow regularly, gradually increasing the height of the blades – if you leave the grass too short during the winter, it will be vulnerable to frost damage.
- Apply autumn feed to help toughen up the grass for the winter.
- Spike or aerate the lawn, and scarify it (see page 268). Top-dress, if need be (see page 266).
- Any edges damaged by overhanging plants during the summer can be repaired now.

Winter

November, December, January

- The lawn can have its final cut of the year now – or perhaps slightly earlier for those who live further north.
- Book your mower in for servicing.
- Continue to clear fallen leaves from your lawn.
- Most important, avoid treading on grass in frosty weather – if you do, the frozen tips will fracture and you'll be left with a damaged lawn. If you need to work on beds or borders in these conditions, lay boards down over the parts of the lawn you will walk across, and especially where you need to manoeuvre a wheelbarrow.

To water or not to water?

New lawns require watering throughout their first season. But established lawns will survive dry summers perfectly well without watering, unless there are extreme drought conditions – at which point there will be a hose-pipe ban, anyway. In a long hot summer lawns will go brown, but when cooler, damper weather arrives they will begin to recover.

Watering a lawn takes copious amounts of water. In dry periods, once you've started you will have to continue, because the lush new growth triggered by watering will need further amounts of water to maintain it.

If you really must water, then make sure you do it either early in the morning or later in the evening – never in between, or the grass will scorch in the sun. Better still, connect a timing device to a sprinkler, set to come on during the night, when every drop of water will be absorbed by the grass instead of evaporating in the daytime heat.

ideal tool

Water timer

Newly sown or newly turfed lawns should be given watering priority in a drought. Use a sprinkler with a timer for easy watering at night. With an established lawn, mow less and don't cut the grass too short – but don't panic. Remember that established lawns will usually recover when the rains return after a drought.

eco watering

Water meters
The majority of water companies in England and Wales require customers who use sprinklers or any unattended garden watering device to have a water meter installed. Contact your water supplier for details.

Tools for easy
lawn maintenance

Having the right equipment, and knowing how to use and maintain it properly, will make a world of difference when it comes to the ongoing task of looking after your lawn.

Edging and cutting tools

It isn't always possible to take a lawnmower right up to the edges of a lawn, so these may need to be trimmed by hand. Edging shears are specially designed to enable you to maintain a neat and well-defined edge around your lawn. Small areas of grass that are awkward to mow are best cut with lawn shears; long-handled versions are the most comfortable to use. For areas of grass that are difficult to reach, look for shears with telescopic extending handles.

An electric or petrol-driven trimmer makes light work of most edging and trimming tasks; choose petrol for bigger gardens and tougher brushcutting. If you want to use a trimmer for edging, choose one that has an edging facility.

An edging iron – also known as a half-moon edger – is useful for cutting away worn or uneven lawn edges along beds and borders and also for cutting turf. Use it with a rocking, sawing motion as you press down to cut.

Most of this work of trimming and cutting lawn edges is eliminated by installing a hard edging around the lawn that lies flush with the ground (see page 267).

Flat-tined rake

Spring-tined rake

Rakes

Lawn rakes are useful not only for clearing fallen leaves and other debris from the grass, but also for drawing out thatch and moss – a process known as scarifying (see page 268). Flat-tined rakes are designed for gathering leaves and twigs. Rakes with spring tines will also scarify and lightly aerate a lawn. Scarifying and raking can be hard work: an electric-powered lawn-raker will make your lawn care much easier.

Electric lawn raker

Spikers

Lawns benefit greatly from aerating or spiking, which improves drainage and reinvigorates growth by allowing air to the roots. You can do this with a garden fork but it is quicker and easier to use a specially designed multi-prong rolling aerator or spiker. Hollow-tined spikers, which extract small plugs of soil, are recommended for use on heavy clay lawns and for grass with obvious drainage problems (see page 268).

Spiker

Long-handled lawn shears

Edging iron

Power trimmers

Edging shears

Rollers and spreaders

Garden rollers are used to level and flatten soil before sowing grass seed or laying turf. They are also useful in spring to flatten patches of turf lifted by frost. For regular maintenance, however, a mower with a roller is sufficient. Over-use of a roller will compact and damage an established lawn.

Convenient and inexpensive, a wheeled lawn spreader makes it easier to distribute grass seed, fertiliser or granular weedkiller evenly and accurately.

Garden roller

Lawn spreader

Choosing a lawn mower

When choosing a mower, you need to take into account the shape and size of your lawn, the finish you want, and what will happen to the clippings. A box for collecting grass clippings will save you time and leave a cleaner lawn. These are traditionally mounted at the front. But if plants and bushes overhang the lawn around the edges, a rear or centrally mounted grass box can make mowing easier and let you cut closer to the edge.

How big is your lawn?
- **Small to medium (up to 100m²)** An electric mower with a cutting width of up to 32cm is usually ideal, though a smaller width of 25–28cm is recommended for very small or awkwardly shaped areas.
- **Medium to large (100m² to 400m²)** Choose an electric or petrol mower with a cutting width up to 40cm. Petrol will give you more power to cope with longer grass and bigger areas. A self-propelled model that you guide – rather than push – makes mowing much less of an effort.
- **Large (over ⅓ acre)** Consider investing in a petrol-powered tractor mower.

Hover
Floating on a cushion of air, a hover mower is particularly easy to use and manoeuvre, especially over uneven surfaces. But it doesn't give the fine cut or striped finish of rotary or cylinder mowers.

safety first
Outdoor electrics
- Never use electrically powered garden tools in a wet garden or when it is raining.
- Always use an RCD (residual current device) with electrical equipment outdoors (see page 21).
- Before inspecting or maintaining a power tool, always disconnect the electrical supply.
- Check that electrical tools are working correctly, and that flexes and plugs are in good condition.

Rotary
The scythe action of a rotary mower's blade gives a closer, finer finish than a hover mower. Wheels support and guide it, so it's easy to keep to straight lines. For a striped finish, choose a model with a built-in roller. Rotary mowers tackle longer grass than cylinder mowers as well as uneven ground. Both electric and petrol models are available, as are self-propelled rotary mowers.

Cylinder
The scissor action of a cylinder mower gives the finest, closest cut of all. All models have a roller for a striped finish. This is a good choice for a fine quality, flat lawn that is mowed regularly. Both electric and petrol models are available, as are self-propelled cylinder mowers.

You can do it...

Easy to steer

Few lawns have straight edges. This electric steerable rotary mower allows you to turn without lifting, mow around obstacles, and even move sideways to cut right up to the edge of the lawn.

B&Q

Petrol mowers
- **Before use** Check fuel and oil levels as well as for any loose and worn parts.
- **After use** Turn off the engine and remove clippings from the top of the upper surface and from the underside. To access the underside, raise the front wheels – don't tip the mower on its side, or oil will flood the air filter.
- **Regular maintenance during the mowing season** Clean or change the air filter; oil wheels and moving parts.
- **Winter storage and spring preparation** Clean thoroughly and drain the petrol. Lubricate where necessary and, if appropriate, oil the cylinder. In spring, change the spark plug and clean or replace the air filter; on rotary mowers, change the oil and, if necessary, the blade, and oil all controls and linkages.

Tractor mowers
A ride-on petrol-powered tractor mower can make light work of cutting even the largest lawn or paddock and is designed to tow useful accessories, such as a roller, tipping trailer and spreader. They are available in a range of sizes and engine powers, with cutting widths of up to a metre and more, saving time over large areas of grass. Always remember to check that the tractor you choose will fit through any gates and into your shed or garage.

Keeping your lawn
fed, level and neat

Feeding a lawn is an important part of keeping it healthy. Top-dressing keeps it tidy by levelling out hollows. And a permanent hard edging is a neat and very practical finishing touch.

A well-fed lawn

Fertiliser is vital for keeping a lawn lush and green. Lawns should only be fed during the growing season and usually need only two feeds a year – in spring and autumn. The spring feed should be high in nitrogen to kick-start the growth of lots of lush new grass, whereas the autumn feed should be high in phosphorus and potassium to toughen the grass up for the winter. Always choose a dry day for feeding, but make sure the ground is not too dry – water first if necessary.

Combined lawn feed and weedkiller

Many lawn feed products combine lawn fertiliser with weedkiller. They are applied in exactly the same way, but you need to be much more cautious to prevent the treatment spreading onto other plants, as it may kill them. The advantage of such a combined product is that well-fed grasses will grow more vigorously to fill gaps where the weeds have died back.

Levelling humps and hollows

If your lawn has humps and hollows, top-dressing will help level it out. This is best done in spring or autumn, or both. You can either buy top-dressing material (sometimes labelled turf dressing) or mix your own, using equal parts of sieved garden soil and sharp sand. On heavy clay soils, horticultural sand (not builder's sand, which contains lime) can be used instead of sharp sand. Rake or brush the material into the hollows, making sure it's no more than 1cm thick – don't bury the grass completely, or it will die.

Feeding your lawn

On smaller lawns, you can scatter granular feed by hand. If you are in doubt about how much and how far to scatter, mark out a square metre with canes and twine. Then measure out the dosage per metre, as instructed on the feed packet, and spread it inside the square – this will give you a visual guide to go by. You can do the same when applying liquid feeds with a watering can or sprayer. Bigger lawns are best fed using granular feed in a wheeled spreader; these cover large areas quickly and ensure you are using the correct amount of feed.

tools materials
- **wheeled lawn spreader**
- granular lawn feed

1 Load the spreader with granular lawn feed. It's best to do this away from the lawn, to avoid spills. Adjust the dial to measure out the correct dosage of feed per square metre.

2 Walk systematically up and down the lawn, pulling the spreader behind you.

1 Sprinkle top-dressing material evenly over the area – a shovel is ideal for doing this.

2 Spread the dressing material with the back of a rake so that it's no more than 1cm thick. The grass beneath it should still be clearly visible.

3 Use a stiff broom to brush the dressing in, making sure the grass isn't buried.

tools materials
- **shovel**
- **garden rake**
- **stiff broom**

- ready-mixed top-dressing; or a mix of sharp (or horticultural) sand and sieved garden soil

Installing stone edging

One of the most trying chores when cutting the grass is maintaining an edge next to a surface that is at a different level. An electric trimmer makes this task very much easier (see page 264) – but for the ultimate low-maintenance solution, install stone edging to create a robust surface that you can mow right over in a single pass.

tools materials

- **gloves**
- **bricklayer's trowel**
- **spirit level**
- **rubber mallet**
- **pointing trowel**
- **pointing iron**
- edging stones
- mortar

1 Lay a bed of mortar next to the path and press the mortar down so that the edging stones will lie flush with the path.

2 Butt the edging stones flush against the path, but leave a 15mm pointing gap between sets of stones.

3 As you work along the path, use a long spirit level to check that your stones are level.

4 Use a rubber mallet to tap the stones into place, making sure they are flush with the path.

5 Smooth the mortar against the edge of the stones to hold the row in place.

6 Use a pointing iron to finish the joints between the stones neatly with mortar.

Turfing or seeding up to hard edging

When laying a new lawn up to hard edging, it's important to make sure the ground level will lie flush with the edging – otherwise you could find yourself hand-trimming after all.

What kind of edging?

All kinds of materials can be used to make low-maintenance lawn edging. Purpose-designed edgings include bricks, terracotta or concrete blocks, plastic strips and pressure-treated timber. Decking boards are ideal for edging lawns alongside planted beds (see page 114).

Turf

Make sure the level of the grass will be at the right height: the top of the soil (not the top of the grass) needs to be level with the edging.

Seed

Before sowing rake the prepared soil and make sure it's level with the top of the edging stones.

Looking after your lawn

Some people's dream lawn is a perfect bowling green. Others are happy with a more natural-looking expanse that includes sprinklings of wild flowers. Whatever your preference, there are ways to make the most of what you have.

Spiking

Spiking or aerating improves drainage and stimulates root growth. Do it in autumn, or if your lawn is getting compacted.

Push spiker

Using a garden fork for spiking is hard work. A push spiker will make the job less laborious and help you to spike more evenly.

Hollow-tined spiker

Purpose-made for aerating, a hollow-tined spiker lifts out cores of grass and soil. When using one, work evenly and methodically across the lawn. Pour horticultural sand into the holes to further improve drainage.

Scarifying

Moss acts like a sponge: it prevents light, water and nutrients from reaching the roots of the grass. Thatch, which consists of layers of dead grass and moss that have accumulated on the surface of the soil, must also be removed to maintain a healthy lawn. Either remove little and often from March to October – except during a drought – or scarify vigorously in the spring and autumn. A week before scarifying, apply a moss killer.

Powered lawnraker

An electric lawnraker makes light work of scarifying and can be used to clear leaves from the lawn in autumn, too. If scarifying by hand, use a spring-tined lawn rake.

You can do it...

Repairing a damaged edge

Crumbling or damaged lawn edges are easy to repair. Remove a square or rectangle of turf including the damaged edge. Turn it round and put it back with the broken edge to the inside. Then fill the damaged area with topsoil and reseed.

B&Q

Dealing with lawn weeds

Even if you love having wild plants in your garden, there are some that need to be dealt with – otherwise you run the risk of them taking over your lawn.

Trefoils, plantain, chickweed, speedwell, clover, creeping buttercup, dandelions, spear thistles and creeping thistles are the ones to get rid of (see opposite). Hand-weeding is fine if there aren't too many – for deep-rooted dandelions, use an old kitchen knife or a weeding tool.

If there are weeds all over the place, treat them with weed-killer spray or granules. Use lawn weedkiller only – any other kind will kill everything, including the grass. There's a range of liquid and granular products available; choose whichever you find easiest to use.

Using a lawn weedkiller

- Don't apply weedkiller during periods of frost or drought – it will scorch the grass and make it turn brown.
- In dry weather, give your lawn a thorough soaking the day before you intend to treat it. If there's no rain for a couple of days after treatment, give the lawn another soaking.
- Avoid mowing your lawn for two or three days before and after treating it with weedkiller. After treatment, don't compost the first four mowings.
- Don't let the weedkiller drift onto flowerbeds and ponds.
- To avoid drifting, don't apply weedkiller on a windy day.
- Keep off the grass for a few days after treatment.
- Never treat a new lawn or one that's less than six months old.

grow

Identifying weeds

Certain weeds thrive in mown grass – and once they germinate, regular mowing rapidly creates an infestation. Invasive weeds are destructive, so should be eradicated by hand or by applications of lawn weedkiller. Other weeds may be tolerated in a less than perfect lawn – daisies are charming, after all.

Invasive lawn weeds

Plantain

Speedwell

Dandelion

Lawn weeds you could learn to live with

Daisy

Yarrow

Chickweed

Clover

Spear thistle

Prunella

Mouse-ear hawkweed

Trefoil

Creeping buttercup

Creeping thistle

Bare or coarse patches

If the lawn is left with bare patches after treatment with weedkiller, these can be reseeded.
- First, spike the area to aerate the soil.
- Next, mix lawn seed with compost at the ratio recommended on the packet and sprinkle it onto the bare patches.
- Water the seeds in, then fix netting over the sown area to prevent it being walked on or birds eating the seed.

Sometimes grass seed drifts into the garden from elsewhere, causing patches of coarse grass. To fix this, fork out the coarse patches, add some topsoil, and reseed them as above.

Pests

If an army of ants has taken over your lawn, you can easily oust them by hosing their nest. On a dry day, worm casts can be scattered with a broom – the worms themselves are beneficial to the garden, so shouldn't be viewed as a problem.

As for moles, if they really are a nuisance, then they can be trapped, or smoked out of their mole hills by dropping in special smoke cones. But there's also a non-lethal organic method that some people swear by. Dig down into the hole and insert a clear glass bottle, with the top half protruding above the ground. Not only will the bottle reflect light down into the run, but the wind blowing over its top will make a whistling sound. The harsh light and noise should be enough to drive the mole from your garden.

Other pests that can damage a lawn include leatherjackets and chafer grubs, whose larvae feed on the roots of the grass and cause it to turn yellowish brown in patches: you may need to need to resort to chemicals to get rid of them.

Fungal disease

Lawns can suffer from fungal disease, which often shows as brown or yellowing patches of dead or dying grass. Anti-fungal treatments are available, but the underlying cause is inadequate drainage. Before treating the affected areas, fork or spike them thoroughly and brush in horticultural sand to improve the drainage – otherwise the problem is liable to rapidly recur.

Fungal disease

A new lawn
from seed

Growing a new lawn from seed isn't difficult, provided the site is well prepared and the new grass is protected from damage and drought.

Planning

Lawn seed should be sown in spring or early autumn. Before laying a new lawn, take some time to think about the part it will play in your overall garden layout. Consider where people will walk, or if there are any obstacles that will get in the way of mowing. Areas likely to be subjected to heavy wear and tear – such as access routes and shortcuts or children's play areas – are better anticipated at the planning stage. If need be, place stepping stones within the lawn, and position children's play equipment on an area of natural play bark instead (see page 116).

Grass in fairly deep shade will always be patchy and prone to moss infestation. In such situations, consider substituting an area of chipped bark, or similar, instead. Overhanging foliage from beds and borders will damage the edges of the lawn and make trimming with shears difficult. A hard edging between lawn and border not only helps avoid this, but if laid flush with the ground will do away with trimming edges completely – you just mow straight over the top (see page 267).

Choosing seeds

There's a wide range of grasses to choose from, according to what you want the end result to be. For a fine ornamental lawn, choose a seed mixture that doesn't contain any coarse grasses, such as ryegrass. But for a lawn that will need to double up as a party venue or football pitch, or that will simply need to withstand regular use, the tougher and coarser grasses are a better option.

Shady and sunny areas may need different types of seed. However, the difference between two types of grass can look obvious. To make this less noticeable, you can seed the bridging area with a mixture of the two seeds.

ideal tool

Powered cultivator
A cultivator can make light work of breaking up and preparing a large area of soil (though it is not suitable for established beds).

Preparing the site

First, clear the ground of all weeds by hand and if necessary by spraying with a non-residual weedkiller (see page 254) – this will reduce weeds later on. Then you can begin to prepare the ground for sowing.

tools materials
- **garden fork**
- **powered cultivator (hire)**
- **rake**

- weedkiller, if required

1 Dig over the entire site with a garden fork. If it's a large area, use a powered cultivator – these can be bought or hired.

2 Rake over the ground to level it, removing any large stones. This preparation work is crucial to achieve a level, even surface.

3 Firm the soil down by 'heeling' it – compressing it with the heels of your boots. Be methodical, to ensure there are no voids in the ground.

4 Use the back of a rake to pull loose soil into any hollows. Repeat until the ground is firm and flat.

Sowing

For a smallish lawn, seed can be sown by hand; for a larger lawn, use a spreader. Use 50g of seed per square metre – if you sow more thickly, that will hamper the lawn's growth.

1 If spreading seed by hand, tie four 1m canes together to form a square – then spread a measured quantity of seed within it. This will show you how densely you need to sow the seed.

2 When you have sown over the entire area, lightly rake the surface of the soil.

3 Finish the sown area by going over it methodically with a garden roller.

Looking after a newly seeded lawn

If the weather is dry, it's essential to keep the new grass seedlings well watered. While the seedlings are very tiny and delicate, it is best to water using a fine mist spray from a hose gun attachment or sprinkler with a mist setting (see pages 250–51). As they grow stronger, you can water with an ordinary sprinkler. Once the grass has grown to 5–8cm, it can have its first cut. The mower blade should be really sharp, otherwise the shoots will tear and lift out of the ground. Set your mower to its highest setting, to take off only the tips, for the first few months. Collect the clippings. As the lawn thickens up, the cutting height can gradually be lowered. Even if weeds appear, you should not apply weedkiller for at least the first six months after sowing.

Seed versus turf

When deciding whether to create a new lawn from seed or to lay turf, you will want to weigh up the advantages and disadvantages of the two methods.

	advantages	disadvantages
Seed	• Low cost • Greater choice of grass types available • Convenience – unlike turfing, sowing can be delayed if the weather is unexpectedly poor	• Takes time to establish – you need to keep off the sown area for some months • Sowing can only be done in spring or early autumn • Slightly more site preparation is needed • Difficult to achieve neat outer edges
Turf	• Instant results • Quick to establish – you need to keep off the new lawn for weeks rather than months • With watering, can be laid at any time of year • Easy to keep an exact line around edges	• Significantly more expensive • Rolls of turf spoil quickly so need to be laid promptly on delivery – unexpected bad weather can be very inconvenient • May be difficult to find matching seed for filling gaps • Shrinks in hot weather unless well watered

A new lawn from turf

Turf will give you an instant lawn. The weather and the quality and freshness of the turf can make a difference – but laying it is relatively straightforward and requires no special skill.

Working with turf

Turf is simply pregrown grass seed that's been cut from the ground with a slice of topsoil. It's a bit like ready-made grass carpeting, rolled up for easy handling – so all you have to do is unroll it, lay it and wait for it to take root. You can tell that this has happened by visible evidence of growth. If in doubt, see if you can lift an edge – if it won't come up, it has taken root. Until the turf has rooted, it will need regular and thorough watering. Don't flood the new lawn but make sure it never dries out, or your turfs will shrink and gaps will appear.

Once it is growing, start to mow it. Keep mower blades set high for the first few cuts and remove clippings. Reduce the cutting height gradually as the lawn becomes established. Avoid applying any moss killers or weedkillers for at least six months.

Ordering turf

Turf is sold by the square metre and delivered in strips. These are usually 1m x 0.3m, but check before ordering as other sizes are sometimes supplied. To work out how much turf you need, measure your lawn then multiply the length by the width to give you the area in square metres. Order about 5% extra, as there's bound to be some wastage.

Before ordering, check weather forecasts. Avoid prolonged wet spells and periods when frost is expected. Generally, the best time to lay turf is from October to February. Provided the weather isn't frosty and the ground isn't waterlogged, October and November are often the best months.

Delay arranging delivery until you have finished preparing the site. If, once the turf has been delivered, you are unable to lay it immediately, don't leave it rolled up or it will turn yellow within a couple of days. Unroll it and lay it flat, somewhere out of full sun, and make sure it doesn't dry out.

Preparing and marking out

Preparing a site for turf is done the same way as for a lawn from seed (see page 270). The aim is to achieve a level surface for the turf to be laid on. Once the ground is cleared and raked flat, you are ready to mark out the exact shape of the new lawn.

Use a board (an old scaffold board is ideal) as a platform to work from. Move it around to avoid churning up the site as you mark it out, and then to avoid damaging turfs you've just laid.

tools materials
- **board**
- **builder's line**
- **wooden stakes or pegs**
- **club hammer**
- **rake**

- turf

1 Mark out the exact boundaries of the lawn, using a builder's line and sharpened wooden stakes or pegs. Use a club hammer to drive them into the ground.

2 Rake over the prepared site one last time, removing stones and making sure it's level.

Laying turf

Start by laying turf along all the edges of the prepared site, then work forwards row by row from one side, working from a board placed on top of the turfs you have just laid.

1 Lay turfs along the boundary of the prepared site, with the longest sides of the turfs parallel to the boundary line.

2 Standing on a board, start laying turfs from left to right, staggering the joints, as in brickwork, from row to row.

3 If you spot a hollow in any of the turfs, lift it with one hand and fill beneath with topsoil.

4 To cut turfs to size, use either a half-moon edging iron or a long-bladed knife.

ideal tool

Half-moon edging iron
The flat half-moon blade is designed for cutting turfs and reshaping lawn edges. Use it with a rocking motion to cut through turf.

5 Tamp down the edges of adjacent turfs with the flat edge of a rake. Butt them up closely together, without any gaps.

6 If there are any gaps between turfs, sprinkle top-dressing material (see page 266) into them, then brush it over with a soft broom to ensure an even coverage.

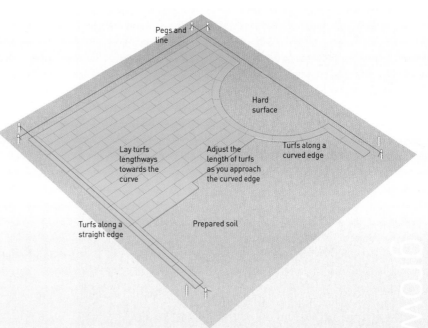

7 Finish by rolling with a garden roller, to level the turf and bed it into the soil.

Laying turf to a curve

Follow the same principles as for laying a square or rectangular lawn. Outline the boundaries with pegs and line, then lay turfs along all the edges – both the straight sides and the one with the curve. You will need to overlap pairs of turfs slightly to form the curve, and then trim the excess.

Next, starting at one of the corners of the lawn, lay rows of turf, working forwards from one of the straight sides and staggering the joints from row to row. As usual, work from a board placed on top of turfs you have just laid.

As with any edge, curved or straight, you may need to adjust the lengths of the turfs as you approach it to avoid finishing with a tiny section. Turfing is not an exact science: expect to lift, recut, adjust and replace the turfs as you proceed.

Pegs and line

Hard surface

Lay turfs lengthways towards the curve

Adjust the length of turfs as you approach the curved edge

Turfs along a curved edge

Turfs along a straight edge

Prepared soil

Wildflower lawns

Wildflower meadows are delightfully colourful, fragrant and attractive, as well as providing a haven for wildlife. Even a small wildflower lawn will dramatically increase the number of birds and insects that visit your garden. This can be your own mini conservation area.

A lawn with a difference

Wildflower lawns are more interesting, colourful and varied than the traditional kind. Unlike conventional lawns, wildflower lawns do not require regular chemical treatments to keep them in optimum condition. They are also more wildlife-friendly, producing lots of pollen, nectar and seed to attract insects and birds. This type of lawn won't withstand much walking on without being flattened – but you can mow a path through it and leave longer grass filled with wild flowers on either side.

A wildflower meadow looks wonderfully picturesque in an orchard, and also attracts insects that will pollinate the trees. Not that everyone has the space for an orchard, but lots of us have room for a quiet corner – perhaps a bench somewhere out of the way, reached by a mown path, that can serve as a perfect spot for reflection and escape, soothed by the hum of insects and the rustle of the breeze through the grass.

Primula veris Cowslip

Muscari Grape hyacinth

Creating a wildflower lawn from scratch

A wildflower meadow can be sown on bare earth, or you can gradually develop one from an existing lawn. If creating a meadow from scratch, whether you are clearing a bed or an area of conventional lawn, it pays to start by spraying with a non-residual weedkiller (see page 254) to eradicate perennial weeds.

You can buy special wildflower-seed mixes that combine grass seed with the kind of flowers found in a meadow. Sow this the same way as any other lawn seed (see pages 270–71), at the concentration recommended on the packet. Some of the flower species will be slower to establish than others, so allow a full twelve months for all of them to germinate.

Choosing seed

Only plant wildflowers native to this country, especially if your garden is near open countryside – many invasive weeds that threaten native habitats are escapees from gardens.

Different mixes of seed are available for different conditions. Be sure to choose one that's suitable for your garden. Flowers that grow on dry grasslands in the wild will not thrive if planted in boggy soil that is prone to waterlogging.

Mixed wildflowers: daisies, bluebells and speedwell

Turning an ordinary lawn into a wildflower meadow

If you are making a meadow from a conventional lawn, you will get the best results by planting flower seedlings amid the grass, rather than sowing seed straight into the ground. Adding new species is best done in the spring.

ideal plants for a wildflower lawn

Moist grassland
Meadow buttercup
  (*Ranunculus acris*)
Great burnet
  (*Sanguisorba officinalis*)
Tufted vetch (*Vicia cracca*)
Cuckoo-flower or Lady's smock
  (*Cardamine pratensis*)
Meadow cranesbill
  (*Geranium pratense*)
Ragged robin
  (*Lychnis flos-cuculi*)
Devil's-bit scabious
  (*Succisa pratensis*)
Foxglove (*Digitalis purpurea*)
Primrose (*Primula vulgaris*)

Dry grassland
White and red clover
  (*Trifolium repens* and
  Trifolium pratense)
Yellow trefoil (*Trifolium dubium*)
Cowslip (*Primula veris*)
Viper's bugloss (*Echium vulgare*)
Wild marjoram (*Origanum vulgare*)
Spiked speedwell
  (*Veronica spicata*)
Field scabious (*Knautia arvensis*)

Greater knapweed
  (*Centaurea scabiosa*)
Lesser knapweed
  (*Centaurea nigra*)
Corncockle (*Agrostemma githago*)
Cornflower, annual
  (*Centaurea cyanus*)
Cornflower, perennial
  (*Centaurea montana*)
Ox-eye daisy
  (*Leucanthemum vulgare*)
Common poppy (*Papaver rhoeas*)
Feverfew (*Tanacetum parthenium*)

Bulbs
Field garlic (*Allium oleraceum*)
Snakeshead fritillary
  (*Fritillaria meleagris*)
Snowdrop (*Galanthus nivalis*)
Summer snowflake
  (*Leucojum aestivum*)
Pheasant's eye daffodil
  (*Narcissus poeticus* var. *recurvus*)
Wild daffodil or Lent lily
  (*Narcissus pseudonarcissus*)
Autumn squill (*Scilla autumnalis*)
English bluebell
  (*Hyacinthoides non-scripta*)

Crocus

Caring for a wildflower lawn

Never add feed or fertiliser to a meadow area. Wildflowers need to grow on fairly depleted soil; if you feed them, the grass will succeed at the expense of the flowers. Also, avoid watering unless the ground is exceptionally dry.

Mowing

Wildflower meadows are mowed the same way as any other lawn, but the timing is different. They should be allowed to grow untrimmed all through spring and early summer, until the flowers are over and have set seed – usually at the end of July or early in August.

By this time the grass will be too long to tackle with any but the most heavy-duty mower. You will need to either scythe the meadow first or cut it with a trimmer; or if it's a very small area, use hand shears. Then rake off the cuttings and finish with a rotary mower. Always remove the severed top growth – if you leave it on the ground, it will feed the grass and kill the flowers.

You then have a choice. You can continue to mow regularly – in effect producing an area of lawn containing plants, such as daisies, that in an ordinary lawn would be considered weeds. Or you can leave the meadow to grow freely until the end of the summer, when it should be cut to allow spring-flowering plants to grow through and be visible.

Weed control

Perennial weeds such as docks and thistles can be left growing, but either remove their seedheads to prevent them spreading or, alternatively, use a weed stick treatment on the leaves of individual weeds.

Wildflower meadow

Growing your own delicious food can take the pleasures of a garden to a whole new level. Simple salads are a great place to start. These are fast-growing, attractive and colourful, and the flavour and texture of freshly picked leaves is uniquely delicious and healthy. A few carefully chosen plants will produce many, many meals. Peas, beans and bush tomatoes are easy to grow – and so are herbs, which add new flavours and colours to the table.

growing for the table

Easier than you think – with fast results

There is no mystery to growing your own food in beds, borders or containers. You will be delighted by how quickly the plants grow. What's more, you can start picking off the outer leaves of lettuce when it is still a young plant, and this same plant will keep producing leaves for two or three months. Just four lettuce plants in a pot, with leaves of different colours and shape, will provide lots of salads.

Small is beautiful

Many vegetable gardens are far too big for most people's needs, wasting valuable space. In fact, you only need a small area, or a few pots, to grow your own vegetables and salads. It's better to use a smaller space and keep sowing or planting as soon as each crop finishes; you can put plants that have gone to seed in your compost bin and then sow others. Full use of your vegetable plot will help keep the weeds down and let you concentrate your watering and attention on the places that really need it.

Be lazy – no digging!

There is usually no need to dig over a vegetable plot at the start or the end of a season. A moist and well-composted soil will be full of worms and organic matter, which contribute to keeping the structure open and aerated. Many gardeners find that their plants grow just as well – if not better – when they don't dig, but instead spread three to five centimetres of garden compost on top of the soil each year. This method is particularly successful for narrow beds, because unlike large, wide plots, the soil here is never trodden down and compacted.

Growing out of season

Every plant has its own growing needs and will thrive best at a certain time of year. For instance, rocket and mizuna (see page 288) usually go to seed in spring or early summer; a spring sowing will yield few leaves, while seeds sown in July or August will reward you with an abundant harvest. Still, it's possible to give plants the environment they need to flourish even when it's not their natural growing season: a greenhouse, coldframe or cloche can all help crops start earlier in the year.

Turning an ordinary lawn into a wildflower meadow

If you are making a meadow from a conventional lawn, you will get the best results by planting flower seedlings amid the grass, rather than sowing seed straight into the ground. Adding new species is best done in the spring.

ideal plants for a wildflower lawn

Moist grassland

Meadow buttercup
   (*Ranunculus acris*)
Great burnet
   (*Sanguisorba officinalis*)
Tufted vetch (*Vicia cracca*)
Cuckoo-flower or Lady's smock
   (*Cardamine pratensis*)
Meadow cranesbill
   (*Geranium pratense*)
Ragged robin
   (*Lychnis flos-cuculi*)
Devil's-bit scabious
   (*Succisa pratensis*)
Foxglove (*Digitalis purpurea*)
Primrose (*Primula vulgaris*)

Dry grassland

White and red clover
   (*Trifolium repens* and
   Trifolium pratense)
Yellow trefoil (*Trifolium dubium*)
Cowslip (*Primula veris*)
Viper's bugloss (*Echium vulgare*)
Wild marjoram (*Origanum vulgare*)
Spiked speedwell
   (*Veronica spicata*)
Field scabious (*Knautia arvensis*)

Greater knapweed
   (*Centaurea scabiosa*)
Lesser knapweed
   (*Centaurea nigra*)
Corncockle (*Agrostemma githago*)
Cornflower, annual
   (*Centaurea cyanus*)
Cornflower, perennial
   (*Centaurea montana*)
Ox-eye daisy
   (*Leucanthemum vulgare*)
Common poppy (*Papaver rhoeas*)
Feverfew (*Tanacetum parthenium*)

Bulbs

Field garlic (*Allium oleraceum*)
Snakeshead fritillary
   (*Fritillaria meleagris*)
Snowdrop (*Galanthus nivalis*)
Summer snowflake
   (*Leucojum aestivum*)
Pheasant's eye daffodil
   (*Narcissus poeticus* var. *recurvus*)
Wild daffodil or Lent lily
   (*Narcissus pseudonarcissus*)
Autumn squill (*Scilla autumnalis*)
English bluebell
   (*Hyacinthoides non-scripta*)

Crocus

Caring for a wildflower lawn

Never add feed or fertiliser to a meadow area. Wildflowers need to grow on fairly depleted soil; if you feed them, the grass will succeed at the expense of the flowers. Also, avoid watering unless the ground is exceptionally dry.

Mowing

Wildflower meadows are mowed the same way as any other lawn, but the timing is different. They should be allowed to grow untrimmed all through spring and early summer, until the flowers are over and have set seed – usually at the end of July or early in August.

By this time the grass will be too long to tackle with any but the most heavy-duty mower. You will need to either scythe the meadow first or cut it with a trimmer; or if it's a very small area, use hand shears. Then rake off the cuttings and finish with a rotary mower. Always remove the severed top growth – if you leave it on the ground, it will feed the grass and kill the flowers.

You then have a choice. You can continue to mow regularly – in effect producing an area of lawn containing plants, such as daisies, that in an ordinary lawn would be considered weeds. Or you can leave the meadow to grow freely until the end of the summer, when it should be cut to allow spring-flowering plants to grow through and be visible.

Weed control

Perennial weeds such as docks and thistles can be left growing, but either remove their seedheads to prevent them spreading or, alternatively, use a weed stick treatment on the leaves of individual weeds.

Wildflower meadow

Growing your own delicious food can take the pleasures of a garden to a whole new level. Simple salads are a great place to start. These are fast-growing, attractive and colourful, and the flavour and texture of freshly picked leaves is uniquely delicious and healthy. A few carefully chosen plants will produce many, many meals. Peas, beans and bush tomatoes are easy to grow – and so are herbs, which add new flavours and colours to the table.

growing for the table

Easier than you think – with fast results

There is no mystery to growing your own food in beds, borders or containers. You will be delighted by how quickly the plants grow. What's more, you can start picking off the outer leaves of lettuce when it is still a young plant, and this same plant will keep producing leaves for two or three months. Just four lettuce plants in a pot, with leaves of different colours and shape, will provide lots of salads.

Small is beautiful

Many vegetable gardens are far too big for most people's needs, wasting valuable space. In fact, you only need a small area, or a few pots, to grow your own vegetables and salads. It's better to use a smaller space and keep sowing or planting as soon as each crop finishes; you can put plants that have gone to seed in your compost bin and then sow others. Full use of your vegetable plot will help keep the weeds down and let you concentrate your watering and attention on the places that really need it.

Be lazy – no digging!

There is usually no need to dig over a vegetable plot at the start or the end of a season. A moist and well-composted soil will be full of worms and organic matter, which contribute to keeping the structure open and aerated. Many gardeners find that their plants grow just as well – if not better – when they don't dig, but instead spread three to five centimetres of garden compost on top of the soil each year. This method is particularly successful for narrow beds, because unlike large, wide plots, the soil here is never trodden down and compacted.

Growing out of season

Every plant has its own growing needs and will thrive best at a certain time of year. For instance, rocket and mizuna (see page 288) usually go to seed in spring or early summer; a spring sowing will yield few leaves, while seeds sown in July or August will reward you with an abundant harvest. Still, it's possible to give plants the environment they need to flourish even when it's not their natural growing season: a greenhouse, coldframe or cloche can all help crops start earlier in the year.

Beds and containers

Even in a small garden, you can grow a wide range of salads and other vegetables. If there's room, you could build a small bed; if not, there are plenty of possibilities for growing in pots or even hanging baskets.

Creating a new bed

A new bed can be created as shown on page 194. As with all new beds or borders, it's best to work on the ground while it's still clear of plants, getting rid of any perennial weeds.

It's also possible to construct a raised bed on any area of lawn or border. The method shown here will work for most crops, but if the soil is compacted or you want to grow root crops such as carrots, you will first need to dig the ground before filling it with compost. For the bed's framework, be sure to use wood that has been safeguarded against rot. One option is pre-treated timber painted with wood preservative or, even simpler, you can buy pressure-treated deck boards. So that the middle of the bed is easy to reach, keep the width to about 1.2m at most; the length can be whatever you fancy.

Basic principles

Creating a healthy environment for plants to grow will reduce the need for chemical sprays – a plant growing in a favourable environment will be able to resist and outgrow the effects of most pests and diseases. Slugs and snails can be a problem, however, and some action may be needed (see opposite). To keep plants healthy, here are a few basic principles to follow:

- Avoid walking on your plot and spread some good soil improver over it once a year (see pages 190–91).
- Try to sow plants in the right season so that they grow in conditions that suit them.
- Rotate your crops – that is, grow a different plant on the same ground from one season to the next so that the soil is not depleted of selective nutrients. This will also prevent the build-up of pests and diseases.
- Water wisely, and never over-water (see pages 250–51).

1 Lay out the deck boards and check the bed isn't skewed by measuring the diagonals with a long tape measure or string. Mark the corners with canes.

2 Remove the boards and join the canes with string to mark out the bed. Cut lines in the grass with a spade, about 10cm from each side of the string. Slide the spade under the turf to cut pieces about 5cm thick, then turn them over and lay them evenly across the bed.

3 Lay the planks side-on along the bare earth outline of the plot and join each corner with one or two galvanised metal brackets and screws, depending on the size of the bed.

4 Empty the sacks of compost and tread it down. If it is at all dry, add enough water to make it evenly moist. The middle of the bed should be slightly higher than the planks to allow for settling.

5 Hammer in enough small sharpened pegs to help hold the boards in place. The strip of bare earth on the outside of the bed will make mowing easier. You might want to fill it with a bark mulch for an attractive finish.

Preparing pots for planting

A patio or pot garden is prepared according to the same principles as a bed, but make sure the container you choose has holes in the bottom for drainage. Compost must be well firmed down and thoroughly moist before you plant or sow.

tools materials
- **pot**
- **gloves**

- multi-purpose or potting compost
- crocks or gravel
- seedlings or plants

1 Cover the bottom of the pot with crocks or gravel to improve drainage (see page 209), then fill it with compost. You could use some rougher garden compost or manure at the bottom of the pot.

2 Wearing garden gloves, press the compost down firmly with your hands, without letting the soil get too compacted. Top up with more compost and press down again; repeat until the pot is full. It is now ready for your seedlings or plants.

Pots for salads and herbs

Any standard pot or planter can be used to grow edible plants. Square pots can be particularly useful for salads and herbs, as the wide top gives more space for leaf growth and makes watering easier. Mature salad plants suck a lot of moisture out of the compost, and it can be difficult to replace this in a pot with a narrow top covered with dense leaf growth.

Working with nature's cycle

All annual plants pass through the same phases of growth: from baby leaves to more mature leaves, to flowering and fruiting, through to seed production and preparing for the compost heap. We can grow plants according to which stage interests us most.

leaves, fruits and herbs

Salad leaves
Grown for their leaves, salads mature quickly and need regular watering. They are normally discarded once they mature to a flowering stem. New ones can then be sown or planted to replace them.

Fruiting plants
Grown for their fruit, plants such as peas and tomatoes need to be cultivated over a longer period than salads. A fertile soil is essential – otherwise the plants will mature more quickly but bear less fruit.

Herbs
Both the leaves and flowers of herbs will add flavour and interest to food. Leaves are generally available in the spring while flowers normally appear in the summer.

Coping with slugs and snails

Slugs and snails, especially if there are a lot of them in your garden, will eat soft-leaved salads and almost any young seedlings of flowers and vegetables.

Prevention
The best strategy for coping with slugs and snails is prevention. Strong, sturdy plants are less susceptible than tender, sappy ones. In high-risk areas you can grow plants that slugs and snails hate, such as tomatoes, spring onions and most herbs. Weeds give extra places for slugs and snails to live, so keep them in check. Sprinkling sharp grit around vulnerable plants, or surrounding containers with copper slug tape, will also help.

Control
If slugs and snails seem to be overrunning your garden, you may have to take further action (see page 255). Although it's impossible to get rid of all of them, you can reduce slugs and snails by picking them off by hand and disposing of them. Use a torch to find them after dusk, or look for them in moist, shady spots such as the bottom of walls in the daytime.

You can also try to encourage natural predators: birds, frogs, hedgehogs and carabid beetles all feed on slugs and snails. Slug pellets should only be used as a last resort – those based on aluminium sulphate are the safest.

Beautiful lettuce

Lettuce is easy to grow and offers a wonderful choice of colours, flavours and textures. Ideally suited to the British climate between March and October, it needs mild, moist conditions with few extremes. It grows quickly, too. Leaf varieties can be picked just six weeks after sowing in summer; the more traditional hearting kinds take longer but are usually sweeter and more crisp.

Sowing lettuce seeds

From late March to the end of August you can sow seeds outdoors, straight into pots or a bed (see page 282). To enjoy your own lettuce as early as May, you will need to start earlier: seed can be sown as early as February provided it has the shelter of a greenhouse, coldframe (see page 284), or simply a propagator hood as shown, which you can place outdoors, provided it's not excessively cold. It's a good idea to sow a few different varieties at the same time, and then use only the strongest plants.

Planting new lettuces

Seedlings can be planted outdoors four to six weeks after sowing, depending on the season. For continuous crops you can go on making new sowings every six weeks or so until late July.

tools materials

- **dibber**
- **modular seed tray**
- **propagator hood**
- seed-and-cutting or multi-purpose compost
- lettuce seeds

ideal tool

Modular seed tray

For planting different varieties of any plant, including lettuces, a modular seed tray is hard to beat. It has individual compartments to keep the roots separate, and you can even label the different modules to keep track of what you've sown.

1 Fill the modules of the seed tray with moist compost. Gently firm or tamp it down, then drop one or two seeds onto the top of the compost in each module. Open the vents once the first leaves begin to grow, and remove the hood once the plants have four to six leaves. Where two plants germinate in one module, pull out the smaller one and dispose of it, ideally in your compost bin.

2 As the plants grow bigger, water daily with a can and rose. Keep an eye out for pests; slug pellets may be necessary around the seed tray in a coldframe. Wait until they reach about 3.5–5cm in height before planting outside; planting them any earlier will make them more vulnerable to slugs. To release a plant from its module, push from the bottom to loosen the rootball then pull out gently, holding the leaves.

3 Use a dibber to make a hole in the ground slightly larger than the rootball. Drop the plant in the hole and lightly firm the surrounding soil with your hands.

4 Allow about 20cm between plants. Water newly planted lettuces daily for a week.

Leaves or hearts?

Lettuces come in both loose leaf varieties and hearted varieties. Loose leaf lettuces form no heart or head. Instead, as their name implies, they grow as a group of loose leaves, which can be picked off without cutting the whole plant (see pages 282–83). Hearted lettuces, on the other hand, form a dense core of leaves that are sweeter and crunchier than the outer leaves, but the whole plant must be cut in order to enjoy them.

Leaves can be picked off loose leaf varieties of lettuce in as little as six weeks after sowing, or two or three weeks after planting (see pages 282–83). Hearts take longer to develop after planting and are ready to be picked after six to ten weeks (see below).

Hearted lettuces

Six or seven weeks after planting, hearted lettuces will start to feel firm at their centre as they fold in and develop into a tight heart of crisp, pale leaves. Now is the best time to harvest them: cut them just above soil level and trim off any diseased outer leaves to reveal the healthy, more densely packed leaves of the heart.

These lettuces can be harvested for another week or two, but if left much later they will start to bolt – that is, the seed-bearing stem will push up from the centre and split open the lettuce, causing the flavour to become more and more bitter. The time taken to reach this stage depends on season, weather conditions and lettuce variety (see table). The golden rule, however, is to water nearly mature lettuces at least every few days, especially in dry, hot weather, as this will encourage them to put on more leaves instead of running directly to seed.

Greenhouses

A greenhouse is not just for expert gardeners – in fact, it can make it easier for anyone to grow and tend plants throughout the year. Greenhouses are available in sizes and shapes to suit all homes, from the traditional stand-alone kind to portable mini-greenhouses, which are great for compact spaces. For complete temperature control, combine a greenhouse heater with plenty of ventilation – windows, louvres and roof vents. Heated greenhouses are perfect for growing seedlings and cuttings, as well as sheltering tender plants over winter.

Choosing hearted lettuce

There are four main types of lettuce hearts: crisp, butterhead, cos and batavia. These different varieties bolt or go to seed at different speeds, while some are easier to grow than others. However, they are all valuable additions to any salad bowl.

Marvel of Four Seasons (centre)

hearted lettuces

Crisp
Slow to bolt and best grown in summer, with a remarkably crisp, densely packed heart. Inner leaves are prone to tipburn, ie when tips turn brown from lack of moisture, so keep well watered. Webbs Wonderful, pictured, produces a large, crisp heart.

Butterhead
Quick to mature but prone to bolting, with soft, thick outer leaves and a round heart, rather like a tender cabbage. Marvel of Four Seasons, pictured, grows well in the summer and can be sown as late as September.

Cos
Quick to bolt and demanding to grow, but with a wonderfully sweet, dense and crisp heart. Sturdy outer leaves are prone to mildew but can be trimmed away. Little Gem, pictured, is small, sweet and quick to mature.

Batavia
Slow to bolt and versatile as can be used for leaves as well as hearts. Sow in spring or autumn for best hearts. Grenoble Red, pictured, will heart up in May if sown in early September but can also be used for leaves if sown from March to August.

Fresh everyday lettuce leaves

You can enjoy fresh salad leaves every day with non-hearting lettuces. Only the outer leaves are picked, so the plant will carry on growing until you are ready for the next harvest.

Clockwise from left: new red fire, Moroccan littlecress, lollo rosso, fristina

Loose leaf lettuce

The great thing about loose leaf lettuce is that while the outer leaves can be picked for the table, the plant will keep on growing and producing leaves for up to ten weeks. Quicker and easier to grow than hearted lettuce, loose leaf lettuce is also more versatile as several different varieties can be picked at once. Seeds sown directly into a bed will need to be thinned when half-grown; this means removing some of them to give the others more growing space and encourage bigger, better leaves. When harvesting leaves, always avoid cutting plants at soil level as they will be unlikely to grow back, making a new sowing necessary.

1 For most loose leaf lettuces, thinning can be done as early as three to four weeks after sowing – put the thinnings in the compost bin. But if you can wait six weeks, the thinnings will be good to eat.

2 Thin the plants by about two-thirds so that you're left with one lettuce every 7.5cm or so. Remove the larger outer leaves of the remaining lettuces by pinching them off at their base. Compost any yellow or slug-eaten leaves.

3 Depending on growing conditions, more leaves will be ready to pick only a week after thinning. You may have to pick off small stems on plants such as purslane, orache and rocket.

Clearing a bed after bolting

After two months or so of being picked over, loose lettuces will start to bolt and develop a taller central stem in the same way as hearted lettuces (see page 281). You can still pick their leaves, though they may be quite bitter. If you have enough younger plants to maintain a succession of leaves, then it is best to remove the plant: hold it firmly at the bottom of the stem and rotate it until it comes clear of the ground along with a few of its larger roots, then tap off any excess soil. The plant can go in the compost bin, while the bed or pot can be levelled off and tamped down, ready for the next sowing or planting.

Choosing salad leaves

Loose leaf lettuces come in a huge variety of flavours, colours and textures. Easy to grow and harvest, many of them would be difficult to find from a commercial producer. Which you choose to grow, and how many, is entirely up to you.

1 **Flat-leaf or Italian parsley** Tasty flat leaves
2 **Aruba lettuce** Dark, pretty oakleaf
3 **Red mustard** Spicy, strong taste
4 **French sorrel** Pungent, lemony taste
5 **Lollo rosso lettuce** Pink-tinged leaves and striking texture
6 **Fristina lettuce** Similar to lollo rosso but bright green
7 **Ruby chard** Vivid red veins, spinach flavour
8 **Frizzy endive** Crunchy and slightly bitter
9 **Pak choi joi choi** Mild, juicy leaves
10 **Red oakleaf** Similar to aruba but paler
11 **Rocket** Strong, slightly spicy flavour
12 **Redina lettuce** Exceptional dark colour
13 **Moroccan littlecress lettuce** Long, pretty leaf and mild taste
14 **Empress of India nasturtium leaf** Aromatic and attractive
15 **Empress of India nasturtium flower** Similar taste to leaf
16 **Celery leaf** A good way to bring celery flavour to salad
17 **Greek basil** Tiny leaves that pack a punch
18 **Orache** Dark red and faintly bitter

Not just lettuce

A salad doesn't have to consist of plain lettuce. There is an amazing selection of other plants – including chard, spinach, orache, purslane and herbs (see page 287) – that will make a delicious, unexpected addition to any salad bowl. Many of these can easily be grown from seed.

Chard

Sow from early April, not before, or it will tend to go to seed. Thin to about 10cm apart. Pick small leaves for salads and larger ones for cooking in the same way as spinach. Seeds are sometimes sold as a mixture called 'Bright Lights', which includes white, ruby (pictured), pink and yellow chards. Sow a row of this and thin out the colours you like least. Note that the white is more vigorous than the coloured chards.

Spinach

Tastiest as a small leaf in salad, though larger leaves can be cooked. Thin to about 7.5cm apart. Success with spinach depends on keeping the soil moist and having the right variety for the season: for example, Matador and Bloomsdale spinaches should be sown from April to June, while Medania spinach is best sown from July to early August for more leaves and less bolting.

Orache

Looks as good in the garden as on the plate. Orache has a vivid colour at a time when red leaves are scarce, since it grows best from a sowing in mid-April for picking in May and June. Sow again in May for summer leaves, picking off the larger leaves wherever they grow on the stem.

eco control

Slugs and snails

Particularly in damp weather, slugs and snails can decimate your lettuce crops. Eco-friendly deterrents include sprinkling eggshells or grit around plants, lining containers with copper slug tape and planting crops slugs hate in with your lettuces – try onions or garlic. The best solution is picking them off by hand (see pages 255 and 279).

Purslane

Pick the shoots – these are the most tender and tasty part. The succulent leaves are extremely juicy but turn bitter after about a month's picking as the plant goes to seed with almost invisible flowers. Sow from May to late July.

Sweet summer vegetables

Summer vegetables such as tomatoes, peas and beans mature more slowly than salad plants, but the waiting is rewarded with mouthwatering flavours in the late summer and autumn.

Lycopersicon lycopersicum 'Tiny Tim' Bush tomato

Growing bush tomatoes

Bush tomatoes form quite compact plants, unlike conventional tomatoes that make a long stem and need staking. Tumbling varieties are for hanging baskets, while bushy ones are best grown in pots. The main colours are red and yellow and most of the fruit are between the size of a marble and a golf ball.

Tomatoes thrive on a little more heat than is usually found in this country; a greenhouse, conservatory or even sheltered patio will provide extra warmth and encourage them to fruit more quickly. Raising tomato seedlings and young plants is quite demanding so you may prefer to buy them as plants in May or early June. Tomatoes are a late summer crop.

Raising tomatoes from seed

Tomato seeds will germinate as early as March with the help of a heated propagator; by April an unheated greenhouse should provide enough warmth. Before being transferred to a pot or modular seed tray, the baby tomato plants will need to be lifted from their original compost using a small stick to help their roots come out. Always hold tomato seedlings by their leaves as their stems are very tender and could be squashed.

tools materials

- **dibber**
- **gloves**
- **modular seed tray or small pot**
- **trowel**
- seed-and-cutting or multi-purpose compost
- tomato seedlings

1 Transfer tender tomato seedlings to a modular seed tray or small pot and allow them to grow under cover for about three weeks.

2 When the plants are about 15cm high with a stem as thick as a pencil, transfer them to a larger pot or bed. Plant them quite deeply, so that the stem is buried up to the first leaves, then water in. The buried part of the stem will grow new roots.

You can do it...

Coldframe

A coldframe is useful for raising seedlings and even for bringing plants on to fruiting. It will protect young tomato plants, for instance, from late spring frosts which would otherwise kill them. Late April is about the right time to start putting tender plants in a frame.

B&Q

Caring for tomato plants

Tomato plants need as much light, warmth and shelter as you can provide, together with regular watering in dry weather and feeding at the flowering stage and beyond. Bear in mind that tomato leaves are susceptible to a fungus called blight; protecting them from the rain will prevent this.

Fruits will form quite quickly over the summer but can seem to take a while to ripen, especially in dull weather. It is worth waiting for the full colour to develop: although a red tomato can be eaten while still pale, the flavour will be much richer, sweeter and juicier if the fruit is left to ripen on the vine before picking. Ripening times will be longer by September; any mature but unripe tomatoes can be picked at the end of the month to ripen in the warmth indoors, although the flavour will be less full.

Peas and runner beans

Sweet and succulent in every way, peas are a high summer crop while beans will be ready in August and September. Both are best picked young and can be enjoyed either raw or lightly cooked. Seeds for peas and beans can be sown directly into the soil, but sowing into modules or pots gives better results; shelter them in a coldframe or window sill until about 5cm high.

Getting the timing right

The natural growth cycle for peas is to put on leaves in April and early May, flower in late May into June and then crop in July. Though peas can be sown at any time between March and July, sowing before mid-April is highly recommended as many, many more peas will be picked from earlier sowings. Sowing later in the year will leave plants vulnerable to pests and diseases such as pea moth and mildew.

Beans are much more sensitive to the cold than peas and will grow best if sown several weeks later, in late May or early June. Don't rush: wait for the soil to warm before sowing as bean seeds in cold soil (below 15ºC) will simply rot. Runner beans tolerate cold better than French beans and will crop for longer if well watered, especially the tall varieties.

Maximising your harvest

Bean and pea plants will crop for longer if you give them plenty of water and keep picking the pods while not too swollen.

Growing traditional varieties

Traditional varieties of runner beans and peas, such as the sugar snap peas shown below, can be supported by a wire obelisk. You may need to add supporting canes to the sides if the plants outgrow the original support. If you have not grown peas before, you will probably be surprised by their sweetness – pea pods' sugars turn into starch as soon as they are picked, so aim to pick them as close as possible to meal time.

tools materials

- **dibber**
- 6 empty plastic bottles
- wire obelisk
- seeds
- plant ties

1 Cut the bottoms and tops off the empty plastic bottles so that both ends are left open. Use a dibber to make six holes around the obelisk, about 25cm apart and 5cm deep. Sow two or three seeds in each hole, fill the holes in, and cover each with the cut plastic bottle to protect seedlings from birds.

2 7–10 days later, the fast-growing stems should be tall enough for you to start twisting them around the support. Secure them gently with plant ties, especially if located in a windy spot.

Hestia Dwarf runner bean

Growing in containers

If you're short of space or want to keep your crops handy outside the kitchen door, try growing one of the many smaller bean and pea varieties in a pot or container.

dwarf varieties for pots and containers

Hestia (dwarf runner bean)

Bean pods are stringless and 15–20cm long – shorter than pods on tall plants. The plant also gives plenty of attractive red flowers. The best time to sow is in late May for cropping in mid-July to end of August.

Sonesta (yellow dwarf French bean)

Delicious, waxy yellow pods, about 10cm long. As with *Hestia*, the best time for sowing is in late May. Pods can be harvested in mid-July to end of August.

Purple teepee (purple dwarf French bean)

Strong colour, most of which disappears in cooking water. Has a shorter harvest period than *Sonesta* but is very easy to pick as the beans grow above the leaves.

Zucolla (dwarf sugar pea)

About 75cm high and worth supporting to keep the fine crop of peas off the ground. Lower yield and shorter harvest period than tall sugar peas. Sow in early April for a July harvest. Grow in a sheltered spot.

eco control

Blackflies

To protect your peas and runner beans from blackflies, plant marigolds or nasturtiums nearby. These will attract hoverflies, which will eat blackflies without touching your pea or bean plants.

Fresh herbs

Herbs are surprisingly easy to grow and their amazing flavours can transform salads and cooked dishes alike.

Raising herbs from seed

Most herbs can be grown from seed and doing this will ensure that your plants are strong, sturdy and full of flavour. April is the best time to sow – regularly watered modules in a coldframe or greenhouse will encourage seeds to grow better and, if correctly labelled, help you keep track of which herbs you are growing. Herbs love full sun and by late May can be planted outdoors into a container or bed.

From left to right: thyme, sorrel, flat-leaf parsley, salad burnet

1 Fill the modules with compost and sow two seeds in each – the weaker seedling of any pair can be removed later. Keep the module tray somewhere sheltered, such as a greenhouse, coldframe or window sill.

2 Most of the seedlings will be well established in three weeks' time. Shown here are sage, thyme, winter savory, summer savory, sorrel, chives and garlic chives.

3 In another three weeks the plants will be ready to transfer to containers or a bed.

tools materials

- **modular seed tray**
- seed-and-cutting or multi-purpose compost
- herb seeds of your choice

Growing herbs

Herbs can be grown in their own bed, in pots or window boxes, or among vegetables and flowers. They respond well to being pruned and kept quite small and are good to have close to hand when cooking. Once established, regular picking will encourage the tender new growth that usually gives the best flavour. Note that sage, thyme and rosemary, if left for a year or two without cutting back, will become leggy – with long, bare stems and new growth only at the tips – and take up much more space than necessary. So be ruthless.

Mixing annuals and perennials

Some herbs are annuals while others are perennials (see table, opposite). Growing the two kinds in one place will give you the best of both worlds: the convenience of trusty favourites that grow year after year, with the flexibility of choosing interesting new varieties to fill any gaps. Most herbs can be grown together in the same container or bed. Only mint, which grows invasively with its roots and can quickly overwhelm a planting area, is best kept on its own.

From left to right: winter savory, red basil, tangerine sage

Basil

Just one of the many herbs you can grow is basil (see table below for more ideas). Tender and fond of warmth, basil will grow well in sheltered spots, though do keep your plants handy – much of the flavour is lost in cooking, so it's best to pick leaves at the last moment.

Sow basil in late spring when the soil is warm and all risk of frost has passed (end of May to early June outdoors; or end of April in a greenhouse, coldframe or conservatory). Water evenly but never to excess and avoid wetting the leaves. Feed in the summer and pinch out flower stems to encourage new leaves.

Terracotta multipot

You can grow many basil varieties in an attractive multipot. Shown here are arrarat, Sweet Genovese, lemon, cinnamon, lime, Greek and Sweet Thai basils.

Hanging basket

Plant about three basils in a hanging basket (see page 210), allowing at least 10cm between them. Lime, Greek and Sweet Thai basils are shown here.

So much choice

Few people realise that there are over a dozen varieties of basil suitable for eating, each with its own distinctive taste; a few of them are in the table below. Even the flowers are edible and, depending on the type, can be bright white, pale pink or a delicate lavender. The flavour of basil flowers is similar to the leaves but slightly milder.

varieties of basil	
Arrarat	Tastes faintly of liquorice. Tall-growing, with purple markings in some leaves.
Cinnamon basil	Distinctive cinnamon taste and smell with purple-veined stems.
Greek basil	Pungent peppery aroma and small leaves.
Lemon basil	Remarkable citrus scent and taste. Worth growing under cover as dislikes too much cold rain.
Lime basil	Superbly scented and ideal for summer salads.
Neapolitana	Strong, even flavour with large, crinkled, deep-veined leaves.
Siam Queen	Purple flowers and pungent, dark green leaves with aniseed and liquorice notes.
Sweet Genovese	The most common type, often sold as sweet basil, with medium-size leaves and strong flavour that is ideal for making pesto.
Sweet Thai basil	More than a hint of aniseed. Dark green leaves with striking purple stems and flowers.

more ideas for herbs

Rosemary

Deeply aromatic perennial, delicious cooked with meats such as lamb or brewed as a tea to stimulate the mind. Leaves make attractive foliage for winter flower arrangements.

Coriander

Dainty annual with delicately perfumed seeds and tasty flat leaves that can be used as an exotic alternative to parsley.

Sage

Mild and aromatic perennial, often used in stuffings and sausages. Striking flowers. Eventually turns woody so needs renewing every 3–4 years. Can be grown from hardwood cuttings once leggy (see page 226).

Mint

Refreshing and stimulating perennial. Good in teas, cold drinks and sweets. Pictured here: pennyroyal, peppermint, spearmint and applemint. Best grown in a pot on its own as it can quickly overwhelm other plants.

Savories

Mainly used to flavour pea and bean dishes. Has small, pale flowers in summer. Winter savory is perennial while the sweeter summer savory is annual.

Sorrel

Leafy perennial with citrus overtones. Smaller leaves, shown here, give a powerful lemony zest, which is good in salads. Larger leaves are better for cooking – try in omelettes.

Marjoram

Powerfully fragrant perennial, used in cooking. Shown here are sweet marjoram (front), common marjoram (middle) and wild marjoram (back), also known as oregano, which is delicious on pizzas.

Thyme

Excellent perennial cooked with poultry and meat. Has small, pretty flowers in late summer and should last 3–4 years before turning woody. Lemon thyme adds zest to dishes and makes a tasty tea.

Parsley

A common garnish, good in soups and stews. Curled parsley (front) is easier to grow than the more flavourful flat-leaf or Italian parsley (back). Biennial.

Dill

Delicately flavoured annual. Feathery texture of leaves complements salads, fish dishes and some sauces. Seeds can be used in pickles.

Pak choi joi choi

Exciting and unusual flavours

Oriental vegetables, grown in autumn, are a delicious and exotic ingredient for salads, stir-fries and other dishes. Many flowers can be eaten raw or cooked and will also make an unusual, colourful garnish. And don't forget strawberries – these succulent fruits are easy to grow in pots or even hanging baskets.

Oriental vegetables

These are truly exciting because there are so many unusual varieties to experiment with. Most are autumn vegetables – they struggle to grow in springtime but come into their own in late summer and autumn. They are best sown in the summer, as they will germinate in warm soil when the days are long, produce leaves as the soil cools and the days shorten, and then lie dormant through winter and go to seed in spring. It's worth protecting them with horticultural fleece following a July or August sowing if the weather is especially hot and dry. Below are three tasty favourites, which will be ready for a first harvest in under six weeks and carry on cropping for up to two months.

Harvest mizuna with a sharp garden knife three weeks after sowing; leave about 5cm of stem so the plant can grow back. For pak choi and red mustard, it's best to pinch off a few outer leaves carefully, then pick the larger leaves every few days.

Ten days after the first cut many leaves will be ready for picking again. Wait a few days more for an even bigger harvest.

Green pak choi

Ideal in salads or lightly steamed, boiled or stir-fried. Sow in August and cut off the outer leaves with a knife when harvesting as twisting them can uproot the whole plant. Another variety, pak choi joi choi (shown top left) has thick white stems and is even more winter-hardy.

Mizuna

Slightly spicy Japanese plant with lovely serrated leaves, similar to mustard leaves but smaller, sweeter and milder. Delicious in salads, stir-fries and soups. Sow in August and allow 20cm between plants.

Red mustard

Deliciously tangy, oriental mustards come in many varieties – all are spicy. Sow between August and September, allowing 5cm between plants, and pick individual leaves when still small.

Flowers for the plate

Another exciting way of enhancing your meals is with flowers, which have eye-catching colours and unusual flavours. All the ones shown here can be eaten or used as a garnish; the stems of garlic chives are also edible.

1 **Oregano marjoram** Pungent flavour
2 **Tom Thumb nasturtium** Rich colour and spicy flavour
3 **Garlic chives** Strong taste of garlic
4 **Pot marigold** Mild and crunchy like all the marigolds
5 **Compact marjoram** Rich herby taste
6 **White borage** Sweet tasting
7 **Gypsy Festival marigold** Best when small
8 **Tangerine sage** Surprisingly sugary
9 **Common thyme** As powerful and aromatic as the leaves
10 **Daisy May marigold** Best when small
11 **Blue borage** Pretty in ice cubes

Flowering rocket

Rocket can be grown for flowers as well as leaves – both are pleasantly aromatic and spicy, with notes of mustard. Cultivated rocket has white flowers while olive leaf and wild rocket have yellow flowers and smaller, more pungent leaves.

Nasturtium

The leaves and brightly coloured petals of nasturtiums such as Tom Thumb (pictured), Empress of India and Peach Melba can be eaten in salads. Pickled, the large seeds look and taste just like capers.

Marigolds

Pot margold's small bright flowers, Gypsy Festival's large pale flowers (pictured) and Daisy May's vividly coloured blooms are all suitable for eating. Note that the flowers of French and African marigolds are much less flavourful.

Courgette flowers

Appealingly crisp in texture, the flowers of squashes, pumpkins and courgettes are delicious deep-fried in batter or added to salads. On courgettes, they grow on the tips as shown or on separate long stems.

Strawberries

Succulent strawberries

Buy and plant a few strawberry plants in March or April for tasty fruit in July – say three plants for a 30cm-diameter pot. They love full sunlight and grow vigorously, so water them generously. When fruiting is finished cut off all the leaves and runners to promote growth the following year; after the second year's crop runners can be rooted into new pots to make new plants.

Plant alpine strawberries in the spring, about 25cm apart – the fruit is currant-size and intensely flavourful, cropping from June to November. Each plant will grow larger in time and develop a large, corm-like root. It will also create new plantlets. After about three years you can pull out the parent plant, leaving the new seedlings to carry on growing.

plant chooser

Understanding
plants

When it comes to deciding what to plant in your garden, it's easy to feel overwhelmed. So here we've featured a selection of recommended plants to inspire and get you started, from trees and shrubs to summer annuals and container plants.

Lavandula stoechas **Lavender**

What plant names mean

Native and common garden plants often have easy English names – like poppy, daisy or foxglove. However, many other native plants have different names in different parts of the country. And in fact most garden plants originally come from overseas. To avoid confusion a universal naming system using Latin enables gardeners to be specific about a particular plant, and to be certain that a name will mean the same in any part of the world. Many Latin names have been adopted as common names, so anemone, camellia, campanula, fuchsia, iris, petunia, wisteria will seem quite familiar, and names like *Lavandula*, *Thymus*, *Rosa*, *Tulipa* require only a small stretch of the imagination.

The two basic parts of a plant name are the genus and the species, so for the Japanese maple these would be *Acer palmatum*. *Acer* refers to the overall 'family' (genus) and *palmatum* is one of the various species which make up that

family. When plants of the same species breed together in the wild, variations in features can result. So a third name or subspecies (subsp.) may be added to describe these variations. Cultivated plants are often artificially bred, to the extent that there may be tens or even hundreds of variations, even though they are all similar enough to fit within the same species. In this case the third part of the name may take the form of a variety or cultivar (which can be one or more words). Thus *Acer palmatum* 'Dissectum Atropurpureum' describes one of many Acers of the species *palmatum*.

A good way to get into using Latin names is to remember just the genus name to start with – *Sedum*, *Hosta*, *Euphorbia* – without getting too tied up with their detailed names.

Growing in the UK climate

Hardy means a plant is able to survive the winter without protection – such as being moved into a greenhouse or indoors, or maybe wrapped in insulating material. The majority of trees, shrubs, climbers and perennials featured in this book are hardy in most parts of the UK. Conditions vary considerably throughout the country, however, so the best way to be sure is to buy locally and seek advice. A few plants in these pages are classed as tender and cannot tolerate prolonged freezing or sub-zero temperatures. These may only survive in southern coastal areas and cities, where it is warmer, or by being brought indoors or protected for the winter.

Getting the conditions right

Although it is best to stick to plants that suit your particular local conditions you will more than likely want to try others that are less suitable. If, for instance, you have a heavy clay soil, but you wish to grow plants such as lavender or thyme, you will get much better results by following the instructions to dig horticultural sand or grit into the soil when planting. This will improve drainage and give the plant the conditions it prefers. Almost all plants will benefit from the addition of soil improver and fertiliser when you plant them. See pages 190–91 for information about soil improvers, mulches and fertilisers. More detailed advice on all kinds of planting can be found on pages 198–227.

Canna 'Picasso' **Indian shot plant**

Using the plant chooser

The following pages feature around 200 garden plants. They are only a tiny sample of the thousands of plants that are cultivated and sold throughout the UK. But they have been chosen because they are outstanding in one way or another, and most are easy to grow, readily available, and suited to the British climate. Each one is accompanied by an essential guide to care and cultivation. If you need to research the needs of any particular plant further, there are lots of specialist books and websites that can help.

guide to symbols

	Grow in shade
	Grow in partial shade
	Grow in full sun
	Width or spread
	Height
	Cultivation notes, including soil type, planting and care

common plant terms

Acid soil
Where pH value is less than 7. Occurs where the mineral content of soil is not alkaline. Often waterlogged or damp, where excess water prevents normal breakdown of dead plant material, producing acid and an accumulation of plant material in the soil forming peat.

Alkaline soil
Usually occurs where underlying rock is limestone or chalk, producing a soil with high calcium content that drains well and has a pH value of more than 7.

Alpine
Term used for rock garden plants. Many such low-growing plants are found on mountains above the tree line in cracks and crevices where there is little soil to sustain larger vegetation.

Annuals
Plants that grow from seed, then flower, set seeds and die all within one year.

Biennials
Plants that grow from seed one year, last through the winter, then flower, set seeds and die in the following year.

Bract
Modified leaf at the base of a flower, usually green, but may be large and coloured, resembling or sometimes replacing petals.

Container-grown
Describes a plant grown or supplied by a nursery in a pot or container.

Corm
Swollen stem below ground, similar to a bulb, that stores food to help the plant to survive through the winter.

Cultivar
Short for 'cultivated variety'. A plant with features which distinguish it from other members of the same species. May either be the result of breeding or a naturally occurring variation.

Deciduous
Shrubs and trees that lose their leaves in winter, for example buddleia, maple, birch and cherry.

Evergreen
Plants that keep their leaves through the winter, for example holly, box and mahonia. A few plants are partially evergreen and may lose some leaves in a harsh winter or exposed spot.

Harden off
The process of gradually accustoming seedlings and plants started indoors to conditions outdoors, for instance by keeping them in a cold frame.

Hardy
Describes a plant that can survive outdoors all year round and doesn't need to be over-wintered in a greenhouse, or protected with insulating material.

Herbaceous
Describes a plant without woody material in its stems that dies down to ground level each year.

Humus
Decayed organic matter from rotting plants in the soil. Important for conserving water and nutrients and helping to give soil an open, crumbly texture. Produced by dead plant matter that falls naturally onto the soil, or by adding compost, manure, bark or wood chips and other organic materials. Vital for healthy plant growth.

Naturalise
Describes the process by which a plant is allowed to spread naturally, often in a semi-cultivated area such as an orchard or wildflower lawn. Only certain plants, including some bulbs, will do this; most cannot compete with more vigorous wild grasses and weeds.

Offset
Small plantlet produced at the base of a plant which is capable of being separated and forming a new plant. May also refer to small bulbs which separate from a larger parent bulb.

Perennials
Plants that live for a number of years without building up much woody material and generally die back to ground level in the winter. Some store food in tubers or rhizomes to help them survive the winter.

Perlite
Sterile, long-lasting volcanic granules added to growing mixes to improve structure, aeration and drainage capacity. *See also* vermiculite.

pH
A scientific scale measuring acidity and alkalinity. The range extends from 1 to 14, with 7 being neutral. Below 7 is acid and above is alkaline. Soil testing kits are cheap and easy to use (see page 189).

Plug
A small plant raised individually, usually in a plug tray – a plastic tray with many compartments filled with soil. Once the plant grows enough roots to bind the soil together a 'plug' is formed.

Rhizome
Swollen underground stem growing horizontally, just below the surface, storing food to help the plant to survive through the winter.

Shrub
Woody plant with multiple stems that grow from the base and no main trunk.

Stamen
The male reproductive part of a flower, often visible in the centre as a number of small stalks with enlarged ends carrying powdery yellow pollen.

Stigma
The female reproductive part of the flower, often seen at the centre as a single stalk with a swollen end that receives the pollen produced by stamens.

Succulent
Plant adapted to life in dry conditions by means of thick, fleshy leaves, and sometimes stems or roots, which retain water.

Sucker
Shoot originating below ground from a plant's roots.

Tap root
A single, strong-growing, main root which usually penetrates deep into the ground.

Tender
Describes plants that can be damaged or killed by low temperatures and therefore need protection.

Tree
Woody plant whose central stem hardens to form a self-supporting trunk from which branches grow.

Tuber
Swollen underground stem or root that stores food to help the plant to survive through the winter.

Variegated
Describes leaves with patches of white, cream or other colours. Rare in wild plants; prized in garden plants.

Vermiculite
Similar properties to perlite, but retains slightly more moisture.

Height and scale
trees

Juniperus scopulorum 'Skyrocket'

① Juniperus
Juniper

Junipers come in a wide range of shapes and sizes, from tall and thin to low and spreading. Their dense, evergreen foliage gives structure and contrast all year round. ☼ Prefers an open, sunny or lightly shaded position. The golden varieties need full sun for best colour, but blues and silvers are often better in partial shade. ✎ Grow in well-drained, fertile soil. Dig in plenty of compost when planting. Water during dry spells, until established. Little pruning is needed other than light trimming to keep in shape. **scopulorum 'Skyrocket'** Pencil-thin cultivar with blue-grey foliage all year round. Excellent as a single specimen plant or used in groups to make pillars. Good for small gardens and in containers when young. Resistant to dry conditions. ↕6m.

ideal plants

Ornamental fruit or berries

Ilex aquifolium Holly No.2

Mahonia aquifolium '**Apollo**' Oregon grape No.37

Malus Crab apple No.12

Prunus laurocerasus Cherry laurel No.45

Prunus lusitanica Portugal laurel No.6

Schisandra rubriflora No.66

Vitis Vine No.71

Ilex aquifolium 'J.C. van Tol'

② Ilex aquifolium
Holly

Easy and fast-growing evergreen with year-round appeal. Cultivars are available with gold or cream variegated leaves. Red or yellow berries in autumn and winter. Some cultivars have separate male and female trees, only females have berries. Can be used for hedging. ☼ Grows best in partial shade but can tolerate full sun. ✎ Prefers moist but well-drained soil.
'**J.C. van Tol**' Dark green leaves with few prickles, masses of red berries in autumn. ↕6m ↔4m.

Arbutus unedo

⑤ Arbutus unedo
Strawberry tree

A slow-growing evergreen tree which looks good all year round. Its glossy, mid-green leaves have toothed edges, set against branches with reddish peeling bark. In autumn clusters of flowers like lily-of-the-valley appear – white, tinged with pink – sometimes followed by rough-skinned red fruits which are edible, but not tasty. ↕8m ↔8m. ☼ Thrives in a sheltered place in full sun. ✎ Grow in rich, well-drained soil with plenty of humus. Plant in autumn. Dig plenty of compost into the planting hole and water frequently during dry spells until well established.
'**Rubra**' Deep pink flowers.

Laurus nobilis

③ Laurus nobilis
Bay tree, Sweet bay

Useful evergreen with waxy, dark green, wavy-edged leaves and dense growth. Small greenish-yellow flowers in summer. Responds well to clipping and is widely used for topiary. Can be hard pruned to keep size in check. Aromatic leaves used in cooking. ↕12m ↔10m. ☼ Prefers full sun or light shade. ✎ Grow in moist but well-drained soil. Dig compost into the planting hole. Growth is slow at first. Water in dry weather until established.

Prunus 'Pink Perfection'

⑥ Prunus
Ornamental cherry

Deciduous and evergreen trees with spectacular white or pink blossom in spring or early summer, often with good leaf colour in autumn. ☼ Grow in full sun or partial shade. ✎ Prefers moist, well-drained soil rich in humus.
'**Pink Perfection**' One of the best flowering cherries. Large clusters of double pink flowers. Foliage tinged with bronze when young. ↕8m ↔8m.
lusitanica Portugal laurel. Handsome evergreen tree with masses of white flowerheads in early summer. Can be grown in containers when small. Leaves are laurel-like, but has small red fruit which turn black, unpleasant to eat and seed kernels are poisonous. ↕20m ↔20m.

Sorbus vilmorinii

④ Sorbus vilmorinii
Chinese rowan

This makes an ideal tree for small gardens. Its branches arch gracefully, with glossy, olive-green, ferny leaves turning orange and red-bronze in autumn. In late spring flat heads of white flowers appear, followed in autumn by bunches of berries which start pink and fade to white, lasting well into the winter. ↕5m ↔6m. ☼ Grow in full sun or partial shade. ✎ Thrives in moist, well-drained soil. Dig well-rotted garden compost into the planting hole and stake firmly.

Magnolia x soulangeana

⑦ Magnolia

Impressive specimen plant with large flowers and lush foliage. There are cultivars with white, cream, yellow or pink flowers, and some are evergreen. ☼ Grow in full sun or partial shade. ✎ Thrives in deeply cultivated, moist but well-drained soil. Generally dislikes alkaline soils although some are lime tolerant.
grandiflora 'Exmouth' Magnificent evergreen tree with tough, glossy, dark green leaves, russet on their undersides, and huge, white flowers 25cm across in late summer and autumn. Often grown as a wall shrub to protect the large, brittle leaves. ↕15m ↔10m.
x soulangeana Spreading shrub or small tree with cup-shaped flowers in shades of white and pink in spring. Dark green deciduous leaves. Will tolerate slightly alkaline soils. ↕6m ↔6m.

Cupressus sempervirens

Eucryphia x nymansensis

Betula utilis var. jacquemontii

8 Cupressus sempervirens
Italian cypress

Striking feature tree forming a thin column of dense evergreen foliage. Effective on its own or in multiples, lining drives or pathways. Can be grown in containers when small. Fast growing. ⬍ 20m ⬌ 2.5m. ☀ Grow in full sun or partial shade. 🌱 Unfussy about soil type as long as it's moist but very well drained.

Gleditsia triacanthos

11 Gleditsia triacanthos
Honey locust

Glossy green, finely divided, ferny leaves and an open habit make this an attractive feature tree. The trunk and branches have sharp spines. Leaves turn vivid yellow in autumn before falling. Fragrant greenish-yellow flowers in summer. ⬍ 12m ⬌ 12m. ☀ Prefers full sun. Tolerates dry conditions and heavy pollution, making it ideal for city gardens. 🌱 Grow in well-drained, fertile soil. Minimal pruning required. **'Sunburst'** The young leaves are rich golden-yellow, darkening to green as they age, but becoming yellow again by mid-autumn.

9 Eucryphia x nymansensis

One of the most desirable garden trees, with compact, upright growth and small evergreen leaves. Masses of single white flowers in late summer make a breathtaking sight. The flowers are highly attractive to bees. ⬍ 10m ⬌ 4m. ☀ Grow in full sun or partial shade in a sheltered position. 🌱 Thrives in well-drained acid to neutral soil. Dig plenty of compost into the planting hole and mulch annually with leafmould or compost. Hardly any pruning is needed as growth is tidy and compact. Remove any damaged or crossing branches.

Malus 'Profusion'

12 Malus
Crab apple

Easy to grow small tree with white or pink spring blossom and abundant ornamental fruit which may be yellow or red, sometimes staying on the branch until early spring. Excellent for winter colour. Fruits enjoyed by birds. ☀ Grow in full sun or partial shade. 🌱 Thrives in moist, well-drained fertile soil. Plant in autumn. Prune out dead or diseased wood in autumn. **'Profusion'** Small, spreading tree. Free-flowering with purplish blossom in spring and berry-like apples 1cm across. ⬍ 10m ⬌ 10m. **'Red Sentinel'** Small tree with white flowers tinged with pink in spring and deep cherry-red apples 2.5cm across in autumn. ⬍ 6m ⬌ 6m.

10 Betula
Birch

Peeling silvery bark and graceful branches with fine leaves make this an appealing garden tree. Leaves are mid-green and open, casting only light shade. Has small catkins in spring. ☀ Grow in full sun or partial shade. 🌱 Does best in damp, humus-rich soil, which is neutral to acid. Plant in autumn. Dig in plenty of compost when planting and mulch each autumn. **pendula 'Laciniata'** Silver birch. Graceful drooping branches. ⬍ 10m ⬌ 3m. **utilis var. jacquemontii** Himalayan birch. Striking white bark and glossy deep-green leaves. ⬍ 18m ⬌ 10m.

Pyrus salicifolia 'Pendula'

13 Pyrus salicifolia 'Pendula'
Weeping willow-leaved pear

One of the best small deciduous trees for any garden. Branches weep to the ground, with long grey-green, willow-like leaves and white blossom in spring, followed by miniature green, inedible pears. Easy to grow. Needs little or no pruning. Slow growing. ⬍ 5m ⬌ 3m. ☀ Grow in full sun or partial light shade. 🌱 Thrives in well-drained, fertile soil. Remove any dead wood in autumn.

Height and scale
trees

Catalpa bignonioides

14 Catalpa bignonioides
Indian bean tree

This elegant, spreading, deciduous tree is grown for its large heart-shaped leaves and impressive heads of white, bell-shaped flowers, splashed purple and yellow, appearing in late spring. In autumn, dark runner-bean like pods form. ⬍20m ◁▷ 10m. ☼ Grow in full sun. ✎ Prefers moist, well-drained soil. Dig plenty of compost into the hole when planting. Pruning is not necessary, unless you need to restrict height or spread.
'**Aurea**' Young leaves have a bronze tinge, later maturing to bright yellow. Makes a stunning combination with bronze or purple-leaved plants such as cotinus or maples. When mature, branches dip gracefully down from the crown.

Acer palmatum 'Dissectum Atropurpureum'

15 Acer palmatum
Japanese maple

Bred for centuries in Japan, these beautiful small trees have coloured leaves from deepest bronze to bright red and lime green; many are variegated or flushed with other colours. Often the leaf colour changes through the season, usually ending with brilliant oranges and reds in autumn before the leaves fall. They make perfect feature plants and are easy to care for. Slow growing, they can take 30–50 years to reach maximum size. ☼ Does best in a position which is shaded in the hottest part of the day. Leaves can scorch in hot sun or wind, especially if the roots become dry. ✎ Adaptable to most soils so long as they are moist. Work in plenty of compost around the roots. Keep well watered during dry spells. Mulch annually with compost. No pruning needed.
'**Dissectum Atropurpureum**' Deep purple-red deeply divided feathery leaves. ⬍8m ◁▷ 10m.

Sorbus aria

16 Sorbus aria
Whitebeam

Whitebeams make tidy and compact trees for the garden, with interesting leaves and plenty of blossom. The leaves are deeply veined and glossy, dark green on top, with a white felty covering of hairs underneath. The white flowerheads appear in late spring, followed in autumn by deep red berries, speckled brown, loved by birds. ⬍10m ◁▷ 7m. ☼ Grow in full sun or partial shade. ✎ Thrives in moist, well-drained soil. Dig plenty of well-rotted compost into the planting hole and stake well. Minimal pruning required.
'**Lutescens**' Young leaves creamy white, later becoming silvery green.
'**Majestica**' ('**Decaisneana**') Large oval leaves.

Eucalyptus gunnii

18 Eucalyptus
Gum tree

Fast-growing trees with spectacular blue-green leaves and coloured bark. For the smaller garden they can be cut down or replaced every few years. ☼ Grow in full sun. ✎ Prefers moist but well-drained, neutral to acid, humus-rich soil.
dalrympleana This slightly tender tree has startling white bark and is also attractive for its display of young blue-green foliage if pruned hard back annually. Tolerates chalky soil.

gunnii Cider gum. Magnificent medium-sized tree with slightly weeping branches. The young leaves are silvery-blue and rounded while the adult leaves become elongated and blue-green on their upper sides. The trunk and branches are covered with peeling bark in many shades of grey, cream, olive and pinkish brown. Not suitable for very cold or exposed areas. ⬍20m ◁▷ 15m.
pauciflora subsp. niphophila Alpine snow gum. Small-growing and hardy tree with spreading branches and striking silver-white bark that peels in late summer, leaving olive, bronze and pinkish brown patches. Leaves are thick, glossy and blue-green, with a broad curving shape. ⬍6m ◁▷ 6m.

Robinia pseudoacacia 'Frisia'

17 Robinia pseudoacacia 'Frisia'
Golden acacia

Grown for its colourful foliage. The deciduous, fine leaves are bright yellow when young, turning greener, then orange in autumn. Compact, upright shape. Severe discomfort if ingested. ⬍20m ◁▷ 9m. ☼ Grow in full sun. ✎ Prefers light, alkaline soil. Can be hard pruned in autumn to restrict height and spread.

ideal plants

Trees for a small garden

Acer palmatum
Japanese maple No.15

Arbutus unedo Strawberry tree No.5

Betula Birch No.10

Eucalyptus pauciflora subsp. *niphophila* Alpine snow gum No.18

Eucryphia x nymansensis No.9

Ilex aquifolium 'J.C. Van Tol ' Holly No.2

Malus Crab apple No.12

Osmanthus x burkwoodii No.23

Prunus 'Pink Perfection' Ornamental cherry No.6

Pyrus salicifolia 'Pendula' Weeping willow-leaved pear No.13

Sorbus aria Whitebeam No.16

Form and structure
shrubs

Phlomis fruticosa

Buxus sempervirens

19 Buxus sempervirens
Box

A hardy evergreen shrub with small, glossy green leaves, well suited for hedging and topiary. Often used for low hedges surrounding borders and herb gardens. Tiny, scented white flowers in spring. Will grow into a large spreading bush if untrimmed. Slow growing and long lived. ⬍5m ◁▷5m. ☀️Prefers light shade but will tolerate some sun where the ground is moist. Becomes dull and scorched in dry conditions. 🌱 Grows best in damp, humus-rich, well-drained soil. Plant in autumn or spring. Dig compost into the bottom of the hole. Mulch with compost in autumn and feed with a slow-release fertiliser or organic bonemeal-based fertiliser. Trim as required to keep in shape through the summer.

Carpenteria californica

20 Carpenteria californica
Bush anemone

Handsome and unusual shrub with glossy, semi-evergreen foliage and large, shining white anemone-like flowers in summer. Slightly tender, especially when young. ⬍2m ◁▷2m. ☀️Plant in a warm, sheltered position, in full sun. Good for growing against a wall. 🌱 Prefers light, well-drained soil. Dig plenty of grit and compost into the planting hole. Little pruning is needed, but one or two of the oldest branches can be taken out annually if plant grows too large.

Osmanthus x burkwoodii

23 Osmanthus x burkwoodii

Makes a lovely compact shrub or small evergreen tree for any garden. The leaves are neat, oval and dark glossy green. In spring it's covered with masses of tiny white flowers which are beautifully scented. ⬍3m ◁▷3m. ☀️Grow in full sun or partial shade. 🌱 Prefers moist, well-drained soil. Plant in autumn or spring. Dig a liberal amount of compost into the planting hole. Mulch with compost each autumn.

Hebe pinguifolia 'Pagei'

21 Hebe pinguifolia 'Pagei'

Easy to grow miniature evergreen spreading shrub which looks good all year round and makes great ground cover for the top of a dry sunny wall, rock garden or path edge. Also useful in containers. The trailing purplish stems, bearing many small glaucous blue-grey leathery leaves, root as they go. Masses of white flowers in short spikes cover the plant in late spring and early summer. Plant in groups for effective ground cover. ⬍15cm ◁▷60cm. ☀️Prefers full sun. 🌱 Thrives in well-drained or dry soil. Plant in spring. Needs no special treatment. Can be trimmed back to restrict size.

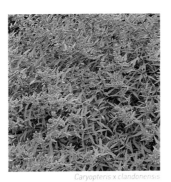
Caryopteris x clandonensis

26 Caryopteris x clandonensis

This lovely small shrub has aromatic silvery-grey leaves and intense blue flowers which cover the plant in late summer and autumn. ⬍90cm ◁▷1.5m. ☀️Grow in full sun. 🌱 Thrives in light, well-drained soil. Dig coarse grit and compost into the planting hole. To maintain a tidy dome-shape, prune hard back in spring as soon as there are signs of growth.

22 Phlomis fruticosa
Jerusalem sage

Small evergreen shrub with soft grey-green leaves and heads of golden yellow flowers in summer. In mild years flowers again in late autumn or winter. ⬍1m ◁▷1.5m. ☀️Grow in full sun. 🌱 Thrives in well-drained soils. Dig grit into the planting hole to ensure good drainage. Prune hard back in early spring otherwise it becomes leggy and straggling.

Convolvulus cneorum

25 Convolvulus cneorum
Silverbush

A charming low-growing shrub with silvery, silky leaves and gleaming white open-trumpet flowers with yellow centres which appear from spring right through to autumn. Makes non-invasive clumps which look good all year round. ⬍30cm ◁▷60cm. ☀️Mediterranean plant which will thrive in a dry, sunny border. Plant in groups for best effect. Also grows well in containers. 🌱 Grow in well-drained fertile soil. Plant out in spring. Work some grit into the planting hole to improve drainage. Trim lightly with shears to keep in shape when flowering has finished.

Form and structure
shrubs

Lavandula stoechas

Perovskia atriplicifolia

Teucrium fruticans

Santolina chamaecyparissus

26 Santolina
Cotton lavender

This low-growing, silver-leaved shrub can be clipped into neat mounds or used as an edging for paths, where its aromatic foliage will scent your way. The feathery leaves are evergreen. In summer yellow button flowers appear, like daisies without petals. ☼ Grow in full sun. ✐ Prefers well-drained, dry, sandy or light soil. Plant in spring. Cut established plants hard back in early spring to retain a neat bushy shape. Trim occasionally with shears after flowering.
'Small-Ness' Small and compact green-leaved cultivar with yellow flowers. ⇕20cm ⬌ 20cm.
chamaecyparissus Silvery grey-green leaves. Yellow button flowers in July. ⇕60cm ⬌ 70cm.
pinnata subsp. neapolitana 'Sulphurea' Silvery leaves and pale sulphur-yellow flowers. ⇕70cm ⬌ 90cm.
rosmarinifolia Green, rosemary-like, needle leaves and yellow button flowers. ⇕60cm ⬌ 80cm.

27 Perovskia atriplicifolia
Russian sage

Whitish stems bear soft, silvery, grey-green leaves and upright spikes of pale lavender-blue flowers in late summer. The flowers attract butterflies and bees, while the strongly aromatic leaves are resistant to rabbits and deer. Flower spikes are good as cut flowers. Easy to grow and will form a slowly expanding clump. ⇕1.2m ⬌ 1m. ☼ Grow in full sun. ✐ Thrives in any well-drained, dry soil. Good for chalk. Dig sand or grit into the planting hole. Cut to the ground in autumn, once the leaves have died.
'Blue Spire' One of the best cultivars with masses of large flower spikes.

Rosmarinus officinalis

30 Rosmarinus officinalis
Rosemary

Rosemary has year-round appeal and is an essential culinary herb that no garden should be without. The pale violet-blue flowers appear from spring to summer and attract butterflies and bees. The needle-like leaves are strongly aromatic and evergreen. ⇕1.5m ⬌ 1.5m. ☼ Grow in full sun. Thrives against a warm wall. ✐ Prefers dry, well-drained, light soils. Dig plenty of coarse grit into the planting hole. Keep in shape by trimming after flowering.

28 Teucrium fruticans
Tree germander

Small evergreen shrub with aromatic, grey-green leaves and spikes of pale lilac flowers. Can be clipped into a low-growing hedge. ⇕1m ⬌ 3m. ☼ Grow in full sun. ✐ Thrives in dry, well-drained, sandy or gritty soil. Plant in spring and dig grit into the planting hole. Cut back in early spring to keep tidy, if required.

Artemisia 'Powis Castle'

31 Artemisia
Wormwood, Mugwort

Wormwoods make good ground cover and their grey-green or silvery leaves combine beautifully with other plants. They are mostly aromatic, shrubby perennials, with insignificant flowers and are well adapted for life in dry conditions. ☼ Grow in full sun. ✐ Soil must be well-drained. Plant in spring. Dig compost and grit into the planting hole. Prune longer woody growths back by about half in autumn to keep tidy.
'Powis Castle' Makes a spreading clump of silvery-grey feathery leaves. ⇕90cm ⬌ 90cm.
arborescens A large, upright bush with fine, silvery, almost white, feathery leaves. ⇕1m ⬌ 1m.
ludoviciana 'Valerie Finnis' Forms a loose mound of very narrow, silvery-grey, pointed leaves. ⇕60cm ⬌ 60cm.
schmidtiana Forms a very low-growing, spreading tuft of white, almost silky, finely divided leaves. ⇕10cm ⬌ 30cm.

29 Lavandula
Lavender

No garden is complete without lavender! Compact, evergreen shrubs which give constant pleasure throughout the year, with their rounded shape, grey-green scented leaves, long succession of usually mauve flowers over the summer and dried flowerheads which can be used in pot-pourri or lavender bags. Bushes can be clipped into tidy mounds or made into hedges. There are several species, including the traditional English lavender and French lavender, with its distinctive ears or tufts on top of the flowerheads. ⇕60cm ⬌ 1m. ☼ Grow in a warm, sunny position. ✐ Prefers a light, well-drained, chalky or alkaline soil. Can be short-lived in heavy soils. Plant in spring. If your soil is heavy or clayey, dig in plenty of sand or grit to improve drainage. Remove dead flowerheads in autumn. Prune back to within 1–2cm of previous year's growth in autumn.
angustifolia English lavender. Pale purple flowers. ⇕60cm ⬌ 45cm.
angustifolia 'Alba' White-flowered form of traditional English lavender. ⇕1m ⬌ 1m.
angustifolia 'Hidcote' Compact, with silvery-grey leaves and deep purple flowers. ⇕60cm ⬌ 45cm.
dentata Produces tall spikes of purple-blue flowers. Strongly aromatic, toothed leaves. ⇕75cm ⬌ 50cm.
stoechas French lavender. Dark purple flowers topped by lighter, vivid purple 'ears'. ⇕60cm ⬌ 60cm.
stoechas 'Blue Star' French lavender. Dark blue-purple flowers, vivid purple 'ears'. ⇕60cm ⬌ 60cm.
stoechas x viridis 'Fathead' Plump, dark purple flowers topped by pale pink 'ears'. ⇕60cm ⬌ 60cm.

Cytisus x beanii

Philadelphus 'Belle Etoile'

Lavatera 'Barnsley'

(32) Lavatera
Tree mallow

Vigorous, easy to grow and reliable. Particularly valuable for its long flowering season, extending from July to November. Mixes well with the whites and pinks of old roses and foxgloves. The leaves are felted grey-green and make a very attractive combination with the pale flowers of cultivars such as 'Barnsley', rather than the commoner pink forms. Fast growing. ⊕2m ◁▷1.5m. ☼Thrives best in a warm, sunny position, although quite tough and able to withstand coastal conditions. ✎Tolerates most soils as long as they are very well-drained or dry. Plant in spring or autumn. Dig in extra grit and sand to improve drainage. Water well until established, after which it can withstand quite dry conditions. The branches are brittle and snap easily in winter winds. Prune quite hard to keep in shape.
'**Barnsley**' Masses of the palest pink flowers with a deep pink eye all summer long.

(33) Philadelphus
Mock orange

Covered in pure white flowers in spring or summer, these small to medium-sized shrubs will fill the garden with a heavenly fragrance. Flowers can be single or double, and have yellow stamens. Leaves deciduous, mid-green. ☼Grow in full sun or partial shade. ✎Prefers light, well-drained, alkaline or neutral soil. Cut away a quarter to a fifth of the oldest wood after flowering.
'**Belle Etoile**' Single white flowers on arching branches. Very fragrant. ⊕1.5m ◁▷2.5m.
'**Lemoinei**' Masses of pure white flowers around mid-summer with a delightful fruity fragrance. Neat and compact. ⊕1.5m ◁▷1.5m.

Exochorda x macrantha

(35) Exochorda x macrantha
Pearlbush

Graceful shrub with arching branches covered with large white flowers in late spring and early summer. Small, medium green leaves turn to shades of yellow and orange in autumn. ☼Grow in sun or partial shade in an open but sheltered position. Makes a good wall shrub if supported by wires or trellis. ✎Prefers moist but well-drained, neutral to acid soil.
'**The Bride**' The best cultivar. Compact and free flowering. ⊕2m ◁▷3m.

(34) Cytisus
Broom

Broom quickly forms a bush with a mass of arching stems which are covered with pea-flowers in late spring and early summer. Makes a spectacular display over several weeks. The deciduous leaves are small and cast little shade. Easy to grow. ☼Prefers a warm, sheltered site in full sun. ✎Plant in well-drained soil. Can withstand drought and poor soil. Plant in spring or early autumn. Brooms are short-lived and dislike pruning, so it's best to replace them every few years. After flowering, the younger stems can be lightly trimmed back to tidy the bush.
'**Lena**' Prolific bright red and deep yellow bi-coloured flowers early to mid-summer. ⊕1.5m ◁▷1.5m.
'**Porlock**' Yellow flowers, very fragrant. ⊕3m ◁▷3m.
x kewensis Low-growing, spreading broom. Creamy white to pale yellow flowers in early summer. ⊕30cm ◁▷1.5m.
x praecox 'Warminster' Compact, with creamy yellow flowers. ⊕1.2m ◁▷1.6m.
purpureus Pale pink to purple flowers in early summer. Dark green leaves. ⊕50cm ◁▷50cm.

Choisya ternata 'Sundance'

(36) Choisya ternata
Mexican orange blossom

Grown for its sweetly scented, white flowers and usually dark, glossy and evergreen leaves. Fast growing. ⊕1.5m ◁▷1.2m. ☼Will grow in full sun or shade. ✎Thrives on any well-drained soil. Plant in spring or autumn.
'**Sundance**' Compact evergreen plant with golden yellow aromatic leaves and sweetly scented white flowers. The best leaf colour is obtained if planted in a sheltered, sunny position. Useful for colour combinations with other plants.

Mahonia x media 'Winter Sun'

(37) Mahonia
Oregon grape

A robust evergreen with striking, spiky foliage and sweetly scented yellow flowers which appear in winter, followed by sprays of blue berries with a grey bloom, giving it 'year-round' appeal. ☼Happy growing in shade. Good under deciduous trees. ✎Thrives in moist but well-drained soil with plenty of humus.
aquifolium 'Apollo' Early spring flowering, good for berries. Can be grown in containers and also makes good ground cover. ⊕1m ◁▷1.2m.
aquifolium 'Smaragd' Compact, low-growing form. ⊕70cm ◁▷1m.
x media 'Charity' Lily-of-the-valley bush. Erect branches with dense spikes of lemony-yellow flowers. Makes an impressive feature plant. ⊕4m ◁▷4m.

Form and structure
shrubs

Elaeagnus pungens 'Maculata'

38 Elaeagnus

Very hardy and easy to grow shrubs useful for their unusually coloured evergreen foliage. Insignificant flowers, sometimes appearing in winter, can have a powerful scent. Fast growing and can be trained as a hedge. ⬦4m ◁▷4m. ☼ Grow in full sun or partial shade. Withstands coastal and exposed planting well. ✿ Prefers moist, well-drained soil. Does not do well on shallow chalk. Plant in autumn or spring. Dig compost into the planting hole and mulch annually. Prune in summer or autumn to limit size if necessary.

'Quicksilver' Scaly, silvery leaves and small, creamy coloured flowers with a sweet scent in summer.

pungens 'Maculata' One of the best cultivars. The rich gold and dark green variegated leaves add a splash of brightness to the garden at all times of the year. Good for arrangements and as a Christmas evergreen.

Cornus alba

41 Cornus
Dogwood

The eye-catching stems of dogwoods, in a variety of colours, provide useful winter colour when many other plants have little to contribute. Multiple stems form a thicket. Leaves are bright green, often with good autumn colour, and white flowers open in early summer. Fast growing. ⬦4m ◁▷5m. ☼ Grow in full sun or partial shade. ✿ Requires moist

but well-drained soil. Plant in spring or autumn. For those grown for winter stem colour, cut back to within 30cm of the soil in early spring to encourage new growth, which has the brightest colour.

alba 'Sibirica' Brilliant crimson winter shoots.

alba 'Spaethii' Bright red stems and attractively variegated leaves in cream, light green and yellow.

controversa 'Variegata' Spectacular small tree. Leaves are green, variegated with creamy margins. White flowers in summer are followed by black berries. Easy, needs no special care. ⬦8m ◁▷8m.

mas Cornelian cherry. Small bunches of yellow flowers on bare twigs in early spring. Leaves follow and in autumn turn rich reddish-purple. Edible cherry-like fruits. ⬦5m ◁▷5m.

Abutilon 'Kentish Belle'

39 Abutilon
Indian mallow

This tender shrub has exotic flowers in reds and yellows hanging like pendants all through summer into autumn. Semi-evergreen, small to medium-sized shrub. ☼ Prefers a warm, sheltered spot against a south-facing wall in full sun. ✿ Grow in well-drained soil with plenty of humus. Dig compost into the soil when planting. Prune only to trim or remove any overgrown branches in spring.

'Kentish Belle' Abundant flowers with apricot yellow petals emerging from deepest red. ⬦2.5m ◁▷2.5m.

megapotamicum Gracefully arching branches with brightly coloured red and yellow flowers. ⬦2m ◁▷2m.

Weigela florida 'Foliis Purpureis'

42 Weigela florida

Popular and easy to grow shrub with attractive flowers and leaves which vary in colour according to variety. Medium sized, but good for both small and larger gardens as can easily be controlled by pruning. ☼ Thrives in full sun or partial shade. ✿ Grow in moist but well-drained humus-rich soil.

'Foliis Purpureis' One of the best forms. Bronze-green leaves make a perfect background for the pink flowers. ⬦1.5m ◁▷1.5m.

'Variegata' Leaves grey-green with cream edges. Rosy pink flowers. ⬦2.5m ◁▷2.5m.

Chaenomeles japonica

40 Chaenomeles japonica
Japonica, Flowering quince

A small deciduous shrub grown for its white, orange or red flowers which appear early in the year, followed in autumn by ornamental yellow fruits, like small apples. Train against a wall, or grow as a small free-standing, spreading shrub. The branches are spiny with mid-green leaves. Fast growing. ☼ Thrives in sun or shade. ✿ Unfussy, but prefers moist, well-drained soil rich in humus. Dislikes very alkaline soil. Dig in compost when planting. Cut flowering/fruiting shoots back to a strong bud after fruiting. On older plants remove a quarter of the oldest branches completely each year.

'Nivalis' Pure white flowers. ⬦90cm.

Escallonia 'Crimson Spire'

43 Escallonia rubra

Escallonias are easy and adaptable shrubs with masses of white, pink or red flowers over a long period in summer and graceful arching stems with glossy evergreen leaves. Grow as a free-standing shrub, against a wall or trained as a hedge. ⬦5m ◁▷5m. ☼ Will grow in full sun or shade and does well in coastal and exposed conditions. ✿ Prefers moist, well-drained soil rich in humus. Plant in late spring to avoid the coldest weather.

'Crimson Spire' A vigorous, erect cultivar with dark glossy foliage. Bright crimson flowers from mid- to late summer.

Viburnum tinus 'Eve Price'

44 Viburnum

Often winter flowering, with delicately scented white or pink blooms, and evergreen or sometimes deciduous leaves, viburnums come in many different forms and offer great value in the garden. ☀ Thrives in full sun or partial shade. ✎ Grow in moist but well-drained soil.
burkwoodii Semi-evergreen. Rounded flowerheads of pinkish white tubular flowers.
⬍ 2.5m ⬌ 2.5m.
plicatum 'Mariesii' Japanese snowball tree. A spectacular spreading shrub with branches growing in horizontal tiers becoming laden with round heads of white flowers in late spring. Strongly veined dark green leaves turning deep red in autumn. ⬍ 4m ⬌ 4m.
tinus 'Eve Price' Laurustinus. Dense evergreen leaves forming a compact bush. Flowers have pink buds opening white. ⬍ 3m ⬌ 3m.
x bodnantense 'Dawn' Deciduous, with deliciously scented pink flowers from autumn to spring.
⬍ 4m ⬌ 3m.

---

ideal plants

Plants for coastal conditions

Artemisia Wormwood, Mugwort No.31
Elaeagnus No.38
Erica Heather No.54
Eryngium alpinum Sea holly No.83
Escallonia rubra No.43
Kniphofia thomsonii
Red-hot poker No.112
Lavatera Tree mallow No.32
Phormium New Zealand flax No.50

Prunus laurocerasus

45 Prunus

Spectacular spring blossom and a range of forms make these smaller ornamental cherries excellent specimen plants for most gardens. There are many cultivars with white, pink or red blossom, often also with good autumn leaf colour. ☀ Grow deciduous cultivars in full sun or partial shade, evergreens will tolerate shade. ✎ Prefers moist, well-drained, fertile soil. Needs only minimal pruning to remove dead or diseased wood or any crossed branches.
'Comet' A dwarf form of flowering almond which can be used in borders, rockeries and containers. Bushy and compact with many branches rising from the base. Branches packed with hundreds of narrow-petalled, starry, pink, fragrant flowers, even on very young plants. ⬍ 1.2m.
laurocerasus 'Otto Luyken' Cherry laurel. Has glossy evergreen leaves and responds well to trimming, which makes it an excellent, fast-growing hedging plant. This cultivar is low growing and will thrive in full sun or partial shade. Cherry red berries are poisonous.
⬍ 1m ⬌ 1.5m.

Fuchsia magellanica 'Riccartonii'

46 Fuchsia

Easy to grow shrub with masses of drooping flowers in rich shades of scarlet, pink and purple, all through summer. Cultivars range from small, trailing and tender, to large, vigorous and hardy. Leaves are deciduous. Fast growing.
☀ Plant in light shade or full sun. ✎ Prefers humus-rich, well-drained soil. Prune in spring. To keep to a manageable size, branches can be cut hard down to the ground in winter, or remove some of the oldest branches each year.
'Versicolour' Deciduous variegated foliage, fairly hardy. Small red flowers. ⬍ 1m ⬌ 1m.
magellanica 'Riccartonii' Stems reddish when young, flowers scarlet and purple. Dark green leaves with a bronze tinge. Very hardy. ⬍ 2.5m ⬌ 2.5m.

Cotinus coggygria purpureus

48 Cotinus coggygria
Smoke tree

Grown for its coloured foliage, which may be deep purple or bright green. The frothy flowers are an added bonus and really do look like a cloud of smoke. Leaves turn bright red in autumn. ⬍ 5m ⬌ 5m. ☀ Grow in full sun or partial shade. ✎ Prefers a moist, humus-rich but well-drained soil.
'Royal Purple' The deep purple leaves of this shrub make it really stand out.
purpureus Light green leaves and pink flowers. Good when grown with 'Royal Purple'.

Salvia 'East Friesland'

47 Salvia
Sage

Sage is a well-known culinary herb, but there are many other cultivars, grown for their blue, mauve, purple or red spikes of flowers, or coloured foliage.
☀ Grow in full sun. ✎ Prefers well-drained soil. Tolerates drought. Dig in grit when planting.
'East Friesland' Purple stems crammed with violet-blue flowers that bloom from mid-summer to late autumn. Blue-green aromatic leaves. ⬍ 60cm ⬌ 60cm.
officinalis 'Icterina' Golden sage. Lovely gold variegated leaves all year. ⬍ 50cm ⬌ 50cm.
officinalis 'Purpurascens' Rich purple leaves lasting through the winter. ⬍ 60cm ⬌ 60cm.
x superba Profuse violet blue flowers. Large wavy-edged sage leaves. ⬍ 60cm ⬌ 60cm.

Ceratostigma plumbaginoides

49 Ceratostigma
Plumbago, Leadwort

Grown for its succession of intense blue flowers in late summer and rich bronzy-red autumn leaf tints, this plant is good grown singly or as ground cover planted in groups. Low growing with wiry reddish stems and bright green leaves. ⬍ 45cm ⬌ 45cm. ☀ Prefers a warm, sunny, sheltered place. ✎ Can be cut back by severe frosts but usually recovers well.
plumbaginoides Intense sky-blue flowers and reddish buds contrast with the olive leaves.
willmottianum Similar to above, though larger and flowering from July, with lighter blue flowers.
⬍ 1m ⬌ 1m.

Form and structure
shrubs

Ceanothus thyrsiflorus

Buddleja davidii 'Black Knight'

Azalea

Phormium 'Rainbow Queen'

50 Phormium
New Zealand flax

Phormiums make spectacular feature plants with sword-shaped leaves which may be arching or erect, in green, olive, bronze or red, often variegated with stripes of cream, pink or white. The leaves are tough and leathery, and form a slowly expanding clump which stands up to wind and coastal conditions well. Cultivars vary widely in size, with leaves under 50cm to over 2m tall. Leaves are great for flower arranging. Spectacular tall spikes of red, yellow or orange flowers on brown or black stems rise above the plant in summer, growing to 3m in some cultivars, producing large black seed pods by autumn. ☼ Grow in full sun. Leaf colours do not develop fully in shade. ✎ Prefers moist, well-drained soil but is unfussy about soil type. Mulch with compost in autumn and cut off any dead leaves. Dead flowerheads are ornamental and can be left on the plant during winter.
'**Rainbow Queen**' Bronze-green leaves with pink-red margins. Upright form with drooping tips. ⇕1.2m.
'**Sundowner**' Upright, broad, bronzy-green leaves with copper-red, pink and cream striped variegation. ⇕1.8m.
cookianum '**Cream Delight**' Mountain flax. Broad, arched leaves with a wide cream-yellow central stripe and green margins edged red. ⇕90cm.
tenax '**Purpureum**' Leaves brownish-purple. Forms large clumps. ⇕2m ⬄2m.

51 Ceanothus
California lilac

Covered in eye-catching masses of intense blue flowers in late spring or early summer, with small, evergreen leaves. Cultivars range from low, spreading forms to tall, upright shrubs, making excellent ground or wall cover. ☼ A warm, sheltered situation in full sun will give the best display of flowers. ✎ Prefers rich, well-drained soil with plenty of humus. Add compost to the planting hole.
'**Italian Skies**' Medium-sized, spreading shrub with deep blue flowers in late spring. ⇕5m ⬄3m.
impressus Deepest blue flowers in early summer and deeply veined leaves. ⇕5m ⬄2.5m.
thyrsiflorus var. repens '**Blue Mound**' Creeping form, covered in light blue flowers in early summer. ⇕1m ⬄2.5m.

Erica carnea 'King George'

54 Erica
Heather

Great ground cover, with many flower and leaf colours. Robust, low-growing, densely spreading shrubs. ☼ Grow in full sun. ✎ Thrives in acid to neutral soils which are well drained. Trim after flowering.
'**Rosantha**' Rose pink flowers in spring, medium green foliage. ⇕15cm ⬄40cm.
carnea '**King George**' Deep pink flowers in winter and dark green foliage. Tolerates alkaline soil. ⇕25cm ⬄25cm.

52 Buddleja davidii
Butterfly bush

Large, fast-growing, deciduous shrub with conical flowerheads from summer to late autumn. Highly attractive to butterflies. Many varieties available, with white, yellow, pink, purple, mauve or deep violet flowers. ⇕3m ⬄5m. ☼ Prefers full sun but will tolerate some shade. Tough plant, survives well in coastal conditions, resistant to pollution. ✎ Grows in most soil types if well drained. Thrives in dry walls, and poor stony soil. Cut down hard to 50cm of soil level in early spring.
'**Black Knight**' Deep purple flowers.
'**Dartmoor**' Light purple flowers.
'**Harlequin**' Magenta flowers with cream variegated leaves.
'**Royal Red**' Rich magenta flowers.
'**White Profusion**' White flowers.

Cistus x corbariensis

55 Cistus
Rock rose, Sun rose

Small, bushy shrubs with exotic single flowers in white, pink or purple, produced throughout the summer. Ideal companion to sages, lavenders and artemisias. Leaves are grey-green and aromatic. ⇕60cm ⬄1.2m. ☼ Thrives in a warm, sunny position. ✎ Soil must be well-drained. Drought tolerant. Dislikes pruning.
x corbariensis White flowers with a yellow centre. Hardy.
x pulverulentus Rose-pink flowers.
x purpureus Pale purple flowers with a maroon spot at the base of each petal.

53 Azalea (Rhododendron)

Small to medium-sized shrubs with a spectacular display of flowers in spring. Azaleas are now included in the same genus as rhododendrons, but are often smaller. Hundreds of varieties with many flower colours and variations in leaf colour. ☼ Grow in full sun or partial shade. ✎ Soil must be moist at all times, well drained, acid and rich in humus. Plant in a shallow hole with plenty of compost or leafmould. Mulch regularly and water in dry spells.
'**Johanna**' Compact evergreen with rich red flowers. ⇕90cm ⬄1.2m.
'**Panda**' Masses of pure white flowers in late spring to early summer. ⇕90cm ⬄1.2m.
'**Vuyk's Scarlet**' Dark glossy evergreen leaves and deep scarlet flowers. ⇕90cm ⬄1.5m.

Phyllostachys nigra

56 Phyllostachys
Bamboo

Outstanding large bamboo with coloured, grooved canes and evergreen leaves. Easy to grow. ☼ Thrives in partial shade. ✎ Grow in moist, clayey or heavy soil. Plant in spring or autumn. Mulch with compost in autumn.
bambusoides '**Castilloni**' Castillon bamboo. Yellow canes with a green stripe running around grooves in the canes at intervals. Spreading growth. ⇕8m.
nigra Black bamboo. Striking glossy black canes and light green leaves, forming a large clump. ⇕3m ⬄3m.

Rosa 'Buff Beauty'

Hydrangea paniculata

Rhododendron 'Baden-Baden'

57 Rosa
Bush roses

For sheer range of flower size, colour and scent, few other plants can match the rose. The family is so diverse that there are roses for practically every situation and to suit every taste. You may be attracted to modern roses, with their refined shape and colour and extended flowering period, or to the charm of classic old roses, which tend to be more heavily scented, or perhaps you may find curiosities such as the moss rose or striped roses fascinating, or you may be drawn to species roses, the ancestors of the rose dynasty. There is much to know about these plants and the more time and effort you devote to them, the more rewarding they become. However, for busy people there are roses which are easy, disease resistant and require little pruning, and which will give good results with minimum effort. ☀ Grow in full sun. Will tolerate partial shade. ✎ Thrive in moist, well-drained fertile soil. Many roses are grafted or budded which will show as a gnarled thickening near the base of the main stem above the roots. It is important when planting to make sure this is well below ground level (5–10cm) to discourage suckers. Dig plenty of well-rotted compost or manure into the planting hole. Keep well watered until established. Deadheading will encourage repeat flowering. Different types of rose benefit from different pruning techniques, but in general pruning should be done in winter or early spring. Remove all dead, congested or crossing branches. Reducing the length of branches will encourage a more compact, tidy growth, and removing a proportion of the oldest branches from the base of the plant each year will make for a more vigorous plant and a better display of flowers (see pages 242–43). Mulch in early spring and again in summer. Feed with rose fertiliser in spring. Well-fed roses are more likely to resist disease.
'Buff Beauty' Vigorous and easy. Flowers pale apricot, creamy yellow and buff, all on the same plant. Can be grown as a bush with regular pruning, or trained up a wall as a climber. ↕3m ◁▷ 2m.
'Eglantyne' Profuse flowering and strongly scented. Modern breeding, but old-fashioned style. Bears clusters of pale pink, ruffled flowers. ↕1.5m ◁▷ 1.3m.
'Flower Carpet' Vigorous modern rose, useful as ground cover. Abundant pink flowers in clusters over a long period. ↕80cm ◁▷1m.
'Iceberg' Modern floribunda rose. Pink flushed buds open to white blooms. Produces lots of flowers over a long period. Makes a good specimen plant for the centre of a border. ↕1m ◁▷ 80cm.
'Mary Rose' Clusters of densely ruffled bright pink flowers and a sweet scent. Modern breeding, but old-fashioned style. ↕1.5m ◁▷ 1.2m.
'Penelope' Hybrid musk rose. Masses of pale pink, scented, flowers fading to white as they age, with golden yellow centres. ↕2m ◁▷ 2m.
'Sweet Juliet' Lovely rose with outer petals palest pink and a central blush of pale apricot and peach. Strongly scented. ↕1.2m ◁▷ 90cm.
'White Pet' A lower growing rose producing masses of white blooms throughout the summer. ↕80cm ◁▷ 80cm.
glauca (rubrifolia) Grown for its wonderful glaucous purple leaves on purple stems, this rose has small single pink blooms like a wild rose, a perfect combination with the rest of the plant. ↕2m ◁▷ 1.5m.

58 Hydrangea

Fast-growing shrubs with showy flower clusters which come late in the summer and last through autumn into winter. Deciduous leaves with autumn colour. Lacecaps have flat heads with tiny florets in the centre surrounded by larger flowers, while mopheads have a mass of uniform flowers in a large ball shape. The papery flowers are good for dried arrangements. Mildly toxic if eaten. ☀ Grow in full sun or partial shade. ✎ Prefers moist but well-drained soil, rich in humus. Plant in autumn or spring.
macrophylla 'Blue Wave' A lacecap hydrangea with wide, flat flowerheads in shades of lilac to bright blue, brushed with streaks of claret as they mature. Flowers dry to an elegant silvery blue. ↕1.5m ◁▷ 2m.
aspera villosa Lacecap flowers in combinations of purple, pink and white, changing as the flowers age. ↕3m ◁▷ 3m.
macrophylla 'Clare Rose' Small violet-blue flowers in flat heads, surrounded by larger white flowers. ↕1m ◁▷ 1.5m.
paniculata 'Floribunda' Cone-shaped flower heads with small florets towards the tip and larger flowers towards the base. ↕4m ◁▷ 2.5m.
quercifolia Oak-leaved hydrangea. Dramatic white cone-shaped blooms consisting of uniformly large florets. More tolerant of dry conditions than other hydrangeas. ↕2m ◁▷ 2.5m.

59 Rhododendron

Massed clusters of brightly coloured, sometimes scented, flowers are the main attraction of rhododendrons. Hundreds of cultivars, with something to suit every size garden and nearly every garden situation. Ranging from small-leaved, small-growing shrubs to large-leaved shrubs or trees, flowering at various times, from winter to summer. The smaller azalea types are often grown in pots and containers. ☀ The larger cultivars generally prefer partial shade and thrive under or near trees. Some smaller types grow well in full sun if their roots are kept moist. ✎ Grow in moist, well-drained, acid soil rich in organic material. Some cultivars will tolerate neutral soil. Will not grow on dry soil. Plant in spring or autumn. Dig compost or leafmould into the planting hole. Mulch well with compost every autumn.
'Baden Baden' Open, waxy, scarlet flowers in trusses, April–May. Glossy evergreen leaves. Medium- to small-sized plant. ↕1.5m ◁▷ 1.5m.
'Yellow Hammer' Mid-yellow tubular flowers in April. Evergreen olive-green leaves. ↕1.8m.

Vertical planting
climbers

Hedera helix 'Buttercup'

60 Hedera helix
Ivy

Common ivy can seem rather dark and gloomy, but there are many good cultivars with gold or cream variegation which make a lighter and more interesting covering for walls, fences and banks, and are less invasive. Some also work well in containers. Adaptable to shade and dry conditions, the evergreen leaves provide year-round cover and interest for difficult areas. All parts of the plant are mildly poisonous and irritant.
☀ There are few places ivy will not grow, although ideal conditions are moist and partially shaded. Leaves show their variegation best when grown in bright light. Great for providing a shelter for birds such as sparrows, robins and wrens. ⚒ Prefers moist, well-drained soil. On variegated cultivars remove any branches which have reverted to plain green leaves. Do not let ivy grow into house gutters or under roof tiles.
'Buttercup' Bright yellow leaves when grown in full sun, becoming greener as they get older or become shaded. ⬍2m ⬌2m.
'Glacier' Leaves grey-green with an irregular cream edging. A smaller-leaved, slow-growing ivy. ⬍2m ⬌2m.
'Goldheart' Small, dark green leaves with a central creamy yellow splash. ⬍8m ⬌4m.

Hydrangea anomala subsp. petiolaris

61 Hydrangea anomala subsp. petiolaris
Climbing hydrangea

Spectacular deciduous climber which in time becomes very large, producing masses of white flowerheads. Clings using aerial roots which are not damaging to sound brick or stonework. Sends out bushy side branches.
⬍25m ⬌25m. ☀ Best for a shaded wall, but can withstand full sun if roots are kept moist. ⚒ Prefers moist, well-drained soil with plenty of humus. Plant in autumn or early spring. Dig compost into the planting hole. Can be slow to establish, but once settled is very vigorous and will spread to cover a large area. Cut back straying branches.

Humulus lupulus 'Aureus'

64 Humulus lupulus 'Aureus'
Golden hop

Fast-growing, twining climber with lovely golden yellow leaves, creating a bright spot wherever it grows. Deciduous. ⬍5m ⬌2m.
☀ Grow in full sun or partial shade. Needs full sun for best leaf colour. ⚒ Thrives in moist but well-drained soils. Plant in autumn or spring. Cut stems to the ground in autumn when leaves have dropped.

Jasminum officinale

62 Jasminum officinale
Summer jasmine

Produces masses of sweetly scented white flowers from mid-summer to early autumn and rampantly twines its way over walls, arbors, fences and porches. Drought and pollution tolerant. ⬍12m ⬌4m. ☀ Grows in sun or partial shade. ⚒ Prefers a moist, well-drained soil enriched with organic matter. Plant in autumn or spring. Trim back any unwanted growth to keep in check. Blooms on new growth.
'Fiona Sunrise' Stunning golden yellow leaves and white flowers. An outstanding yellow climber. ⬍4m ⬌4m.

Campsis x tagliabuana

65 Campsis
Trumpet creeper

Vigorous, tender climber with exotic-looking orange trumpet flowers and bright green leaves. Leaves and stems can cause skin irritation. ⬍10m ⬌10m. ☀ Grow in full sun in a sheltered place. ⚒ Prefers moist soil. Dig plenty of compost into the planting hole and mulch in autumn and late spring. Stems need tying in until self-clinging aerial rootlets develop.
radicans Orange-red flowers from late summer to autumn.
x tagliabuana 'Madame Galen' Flowers late summer to autumn.

Tropaeolum speciosum

63 Tropaeolum speciosum
Flame creeper

This lovely perennial climber is a classy relative of the common nasturtium. The flame-red petals are widely spaced and blend well with the greyish-green leaves which are divided into five leaflets. Dies down completely in winter.
⬍3m ⬌3m. ☀ Grow in full sun, preferably against a south-facing wall, but likes to have its roots cool and shaded. ⚒ Prefers moist, humus-rich, acid soil which is well drained. Plant in spring. Slow to start but once the tubers begin to put on deep growth it will become vigorous. In late autumn remove dead stems and foliage and mulch well with compost to protect tubers from frost.

Schisandra rubriflora

66 Schisandra rubriflora

Unusual and charming climber with deciduous dark green leaves and twining red shoots. Deep crimson flowers on hanging, cherry-like stalks appear in late spring and early summer, followed by strings of red berry-like fruits. Separate male and female plants are needed for fruit to set. ⬍10m ⬌8m. ☀ Grow in full sun or partial shade. ⚒ Prefers moist, well-drained, fertile soil. Tie straying shoots in to supports. No pruning needed.

Solanum crispum 'Glasnevin'

67 Solanum crispum 'Glasnevin'
Chilean potato vine

Just what you want from a climber – easy to grow, modest size, semi-evergreen leaves and the whole plant is covered with cascades of pretty lilac flowers from mid-summer until late autumn. ⬍6m ◁▷2m. ☼Grow in full sun on a warm wall. ⚘Thrives in moist, well-drained, light soil, neutral or alkaline. Not self-clinging so needs to have its main stems tied to wires or a trellis. Can be cut hard back to reduce growth if necessary, otherwise no pruning needed.

Actinidia kolomikta

70 Actinidia kolomikta

Unusual and elegant deciduous climber with leaves that start green, then become half white and splashed with pink at the tips as the summer goes on. Small, white, faintly lemon-scented flowers open in May. ⬍5m ◁▷5m. ☼Grow against a sunny, sheltered wall for best leaf colour. ⚘Prefers well-drained neutral soil. Support the twining stems on mesh or wires and tie in any straying shoots. Mulch with compost in autumn.

Wisteria sinensis

68 Wisteria

Vigorous climber grown for its magnificent cascades of perfumed flowers. The twisted woody stems can be supported on nails or wires. Most varieties flower in spring, followed by soft, light green foliage throughout spring and summer. Bean-like seed pods are produced after flowering. Leaves are deciduous. Poisonous.☼Grow in full sun. Looks great climbing over archways and pergolas and can also be grown as a free-standing standard. ⚘Prefers moist, but well-drained soil. Slow to start, but once established is fast growing and needs strong support. Prune in late winter and after flowering if needed to tidy and keep in check.
floribunda 'Alba' White-flowered Japanese wisteria. Long, drooping fragrant flower sprays up to 60cm long. Flowering early summer. Less vigorous than Chinese wisteria. ⬍9m ◁▷3m.
sinensis Chinese wisteria. Pale lilac flowers late spring to early summer up to 30cm long. Lightly scented. ⬍10m ◁▷4m.

ideal plants

Climbers and shrubs for shady walls

Chaenomeles japonica Japonica, Flowering quince No.40

Clematis Old man's beard, Traveller's joy No.73

Hedera helix Ivy No.60

Humulus lupulus 'Aureus' Golden hop No.64

Hydrangea anomala subsp. *petiolaris* Climbing hydrangea No.61

Lonicera japonica 'Halliana' Honeysuckle, Woodbine No.69

Lonicera x heckrottii

69 Lonicera
Honeysuckle, Woodbine

Woodland plants with usually deliciously scented flowers which will rapidly cover walls, trellis or archways, and look great twining into trees. Combine with clematis and roses. Many cultivars are available, with white, cream, yellow or orange tubular flowers, often flushed red or a darker shade on the outside. Some have evergreen leaves. ☼Grow in full sun or partial shade. Prefers to have its roots in cool, damp shade. ⚘Thrives in moist, well-drained soil, rich in humus. Dig a generous amount of compost into the planting hole. Provide wires or support for the plant to twine around. Mulch with compost in autumn.
japonica 'Halliana' Japanese honeysuckle. Fast growing, with small white flowers which turn yellow as they age. Evergreen foliage. ⬍10m ◁▷2m.
periclymenum 'Graham Thomas' Cultivar of common honeysuckle. Produces very full flowerheads throughout the summer, flowers open white, becoming yellow as they age. Deciduous green leaves. ⬍7m ◁▷2m.
periclymenum 'Serotina' Dutch honeysuckle. Flowers pale cream inside, deep purplish-pink outside. Deciduous green leaves. ⬍7m ◁▷2m.
sempervirens Coral honeysuckle. Flowers coral red on the outside, yellow-orange on the inside. Compact growing with dark green leaves and orangey-red berries. ⬍4m ◁▷2m.
x brownii 'Dropmore Scarlet' Flowers scarlet outside, orangey-yellow inside. Blue-green semi-deciduous leaves. ⬍4m ◁▷2m.
x heckrottii Flowers dusky pink outside, orangey-yellow inside. Dark grey-green semi-deciduous leaves. ⬍4m ◁▷2m.
x tellmanniana Flowers rich coppery-yellow outside, yellow inside. Deep green semi-deciduous leaves. ⬍4m ◁▷2m.

Lonicera sempervirens

Vertical planting
climbers

Vitis coignetiae

71 Vitis
Vine

Vines can be ornamental and fruitful, sometimes both at once. Great for covering a wall or pergola. Can also be grown in large pots or tubs. ☀ Thrives in full sun or partial shade. ✎ Does well on almost any well-drained soil. Vines have shallow, spreading roots so if your soil is not well drained it's worth digging a generous amount of grit into the soil half a metre or so around the plant. Vines grown for fruit should be allowed to develop one or two main stems. All branches should then be cut back to within two buds of the main stems when the plant is dormant. Ornamental vines can be allowed to grow at will, and cut back as required, although woody growth should only be cut in winter or the wound will 'bleed'.

'**Brant**' Vigorous ornamental vine which produces many bunches of small, sweet, black grapes which are edible though full of pips. Decorative leaves turn deep red in autumn. ⇕7m ⬌ 7m.
coignetiae Crimson glory vine. Vigorous ornamental vine with huge leaves which develop striking autumn colours. Needs a large space so not suitable for small gardens. ⇕15m ⬌ 15m.
vinifera 'Purpurea' Grape vine. Outstanding ornamental vine with leaves developing a bronze-purple colour, powdered silver, becoming deep plum by autumn. Has bunches of small purple grapes which are bitter, but attractive. ⇕6m ⬌ 6m.

Rosa 'Guinée'

72 Rosa
Climbing roses

Roses are among the loveliest of climbers, with spectacular displays of flowers over a long period and often wonderfully scented. Useful for covering walls or fences, or can be grown through trees or over pergolas. Combinations of climbing roses and clematis can be particularly successful if carefully chosen. ☀ Grow in full sun or partial shade. ✎ Prefers moist, well-drained, fertile soil. Dig plenty of well-rotted compost or manure into the planting hole. Mulch with compost regularly and feed with rose fertiliser. Train branches on wires or nails.

'**Blush Noisette**' Repeat flowering throughout the season. Can be grown as a bush or climbing rose. Flowers in clusters opening from crimson buds fading to white. ⇕2.5m.
'**Gloire de Dijon**' Old climbing tea rose. Repeat flowering from summer to autumn. Full cup-shaped blooms in shades of salmon, buff-yellow, pale yellow and fawn. ⇕5m.
'**Guinée**' Modern climber. Deep crimson blooms, strongly scented. Flowering in mid-summer. ⇕3.5m.
'**Mme Alfred Carrière**' First-class climbing rose with vigorous growth. Begins flowering very early and continues until the beginning of winter. Abundant flowers open pale pink, ageing to pure white. Very sweetly scented and long lasting. ⇕5m.
'**New Dawn**' Rambler. Extremely vigorous with dark glossy green leaves and medium-sized pale pink blooms which are lightly scented. Flowers from mid-summer through to winter. ⇕5m.

Clematis 'Ville de Lyon'

73 Clematis
Old man's beard, Traveller's joy

Clematis have become hugely popular. They create a spectacular show, with blooms in almost every colour. By selecting from the vast range of varieties you can have clematis flowering almost throughout the year. Easy to grow and taking up little space, clematis are equally appealing for the beginner with a small garden or the expert with plenty of space to fill. Apart from climbers there are some herbaceous clematis that will sprawl happily in a border, mixing well with other plants. Some cultivars set attractive feathery seedheads in autumn. All parts are poisonous if eaten and mildly irritating to the skin. Cultivars listed are deciduous unless described otherwise. ☀ Grow in full sun or partial shade – ideally roots in cool shade and top in sun. ✎ Thrives in moist but well-drained soil, rich in humus. Dig plenty of well-rotted compost or manure into the planting hole. Mulch in autumn and early summer. For pruning see page 241.

'**Huldine**' Flowers mid- to late summer. Many small single white flowers with faint mauve stripes. ⇕5m.
'**Jackmanii Superba**' Flowers early to late summer. Lovely large velvety, deep mauve single flowers. ⇕4m.
'**Niobe**' Flowers late spring to early autumn. Rich, deep, velvety, ruby red single flowers. ⇕3m.
'**Perle d'Azur**' Flowers prolifically mid- to late summer. Outstanding vigorous plant with large violet-blue single flowers. ⇕4m.
'**Prince Charles**' Flowers early summer to early autumn. Prolific purple-blue flowers. Can be grown in containers. ⇕2.5m.
'**Ville de Lyon**' Free flowering, early summer to early autumn. Deep vibrant red single flowers. ⇕4m.
armandii Flowers early to mid-spring. Clusters of small single white flowers. Evergreen. Does best on a warm sunny wall. ⇕6m.
cirrhosa balearica Flowers mid-winter to early spring. Bell-shaped single creamy-white flowers with maroon speckles. Evergreen, divided, ferny leaves. Does best on a warm sunny wall. ⇕7m.
x durandii Flowers early summer to early autumn. Vigorous. Violet-blue four-petalled single flowers with yellow stamens. ⇕1.8m.
florida 'Alba Plena' Flowers on and off between late spring and early autumn. Single white flowers on hairy stalks. Deep glossy green leaves. Half-hardy. ⇕3m.
montana 'Alba' Flowers profusely from late spring to early summer. Small single four-petalled flowers. Vigorous grower. ⇕8m.
orientalis 'Bill Mackenzie' Flowers mid-summer to early autumn. Single bell-shaped flowers with four upturned petals, yellow to greenish yellow. ⇕3.5m.
texensis 'Duchess of Albany' Flowers mid-summer to early autumn. Goblet-shaped flowers with joined petals which only open slightly, orangey-red on the outside, creamy white inside. Alkaline soil. ⇕2m.
viticella 'Alba Luxurians' Flowers mid-summer to early autumn. Open single flowers with four widely spaced white petals, shaded green at the tips. ⇕4m.
viticella 'Betty Corning' Flowers early summer to early autumn. Open bell-shaped flowers with four deeply veined petals, pale mauve-pink on the inside, deeper violet-pink on the outside. ⇕3m.
viticella 'Etoile Violette' Flowers mid- to late summer. Vigorous. Abundant single rich purple flowers with slim, widely spaced petals and yellow stamens. ⇕4m.
viticella 'Purpurea Plena Elegans' Flowers mid-summer to early autumn. Rose-like double blooms, petals dark magenta, curved outwards. ⇕4m.

Framework planting
perennials

Hyssopus officinalis

Matteuccia struthiopteris

Dryopteris filix-mas

Acanthus mollis

(74) Acanthus
Bear's breeches

Bold architectural plant with prickly, thistle-like leaves and tall spikes of spiny flowers in summer. Flowers are white, lightly shaded with pink or purple under purple-shaded bracts. Makes a slowly expanding clump. ⇕1.5m ⬦1m. ☀Good in full sun but can tolerate light shade. ✐Grow in well-drained soil. Plant in autumn or spring. If clumps become too large divide in autumn.

mollis Deeply cut, dark green, shiny leaves. Flowers mid- to late summer.

spinosus Graceful, arching, dark green, spiny leaves up to 1m long. Flowers late spring to mid-summer.

(75) Dryopteris filix-mas
Male fern

Sends up many stiff fronds to make a bold feature-plant for shade, or a fill-in for the back of shady borders. The mid-green fronds unfurl from coiled buds in spring and last through until the hard frosts of winter. Makes a large clump with several crowns after a few years. ⇕1m ⬦90cm. ☀Grow in full or partial shade. ✐Prefers moist, well-drained soil, rich in humus. Mulch with compost or leafmould in autumn. Cut down dead foliage in spring, being careful not to damage the new shoots.

Polystichum setiferum

(78) Polystichum setiferum
Soft shield fern

A pretty fern with deeply divided, pointed fronds giving a soft, feathery effect. The light green fronds will last through to the coldest part of the winter. Good ground cover for a damp, shady corner. ⇕60cm ⬦80cm. ☀Grow in full or partial shade. ✐Prefers moist, well-drained soil, rich in humus. Dig in leafmould or compost when planting. Cut down dead foliage in spring before growth starts. Mulch with compost or leafmould in autumn.

(76) Matteuccia struthiopteris
Shuttlecock fern

A beautiful sight in spring, the lush, pale green fronds really resemble a shuttlecock. Look great in groups. ⇕1.5m ⬦1m. ☀Like most ferns, it thrives in the shady or partially shady, moist atmosphere under trees or shrubs. ✐Grow in damp, humus-rich soil. Plant in spring. Dig a generous amount of leafmould or well-rotted compost into the planting hole and mulch in autumn with leafmould or compost.

Brunnera macrophylla

(79) Brunnera macrophylla
Siberian bugloss

Good ground-cover plant, making a spreading layer of hairy, mid-green leaves, with bright blue flowers in mid- to late spring. ⇕45cm ⬦60cm. ☀Being a woodland plant, it prefers cool shade, but will thrive in a partially shaded border. ✐Does best in damp, humus-rich soil. Cultivate from plants in spring. Gradually spreads, year by year. Divide or dig up to control excessive growth.

'Jack Frost' Heart-shaped leaves, 9-12cm wide, variegated with silver overlay and light green veins. Clear blue flowers with yellow centres grow to ⇕45cm.

(77) Hyssopus officinalis
Hyssop

Perennial herb with scented leaves and blue flowers good for edging paths or borders. Thrives in poor, dry conditions. Compact and bushy, will grow into a mound. Can be kept in shape by clipping, or trimmed to make a low-growing hedge. Attractive to bees and butterflies. ⇕60cm ⬦80cm. ☀Prefers full sun. ✐Grow in well-drained, dry garden soil, neutral to alkaline. Dig coarse grit into the planting hole to improve drainage. In autumn cut back flowered shoots to 1–2cm of this year's growth.

Alchemilla mollis

(80) Alchemilla mollis
Lady's mantle

A trouble-free ground-covering plant forming neat mounds of rounded, greyish-green leaves which look good spilling over the edges of paths and borders. Small greenish-yellow flowers are borne in light sprays above the leaves for most of the summer. ⇕50cm ⬦70cm. ☀Grow in full sun to partial shade. Will tolerate dry conditions but needs moisture to thrive. ✐Being a woodland plant, it prefers humus-rich soil. Grow from plants. Self-seeds and spreads easily.

Framework planting
perennials

Echinops ritro

Festuca glauca

Sedum 'Autumn Joy'

Eryngium alpinum

(81) Sedum

Sedums are grown for their interesting fleshy leaves and colourful heads of flowers which appear in late summer and which are attractive to bees and butterflies. The taller-growing species are good for borders and wild planting. ☼ Grow in full sun. 🖉 Thrives in any well-drained or dry soil. Tolerant of poor shallow soils. Plant in spring. Dig plenty of horticultural grit into the planting hole to ensure good drainage. In the first year water in dry weather until the plant becomes established. You can leave the dead flowerheads into winter, or cut them down in late autumn, being careful not to damage next year's shoots which will already be pushing through.
'Autumn Joy' ('Herbstfreude') Thick stems with blue-green leaves make slowly expanding clumps. Flat heads of deep pink starry flowers in late summer. ⬍50cm ◁▷70cm.
'Ruby Glow' Purplish leaves on low-growing straggling stems. Crimson flowers from late summer to early autumn. ⬍20cm ◁▷50cm.
telephium subsp. ruprechtii Glaucous purple leaves and stems with pink flower buds opening to cerise starry flowers. ⬍50cm ◁▷70cm.

(82) Festuca glauca
Blue fescue
Easy to grow ornamental grass with an eye-catching bluish tinge. Makes uniform, neat clumps which can be used in formal designs or randomly in mixed ground cover with other plants such as sedums and hardy geraniums. Also useful for rock gardens and containers where the blue colour is particularly good with terracotta. Plumes of white flowers in summer. ⬍20cm ◁▷15cm. ☼ Grow in full sun for best colour. 🖉 Prefers well-drained soil. Drought resistant. Plant in spring.

Stachys byzantina

(85) Stachys byzantina
Lamb's ears
This well-known perennial is popular as an easy ground-cover plant, forming a mat of soft, fluffy, silvery leaves which last late into the year. Throws up spikes of small purple-pink flowers in summer which are somewhat hidden by felty leaves. ⬍35cm ◁▷50cm. ☼ Grow in full sun. 🖉 Prefers dry, well-drained, light soils and once established withstands drought well. Plant in spring. Divide large plants in spring.

(83) Eryngium
Sea holly
Bold feature plants with tall, branched stems surrounded by collars of deeply cut, spiny leaves, ending in cone-shaped flower heads. Plants are often silvery with a bluish tinge. Flowers develop in mid- to late summer and last well into the autumn as they dry out on the plant. Excellent for fresh or dried arrangements. Good for combining with plants like rudbeckia, achilleas and grasses. ☼ Plant in an open, sunny position. 🖉 Prefers well-drained, moderately fertile soil. Plant in spring. Develops a deep tap root and dislikes being moved.
alpinum Many branches, topped by greenish flowers surrounded by a rosette of silver-blue feathery leaves. ⬍70cm ◁▷60cm.
bourgatii A lower-growing, spreading sea holly making a clump with violet-blue stems bearing greyish-blue or green flowers surrounded by a rosette of spiky grey-green leaves. ⬍50cm ◁▷40cm.
bourgatii 'Picos Blue' Very sturdy stems are topped by large deep amethyst-blue flowers which intensify in colour as they age. ⬍50cm ◁▷50cm.
planum Many branched stems bear spherical pale blue flowers surrounded by blue-green divided leaves. ⬍90cm ◁▷50cm.

(84) Echinops ritro
Globe thistle
Sturdy thistle with steely blue globe flowers and spiny, grey-green, divided leaves. Makes a good feature plant near the back of a border. Flowers from late summer to early autumn. Attractive to butterflies. Good for cut flowers. ⬍90cm ◁▷60cm. ☼ Grow in full sun or partial shade. 🖉 Prefers light, well-drained soil that is moderately fertile. Plant in autumn or spring. Divide large clumps and replant from autumn to early spring.
'Veitch's Blue' Cultivar with slightly darker vivid blue flowers and more abundant flowering.

Macleaya microcarpa 'Kelway's Coral'

(86) Macleaya microcarpa
Plume poppy
This huge perennial is bound to impress, with its tall stems, unusually shaped and coloured leaves and spectacular plumes of creamy white or pink flowers. The grey-green leaves are rounded and lobed. ⬍2.5m ◁▷1m. ☼ Grow in full sun or partial shade. Plant where there is plenty of space as it will develop into a large clump. 🖉 Not too fussy, but prefers a moist but well-drained soil. Plant in spring. Once established becomes very vigorous and spreads.

---

ideal plants

Blue-grey, grey or silver leaves

Artemisia Wormwood, Mugwort No.31
Convolvulus cneorum Silverbush No.25
Eryngium Sea holly No.83
Festuca glauca Blue fescue No.82
Hosta sieboldiana elegans No.141
Lavandula angustifolia Lavender No.29
Melianthus major Honey bush No.91
Nepeta 'Six Hills Giant' Catmint No.122
Perovskia atriplicifolia 'Blue Spire' Russian sage No.27

Astrantia major

87 Astrantia major
Masterwort

Charming papery flowerheads, like miniature pincushion posies, in greenish-white, cream, pink or red, appear in early summer on slender stems and last for weeks. Easy and reliable, needs no special care. ⬍80cm ◁▷50cm. ☼ Prefers full sun or light shade. 🌱 Does best in fertile, damp, humus-rich soil. Mulch with compost in autumn when the leaves have died down.
'Hadspen Blood' Flowerheads deep red.

Melianthus major

91 Melianthus major
Honey bush

Grown for its handsome, attention-grabbing, divided and serrated blue-green leaves, this tender perennial is hardy in mild areas. Can be overwintered indoors or treated as a half-hardy annual and planted again each year. Spikes of deep red flowers from late spring to mid-summer. Use as bedding or a container plant. ⬍2m ◁▷2m. ☼ Grow in full sun. 🌱 Prefers moist but well-drained soil. Grow from plants or seeds. Dig sand into planting hole or mix into potting compost. Overwinter at a minimum of 5°C.

Galtonia candicans

88 Galtonia candicans
Summer hyacinth

Reminiscent of a white hyacinth, this plant is much larger and more majestic, with bold, strap-shaped leaves and heads of white, scented flowers in late summer, rising to over 1m tall. Slightly tender. ⬍1.2m ◁▷40cm. ☼ Grow in full sun. 🌱 Prefers light, well-drained alkaline soil. Plant bulbs 20cm deep, working grit into the soil to improve drainage. Mulch thickly in autumn to protect from freezing.

Crocus tommasinianus

92 Crocus tommasinianus
Early crocus

Delightful dwarf crocus which brings winter cheer early in February. Useful in beds and borders, rock gardens and containers. Naturalises easily and increases quite rapidly. The flowers are intense lilac and open widely in sun to reveal bright orange-yellow stamens. The leaves also are decorative, with a central silver stripe. Withstands frost and cold winds. ⬍10cm ◁▷8cm. ☼ Thrives in full sun but can take a little shade. Does well under deciduous plants where it will get all the sun it needs early in the year before it becomes shaded. 🌱 Prefers well-drained coarse or gritty soil. Plant bulbs in early autumn.

Lamium maculatum 'White Nancy'

89 Lamium maculatum
Dead nettle

Lamiums make great low-growing ground cover and will quickly carpet the space under shrubs and trees. Pretty silver and green or golden variegated leaves last for most of the year. Pink or white flowers in summer are an added bonus. The white flowered cultivars are the best. ⬍15cm ◁▷1m. ☼ Grow in full or partial shade. 🌱 Prefers moist soil, rich in humus. Dig compost into the planting hole and water in dry weather. Mulching with compost around the plant will encourage faster, spreading growth.
'White Nancy' Silver variegated leaves with a thin green margin and pure white flowers in summer.

Carex morrowii

93 Carex
Sedge

With their coloured or variegated grassy leaves, sedges add texture to a garden and make trouble-free garden plants. ☼ There are cultivars for shade through to full sun. 🌱 Some prefer damp, boggy conditions, others like it hot and dry.
flagellifera Glen Murray sedge. Grow in moist, well-drained soil in full sun. Forms dense tussocks of slender, red-brown leaves. ⬍1m ◁▷90cm.
morrowii Evergreen clumps of broad, glossy, light green leaves with cream margins and stripes. ⬍50cm ◁▷40cm.

Puschkinia scilloides

90 Puschkinia scilloides
Striped squill

Unusual spring-flowering bulb with the palest blue starry flowers, each petal having a thin, darker blue central stripe. Trouble-free and easy to grow. Good for mixed spring planting in borders, rock gardens, containers and for naturalising in wild meadows. ⬍20cm ◁▷5cm. ☼ Grow in full sun. 🌱 Prefers moist but well-drained soil in spring and hot dry conditions in summer to ripen bulbs. Plant bulbs in autumn. Dig in compost or leafmould before planting.

Galanthus caucasicus (elwesii)

94 Galanthus
Snowdrop

One of the first and most welcome flowers to appear when the winter weather is still harsh, these milk-white flowers never lose their charm and signal that spring is not far away. ⬍10cm ◁▷10cm. ☼ Plant in full sun or partial shade. Does well under deciduous shrubs and trees. 🌱 Thrives in humus-rich, damp soil, although fairly tolerant of most soils. Plant bulbs in autumn or pots of plants in spring.
x atkinsii Has heart-shaped green marking on inner petals.
caucasicus (elwesii) Slightly larger-flowered than the common snowdrop and with broader, more vigorous leaves.
nivalis The common snowdrop.

Framework planting
perennials

Anthemis tinctoria

95 Anthemis
Chamomile
Covers any sunny border, wall or bed with a mass of aromatic feathery leaves, topped with yellow or white daisy flowers all summer long. The flowers last well in water. ☼ Grow in full sun. Dislikes damp and shade.
🌱 Thrives in well-drained, fertile soil. Cultivate from plants in spring. Improve drainage with plenty of grit, and add some slow-release fertiliser.
carpatica 'Karpatenschnee'
A dwarf-growing chamomile forming compact tufts of bright green leaves topped with pure white daisy flowers with yellow centres. Good rock garden plant. ↕15cm ◁▷30cm.
punctata subsp. cupaniana
A larger chamomile with silver-grey feathery leaves forming a spreading mound ↕15cm, with white daisy flowers on stalks to ↕30cm. Suitable for wall and borders.
tinctoria 'E.C. Buxton' Produces masses of lemon-yellow daisies with darker yellow centres for many weeks through the summer. ↕70cm.

Cortaderia selloana 'Pumila'

96 Cortaderia selloana 'Pumila'
Dwarf pampas grass
A smaller version of the familiar pampas grass producing masses of creamy, feathery plumed flowers towards the end of the summer. The flowers last well, adding interest to the autumn and winter garden. A mature clump can produce up to 100 flower stalks. Use gloves when handling – sharp-edged leaves can cut.
↕1.4m ◁▷1m. ☼ Drought-resistant and good for coastal locations. Grow in full sun or very light shade.
🌱 Thrives in rich, well-drained to dry soil. Plant in spring. Dig coarse grit into the planting hole.

Stipa gigantea

99 Stipa gigantea
Giant oats, Golden oats
This lovely ornamental grass is grown for its tall stems of feathery flowers which turn golden in autumn and splay out sideways, creating a spectacular, shimmering display. The long-lasting flowerheads can be left on the plant to add interest to the winter garden. The leaves are gracefully arched. Forms a clump which expands slowly. Makes an excellent specimen plant. ↕2.5m ◁▷1.2m. ☼ Grow in full sun. 🌱 Prefers moist, well-drained soil. Drought resistant once established.

Lysimachia ephemerum

97 Lysimachia ephemerum
Silver loosestrife
Elegant, narrow spikes of starry, pearly white flowers are perfectly set off against waxy grey foliage in August and September. Can be used as a cut flower for indoor arrangements. Makes a slowly expanding, non-invasive clump, year by year. ↕1m ◁▷80cm.
☼ Prefers partial shade but will tolerate sun if roots are kept damp. 🌱 Thrives in moist, fertile soil. Plant in spring. Dig compost into the planting hole and mulch with compost in autumn.

Erythronium 'Pagoda'

100 Erythronium 'Pagoda'
Dog's-tooth violet
Unusual and delightful spring-flowering bulb, with green leaves faintly mottled with bronze and yellow 'fairy cap' flowers hanging from gracefully arched stems. Erythroniums also come with pink or cream flowers, but this cultivar is particularly vigorous and quickly naturalises by self-seeding. ↕30cm ◁▷15cm.
☼ Grow in partial or full shade. Deciduous woodland is its natural habitat. 🌱 Thrives in most soils as long as they are moist and rich in humus. Plant bulbs in autumn. Dislikes being moved, but divide clumps after flowering if too large. Mulch with compost or leafmould in autumn.

Primula vulgaris hybrid

98 Primula vulgaris
Primrose
Once you have primroses in your garden they'll look after themselves and give a generous display of flowers each spring. Great for damp, shady corners. The wild, creamy yellow primrose is lovely, but many coloured varieties, including doubles, have been bred since Victorian times and before, and some of these are highly prized, although less vigorous than the wild plant.
↕20cm ◁▷35cm. ☼ Grow in full sun to full shade. 🌱 Thrives in damp soil rich in humus. Plant out in autumn. Dig compost into planting hole and mulch in autumn with compost.

Narcissus 'Hawera'

101 Narcissus
Daffodil
These bulbs although common are none the less welcome, being among the first to bring colour to the spring garden, with varieties to suit every taste, from big and brash to small and dainty. Prefers moist but well-drained soil, although not too fussy about soil type. ☼ Grow in full sun or partial shade. 🌱 Plant bulbs in autumn at three times the depth of the bulb. After flowering do not remove leaves until they wilt and die back.
'Dutch Master' Giant trumpets of deep yellow. ↕45cm ◁▷15cm.
'Flowerdrift' Double white petals, orange-yellow cup. ↕45cm ◁▷15cm.
'Hawera' Dwarf daffodil in shades of acid yellow. ↕18cm ◁▷8cm.
'Winston Churchill' Double with creamy white petals. Scented. ↕30cm ◁▷15cm.

Rudbeckia 'Marmalade'

102 Rudbeckia
Coneflower

Grown for its bright yellow and orange daisy flowers with large, brown, domed centres, helping to fill and brighten the autumn border. Many cultivars are available. Size varies according to cultivar. ⊕30–150cm ◁▷ 20–100cm. ☼ Grow in full sun or partial shade. ✎ Prefers moist, heavy soil which does not dry out. Grow from seeds indoors in early spring, or divide established plants in autumn or spring.

Kirengeshoma palmata

106 Kirengeshoma palmata

Unusual but easy perennial for a shady spot. Forms a loose clump with tall thin stems supporting widely spaced, maple-shaped leaves. Has yellow bell flowers in autumn at the tips of the stems. ⊕90cm ◁▷ 75cm. ☼ Grow in partial to full shade. ✎ Thrives in moist, well-drained acid soil. Mulch with compost or leafmould in autumn.

Crocosmia 'Citronella'

103 Crocosmia
Montbretia

These easy perennials produce masses of flame-coloured flowers through the summer, growing from clumps of sword-shaped leaves. The common orange montbretia can be invasive, but there are many other varieties, in yellows, oranges and reds, which are less so. Blends well with grasses and summer annuals, and good in wild plantings. ☼ Thrives in full sun though it can stand light shade. ✎ Unfussy about soil so long as it's not waterlogged. Plant bulbs in early spring, or container-grown plants during the growing season. Mulch with compost in autumn. Divide clumps when they become too large.
'Citronella' ('Golden Fleece') Large lemon-yellow flowers in late summer. Mid-green leaves. ⊕70cm.
'Fire King' Bi-coloured orange and yellow flowers, late summer. ⊕60cm.
'Lucifer' Intense red flowers in bold spikes, mid-summer. Bright green leaves. Very hardy. ⊕1m.
'Solfatare' Apricot yellow flowers, greyish bronze-tinted leaves. ⊕60cm.

Papaver orientale

104 Papaver orientale
Oriental poppy

With their huge, vibrant blooms in red, pink or white, these poppies are spectacular and a must for any cottage-style planting. Petals often have black splotches at the base, adding to the dramatic effect. Double varieties are available. ⊕1m ◁▷1m. ☼ Grow in full sun. ✎ Prefers moist but well-drained soil. Grow from plants in spring.
'Patty's Plum' Soft plum-purple flowers like crumpled silk. ⊕90cm ◁▷ 90cm.

Eremurus stenophyllus

107 Eremurus stenophyllus
Foxtail lily

Spectacular and unusual, this plant throws up sturdy spikes packed with hundreds of dark yellow, star-shaped flowers, fading to orangey-brown in early summer. Narrow grey-green leaves form clumps early in spring but die down as the plant starts to flower. ⊕1m ◁▷ 60cm. ☼ Plant in full sun in a warm, sheltered corner. ✎ Good drainage is essential. Thrives in dry, moderately fertile to poor soil. Dig in plenty of coarse grit when planting and lay the tubers on a layer of pure sand or grit.
'Bungei' Brighter, lemony-yellow flowers and larger growing. ⊕1.5m ◁▷ 70cm.

Hemerocallis 'Summer Wine'

105 Hemerocallis
Daylily

Trouble-free plants giving a long-lasting display of lush lily flowers year after year with virtually no maintenance. Although each bloom lasts for only one day, an established plant will produce hundreds of flowers in succession. While the common orange daylily is attractive, there are many more interesting varieties with flower colours in white, yellow, orange and pink, often veined or shaded with darker colours. Deciduous, strap-shaped leaves form a slowly expanding clump over the years. ☼ Thrives in full sun or partial shade. ✎ Will grow in almost any soil but prefers it moist and well drained. Plant container-grown stock in autumn or spring. Dig plenty of compost into the planting hole. Tidy plants in autumn by removing dead flower stalks and remove dead foliage in early spring.
'Black Magic' Deep dusky pink flowers with greenish-yellow centres. ⊕90cm.
'Children's Festival' Flower petals are soft rose-pink at their tips and apricot at their bases, shading through every colour in between. ⊕60cm.
'Pandora's Box' Pale cream flowers with a purple eye. ⊕60cm.
'Peach' Pale peach-coloured flowers in mid-summer. ⊕75cm.
'Pink Damask' Salmon pink petals with a lighter rib running down the centre. ⊕75cm.
'Summer Wine' Dull magenta-pink flowers with a golden throat. ⊕60cm.
lilioasphodelus Bright lemony flowers for weeks through the summer. ⊕60cm.

Framework planting
perennials

Potentilla 'Gibson's Scarlet'

108 Potentilla 'Gibson's Scarlet'
Cinquefoil

Glorious bright red flowers all summer long hover over a low, spreading clump of strawberry leaves. A 'must-have' for informal planting in borders, along dry-stone walls and in rock gardens. Easy to grow. ⊕45cm ◁▷ 70cm. ☼Prefers full sun. ✐Thrives in well-drained soil. Good drainage is essential. Grow from plants in spring. Dig in plenty of grit when planting.

Osteospermum 'Buttermilk'

109 Osteospermum
African daisy

Masses of daisy flowers throughout the summer create a mat which will cover banks and dry-stone walls. Many cultivars are available, with yellow, pink or purple flowers. Slightly tender. ⊕50cm ◁▷ 70cm. ☼Grow in full sun. ✐Thrives in light, well-drained soil.

'Buttermilk' Creamy-yellow flowers, almost white in the centre, with a brown eye.

jucundum Flower colour variable, but can be soft pink with a violet tinge, lighter in the centre with a yellowish-brown eye.

Scabiosa columbaria

111 Scabiosa
Pincushion flower

Few border plants produce such a plentiful display of flowers over such a long period. Makes a tidy clump of foliage from which the pincushion flowerheads grow on taller stems. Attracts butterflies. ☼Grow in full sun. ✐Prefers moist but well-drained, sandy or light soil, especially chalk. Named varieties are available as plants. For best display of flowers deadhead as often as possible.

'Pink Mist' Masses of pink flowers from June to October. ⊕30cm ◁▷ 30cm.

Kniphofia hybrid

112 Kniphofia
Red-hot poker

Bold feature plants with sword-shaped leaves and tall, sturdy flower spikes in vibrant reds, oranges and yellows, also white and greenish-cream. Flowers are attractive to bees. Forms a slowly expanding clump year by year. ☼Grow in full sun. ✐Prefers moist but well-drained sandy soil with plenty of humus. Remove dead stems after flowering.

thomsonii var. snowdenii Individual flowers begin green at their bases, changing through yellow to glowing orange at their tips. Long flowering period from mid-summer to late autumn. ⊕90cm ◁▷ 50cm.

Digitalis x mertonensis

110 Digitalis
Perennial foxglove

Tall spires of foxglove flowers are a pleasure in any garden and an essential ingredient for cottage gardens. Easy to grow and good for the back of a border or any shady corner. Flowers in white, cream, yellow, salmon, pink and shades of purple are produced from late spring to summer and are attractive to bees. All parts are poisonous. ☼Prefers a damp, slightly shady situation although will self-seed and spread to most parts of the garden. ✐Thrives in moist but well-drained soil rich in humus. Dig plenty of compost into the soil when planting.

lutea Perennial foxglove with dark green glossy leaves and spikes of pale yellow flowers in early summer. Will grow in sun or partial shade but prefers alkaline soil. ⊕60cm.

x mertonensis Similar to the common foxglove but perennial, and with larger, dusky-pink flowers. ⊕75cm.

Anemone x hybrida 'Honorine Jobert'

113 Anemone hupehensis
Japanese anemone

As the flowers of many other plants are coming to an end, Japanese anemones are just getting into their stride, filling the autumn border with masses of blooms. These long-lived perennials form a clump of leaves in spring out of which grow tall, branched stalks of flowers later in the year. They need almost no attention, have few pests or diseases, and increase in size slowly from year to year. The cultivars listed have all the virtues of the common pink form, but with more interesting flowers. ⊕90cm ◁▷ 50cm. ☼Grow in full sun or partial shade. ✐Adapts well to most soils. Mulch with compost every autumn. Grow from plants in spring. Dig in plenty of compost when planting.

'Hadspen Abundance' Classy deep pink petals fading towards the edges, yellow stamens.

x hybrida 'Honorine Jobert' Flowers pure white with a greenish centre and yellow stamens. Flower stalks can grow to ⊕1.5m.

var. japonica Violet-pink with a ring of bright yellow stamens.

Rodgersia podophylla

114 Rodgersia

Bold feature plant with huge leaves and sturdy spikes of cream or pink flowers, reminiscent of horse chestnut. ☀ Best in partial shade. ✐ Prefers moist, rich soil with plenty of humus. Dig compost into the planting hole. Mulch in autumn.
pinnata 'Superba' Strong pink flowers perfectly set off by the bronze-green foliage. ⌀1.2m ◁▷90cm.
podophylla Vigorous spikes of creamy flowers in summer. Leaves green, turning bronze-red in autumn. ⌀1.5m ◁▷1.5m.

ideal plants

Especially long-flowering plants

Abutilon Indian mallow No.39

Achillea Yarrow No.138

Anemone hupehensis Japanese anemone No.113

Argyranthemum No.192

Bougainvillea No.197

Erysimum Perennial wallflower No.139

Fuchsia Fuchsia No.46

Hemerocallis Daylily No.105

Lavatera Tree mallow No.32

Penstemon No.135

Scabiosa Pincushion flower No.111

Solanum crispum Chilean potato vine No.67

Verbena bonariensis No.116

Echinacea purpurea

115 Echinacea purpurea
Purple coneflower
A fine border plant which has large purple or white flowers with dark, domed centres from mid- to late summer. Looks good in a large group or in wild plantings. Excellent for cut flowers. ⌀1.2m ◁▷80cm. ☀ Grow in full sun. ✐ Prefers well-drained soil. Plant seeds in early spring for flowering next year, or plants in spring for flowering the same year.

Fritillaria meleagris

118 Fritillaria meleagris
Snakeshead fritillary
Always fascinating, these spring bulbs have flowers which are an odd, angular shape, as if folded out of paper, and chequered in dull purple and white, or just pure white. The flowers emerge on thin stalks about 30cm tall from April to May. ⌀30cm ◁▷10cm. ☀ Prefers open sun or very light shade. Ideal for wild plantings in grass, where it will naturalise and increase. ✐ Does well in damp, acid to neutral soil. Plant bulbs in autumn. Dig a liberal amount of compost into the soil when planting. Avoid moving once established.

Verbena bonariensis

116 Verbena bonariensis

No matter how full your garden is, there's always room for a few plants of this charming perennial, which throws up heads of tiny purple flowers on tall, wiry stems. The flowers are highly attractive to butterflies and bees and it will self-seed. ⌀2m ◁▷50cm. ☀ Grow in full sun. ✐ Prefers moist, well-drained soil. Grow from plants or seed in spring. When finished flowering cut stems off to almost ground level. New stems will grow the following year.

Foeniculum vulgare

119 Foeniculum vulgare
Fennel
Easy to grow feature plant forming a tall clump of fine, feathery foliage, increasing in vigour and size from year to year. ⌀1.8m ◁▷60cm. ☀ Grow in full sun. ✐ Will grow in most soil types if moist and well drained. Plant in spring. Self-seeds frequently. Transplant seedlings while they are less than 15cm tall to avoid damaging the tap root.
'Purpureum' This bronzy-purple cultivar is much more interesting than the plain green form and makes a perfect backdrop for orange and violet-blue flowers.

Pulmonaria saccharata

117 Pulmonaria
Lungwort
One of the first perennials to bloom, giving a long succession of pink, blue or white flowers from late winter to early summer. Handsome, often evergreen leaves spotted with silver give colour and interest all year round. Good for planting with primroses and spring bulbs. Attractive to bees. ⌀25cm ◁▷50cm. ☀ Prefers partial or full shade. ✐ Thrives in moist, humus-rich, heavy soil. Mulch with leafmould or compost in autumn.
'Majeste' Leaves almost entirely silvery apart from edge and veins. Flowers pink becoming blue.
'Raspberry Splash' Dark green leaves, speckled silver. Intense raspberry-coloured flowers.
'Sissinghurst White' White flowers, spotted leaves.
rubra Plain pale green leaves with narrow silver edge. Coral-red flowers.
rubra 'Bowles Red' Sprays of coral-pink flowers.

Eupatorium purpureum

120 Eupatorium purpureum
Joe-pye weed
Huge pink, purple-pink or cream flowerheads on towering stems make this a spectacular feature plant and a magnet for bees and butterflies. Flowers from mid-summer to autumn. ⌀2.5m ◁▷1m. ☀ Grow in full sun. ✐ Will grow in most soil types as long as not waterlogged. Plant in spring. Dig compost into the planting hole.

Framework planting
perennials

Delphinium 'Pacific Giants Mixed'

Nepeta 'Six Hills Giant'

Iris 'Black Swan'

Ajuga reptans 'Braunherz'

121 Delphinium

This classic cottage garden perennial makes a long-lasting display of tall flower spikes through the summer in pinks, mauves, blues, white and even yellow. All parts of the plant are poisonous and can irritate the skin. Can be fatally toxic if eaten. ‡1.8m ◁▷1m. ☼ Grow in full sun. ⚲ Prefers rich, fertile soil. Plant container-grown stock in spring. Can also be grown from seed but will take a year or two to establish and flower. Often needs staking and slugs can be a problem.
'Pacific Giants Mixed' Densely packed spikes of flowers to ‡1.8m in shades of blue, violet, purple and white, often with contrasting centres.

122 Nepeta
Catmint

With spikes of pale violet-blue flowers from early to late summer, perfectly set off by grey-green leaves, this bushy perennial makes a wonderful edging for a border or path. Cats love to roll around on it. Attracts bees. ☼ Grow in full sun or partial shade. ⚲ Prefers well-drained, dry, sandy or light soil. Use short canes to reduce cat damage and support the plant if necessary. Trim dead flower spikes. Cut hard back in autumn to encourage a neat bushy plant.
'Six Hills Giant' Large and vigorous form. ‡90cm ◁▷90cm.
x faassenii Common garden catmint. Light blue flowers, grey-green leaves. ‡50cm ◁▷50cm.

123 Iris

A drift of irises in full bloom can be a breathtaking sight, and there are very many cultivars to suit every situation. ☼ Grow in full sun. ⚲ Prefers moist, well-drained, fertile soil.
'Black Swan' Dusky maroon and brown flowers. ‡1m.
'Jane Phillips' Delicate blue flowers early to mid-summer. ‡90cm ◁▷60cm.
'Kent Pride' Petals red-brown, white and yellow. ‡1m.
'White City' Pale blue flowers fading to white. ‡1m.
pallida 'Variegata' Grey-green leaves variegated cream. ‡30cm.
sibirica 'Flight of Butterflies' Flowers in late spring, mid-violet-blue upper petals, gold fading into white lower ones, veined deep blue. ‡90cm ◁▷50cm.

124 Ajuga reptans
Bugle

A tough and colourful ground-cover plant for damp places. Spreads quickly, making a low-growing mat of evergreen or semi-evergreen leaves with spikes of blue flowers in spring. Leaf colours depend on variety. ‡15cm ◁▷30cm. ☼ Prefers partial or full shade. ⚲ Thrives in damp soil. Dig in compost when planting.
'Arctic Fox' Attractively cream and grey-green variegated.
'Atropurpurea' Bronze-purple leaves.
'Braunherz' Deep purple-brown leaves.
'Burgundy Glow' Leaves silver-green, pink and magenta, edged with cream.
'Variegata' Leaves silver-green and cream.

ideal plants

Low-growing ground cover

Ajuga reptans Bugle No.124
Alchemilla mollis Lady's mantle No.80
Alyssum montanum Mountain madwort No.154
Anthemis carpatica 'Karpatenschnee' Chamomile No.95
Brunnera macrophylla Siberian bugloss No.79
Ceanothus thyrsiflorus var. *repens* 'Blue Mound' California lilac No.51
Erica Heather No.54
Geranium 'Johnson's Blue' Hardy geranium No.130
Hebe pinguifolia 'Pagei' No.21
Heuchera micrantha Coral flower No.136
Juniperus Juniper No.1
Lamium maculatum 'White Nancy' Dead nettle No.89
Pulmonaria Lungwort No.117

Muscari armeniacum

Ophiopogon planiscapus 'Nigrescens'

Agapanthus Headbourne hybrids

125 Muscari armeniacum
Grape hyacinth

Reliable and easy to grow spring flowering bulb which mixes well with primulas and other spring flowers. Spreads freely. ‡20cm ◁▷10cm. ☼ Grow in full sun. ⚲ Thrives in any well-drained soil. After planting requires no further attention. Allow the leaves to die down naturally after flowering.

126 Ophiopogon planiscapus 'Nigrescens'
Lilyturf

One of the few plants with truly black leaves. Small and easily overgrown by larger plants, it is best in a rock garden or in pots. The young grass-like leaves are purplish green, darkening to black as they grow older. Flowers are lilac or white. ‡20cm ◁▷30cm. ☼ Develops best colour when grown in full sun. ⚲ Prefers moist, well-drained, neutral to acid soil. Left alone it will form spreading clumps which can be split. Mulch in autumn with sieved compost.

127 Agapanthus
African lily

Exotic-looking summer feature plant with imposing heads of blue or sometimes white flowers on tall stalks rising above glossy, strap-shaped leaves. ‡1.2m ◁▷50cm. ☼ Thrives in containers or in a warm border at the base of a south-facing wall in full sun. ⚲ Plant in well-drained soil enriched with plenty of compost. Plant bulbs in spring avoiding heavy frosts or freezing conditions. Warmth is essential for flowering. Most hybrids are hardy but a thick mulch of compost applied in the autumn will protect against winter frosts. Overwinter indoors if there are long periods of below zero temperatures.

Tulipa 'White Triumphator'

Tulipa
Tulip

Valued for their huge range of brightly coloured flowers on tall stems. Mix happily with lower-growing plants such as wallflowers and forget-me-nots. ☀ Grow in full sun. 🌱 Prefers moist, well-drained soil. Dislikes waterlogged or poorly drained soil. Plant bulbs in November at two to three times their own depth. Allow leaves to die down naturally in the summer.

'Angelique' Superb late double with blush-pink, white and green peony-like flowers. Weatherproof. Individual flowers last up to three weeks. Great for cut flowers. ⬍35cm.

'Apricot Beauty' Single early tulip. Flowers are soft translucent apricot flushed with rose in April. ⬍45cm.

'Swan Wings' White flowers with fringed petals. ⬍60cm.

'Negrita' Deep purple tulip with darker veins. Stunning planted in large groups but also good for plantings of mixed colours. Flowers mid-spring. ⬍45cm.

tarda Small tulip with up to six flowers on a single stem. Petals white with a daffodil-yellow base. Flowers for a long time. Good for rock gardens, raised beds, containers and pots. ⬍15cm.

Dicentra 'Stuart Boothman'

Dicentra

Easy and reliable perennial with flowers lasting for many weeks from early until late spring. Finely divided, ferny leaves. Ideal for damp, shady corners. All parts are mildly toxic. ☀ Grow in partial shade. 🌱 Unfussy about soil type but does best in rich, moist soil. Dig compost into the planting hole and mulch each year with compost,

'Adrian Bloom' Bright rose pink flowers in spring, mid-green leaves. Will tolerate drier conditions than some. ⬍40cm.

'Stuart Boothman' Pale pink flowers and lovely greyish-green leaves. ⬍40cm.

formosa 'Luxuriant' Red flowers, apple-green leaves. ⬍40cm.

spectabilis Bleeding hearts. Graceful sprays of rose and white locket flowers. ⬍60cm.

spectabilis alba Pure white-flowered form of above. ⬍60cm.

Corydalis flexuosa

Corydalis
Fumitory

Woodland plant which thrives in damp shade. Clumps of deciduous ferny leaves are topped by a profusion of delicate tubular flowers from late spring to early summer. ⬍30cm ◁▷30cm. ☀ Grow in partial to full shade. 🌱 Prefers moist, humus-rich, but well-drained soil. Plant in spring. Dig plenty of compost into the planting hole.

flexuosa Brilliant sky-blue flowers.

Geranium cinereum 'Ballerina'

Geranium
Hardy geranium

The fleshy stemmed, bright red- and orange-flowered tender pot plants often known as geraniums are more correctly called pelargoniums. The true geranium is a long-lived hardy perennial available in hundreds of cultivars ranging from tiny plants which thrive in dry, rocky crevices to lush-growing metre-high border plants, all with colourful flowers in a range from white through pinks, red, violet to blue. Tough, adaptable and easy to care for, there is a geranium for almost every garden situation. ☀ The smaller cultivars are generally adapted to dry, sunny situations while the larger species prefer more moist surroundings which can be helped by partial shade. 🌱 Soil preference ranges from dry and gritty to moist but well-drained, fertile and humus rich. Once established they will grow for years with almost no attention. Trim with garden shears to keep tidy as needed. This often stimulates fresh growth and continued flowering. Large clumps can be dug up and divided.

'Johnson's Blue' Outstanding cultivar. Forms a mound covered in vivid blue, cup-shaped flowers for several weeks around mid-summer. ⬍40cm ◁▷40cm.

cinereum 'Ballerina' Exquisite cultivar with pale pink flowers darkly veined with maroon complemented by slightly greyish-green leaves. Flowers all summer and autumn. useful for front of borders, rock garden or patio containers. ⬍15cm ◁▷15cm.

clarkei 'Kashmir White' Large white flowers veined with pink through most of the summer. Sun or partial shade. ⬍50cm ◁▷50cm.

macrorrhizum 'Ingwersen's Variety' Aromatic light green leaves with pale pink flowers. ⬍50cm ◁▷70cm.

phaeum Upright growing with deep purple, almost black flowers. Leaves sometimes blotched. Expands into large-sized clumps and self-seeds. Useful for dry shade. ⬍80cm ◁▷50cm.

phaeum 'Samobor' Light green leaves marked with variable maroon blotches, topped by modest burgundy-coloured flowers on upright stems making a pleasing combination. ⬍80cm ◁▷50cm.

wallichianum 'Buxton's Variety' Superior border plant. Stunning china-blue flowers with luminous white centres and dark stamens over luxuriant, lightly mottled foliage. ⬍30cm ◁▷1m.

Framework planting
perennials

Penstemon 'Garnet'

Eurhorbia characias subsp. *wulfenii*

Helleborus niger

Canna 'Picasso'

132 Canna
Indian shot plant

Popular in Victorian times for their large, coloured leaves, these exotic feature plants are in fashion again, with many varieties available in a range of sizes and colours. Thick stems grow from underground corms bearing leaves which vary from bright green to deepest bronze, often with cream or pink stripes. Flowers in shades of red, through orange to apricot and yellow. ☼ Cannas need a warm, sunny situation to flower well. A sheltered border against a wall, or a container in a warm corner or conservatory are ideal. ⚒ Grow in fertile, humus-rich soil. Keep moist at all times. Plant corms in spring. In milder areas overwinter in the ground outside, well mulched to protect from frost. Otherwise lift before hard frosts and store in a cool but frost-free place.

'Durban' (C. tropicana) Orange flowers, leaves striped red, yellow and green. ≜2m.
'Picasso' Large yellow flowers spotted red. ≜1m.
'Striata' Green foliage veined cream or yellow, yellow flowers. ≜2m.
'Wyoming' Imposing, with huge bronze leaves and vivid orange blooms. ≜2.5m.
iridiflora 'Ehemanii' Giant banana-like mid-green leaves and drooping cerise pink flowers. One of the hardiest. Overwinter in most areas with just a thick mulch. ≜1.5m.

133 Euphorbia
Spurge

There are many widely different forms of euphorbia, some of which make outstanding garden plants. Most are poisonous if eaten and the sap is a skin and eye irritant, so best handled carefully wearing gloves. Robust and easy to grow, these plants have few pests and diseases. Deer- and rabbit-proof. ☼ Most euphorbias prefer full sun. ⚒ Grow in well-drained, moist to dry soil.

'Redwing' Small and compact. Showy yellowish-green flowerheads with reddish colour in spring. Good for growing in containers. ≜50cm.
characias subsp. wulfenii Bold feature plant with impressive heads of yellowish-green flowers. ≜1m ◁▷1m.
griffithii 'Fireglow' Brilliant reddish-orange flowerheads in late summer are perfectly complemented by dark bluish-green leaves. ≜80cm ◁▷80cm.
myrsinites Bluish-green fleshy leaves on sprawling stems which stand up at the ends, producing yellow flowers in spring. ≜10cm ◁▷30cm.
polychroma From mid- to late spring the sulphur-yellow flowers and narrow, curvy-edged leaves with a bluish tint make a tidy, low-growing mound. ≜40cm ◁▷50cm.

134 Helleborus
Christmas or Lenten rose

Hellebores are invaluable for their long-lasting winter flowers and evergreen foliage. All parts of the plant are poisonous. ≜40cm ◁▷40cm. ☼ Prefers partial shade. Protect from cold winter winds. ⚒ Grow in deep, fertile, well-drained soil rich in humus. Dig compost into the planting hole. Remove dead leaves in autumn and mulch with compost.
niger Christmas rose. White flowers from early winter through to early spring.
orientalis Lenten rose. Flowers from mid-winter to mid-spring, green or cream, splashed or shaded with maroon or pink.

Heuchera micrantha var. *diversifolia* 'Palace Purple'

136 Heuchera micrantha
Coral flower

Heucheras are wonderful ground-covering foliage plants which are happy in shade. There are many cultivars with varying leaf colours and sizes. ☼ Prefers light shade, but will tolerate full sun if soil is damp at all times. ⚒ Grow in moist, well-drained soil.
'Green Spice' Large, evergreen leaves, olive-green shaded with silver and bronze, strong burgundy veins. ≜35cm ◁▷25cm.
'Helen Dillon' Tall plumes of coral-pink flowers in summer over silver-green leaves veined in deeper green. ≜45cm ◁▷25cm.
var. diversifolia 'Palace Purple' Deep purple or bronze leaves all year round. ≜45cm ◁▷25cm.

135 Penstemon

Penstemons give a constant show of flowers from late spring until the first frosts. In milder areas grow as perennials. In colder areas grow from seed each year. ☼ Thrives in full sun. ⚒ Prefers moist, well-drained, light soil. Cut back in spring.
'Evelyn' Small rose-pink flowers, lighter on the inside, veined in darker pink. Hardy. ≜60cm ◁▷30cm.
'Garnet' Deep cerise flowers. Bushy plant. Hardy to half-hardy. ≜70cm ◁▷70cm.
'Volcano Kilimanjaro' Flowers rich cream on the outside, white inside. Hardy. ≜70cm ◁▷70cm.

Allium hollandicum 'Purple Sensation'

137 Allium
Ornamental onion

Ornamental cousins of the common onion, with impressive ball-shaped or flat flowerheads on tall stalks. Individual flowers are star- or bell-shaped. Colours vary according to cultivar, with white, pink, mauve, blue or yellow. Dead flowerheads are often ornamental and can be left on the plant or cut for dried arrangements. ☼ Grow in full sun. ⚒ Thrives in fertile, well-drained soil. Plant bulbs from early autumn.
cristophii (A. albopilosum) Each bulb makes a spherical head of dusky pink flowers up to ◁▷20cm on ≜60cm stalks in early summer.
hollandicum 'Purple Sensation' Dense heads of star-shaped purplish-pink flowers up to ◁▷10cm, on ≜1m stalks in summer.

Achillea millefolium 'Cerise Queen'

138 Achillea
Yarrow

Grown for its large, flat flowerheads in bright yellow, cerise, cream or pink, on tall stems, giving colour all summer long. Attracts butterflies, bees and other insects. ☀ Thrives in a warm, sunny border but can stand a little shade. ⚘ Not fussy about soil type but needs good drainage. Grow from plants in spring. Loosen clayey soils by digging in some sand or grit when planting. Mulch with compost in autumn.

'Salmon Beauty' Lots of pale salmon-pink flowerheads in summer, fading to creamy white. Feathery grey-green leaves. ⇕90cm ⇔60cm.

filipendulina 'Cloth of Gold' Rich, deep golden flowerheads above bright green ferny leaves. ⇕1.5m ⇔1m.

millefolium 'Cerise Queen' Makes a vigorous spreading mat of deep grey-green, feathery leaves topped with masses of intense pink flowerheads. ⇕90cm ⇔60cm.

Erysimum 'Apricot Delight'

139 Erysimum
Perennial wallflower

Forms a slowly expanding evergreen clump, flowering profusely for a long period over the summer. Flowers are scented on warm days, though not as strongly as its biennial cousin, the familiar wallflower. ☀ Prefers full sun or partial shade. Grows best in poor, well-drained neutral or alkaline soil. ⚘ Grow from plants in spring. Plants become leggy and straggling and benefit from hard pruning. Short-lived and are best replaced regularly.

'Apricot Delight' Orange flowers and bright green leaves. ⇕50cm ⇔50cm.

'Vulcan' Deep blood-red flowers. ⇕50cm ⇔50cm.

Camassia leichtlinii

142 Camassia leichtlinii
Quamash

Wands of star-shaped flowers in white, purple or blue from late spring to early summer are an asset to any border or wildflower meadow and take up little space. Leaves are strap-shaped. ☀ Plant in full sun or light shade. ⚘ Prefers a moist, humus-rich soil. Plant bulbs in autumn.

caerulea 'Electric Blue' Star-shaped flowers on spikes ⇕80cm.

Lupinus 'Gallery Red'

140 Lupinus
Lupin

Perfect for cottage gardens, these traditional border plants produce bold spikes of colourful flowers over several weeks in summer. Flowers can be white, cream, yellow, pink, red, mauve and blue, often bi-coloured. Seeds poisonous. ⇕90cm ⇔70cm. ☀ Prefers full sun or partial shade. ⚘ Grow in well-drained fertile soil. Remove flowerheads as soon as flowers are over for repeat flowering.

'Chandelier' Bright yellow flowers. ⇕90cm.

'Gallery Red' Glowing orangey-red flowers in early summer. ⇕90cm.

arboreus Tree lupin. Evergreen leaves, yellow or blue flowers, woody stems making a bush. ⇕2m ⇔2m.

Miscanthus sinensis

143 Miscanthus sinensis

A spectacular grass, forming bold clumps of coloured foliage. Grow as a specimen plant or grouped in a border. ☀ Prefers full sun or partial shade. ⚘ Thrives in moist, well-drained soil.

'Malepartus' Robust clumps of leaves, mid-green, turning deep bronze in late summer. Large feathery blooms, opening purplish-pink and turning silver. ⇕2m ⇔2m.

'Zebrinus' Zebra grass. Attention-grabbing grass, unusually striped across the leaves. ⇕1.2m ⇔90cm.

Hosta fortunei

141 Hosta

Hostas are grown for their large, luxuriant leaves which are variously coloured and variegated. They thrive in moist shade and are great for brightening dull corners, or for use individually as feature or container specimens. Spikes of lilac or white flowers grow above the leaves in summer. ☀ Grow in shade or partial shade. ⚘ Prefers moist soil, rich in humus. Plant in autumn or spring. Dig plenty of compost into the planting hole. Slugs are the main pest and need to be kept under control from the start.

'Gold Standard' Golden yellow-green leaves with darker green margins. Lavender flowers. ⇕60cm ⇔75cm.

'Great Expectations' Leaves with gold centres fading to creamy white with age and broad blue-green margins. Almost white flowers in summer. ⇕60cm ⇔1.2m.

'Sum and Substance' Large hosta with golden-green leaves fading to golden-yellow. Lavender flowers on tall stalks during August. ⇕90cm ⇔1m.

fortunei 'Albopicta' Large heart-shaped leaves splashed with shades of cream, yellow and green. Lilac flowers in mid-summer. ⇕50cm ⇔1m.

fortunei 'Francee' Predominantly green, heart-shaped leaves with narrow white margins. Lavender flowers in summer. ⇕55cm ⇔1m.

sieboldiana elegans Broad heart-shaped glaucous grey-blue leaves with a deeply puckered texture. ⇕1m ⇔1.2m.

sieboldiana 'Frances Williams' Large leaves with wide yellow margins surrounding blue-green centres. Grow in shade for best colour. White flowers from July to August. ⇕60cm ⇔1.5m.

Water gardening
pond and bog plants

Zantedeschia aethiopica

(144) **Zantedeschia aethiopica**
Arum lily

Few flowers are as impressive as those of the white arum, and with bold, glossy green leaves to match, this is an imposing architectural plant for the edge of a pond or stream. Good also for cut flowers. All parts are poisonous and irritant to eyes and skin. ⇕1m ⬌60cm. ☼Prefers full sun. ⚘ Grow in moist or boggy soil. Plant in spring. The plant is tender and will die down completely in the autumn. Protect from frost with a thick mulch in autumn.

Carex elata 'Aurea'

Gunnera manicata

(145) **Gunnera manicata**

One of the most impressive architectural perennials, with leaves up to 2m across, often described as 'giant rhubarb'. In spring leaves and flower stems emerge from massive hairy buds and rapidly expand to gigantic proportions. Leaf undersides and stems are covered in dense prickles. Only suitable for a large garden. ⇕2.5m ⬌3m. ☼ Thrives in full sun or partial shade. ⚘Grow in boggy soil at the edge of a pond or stream in waterlogged soil. As winter begins pile the dead leaves over next year's buds to protect them from hard frosts.

Ligularia przewalskii

(147) **Carex elata**
Golden sedge

The golden leaves of this damp-loving grass are great for adding a bright highlight to a pond edge or bog garden, contrasting well with darker-leaved plants. The deciduous leaves arch gracefully, forming a wide tuft. ☼For best leaf colour grow in full sun. ⚘Roots need to be damp at all times or even submerged. Humus-rich, boggy soil. Remove previous year's foliage in early spring before growth starts. 'Aurea' Bowles' golden sedge. Bright yellow leaves with narrow green edge. ⇕75cm.

(148) **Ligularia**

Bold clumps of large leaves and heads of yellow flowers. Good near ponds or in bog gardens. ☼Grow in full sun or partial shade. ⚘Prefers moist or wet soil, rich in humus. Dig compost into the planting hole. Attractive to slugs, which will quickly ruin the foliage. Do not allow roots to become dry in summer. dentata 'Desdemona' Large, rounded, bronze-green leaves, purplish underneath, and vivid orange flowerheads. ⇕1.5m ⬌1m. przewalskii Deeply toothed mid-green leaves, tall spikes of yellow flowers on deep purplish stems. ⇕1.5m ⬌1.5m.

Astilbe 'Bressingham Beauty'

(146) **Astilbe**

Grown for its delicate, feathery plumes of flowers rising on tall stems in early to mid-summer above a mass of mid-green, ferny leaves. Flowers are white, pink, red or purple according to variety. Makes good ground cover beside a pond or anywhere that is damp. ⇕60cm ⬌45cm. ☼Grow in sun or shade. ⚘Thrives in damp, humus-rich soil, or boggy conditions. Dislikes alkaline or dry soils. Mulch with compost. Water during dry spells. 'Bumalda' Cream flowers, tinged pink, bronze leaves. ⇕45cm. 'Venus' Coral-pink plumes of flowers. ⇕1m.

Lobelia cardinalis 'Queen Victoria'

(149) **Lobelia cardinalis**
Cardinal flower

Tall, erect plants with purplish foliage and flame-coloured flowers make spectacular bog garden or pond-side plants when grown in groups. Although related, this plant is quite different from the popular lobelia used in baskets and bedding. All parts of the plant are poisonous. ⇕90cm ⬌30cm. ☼Grow in full sun. ⚘Thrives in damp, boggy conditions. Plant in spring. Water if the soil becomes dry. Mulch well with compost to retain moisture. Trim dead flower stems to ground level in late autumn. 'Queen Victoria' One of the best cultivars. Stout, upright flower spikes bearing bright crimson flowers from late summer to early autumn. Stems and leaves deep reddish-purple.

Detail planting
alpine and rock garden

Thymus serpyllum var. albus

Oxalis adenophylla

150 Oxalis adenophylla

Small, compact and charming, this plant makes mounds of pleated, clover-like, grey-green leaves, the perfect background for the single flowers which have petals shaded from white at the base to violet-pink at their tips, veined with deep pink. Good for rock gardens and alpine troughs. ⬍10cm ◁▷15cm. ☀Grow in full sun or partial shade. ✎ Prefers moist, well-drained, light soil. Grow from plants bought in spring. Plant in a mix with 40% horticultural grit, 60% loam-based potting compost.

Lewisia

151 Lewisia
Bitter root

Small but eye-catching plants forming neat rosettes of leaves from which grow stalks bearing heads of flowers in bright pink, magenta, yellow and orange, with petals outlined in white. ⬍20cm ◁▷20cm. ☀Grow in full sun or partial shade. ✎Thrives in well-drained, gritty soil. Protect from winter wet. Plant seeds, or buy plants in spring. Grow in a mix of 50% compost, 50% coarse grit.
'Rainbow' Semi-double flowers, from white and yellow to pink, red-orange to purplish-red.

Alyssum montanum

154 Alyssum montanum
Mountain madwort

Covers walls and rockeries and fills gaps in paving with a neat, low-growing, evergreen carpet, bursting into a mass of yellow flowers in spring. ⬍12cm ◁▷50cm. ☀Thrives in dry, sunny places. ✎ The poorest soil is sufficient, as long as it's well drained. Grow from seeds from autumn to early spring or plants in early spring.
'Mountain Gold' Fragrant golden yellow flowers in spring.

Erigeron 'Rosa Juwel'

152 Erigeron
Fleabane

Low-growing erigerons are great for naturalising in dry places. They make a spreading mat covered in colourful daisy flowers, and will tumble over dry-stone walls, paths and rockeries. ☀Thrives in a warm, dry, sunny situation. ✎ Grow in moderate to poor, sandy or gritty soil.
'Pink' Pink petals surrounding a yellow button. ⬍10cm ◁▷50cm.
'Rosa Juwel' Semi-double pink flowers with yellow centres. ⬍60cm ◁▷45cm.
karvinskianus Pink flowers, fading to white, thriving in the poorest, driest corners and seeding around. ⬍20cm ◁▷10cm.

Pulsatilla vulgaris

155 Pulsatilla vulgaris
Pasqueflower

Outstanding rock garden plant with feathery, silky leaves and purple flowers with yellow centres. Feathery seedheads follow the flowers. Pure white and red-flowered varieties are also available. Good for rock gardens or dry banks, or anywhere that is well drained and sunny. ⬍20cm ◁▷20cm. ☀Grow in full sun or partial shade. ✎Prefers humus-rich, sandy, well-drained soil. Will grow in alkaline soil. Once established it should be left alone as it dislikes root disturbance.

153 Thymus
Thyme

Culinary thyme has plenty of ornamental relatives, grown for their evergreen, coloured leaves and small flowers which attract bees. Creeping thymes are great for planting in a path, releasing their scent when you tread on them. Bushy thymes make a good edging for borders and can be clipped into a low-growing hedge. ☀Grow in full sun. ✎ Prefers very well-drained neutral to alkaline or chalky soil. Dig in grit or sharp sand when planting. Trim larger-growing thymes after flowering to neaten shape.
'Doone Valley' Foliage randomly splashed with golden variegation. Purple-pink flowers and tangy lemon scent. ⬍12cm ◁▷20cm.
'Goldstream' Vigorous low-growing mat. Fragrant leaves, variegated light green and yellow. Lilac flowers. ⬍12cm ◁▷20cm.
x citriodorus 'Silver Queen' Upright bushy habit. Cream variegated leaves with strong lemon scent and pale mauve-pink flowers in June. ⬍15cm ◁▷15cm.
lanuginosus Grey leaved, creeping thyme. Pink flowers in mid-summer. ⬍5cm.
pulegioides 'Archer's Gold' Pink flowers, bright green leaves turning gold. Dense, upright, bushy habit. ⬍15cm ◁▷15cm.
pulegioides 'Bertram Anderson' Bright golden-yellow leaves with pale mauve flowers. ⬍5cm.
serpyllum var. albus Vigorous trailing strands of bright green leaves, forming a dense, colourful mat. White flowers in June. ⬍12cm ◁▷30cm.
serpyllum var. coccineus Crimson-pink flowers. Trailing stems of bright green leaves form a dense mat. ⬍12cm ◁▷45cm.
vulgaris 'Silver Posie' Upright bushy growth. Pink flowers. Silver and green variegated leaves. ⬍15cm ◁▷15cm.

Detail planting
alpine and rock garden

Viola labradorica 'Purpurea'

 Viola

There are hundreds of viola cultivars ranging from small-flowered violets through to large, showy pansies. Violas and pansies are particularly useful for winter bedding and for baskets and pots. Violets add colour and scent to the spring garden.
cornuta 'Alba' Small, vigorous viola, with starry white flowers, which will spread and self-seed. Useful in shade and inhospitable areas. ⬍15cm ◁▷15cm.
labradorica 'Purpurea' Purple-leaved viola. Flowers in spring and again in autumn, and often through mild winters. Grow in shade or sun. Self-seeds and spreads. ⬍5cm ◁▷5cm.

Veronica 'Crater Lake Blue'

 Veronica
Speedwell

Low-growing veronicas are great for making a colourful, ground-covering mat for border and path edges, rock gardens and walls. ☼Grow in full sun or light shade. ♂Prefers moist soil which is well drained.
'Crater Lake Blue' Neat mounds with spikes of ultramarine flowers May to July. ⬍25cm ◁▷30cm.
'Ionian Skies' Bright blue flowers in summer. ⬍25cm ◁▷25cm.
prostrata Dense, mid-green mat. Flowers vary from pale to dark cobalt blue. Prefers partial shade to full sun. ⬍15cm ◁▷40cm.

Dianthus 'Whatfield Joy'

 Dianthus
Pink

Relatives of the carnation, these plants make a low-growing mat of silvery-green leaves and flower throughout summer and autumn. Flowers white, pink or red with a rich scent. Good for rockeries and border edging. ☼Grow in full sun. ♂Prefers well-drained, alkaline soil.
'Flashing Light' Flowers ruby red. ⬍15cm.
'Fusilier' Fragrant, dark red, flowers in summer. ⬍15cm.
'Pike's Pink' Dwarf alpine with pale pink flowers, darker in the centre, scented. ⬍15cm.
'Whatfield Joy' Deep rose pink single flowers with a ruby eye. ⬍15cm.

Saxifraga

 Saxifraga
Saxifrage

Saxifrages are great for walls, rock gardens and troughs, making neat clumps that blend well with small sedums and sempervivums.
❁Most saxifrages prefer partial shade. ♂Thrives in dry, well-drained, sandy or gritty soil.
'Cloth of Gold' Compact, mossy cushion of golden-yellow leaves with short-stemmed red flowers in late spring. ⬍5cm ◁▷8cm.
'Elf' Small, compact cushion with pink flowers on short stems. ⬍5cm ◁▷8cm.
'Silver Cushion' Spreading mat of pretty silvery-green leaves. Pale pink flowers on short stems. ⬍10cm ◁▷15cm.

Assorted Sempervivums

 Sempervivum
Houseleek

These fascinating plants make a great year-round display on dry-stone walls or in rock gardens, troughs and containers, or even on roofs, where they were once grown to ward off lightning and evil magic! The fleshy, pointed leaves grow in a rosette and the plant forms a gradually expanding clump or mat of many rosettes. Heads of star-shaped flowers rise on taller stalks in summer. Leaf colour varies with cultivar, and leaves may be hairy or have 'cobwebs'. ☼Prefers full sun. ♂Grow in very well-drained soil. Survives in crevices where there is hardly any soil. Improve drainage by adding plenty of horticultural grit when planting.
arachnoideum Leaves green, heavily tinged red-purple with white 'cobweb' hairs between leaf tips. Pink flowers in summer. ⬍8cm ◁▷30cm.
tectorum Common houseleek. Blue-green leaves, lightly tinged red. Heads of red-purple flowers in summer. ⬍15cm ◁▷50cm.

Sedum spathulifolium 'Cape Blanco'

 Sedum
Stonecrop

Small sedums are tough and well adapted to survive in the poorest, driest crevices, where they will spread into a mat of coloured, succulent, evergreen leaves. In summer, heads of star-shaped flowers appear on short stalks in white or shades of pink, red or yellow. Sedums make good plants for troughs or terracotta pots and blend well with pebbles and gravel. Also great for dry, sunny walls. Easy and trouble-free.
☼Grow in full sun or partial shade. ♂Prefers moist, well-drained gritty or sandy soil. Dig grit into soil when planting. For containers plant in a mix of at least 50% grit to compost.
acre 'Aureum' Golden-leaved form of British native species. Makes a low-growing mat of small leaves with bright yellow flowers in summer. ⬍5cm ◁▷30cm.
spathulifolium 'Cape Blanco' Clumps of evergreen grey-green leaves in rosettes, dusted with a white bloom in their centres. Yellow flowers in summer. ⬍10cm ◁▷50cm.
spathulifolium 'Purpureum' Clumps of evergreen, grey-green leaves in rosettes turning to shades of purple as they grow larger. Older leaves turn bright red in autumn. ⬍10cm ◁▷50cm.

Summer colour
annuals and biennials

Consolida ajacis

165 Consolida
Larkspur, Annual delphinium
Closely related to delphiniums these annuals produce a colourful display of flower spikes in summer. ☼ Grow in full sun. ✎ Prefers light, well-drained soil. Sow seeds in flowering position, either in spring, or in September to produce vigorous plants for flowering the following year. Deadhead to increase flowering. **'Dwarf Rocket Mixed'** Easy to grow dwarf larkspur with spikes of pink, white, pale blue and dark blue flowers. Good for cut flowers or drying. ≜ 40cm.

Papaver rhoeas

164 Papaver rhoeas
Shirley poppy
Bred from the cornfield poppy, these cheerful summer annuals have pink, orange and red single and double blooms which fade to white in the centre, where there is a compact ring of yellow stamens. Easy to grow. ≜ 90cm ◁▷ 30cm. ☼ Plant in full sun. ✎ Prefers light, well-drained soil. Sow seeds in spring in finely raked soil where they are to grow. Thin to 20cm spacing and keep weed free. **'Shirley Single Mixed'** Single poppies in mixed colours.

Tropaeolum majus

163 Tropaeolum majus
Nasturtium
One of the easiest annuals to grow, with red, orange, yellow or cream flowers all summer long. Round green, sometimes bluish, leaves. ☼ Grow in full sun. ✎ Thrives in poor, well-drained or dry soil. Plant seeds in late spring or early summer, where plants are to grow.
'Empress of India' Lovely deep red flowers. ≜ 30cm ◁▷ 45cm.
'Red Wonder' Scarlet flowers and round, dark blue-green leaves. Compact plants. ≜ 25cm ◁▷ 25cm.

Matthiola bicornis

162 Matthiola bicornis
Night-scented stock
Very easy to grow annual which has a wonderful spicy scent in the evening, so good near seats and paths. The flowers are rather insignificant, coloured pale pink, mauve or purple. Leaves grey-green. ≜ 30cm. ☼ Does best in a warm, sheltered position in full sun or partial shade. ✎ Prefers well-drained soil which is moist to dry. Plant seeds where they are to grow from March onwards.

Campanula medium

168 Campanula medium
Canterbury bells
This biennial provides a long-lasting display of large blue, pink or white cup-shaped flowers from early to mid-summer. There are also perennial campanulas that give good garden value. ≜ 1m ◁▷ 40cm. ☼ Thrives in full sun or light shade. ✎ Prefers fertile, well-drained soil. Grow from plants in spring to flower the same year, or from seeds planted mid- to late spring for flowering the following year. Prepare planting area by digging in compost. Staking or support is necessary in all but the most sheltered gardens. Deadhead to prolong flowering.
'Blue' Showy, bright blue bell flowers in early summer.

Eschscholzia californica

167 Eschscholzia californica
Californian poppy
A cheerful, easy annual poppy that will brighten any border with a blaze of colour throughout the summer. Looks wonderful in a dry, wild planting with grasses, achilleas, erigeron and crocosmia. ≜ 30cm ◁▷ 30cm. ☼ Grow in full sun. ✎ Prefers poor, dry soils. Dislikes being moved. Sow seeds in flowering position in spring. Self-seeds freely but eventually reverts to the plain orange form.
'Special Mixture' Silky flowers in shades of orange, yellow, pink, red and cream against blue-green feathery leaves.

Calendula officinalis

166 Calendula officinalis
Marigold, Pot marigold
Easy to grow annual with large daisy-like flowers in cheerful orange or yellow, sometimes with a darker brown centre. Popular in cottage gardens, informal borders and containers. Grows fast and flowers all summer. Good for cut flowers. ☼ Prefers full sun but will tolerate light shade. ✎ Adaptable to different soils but does well in poor, dry conditions. Plant seeds where they are to flower from March to May.
'Orange King' Intense orange flowers with orange or brown centres. ≜ 45cm.

Summer colour
annuals and biennials

Impatiens walleriana 'Accent'

(169) Impatiens
Busy lizzie

Masses of colour throughout spring, summer and autumn make these a popular choice for pots, hanging baskets and containers. Also useful as bedding and for indoor plants. Very easy to grow. Flowers can be white, pink, red or orange. Plant outdoors from late spring to early autumn. Killed by frost. ☀ Thrives in full sun or shade. Becomes leggy if too shaded. ✐ Use standard potting compost. Grow from plugs or plants in spring.
'**Accent**' Mixed flower colours. Compact bushy plants. ‡25cm.
'**Cajun**' Mixed flower shades on bushy, compact plants. ‡30cm.
'**Super Elfin Series**' Dwarf-growing bushy plants with flowers in mixed shades. ‡20cm.

Linaria maroccana

(170) Linaria
Toadflax

Charming small annual with multi-coloured, miniature snapdragon flowers. Easy to grow. Good for filling space near the front of a warm, sunny border. ☀ Prefers full sun. ✐ Unfussy about soil. Sow seeds in spring where plants are to grow.
'**Fairy Bouquet**' Flowers in yellow, pink, salmon, orange, magenta, mauve, cream and white. ‡20cm.

Lathyrus odoratus

(171) Lathyrus odoratus
Sweet pea

An old favourite which never loses its charm. Highly fragrant and colourful flowers are wonderful for cutting. Seeds in miniature pea-pods are poisonous. ☀ Grow in full sun or partial shade. ✐ Prefers a rich soil with plenty of organic matter. Sow seeds indoors from January or outdoors where they are to grow from April. To get more flowers, pinch out growing tips after four pairs of leaves have grown. Can grow to ‡2m. Support with canes, net or peasticks. Pick flowers regularly or deadhead to prolong flowering.
'**Special Mixed**' Easy to grow, scented flowers in shades of cream, mauve and pink.

Petunia multiflora 'Resisto'

(173) Petunia

Making colourful cascades of flowers all summer, these easy annuals are popular for hanging baskets and containers. Flowers in almost every colour and often also striped or deeply veined. Both bushy and trailing types are available. ☀ Prefers full sun. ✐ Grow in well-drained potting compost. Widely available as plants or seeds. Plant out in spring after last frosts.
'**Hurrah Series**' Compact and heavily branched with many small flowers. Weather resistant.
'**Resisto Series**' Mixed colours.

Antirrhinum majus 'Maxi'

(172) Antirrhinum
Snapdragon

A cottage garden favourite, with 'snapdragon' flowers ranging from white through yellow and orange to pink and red, sometimes bi-coloured. ☀ Grow in a sunny place. ✐ Prefers fertile, well-drained soil. Sow seeds indoors in early spring or outdoors from May onwards. Deadhead to prolong flowering.
'**Intermediate Mixed**' Colourful mix of flowers up to ‡40cm.

---

ideal plants

Fragrant flowers

Jasminum officinale Summer jasmine No.62

Lathyrus odorata Sweet pea No.171

Lonicera japonica Honeysuckle, Woodbine No.69

Matthiola bicornis Night-scented stock No.162

Nicotiana 'Evening Fragrance Mixed' Ornamental tobacco No.176

Rosa Bush rose No.57

Digitalis purpurea hybrids

174 Digitalis
Foxglove

Tall spires of foxglove flowers are a pleasure in any garden and an essential ingredient for cottage gardens. Good for the back of a border or any shady corner and loved by bees. Flowers in white, cream, yellow, pink, salmon and purple from late spring to summer. All parts are poisonous. ☀ Thrives in damp, shady places although they will self-seed and spread to most parts of the garden. 🖌 Prefers moist but well-drained soil rich in humus. This biennial form flowers in the second year from seed.
purpurea 'Excelsior Hybrids' Densely packed spires of flowers in early to mid-summer in pastel shades of cream, purple, pink and white. ⇕1–2m.

Verbascum 'Cotswold Beauty'

175 Verbascum
Mullein

Verbascums have large, sometimes woolly leaves which grow in a neat rosette. One or more tall flower spikes rise from the centre. There is an increasing range of cultivars with flowers in various colours. Some are best treated as biennials, though others are short-lived perennials. ☀ Grow in full sun. 🖌 Prefers light, well-drained soil. Drought resistant once established. Takes two years to flower from seed, or will flower the same year from plants.
'Cotswold Beauty' Apricot-, pink- and peach-flushed flowers on branching spikes. ⇕1.3m.

Nicotiana 'Lime Green'

176 Nicotiana
Ornamental tobacco

Tender, tall-growing annuals flowering in summer. Some are scented. Single flowers with five petals, each with a central crease. All parts are poisonous. ☀ Grow in full sun or partial shade. 🖌 Prefers moist, well-drained soil. Plant seeds in trays indoors in spring.
'Evening Fragrance Mixed' Flowers red, pink and white, scented. ⇕90cm.
'Lime Green' Unusual lime green flowers. Unscented. ⇕60cm.
alata 'Domino' Neat and compact plants. Flowers red, pink, white, green, purple and salmon, some with contrasting eyes. ⇕45cm.

Lobelia erinus

177 Lobelia erinus

Grown for their profusion of colourful summer flowers these low-growing bushy or trailing plants are popular for hanging baskets, planters, pots and for bedding. Flowers can be white, pink, red, pale blue or dark violet-blue. Leaves dark green, often bronze tinged. ⇕10–25cm ⇔10–20cm. ☀ Prefers full sun or partial shade. 🖌 Will grow in any moist, well-drained soil. For containers and hanging baskets use a general potting compost. These plants do not survive the winter, so need to be planted each year. Easy to grow from seeds started indoors in spring or widely available as plants.

Alcea rosea hybrids

178 Alcea rosea
Hollyhock

A familiar cottage garden plant with tall spires of large single or double flowers in various colours. Attracts bees and butterflies. ⇕2.5m ⇔60cm. ☀ Prefers a warm, sunny position. 🖌 Grow in well-drained soil. Will flower from plants in the same year, or from seed in the following year. Staking is required in all but the most sheltered spots.
'Mixed' Mixed colours – white, cream and pink.

Indoor and out
container plants

Cycas revoluta

179 Cycas revoluta
Sago palm

Little changed from its prehistoric ancestors, this makes a fascinating and easy to grow container plant. The finely divided palm leaves arch gracefully in a rosette from a woody trunk, which will eventually grow to 2m after many years. The female flower and male cone are produced on separate plants from the central rosette, but only grow on mature plants kept in good conditions. ⬥1.5m ◁▷1.5m. ☼ Grow indoors in bright light, but shade from direct sunlight. Can be moved outdoors for the summer to a lightly shaded spot. Will not stand cold, damp conditions and should be moved indoors before the first autumn frosts. ✎ Grow in moist, well-drained soil, preferably a loam-based compost. Aim to keep the soil slightly damp during the growing season by watering two to three times per week. Water much less frequently in winter.

Philodendron 'Cannifolium'

180 Philodendron
Swiss cheese plant

Luxuriant, large-leaved foliage plants for indoor containers. The commonly grown Swiss Cheese plant is just one cultivar in a varied range. Leaves are heart shaped, glossy green or sometimes reddish or golden, and may be divided. Toxic. ⬥25cm–5m. ☼ Prefers diffused light, never direct sunlight. ✎ Grow in moist, well-drained compost. Water frequently when in growth and keep humidity high with gravel trays or by spraying regularly. Give a liquid feed every two to three weeks.

Aspidistra elatior

183 Aspidistra elatior
Cast-iron plant

An attractive container plant grown for its broad green leaves and tolerance of low light conditions. In milder areas can be grown outdoors all year round and makes good ground cover for shade. Flowers are borne at ground level and are rarely seen. ⬥60cm ◁▷ 60cm. ☼ Grow in sun to deep shade. Tolerates frost down to -5°C. ✎ Humus rich but well-drained soil. Keep damp but not saturated during the growing season, water infrequently in winter.

Ficus benjamina

181 Ficus benjamina
Weeping fig

This makes a great feature plant for a conservatory or large greenhouse, with graceful weeping branches and glossy, dark green leaves, sometimes variegated. Wear gloves when handling as plant is a skin irritant. ⬥30m ◁▷ 20m. ☼ Grow in bright but diffused light, do not expose to full sun. Prefers a still, humid atmosphere with no draughts. ✎ Grow in a container filled with loam-based compost. If the soil feels moist, do not water. In winter water sparingly. To improve drainage and air humidity stand the plant in a tray of gravel, but never allow roots to stand in water. Dislikes being moved.

Echeveria sp

184 Echeveria

These succulent plants look good in old clay pots, stone troughs or containers mixed with sempervivums and saxifrages. The greyish-green leaves grow in rosettes to form a slowly expanding clump. In summer, flowers appear on tall stalks in bright yellows, oranges and pinks. ⬥5–15cm ◁▷ 20cm. ☼ Full sun and warmth is essential. Grow indoors or outside in mild areas. Protect from frost. ✎ Plant in a mix of 50% coarse grit, 50% potting compost. For planting outdoors mix plenty of grit into ordinary garden soil. Requires little attention. Repot when container becomes overcrowded.

Sansevieria trifasciata

182 Sansevieria trifasciata
Bowstring hemp, Mother-in-law's tongue

This plant can look spectacular when grown well and will thrive outdoors in containers over the summer. Erect, strap-shaped leaves rise straight from the base of the plant. The leaves are dark green with cream edges and silvery, horizontal stripes ⬥1m. ☼ Grow in partial or full shade. ✎ Prefers moist but well-drained potting compost. Overwatering causes rotting of the leaf bases. Keep the compost damp but never allow to stand in water. Feed with liquid fertiliser every two weeks through the growing season. Water less frequently in winter.

Dracaena draco

185 Dracaena

Exotic-looking but easy to grow feature plants with strap shaped leaves arching gracefully from a single trunk. New leaves continually grow from the central bud while lower down the older leaves die and fall away revealing the gradually extending trunk. ⬥50cm–15m. ☼ Grow in full sun to light shade. In milder areas can be grown outdoors. In colder areas may be killed or cut back by hard frosts. ✎ In a container use rich, well-drained loam-based compost. Plant outdoors in well-drained soil. Water when compost gets dry but do not stand in water. Water sparingly in winter. To keep the plant tidy regularly trim away the old, dead leaves. Repot into a larger container annually in winter or early spring.

Spathiphyllum wallisii

Musa maurelii

186 Peperomia

Easy to care for foliage plants, useful for creating interesting leaf textures for indoor planting. The rounded leaves are sometimes smooth, glossy and variegated, while others are deeply and darkly veined with silver highlights. ⌀10cm–50cm. ☀ Grow in partial shade. Does not like direct sunlight. ✎ Prefers moist, well-drained potting compost mixed with 25% sand.
argyreia Handsome rounded, deep green leaves with tapering silver bands. Rat's tail-like flower stalks.

Peperomia argyreia

187 Spathiphyllum wallisii
Peace lily

Deep glossy green leaves and white flowers like arum lilies on tall stems make this an outstanding indoor plant. Flowers appear in summer and can last for up to six weeks or more. ⌀65cm ⬌50cm. ☀ Perfect for a shady spot indoors. Keep away from direct sunlight and cold draughts. ✎ Grow in loam-based potting compost. Keep compost moist at all times. Water sparingly in winter.

188 Musa
Banana

One of the largest-leaved plants available to gardeners, the banana really stands out as an exotic-looking feature plant. The leaves are an elongated oval shape, ribbed across and bright green. Flowering is unlikely in temperate climates unless grown in a heated greenhouse. ☀ Although they can be kept outside during the summer, most bananas are susceptible to freezing temperatures and need to be overwintered in a frost-free greenhouse or conservatory. They make tough indoor plants and are easy to care for. ✎ Grow in well-drained sandy soil or compost. Grow outdoors in summer but overwinter in a frost-free place.
basjoo Huge bright green leaves on arching stems. Large creamy-yellow flowers. ⌀5m ⬌4m.

Chlorophytum

189 Chlorophytum
Spider plant

Popular and nearly indestructible indoor plant. When well watered and fed it produces broad, striped, grass-like foliage and throws out long white stems with white flowers. ⌀20cm ⬌30cm. ☀ Grow in bright natural light but not full sunlight. Can be used as summer bedding. ✎ Thrives in moist, well-drained soil. Grow in pots or containers with good drainage using standard potting compost. Water regularly with distilled or rain water as tap water can cause browning of the leaf tips.

Agave americana 'Marginata'

190 Agave americana
Century plant, Maguey

A Mexican desert succulent which makes a good feature plant for a container. The fleshy leaves form a rosette and are greyish green and strap shaped, tapering to a point, with very sharp spines along the edges. ⌀1.5m ⬌1.5m. ☀ Grow in a container situated in a warm sunny place, indoors or outdoors. It can stand any amount of sun. Overwinter indoors in a frost-free greenhouse or conservatory. ✎ Needs very well-drained soil. Plant in a mixture of 50% sharp grit and 50% compost.
'Marginata' The grey-green leaves are attractively edged with cream variegation.

Aloe vera

191 Aloe vera
Medicinal aloe

Spiky feature plant with light green, succulent leaves. Aloes are desert plants and will survive in poor, dry soil, making them easy to care for. Given regular weekly watering and plenty of pot room they will throw up tall spikes of tubular yellow flowers in summer. ⌀50cm ⬌60cm. ☀ Thrives outdoors in a warm corner through the summer, making a gradually expanding clump. Overwinter indoors in a frost-free place. Cannot tolerate freezing. ✎ Grow in well-drained soil. Use 50% coarse grit mixed with potting compost. Baby plants appear around the plant and can be left to grow, or separated and started on their own. Give a liquid feed every few weeks through the summer. Water only every two to three weeks in winter.

Indoor and out
container plants

Argyranthemum frutescens

(192) Argyranthemum

This popular 'daisy bush' produces an endless display of flowers through the summer. Can be planted in containers or borders. ⊕1m ⬦1m. ☼Thrives outdoors in a warm spot during the summer. Can be left out in milder parts but best overwintered in a frost-free greenhouse or conservatory if temperatures drop below -5°C. Usually regrows from the base if cut by frost. ⚘Prefers well-drained, fertile soil. Plant in a mixture of about 20% horticultural grit to 80% standard potting compost with gravel or broken pots at the bottom to improve drainage. Deadhead frequently. Feed occasionally. Can be trained as a standard. Mulch well in autumn if left outdoors. Trim back untidy growth.
'Jamaica Primrose' Primrose yellow flowers with a golden yellow 'button', bright green divided leaves.

Lilium 'Odeon'

(193) Lilium
Lily

Lilies are grown for their exotic flowers and there are many cultivars which vary widely in size and flower colour. Some are scented. They can be grown indoors or out and are excellent for cut flowers and in containers. ☼Prefers full sun, but does best with roots cool and shaded, so growing between other plants works well. ⚘Grow in well-drained, rich soil. Plant bulbs in autumn in a hole two to three times their own depth. Dig compost into planting hole and can add a layer of horticultural grit at the bottom to improve drainage. In containers plant bulbs in loam-based compost.
regale Regal lily. Tall lily with dark green leaves and heads of white trumpet-shaped flowers which are strongly fragrant. ⊕1.5m ⬦45cm.

> ### ideal plants
>
> #### Exotic looking feature plants
>
> *Abutilon* Indian mallow No.39
> *Agapanthus* African lily No.127
> *Allium cristophii* Ornamental onion No.137
> *Callistemon citrinus* Bottlebrush No.195
> *Campsis x tagliabuana* 'Madame Galen' Trumpet creeper No.65
> *Canna* Indian shot plant No.132
> *Cycas revoluta* Sago palm No.179
> *Cymbidium* Orchid No.200
> *Dracaena* No.185
> *Eremurus stenophyllus* Foxtail lily No.107
> *Lilium* Lily No.193
> *Nerium oleander* Oleander, Rose bay No.196
> *Phormium* New Zealand flax No.50
> *Tropaeolum speciosum* Flame creeper No.63

Brugmansia arborea

(194) Brugmansia (Datura)
Angel's trumpets

Spectacular indoor feature plant with huge, hanging trumpet flowers and hypnotic scent. Various cultivars are available with white, cream, yellow or orange flowers. All parts are highly toxic. ⊕4m ⬦2m. ☼Prefers full sun or light shade. Containers can be placed outside in summer but need to be overwintered in a frost-free greenhouse or conservatory. ⚘Grow in moist, but well-drained, humus-rich soil or loam-based potting compost. Grow from plants or seeds. Can be pruned to keep size under control.

Nerium oleander

(196) Nerium oleander
Oleander, Rose bay

Tender, exotic looking evergreen shrub with showy clusters of white, pink or red funnel-shaped, fragrant flowers. Leaves are dark green, glossy, long and narrow. All parts are poisonous. ⊕2–5m ⬦2–3m. ☼Grow in a container which can be placed outside in a warm, sheltered place in summer and taken indoors for overwintering in a frost-free greenhouse or conservatory. ⚘Prefers moist but well-drained soil. Water before the soil dries out during the growing season. In winter water infrequently and keep compost fairly dry.

Callistemon citrinus

(195) Callistemon citrinus
Bottlebrush

Evergreen Australian shrub with colourful bottlebrush flowers in red, pink, white or purple all summer long. Each flower produces small woody fruits which form in clusters along the stem and last for many years. New leaves are often coloured. ⊕2m ⬦4m. ☼In mild areas plant in a warm sunny corner or at the base of a south-facing wall. Otherwise grow in a container in full sun. Overwinter in a frost-free greenhouse or conservatory. ⚘Plant in well-drained but moist compost. Dislikes alkaline soils. Apply low-phosphorous fertiliser and mulch in spring and autumn.

Bougainvillea

(197) Bougainvillea

These exotic climbing plants put on a spectacular display of vibrant colour which lasts for weeks. The small tubular flowers are surrounded by three brightly coloured bracts in shades of red, purple, orange or white according to variety. Main requirements for flowering are warmth and a high light level. ⊕10m ⬦10m. ☼Grow in a frost-free conservatory or greenhouse. Can be lightly shaded in summer. ⚘Add 20% finely shredded bark or Perlite to 80% compost to improve drainage. Flowers best if kept slightly on the dry side and root bound. Water sparingly in the winter, when there will be some leaf loss due to low light conditions. Light pruning when required will keep plants under control.

Saintpaulia

198 Saintpaulia
African violet
Popular indoor pot-plant flowering all year round if conditions are right. Has velvety, hairy leaves and delicate flowers in many shades, from white through pinks and mauves to dark purple. Grow in plastic pots in moist, rich, well-drained compost. Add 25% sand or vermiculite to 75% compost to improve drainage.
⇕15cm ◁▷ 15cm. ☀ Prefers bright, filtered light, never full sunlight. Thrives in a constant room temperature. Avoid cold, draughty windowsills. Place on trays of moist gravel for extra humidity. ✎ Avoid wetting leaves or flowers; stand in a tray of water for a few minutes then drain. Never leave standing in water. Add liquid feed every two weeks except in winter.

Lithops

199 Lithops
Living stones
Fascinating small desert plants which look like rounded pebbles. The fat, succulent leaves grow half-buried and have a translucent 'window' at the top which is coloured and marked in stony greys, greens and browns, according to variety. One or two daisy-like yellow or white flowers may be produced in summer. Can be kept outdoors in summer but will be killed by winter frost and freezing temperatures. Very slow growing. ⇕1–2cm ◁▷ 2–3cm. ☀ Prefers a hot sheltered situation in full sun. ✎ Grow in coarse, gritty compost or buy special cactus mixture. Can be grown from seed in a very warm place. Water sparingly in the growing season and stop watering in winter.

Cymbidium

200 Cymbidium
Orchid
Orchids have exotic, waxy flowers, often in contrasting colours, which last for weeks. Challenging to grow, but very rewarding if you are prepared to take time and trouble over their care. There are many cultivars with flowers in most colours or colour combinations. ⇕25cm–90cm. ☀ Grow in a greenhouse or conservatory. Will grow in fairly dim light, but needs bright light leading up to flowering. Shade from direct sunlight. ✎ Use special orchid compost. Keep soil moist at all times, but do not allow to become waterlogged.

Campanula isophylla

201 Campanula isophylla
Falling stars, Italian bellflower
Charming and easy pot-plant producing a trailing mat of leaves which become covered with a mass of blue or white bell flowers lasting many weeks. Can be left outside in summer if protected from strong sunlight and good for hanging baskets. Killed by frost so overwinter indoors. ⇕20cm ◁▷ 30cm. ☀ Thrives in bright light but not full sun. ✎ Grow in well-drained compost. Keep damp at all times but not waterlogged. 'Alba' Cascades of white flowers. Very prolific.

Asparagus densiflorus

202 Asparagus densiflorus
Asparagus fern
Grown for its trailing, bright green, feathery foliage. Flowers are white and insignificant. ⇕70cm ◁▷ 70cm. ☀ Shade from full sun. ✎ Grow in moist, humus-rich soil or potting compost. Keep moist while in growth, but avoid roots becoming waterlogged. Can be grown from seed but quicker and more reliable from bought plants.

Tradescantia albiflora

203 Tradescantia
Trailing tradescantias have interesting foliage and are extremely easy. Often grown as single pot plants, they are also excellent when allowed to roam freely in mixed plantings in a conservatory or greenhouse, where they will trail and hang to form a lush mass of foliage. There are many cultivars with leaves which are coloured or variegated. Fast growing. ⇕15cm ◁▷ 30cm. ☀ Grow in full sun or shade. ✎ Thrives in moist but well-drained soil, rich in humus. For lush foliage keep well watered and maintain a humid atmosphere. Easy to grow from cuttings.

Container plants 327

enjoy

There are so many ways to make more of your outdoor space – you can use the garden as a playroom, a workspace or as a venue for relaxing and entertaining by day or by night. Introducing the tranquil sound of running water will transform the garden into a calm, peaceful place, while the flickering flames of a fire will prolong a party into the cool of the evening.

a garden for all seasons

Bringing the outdoors in

One of the nicest ways to enjoy the pleasures of outdoors in indoor comfort is in a conservatory. This is the ultimate room with a view: bright and sunny by day, warm and moonlit by night, a conservatory allows you to enjoy the garden from the comfort of your home. If you add a table and chairs, it becomes a room for dining and entertaining, whether it's a lazy Sunday morning brunch, an informal lunch, a romantic candlelit dinner for two or a celebratory family feast.

Another way to get more enjoyment from your outdoor room is with a summerhouse where you can get away from it all and relax. Install heating and lighting, and you can use it all year round, as office, workshop, teenage den – whatever suits you and your family. A sheltered terrace or patio can also be a perfect place to relax on a sunny day regardless of the season: patio heaters provide warmth at any time of the year.

Taking the indoors out

Don't go indoors just because the sun has set. Instead, create a little drama in the garden with candles, hurricane lanterns and oil burners. Light up decking and terraces with multicoloured lights; spotlight decorative features like sundials, statues, fountains and ponds to create a dramatic backdrop for your garden parties; light your guests' path through the garden with torches or coloured paper lanterns. Even when it's much too cold, dark and frosty to be in the garden, outside lights will welcome your visitors. They also prevent interior windows becoming 'black mirrors' after dark. You could highlight the garden's structures by draping a sparkling trail of tiny, twinkling fairy lights over a gazebo, trellis or wall, or stringing them through the bare winter branches of the trees.

An outdoor room all year round

A really successful outdoor room is one where style and comfort are all part of the plan, making this a space you will enjoy for more hours of the day and more days of the year than you ever have before.

Conservatory living

Having a conservatory means that you don't have to brave the elements to enjoy the colours, scents, textures and sounds of the outdoors; you can use it to extend your social and family life beyond the house, whatever the weather.

Design for living

Imagine your conservatory with a table set for breakfast or a leisurely Sunday brunch in the sunshine. In the evening, with some lamplight and lots of candles, and sparkling china and glass set on a crisp linen tablecloth, the conservatory becomes a romantic setting for supper under the stars. At Christmas and other holidays, decorated with lights and ornaments, it will look like a fairy-tale scene.

A garden under glass

No conservatory is complete without plants. A hot, sunny conservatory is ideal for cacti and blossoms, especially Mediterranean plants such as bougainvillea (see page 326). A shady conservatory will encourage leafy palms and ferns to thrive. Both will have room for tubs or pots, either singly or massed together in groups, scented climbers such as jasmine, and hanging baskets filled with flowers or even tomato and strawberry plants. The conservatory is an ideal place to overwinter tender specimens such as olive and citrus trees and banana palms. See pages 172–73 for more ideas.

Traditional elegance, contemporary chic

Elegant and sometimes ornate Victorian and Edwardian styles of conservatory are enduringly popular, and are particularly appropriate when they are built onto houses from the same period. The range of styles, shapes and sizes of conservatory available today, however, demonstrates how the concept of the glass house has been reinterpreted to provide gracious living space that complements all architectural styles, ranging from the old and familiar to the cool and contemporary. For clean, modern lines, you could choose floor-to-ceiling glass panels; for a more integrated, traditional look, go for a conservatory built on dwarf walls that match the existing masonry. Tough, modern PVCu frames are available in brilliant white, or in maintenance-free woodgrain finishes to match the exterior doors and windows of your home.

Comfort zone

Conservatories receive more daylight and sunshine than other rooms, so bear this in mind when choosing colours and furnishings: you want to be cool in summer and warm in winter. You will also want to use your conservatory after dark, so give some thought to the type of lighting needed. Light will be lost through the glass walls and ceiling, so a number of low-intensity lamps will create a more subtle effect than a few very bright ones.

Their glass construction means that conservatories lose heat rapidly in winter but can heat up excessively in summer. So both heating and ventilation are a must. Extending existing central heating or adding an independent heat source will keep you cosy and warm on a cold day – a particular priority in a north-facing conservatory. A south-facing conservatory, on the other hand, is more likely to suffer excessive summer temperatures. So at least a third of the windows should open and the doors should fold right back. Blinds, roof vents and fans will help, and you could also install an air-conditioning unit. Getting the temperature just right will mean you can enjoy the space all year round. An even temperature will benefit your plants too. See also pages 170–73.

Planning permission

You may need planning permission and Building Regulations approval to add a conservatory to your home. The Planning Department and Building Control officer of your local council will be able to advise you (see page 373).

Building costs

Most conservatories are assembled from pre-manufactured components, often with each element priced individually according to size, finish (hardwood or PVCu) and glass specification. This means that many conservatories can be self-built, and it's easy to calculate the basic cost of the structure. But don't forget to factor in other costs: any planning permission that may be required; the construction costs of building a foundation and laying a damp-proof course, if needed; as well as the cost of installing pipework for central heating and cabling for extending the electrical supply from your home. If you plan to do the electrical work yourself, you must inform your local Building Control Department first (see page 373).

Your choice

Before you invest in a conservatory consider which type will best suit the style of your home and the needs of your family. Factors such as the type of glazing and the frame material used are also important.

Mahogany effect

Bright white

Pavilion-style

B&Q

Summerhouse style

An attractive summerhouse is a focal point in the garden, and provides a place from which the rest of the garden can be admired.

Shelter in style

The summerhouses of the grand gardens of the past were often brick-built, but today wood is the most popular material. Hardwoods such as cedar are more costly than softwoods, but are exceptionally durable. Softwood structures need to be treated with wood preservative to extend their life, and they can also be be painted, stained or varnished. A summerhouse will acquire a different personality depending on the colour it is painted: pale pastels for a seaside look; vibrant blues, greens and pinks in a sunny spot will suggest the Caribbean; dark green will bring to mind a cabin in the woods. By adding colour you can make a summerhouse into a spectacular feature or blend it into surrounding nature.

Shapes and sizes

Summerhouses and wooden garden buildings come in a wide range of sizes and shapes – including square, rectangular, round and hexagonal. Some are partitioned into internal rooms, providing both living space and garden storage. A summerhouse is a sheltered spot in which to sit, read, relax, practise yoga or meditation or even entertain. The walls will usually be extensively glazed, so it's a good idea to site it in a sunny location: in summer you can open the windows and the door to let in a cool breeze, while in winter you can still enjoy the sun.

You can do it...

Outdoor kids' playroom

Kids love the fun and adventure of their own garden playhouse. There are lots of different sizes and styles to choose from – including playhouses on stilts. Check for shatterproof glazing and non-toxic wood treatments before you buy.

B&Q

Larger structures

A bigger wooden building can be used as an annexe to your home, providing more space for work or leisure, or even serving as a garden guest house. Such buildings often have fewer and smaller windows so they look more like little houses, ranging in style from traditional chalet to New England cabin or sleek Scandinavian lodge. These structures are also sturdy and windproof, making them ideal for year-round use. A solidly constructed and properly insulated building is particularly appealing if you are planning to work or run a business from home, but need the psychological transition of leaving the house to go to work each day. A dining table and chairs, soft furnishings, rugs and curtains will all make the space more inviting. Power for lighting, heat and electrical equipment can be brought from your home. The cabling must be installed or certified by a qualified electrician (see page 373).

Optional extras

Some summerhouses, big and small, have a veranda to provide protection from the glare of the sun. Others have a built-in patio in front – ideal for lounging or al fresco dining. The option of an attached store room means that your beautiful garden room won't become the depository for garage or household overspill.

Planning permission

Depending on a number of factors, including the size of the garden in which you want to erect the summerhouse, and the size, location and intended use of the structure, you may require planning permission and Building Regulations approval (see page 373). Always check with the Planning Department of your local council before you begin construction or installation.

Easy construction

Many summerhouses are available flatpacked for self-assembly and come complete with pre-glazed and pre-hung doors to make the construction process as easy as possible. Although they often have a wooden floor, you need to prepare a solid, level base or platform for them to sit on: siting a wooden structure on bare earth will cause it to rot quickly. (See pages 106–7 and 118–19 for more information on assembling different types of summerhouse.)

It's a good idea to choose a sheltered spot as this will minimise the risk of structural damage in storms or high winds: sturdy as they are, most summerhouses, especially the self-assembly variety, are not anchored to the ground.

Once the summerhouse has been constructed, all it needs is a few finishing touches: decorative wood preservative, paint or stain. Add some comfortable chairs, a table, perhaps a radio, and settle down in your new room.

Your outdoor dining room

An area of hard surfacing such as a patio or deck provides a practical, low-maintenance platform for outdoor dining. Unlike lawns, hard surfaces dry off within minutes of the sun coming out, so can be used no matter what the weather has been like. Add comfortable furniture, lighting, an outdoor heater, good food and a few close friends, and your outdoor room is equipped for stylish al fresco dining.

Using your space

It's a good idea to site the dining area in your outdoor room in a spot where there is good access from the house or barbecue area – carrying plates, glasses, bottles and food can be difficult if you have to negotiate your way round shrubs, pots or water features. If your patio or deck is adjacent to, and on the same level as your indoor kitchen or dining room, then it may be possible simply to move your indoor dining furniture outside.

Be realistic about how many people you will want to seat at the same time – there's little point filling a space with a huge table that seats ten if you usually entertain no more than two or three friends together. But if you are looking to entertain bigger groups in a tight space, remember that more people can sit around a circular dining table than a square or rectangular one of an equivalent size. A folding wooden picnic table is ideal for buffet snacks and drinks.

While it may seem an attractive option, setting out a dining table and chairs on a lawn can be less successful than using a hard surfaced area such as a deck, terrace or patio. A lawn can be damp even on the sunniest day, and chair and table legs will sink into the ground. Lightweight furniture can be a perfectly adequate option for a hard surface but is likely to wobble on the usually slightly uneven surface of a lawn.

In small or awkwardly shaped spaces, deck tiles that slot into an easily assembled frame make terrific mini decks that are ideal for a dining table and chairs.

Choosing wooden furniture

The good looks and durability of teak makes this one of the most popular hardwoods for outdoor use. A light coating of teak oil is all that is needed for maintenance and weatherproofing. Other hardwoods, such as oak, redwood and cedar, offer the same qualities in a range of different wood tones to harmonise with your colour scheme. Much of this wood has been tanalised – impregnated under pressure with tanalith oxide preservative, which protects the wood from dry and wet rot and woodworm, and offers a surface that can be oiled, stained or painted. Softwoods such as pine are much cheaper, but they may also require a coat of wood preservative each year to stop them deteriorating.

When buying wooden furniture, look for the stamp of the FSC (Forest Stewardship Council): this guarantees that the wood has come only from an independently certified, responsibly managed and sustainable source that isn't contributing to global deforestation and climate change.

Metal options

Garden furniture made of powder-coated steel is sleek, contemporary and hard-wearing. Because the steel will withstand extremes of heat and cold, the frames can be left outdoors all year round. When you are not enjoying al fresco dining, the metal table can double as a potting table or as a showplace for magnificent displays of pot plants and blooms.

Painted metal furniture is functional and very stylish, ranging from simple café style chairs and tables, through sleek, modern forms in nylon and tubular aluminium, to the more elaborately patterned Victorian-styled wrought-iron pieces. Wrought iron can be expensive – and it is also extremely heavy. If you want to follow the sun in your outdoor dining room, or need to store your furniture during the winter, choose a more lightweight and portable material.

Metal hinges on chairs and tables do need to be protected from rusting and should be oiled regularly to keep them in good working order.

Creating shelter

Shelter, whether from a hot sun, a cool breeze or from overlooking buildings, will help make your outdoor room a more comfortable and enticing space.

Summer shade

Parasols not only look elegant but are practical too, offering protection from the sun while you dine or relax outdoors. They come in a big variety of sizes, styles and materials: from classic hardwood and canvas to sleek aluminium and lightweight resin. A swing bench with a canopy provides a relaxed, intimate spot of shade. A temporary gazebo is like a mini marquee and is a great way to extend your outdoor entertaining space. Gazebos can be erected on lawns, patios and decked areas. They make great play tents and paddling pool shelters, protecting kids from over-exposure to the sun, and are also ideal for housing a temporary bar or buffet. Larger gazebos can be used for bigger parties and outdoor celebrations. There's also a heatproof variety that can be erected over a patio heater, so even if there's a chill in the air, you'll be cosy and comfortable.

Permanent structures

Pergolas are a timelessly classic garden feature, and make a perfect support for climbing plants such as roses, wisteria, clematis or grapevine; or you could train scented jasmine over the structure for a glorious evening perfume. Wooden pergolas remain the most popular type, and can be bought in modular units so that you can easily get the right size for your needs.

Shady places

True pergolas are free-standing structures, but there are also overhead or lean-to pergolas which are connected to the exterior of the house and form a colonnade that extends out into the garden. These are particularly useful, not just for providing shade, but for creating privacy, as they will screen off an area from overlooking windows in neighbouring buildings.

An arbour resembles a pergola, but instead of being a walkway, it is a sheltered seating area. The framework can be very simple: traditional wooden trellis is ideal, but metal arbour frameworks can be even easier to install. An arbour can support a canopy of plants and will be particularly attractive if the plants are scented.

Private spaces

Dividing the garden into a number of smaller areas adds a quality of mystery and discovery, as well as providing the opportunity to create a series of differently themed garden rooms within a single space. Allow glimpses from one area to the next with features such as a moon gate, which is a wall with a round hole cut into it, or a panel of trellis with a circle cut out. A lacy pierced screen of stone or concrete blocks will soften breezes, let dappled light through and add an exotic Moorish touch to a private terraced area. Rose-covered arches, climbers supported by panels of trellis, or even walls of semi-opaque glass bricks can mark out the divisions in a garden – as well as providing screening from the wind, and privacy from overlooking buildings.

Garden walls

As an alternative to traditional brick or stone, cement-rendered or cast-concrete partition walls can be elegant and sculptural: painted brilliant white or a bright, funky colour, they can be used to divide up a space or to hide an otherwise unattractive feature or view. Such walls don't need to be high: a low one may be enough to define a space and provide some privacy.

Living partitions

Hedges don't have to be limited to the traditional privet, box or beech: shrub or rambling roses will grow into a charming informal hedge, as will the hardy *Fuchsia magellanica* 'Riccartonii' (see page 301). Rows of lavender or rosemary make a low, fragrant living partition that releases a heady scent as you brush past.

Outdoor heaters

Don't be driven indoors by a nip in the air.
An outdoor heater can make the garden
a cosy environment, day or night.

Real flames

At the end of a barbecue, there will always be a group of
friends happily snuggled up enjoying the dying embers of
the coals. There are few things as mesmerising as the sight
of glowing coals or flames leaping in the dark. You don't
have to have a barbecue every night – there are other ways
of getting real flames into your outdoor room, providing
warmth and light throughout the year.

Outdoor fireplaces using solid fuel – either wood or
coal – are portable, so they can be moved (when not in use)
for maximum visual and heating effect, and can be safely
stored away when not required. And the attractive design
of many outdoor fireplaces makes them a feature in their
own right.

Fire bowls and chimineas

Fire bowls are shallow metal containers in which you can burn
logs. If you throw on clippings of woody herbs such as thyme,
rosemary or lavender, the air will be filled with scent. However,
unprotected flames must never be left unattended, and are not
safe with young children around. A sturdier alternative to a fire
bowl is a wood-burning chiminea. These attractive pot-bellied
stoves come in clay, terracotta and cast iron in a range of sizes
to suit every space. For safety they must be placed on a hard,
level surface, and kept well away from any flammable PVCu or
wooden structures such as fences, pergolas or conservatories.

Solid fuel releases less greenhouse gas than propane gas,
so is the better option for the environment. But do check that
firewood is certified as coming from a well-managed source.

Café society

We've become used to dining al fresco at pavement cafés kept
warm by giant mushroom-shaped heaters. Patio heaters are
now available in a range of sizes, styles and colours for use
at home. Not only do they create a cosy circle of warmth, but
they look good and are easy to use and store.

Added extras

Patio heaters not only raise the temperature, but some also
have lights and foot warmers so that you can stay out long after
dark. For the ultimate in luxurious outdoor living, you can add
a specially designed cooking grill and circular table: using the
same gas cylinder as the heater, you can cook food at the table.

The right heater for you

When buying a patio heater, make sure you choose the correct gas cylinder. Patio heaters run on propane gas, which doesn't freeze in cold weather. Propane for domestic use is usually labelled 'patio gas' – look out for it in green cylinders with an orange top.

The sturdy construction of patio heaters combined with the weight of the gas cylinder at the base makes them very stable, but it's a good idea to choose a model with a tilt-switch and a flame failure device that will automatically cut the flow of fuel if the heater gets knocked over or if the flame is extinguished by the wind. As with any gas appliance, it is essential to follow the manufacturer's instructions for safe operation and storage.

Patio heaters come in different sizes that give off different amounts of heat. A 15kW heater will radiate warmth over about 20 square metres: if you have a large space to heat, this is the one for you – but choose a model with wheels so that you will be able to move it into position easily. For a medium-sized area, a heater around 13kW is ideal, or for a smaller space opt for an 11kW version. The smallest patio heater is a table-top model, a stylish mini-heater which will keep all your guests cosy around a big table. But bear in mind that these must only be used on wooden or metal tables, not plastic or glass.

Lighting the garden

Garden lighting can create a magical atmosphere at night. And it means that outdoor living and entertaining can be extended long after sunset.

Candlelit atmosphere

The flickering light cast by candles is both romantic and flattering. Dozens of night lights in small holders look magnificent lined up in rows along a path, the edges of garden steps, or on top of a wall. A flotilla of floating candles on a small pond or on a shallow glass bowl of water is a very effective way of introducing some atmospheric lighting. Concertina-style Japanese lanterns in gorgeous colours, and storm lanterns in a range of styles, from utilitarian to highly decorative, are attractive and also practical because their flames are protected from wind.

Garden flares and oil-burning torches look spectacular when grouped together in large terracotta pots or galvanised buckets filled with sand, spaced a safe distance apart. They are also designed to withstand a certain amount of wind. Garden flares will burn for several hours and many are impregnated with citronella or eucalyptus oil, which will help keep mosquitoes and gnats at bay.

Lighting choices

While candles, torches and flares are an atmospheric addition to the night-time garden, they burn out quickly and have to be replaced frequently. It is also essential to be alert to safety at all times. A more long-term solution is to install a lighting system that will fill your outdoor room with light at the flick of a switch – or even one that is switched on automatically by movement-activated sensors. Alternatively, you could go for solar-powered lights, which don't require any wiring or complex installation. Whichever option you choose will depend on your particular lighting needs.

Electric lighting

Outdoor lights that run at mains voltage must be powered using steel-wire-armoured cable (SWA), buried at a minimum depth of 450mm (see page 163). Low-voltage systems take their power via a transformer which steps down the electrical supply to a very low voltage. This means that even if you cut through a low-voltage cable accidentally, there's no risk of electrocution. Nonetheless, it's generally better to run them in protective conduit and bury them to avoid tripping or accidental damage.

All outdoor electrical fittings must be fully weatherproof and suitable for the location (see page 373). If you plan to install or make changes to an outdoor power or lighting circuit, you must inform your local authority's Building Control Department first (see page 373).

Solar-powered lighting

Solar-powered lights need no wiring as they store the energy of sunlight in a battery. They are not a powerful light source, so if you want to light a large area, you'll need quite a number of them. As their power fades, so does their light, heralding a natural end to an evening in the garden.

Painting with light

Spotlights, which are designed to direct a beam in a single direction, are useful for highlighting particular features: they can be mounted on a wall or on spikes that can be pushed into the earth or in among the leaves of a potted plant on a terrace or patio. When placed under trees or shrubs they highlight leaf and branch structure; directed downwards they create a soft, functional light for picking out steps and paths and for illuminating the edges of patios and terraces. Lighting can also be directed at the water in a pond or used to highlight the plants and ornaments at its edge; submersible pond lights add drama and can draw attention to a waterfall or fountain.

Low-voltage recessed lights are very elegant along walls, down steps, or set into decking, emitting a glow that is bright enough to illuminate the surrounding area without creating blinding upward shafts of light. If your outdoor space has a large tree or a pergola you can create a night-time canopy of twinkling stars with low-voltage weatherproof net lights.

Considerate lighting

Whatever type of lighting you choose for your outdoor room, be sure to direct the beams in a way that your neighbours will not find intrusive. Choosing lower-wattage bulbs outdoors will lessen light pollution and allow you to see more stars on clear nights.

B&Q

Use your individual style to bring colour, pattern and texture into the outdoor room, making it a beautiful and enticing place for al fresco living. You can decorate this space using all kinds of objects and finishes, including paint, pebbles, glass, metal, and running or still water, in ways that will reflect your unique personality and taste.

decorating the outdoor room

Colour, pattern and texture

Coloured paints and stains will brighten up all kinds of surfaces in the garden. Paint can make a feature out of a bland wall or fence, and can be used to highlight containers and garden furniture. Stain and varnish will bring out the natural beauty of decking or wooden furniture. Hard paving materials such as blocks and slabs are produced in a huge selection of finishes and colours.

Decorative aggregates – chippings, pebbles and gravel – can add colour and texture to an outdoor room. They look good on paths and can also provide ground cover over bigger areas. You can plant through them, and lay them over weed-control fabric for a really easy-care surface. Gravel ranges in colour from white to golden yellow to dark grey; it can be water-washed and smooth, or rugged and crushed from larger pieces of stone. Granite and marble chips are available in even more striking colours. Coloured rockery stones in different shapes and sizes create a strong contrast with plants and foliage. They will add sparkle when strewn at the base of a water feature, or use them to dress the tops of plant pots, where they will help to retain moisture.

Individual style

Table tops and other surfaces can be decorated with mosaics made from broken ceramic tiles, shells, pebbles or glass marbles. You could even use mosaic to add interest and individuality to a slab patio: simply raise one paving slab and lay a mosaic in your own design in a soft concrete mix.

Sculptures, statues, figurines, urns, found objects like sun-bleached driftwood, sundials, hanging mobiles and other ornaments will all add extra character to an outdoor room. They can be used as focal points, or positioned to flank a door or pathway, and will look spectacular at night when illuminated. And don't overlook pots, tubs and planters when it comes to adding finishing touches. There are containers to suit every style of garden, from traditional terracotta, stone and glazed earthenware to brightly coloured contemporary designs in metal, concrete, glass and plastic.

Coloured paints
and stains

Furniture, decking, fencing, trellis and even walls and containers can all be coloured to produce subtle harmonies or a dramatic contrast with their surroundings.

Using colour outdoors

Coloured paints and stains can be very effective in an outdoor space. Painting garden walls or fences the same colour as the exterior of your house, or the same colour as external features such as window frames or doors, is one way to create a visual link between the house and the garden.

You can also use colour to create optical effects: green or wood-coloured boundary walls or fences can make a small space seem larger as they give the impression of disappearing into the surrounding foliage. A shed, summerhouse, gazebo or bench painted in cool pastel colours will appear further away than it actually is, and this can help to make a small garden feel more spacious. Hot or strong colours like reds, vibrant pinks and bold blues will make objects stand out and be noticed, especially if they are in the sun. Give some thought to the colours of your planting, too: painted fencing or trellis can provide a backdrop that will either contrast or harmonise with the predominant colours of your flowers and foliage.

Think of your decking, patio or terrace as a floor covering or carpet and add colour there too. Patio or specialised floor paints can transform the uninteresting concrete floor of a basement courtyard into a pleasing, inviting area. Decking can be stained to blend in with the grass, gravel or paving that surrounds it.

Wooden and metal garden furniture can also be painted or stained in colours that echo those used elsewhere in the garden, helping your design to 'hang together'.

Colour effects

If you want to create fresh, fun spaces outdoors think cheerful bright colours, especially for children's playhouses and climbing frames. Conjure up sun-baked days and sultry nights with warm terracottas and deep reds, or chill out in a minimalist zone of silvery whites, blues and greys. Colour is the key to creating moods by day and by night, all through the year. If you get bored with a particular effect you can always change a colour to create a new mood.

Choosing your materials

There is a wide choice of oil- and water-based exterior and masonry paints. Water-based paints dry quicker than oil-based varieties, are less harmful to the environment and produce less odour, and you won't need white spirits or turpentine to clean your brushes afterwards. Modern oil-based paints are available in gloss, satin and flat finishes for use on wood, metal and other surfaces such as concrete. They will often require the application of an appropriate undercoat and you will need to have white spirits or turpentine to hand to clean brushes and mop up any accidental spillages.

Wood stains and decking stains come in a range of colours, many designed to imitate the natural colours of timber. Most also contain a timber preservative. Bear in mind, though, that the final colour may not quite match the one on the tin, since it will be affected by the original colour of the wood.

Using them safely

Keep these products out of the reach of children. Wear gloves to apply them, and avoid contact with exposed skin. Many oil-based products contain volatile solvents and give off unpleasant fumes while drying. Avoid smoking, drinking or eating while using them, and never use them if you have any kind of breathing difficulty. Cloths impregnated with oil-based paints, varnishes, stains and turpentine or white spirits can self-ignite: they should be soaked in soapy water and disposed of outside the home. Never pour paints and solvents down the drain. Contact your local council for information about safe disposal.

Garden ornaments

Sculptures and fountains, sundials and bird feeders, plant pots and containers will all provide the individual finishing touches to your outdoor room.

Personal style

The ornaments and decorative objects you choose to put in your outdoor room – whether they're traditional or contemporary, old and weathered or shiny and new – will be determined by your personal taste and style. Part of the fun of furnishing this space is the search for new decorative treasures.

Positioning your ornaments

Sculptures, obelisks, columns or large urns can act as focal points at the end of a walkway or vista. In pairs they can give a touch of grandeur to a doorway or entrance. Or they can be placed so that they will be discovered half-hidden in foliage around a corner or in a niche or alcove, adding a little bit of mystery and surprise to the experience of your outdoor room.

Traditional garden ornaments

Sundials have been in use for thousands of years, and although we no longer rely on them to tell the time, they are a satisfying reminder of times past. Stone sculptures of humans or animals have also long been popular. Antique pieces can be forbiddingly expensive, but it's now possible to buy modern reproductions made from reconstituted stone which, in time, becomes weathered and mellows to blend in with its surroundings. There are also bronze-effect resin sculptures that look completely authentic, but are a fraction of the weight or cost of real bronze, enabling you to create as grand or classical a look as you like.

Abstract and living art

Found or reclaimed objects work particularly well in informal and cottage-style gardens: sun- and sea-bleached driftwood set on a stretch of shingle or gravel; old chimney pots planted with bright geraniums; or a mobile made from sea shells, or small pebbles with holes. If you're looking for a more modern or abstract style, you'll find spheres, cubes and pyramids of various sizes and colours in stone, metal, glazed ceramics and glass, as well as cairns – towers of stones held in place on hidden steel poles.

Outdoor art can also be made from natural materials. Willow can be woven into sculptures – of animals, people or abstract forms – and into arbours with built-in seats, arches, and delightful play tunnels for kids. Encourage birds to come into your garden with feeders, baths and nesting boxes that will attract them – and look attractive – all year round.

Decorative techniques

Inexpensive, mass-produced terracotta pots – which look shiny and new – can be artificially aged and made to look antique by painting them with live yogurt. Put the pots out in the sun to dry if you want a whitened effect, or place them in a shady spot if you want a green, mossy finish. Plastic pots can also be transformed with a little imagination and a few pots of paint, including shiny metallics – they can be painted a solid colour or livened up with stripes or spots or with paint effects such as stencilling or sponging. Make your pots unique by decorating them with pebbles, glass beads, sea shells or even bright fragments of broken crockery.

Protecting your ornaments

Consider the effects of the weather on your garden decoration: sunlight and rain will weather materials like wood, stone and even metal, while frost may cause damage to unglazed earthenware and terracotta. If you plan to keep your pots and other decorative items outdoors throughout the year, check that they are frost-proof.

Regrettably, while your ornaments will draw admiring looks, they may also attract the attention of thieves. The increasing number of thefts from gardens – of furniture, sculpture, pots and urns as well as plants – means that it pays to make sure they are secure (see pages 163 and 372).

Pots and containers

Like sculptures, pots and containers can be beautiful additions to an outdoor room – even when they are left unplanted. Decorative pots work well either singly or in collections of various shapes and sizes, while a large pot or urn can be used to impressive effect to form a focal point, or be hidden among lush foliage for an elegant surprise. Arranged on holders up a drainpipe or other vertical structure, potted plants can transform otherwise unattractive features with colour and foliage.

safety first

If you place statues, pots and urns on plinths to raise them above ground level it is vital to ensure that they are secure and stable, so that they won't fall and cause injury.

You can do it...

More choice

There is a wide range of sculptures that have been specifically designed for outdoor conditions.

Urns and pots of all sizes can be used as planters, for lighting effects or as part of a water feature.

Outdoor artefacts can lend a traditional or ancient look, or one that is boldly modern.

Water features

Water can create a range of different moods, from the meditative calm of a still pool to the exciting thrill of cascades and fountain jets.

Adding water

Most of us don't have a natural stream or pond in our garden, but that doesn't mean that one can't be introduced, even into the smallest outdoor space. This could be a wildlife pool, a bubbling urn or pebble fountain, a raised pool on the patio, a rill or canal, or even a wall-mounted water spout.

Ponds and pools

A pond provides an area of tranquillity while attracting useful wildlife: hedgehogs, toads and frogs will dine on slugs, snails and insects, while birds that come to bathe and drink will also feast on insects.

Symmetrical, geometric shapes work extremely well with formal and modern minimalist designs, while an organic shape will look great in a more informal setting. Even in a small space, a beautiful basin, a wooden half-barrel or a reclaimed stone or ceramic butler's sink will be large enough for a few miniature water lilies to thrive in.

safety first

A child can drown in just an inch or two of water. If you have small children, it is advisable to avoid installing any water feature that involves an open pool of water and to opt instead for bubble or wall fountains, which incorporate hidden, underground reservoirs.

Shallow pools

The bottom of a shallow pool can be decorated with a pattern of pebbles, a mosaic, or coloured glass chippings (though these can be harmful to fish: do check the manufacturer's guidelines). To enhance reflections of the sky, clouds and overhanging plants, use a black pool liner or a mirror on the bottom (it will need to be a shallow pool for this to work).

Raised pools surrounded by paving are ideal for small spaces and patios, especially those bounded by high fences or walls, as they will introduce reflected light and make the space feel larger.

Construction and siting

Still ponds and pools need to be positioned where there is enough sunshine to warm the water and enough shade to discourage algae from growing. But avoid overhanging trees: leaf fall will lead to a thick layer of decomposing vegetation at the bottom of a pond or pool, which, as it rots, will emit methane gas, which is harmful to fish. The leaves of yew, holly, willow and laburnum are poisonous to water plants and animals. Watch out for wind when siting fountains, especially if the water shoots up high, as you'll risk a soaking when you pass by – and you'll have to keep topping up the reservoir.

Fountains

Fountains range from simple bubbles and gentle cascades over a mound of pebbles, slates or stones, to wall fountains and more elaborate water tiers, plumes, bells, columns and spheres. Incorporating a fountain into a pool is a good way of keeping the water moving. All fountains need a reservoir of water, which can either be hidden below ground, or be part of the overall design – for example a barrel or large terracotta urn – and an electric pump to circulate the water. Once installed and filled, fountains make little demand on mains water supplies (just the occasional topping up of the reservoir) and don't need much maintenance. There are even solar-powered fountains which cost nothing to run.

Creating ponds and water features

Creating a water feature is easy: there are rigid fibreglass and reinforced plastic pre-formed ponds and stream units with header pools in a range of shapes and sizes that are simple to install. Flexible liners, available in a variety of sizes, thicknesses and colours can be used for creating informal ponds. Raised ponds, where the whole body of the pool sits above ground, need strongly constructed foundations and walls as they will have to bear the weight and withstand the outward pressure of the water.

Waterfalls

Installing a waterfall in your outdoor room will introduce the calming and harmonious sound of running water. The constant movement of the water will aerate the pond or pool into which it flows, allowing pond life to thrive.

The new-found British passion for good food is reflected in what, and how often, we are cooking. Nowhere is this more evident than in our idea of a barbecue, which has evolved dramatically in recent years from a slap-up meal of charred sausages, to something altogether more varied and exciting that is inspired by outdoor cooking traditions from around the world.

cook outdoors

Simply delicious

Almost every culture has dishes that incorporate grilling and barbecuing techniques: think Mediterranean grilled koftas; American pit-cooked barbecue pork; Caribbean jerk-spiced grilled meats. The list goes on, and is infinitely diverse and delicious. The beauty of outdoor cooking is that almost anything goes. While hamburgers and sausages are simple, tasty options, there are many other mouth-watering possibilities – from meat and fish, to vegetables and fruit.

Holiday every day

Modern life can be hectic and stressful, but relaxing and entertaining in your garden is the ideal antidote. There is something deeply satisfying about cooking outdoors; it's a pleasure that evokes summer holidays and getting away from it all. With the British passions for travel and home improvement now rivalled by our new-found love of good food, the garden is a place where all these pleasures can come together.

Easy living

Gone are the days when a barbecue was just a big weekend party thrown once each summer for friends and family. The latest gas-fired models offer almost instant results, making it easy to come home in the evening and decide to grill without much forward planning. A relaxed candlelit dinner outdoors is a great way to unwind and restore your perspective after a long day's work.

Fresh is best

Cooking on a barbecue is perfect for people who don't think of themselves as cooks and who loathe the thought of slaving over a hot stove. Barbecue food can be as complex or as simple as you want it to be. What could be easier than throwing some freshly made kebabs from your butcher on the grill, and enjoying a glass of wine while they cook?

If there is any secret to barbecue success it is in the ingredients. Barbecue food is often unadorned and simply prepared, so you'll get the best results with flavourful fresh ingredients. Head for your local weekend farmers' market or a good butcher; select locally sourced foods from your supermarket; grow your own herbs and vegetables and pick them as you need them. Foods lose their flavour quickly, so fresh tastes best.

Know your barbecue

Barbecuing is easier and more popular than ever before and brings an air of festivity to almost any occasion.

Choosing the right barbecue

Before you start, you'll need to decide which type of barbecue will best suit your needs: multi-tiered; built-in; disposable; kettle; one on wheels...the list of options is a long one. You can even barbecue on some models of chiminea if you add a grill attachment. You'll also have to think about how much money you want to spend; how much space you want to devote to a barbecue; how often you will use it; and how quickly you will need to access it.

How to choose between gas and charcoal? Charcoal barbecues are usually cheaper than their gas counterparts, so they suit any budget. And charcoal will give you that authentic char-grilled taste. Smoking aids such as wood chips work better on charcoal, where they smoke, rather than burn. However, gas barbecues do have the distinct advantage that they can be lit almost instantaneously. You can come home from work, decide to barbecue, and have a meal ready in under an hour. If you are cooking for an extended period, charcoal will need to be replenished, while gas will burn for as long as there is fuel in the cylinder. Still, if you really find it impossible to choose, you can always buy one of the latest dual-fuel versions.

Once you decide which type of barbecue is right for you, you'll need to think about where to place it so that it's safe and accessible. Keep it away from overhanging trees or shrubs and place it on level ground away from the house. Always keep a fire extinguisher to hand and never leave children and animals unattended while the barbecue is lit.

Getting started

A gas grill is easily started by turning on the gas at the cylinder, opening the valve and clicking the starter ignition. Charcoal takes a little longer to get going, but there are now many quick-lighting varieties that are ready for cooking in 15–20 minutes, as well as charcoal that you light by setting fire to the paper bag – a particularly easy and clean option. Stacking charcoal in pyramids will speed up the lighting time as air will circulate, encouraging the flames. Placing firelighters at the base of the charcoal pyramids will help ignite the fuel (always let these go out completely before you start cooking). Once the coals are glowing, you can add flavour enhancers such as wood chips.

To judge the temperature of a barbecue, check the colour of the coals: they will begin to turn ash-grey when hot enough for you to start cooking. Before adding food to the grill, brush the grates with a little oil to keep the food from sticking.

Cooking methods

There are many different ways to cook on a barbecue; the more you use yours, the more you will find your own methods of achieving great results. While some people use their barbecues only to cook smaller cuts of meat like steaks or burgers, if you have a closed-top barbecue and enough room in the grill to use indirect heat, you could cook large pieces of lamb or pork, or even a whole chicken. To do this, light the charcoal on the outside edges of the barbecue with a drip pan in the middle. When hot, set the meat over the pan and close the grill. If you have a gas barbecue with two heat controls, you can achieve the same effect by turning off the flames on one half of the grill. Alternatively, you could invest in a rotisserie attachment for cooking whole chickens.

Looking after your barbecue

Use wire brushes to clean the grill when it has cooled down and occasionally clean the inside of the barbecue with soapy water to remove the grease that will build up with heavy use. This will help to rid the grill of any residue that may cause food to stick, or even burn. To protect your barbecue from the weather, cover it once it has cooled down completely.

safety first

If you have a gas barbecue, always turn the gas off at the cylinder when not in use. This should stop the gas leaking and will prevent a dangerous flare-up when you light the barbecue. In case of fire, disconnect the gas immediately and move the cylinder away from the barbecue. Allow the flames to die down – do not use water to extinguish them.

Barbecue cooking

There is something especially appetising about food cooked outdoors, and the simpler the food, the better it tastes. Barbecuing allows cooks of almost any experience to introduce a wide variety of flavours, with inspiration from any number of good quality cookbooks.

Bringing garden freshness to your barbecue

Grilling is an ideal cooking method for vegetables; they retain their flavour and colour, and peppers and tomatoes release natural sugars. You can barbecue almost any vegetable, even some lettuces such as radicchio or endive, which are delicious when cooked on the grill.

Even the most dedicated carnivore will admire barbecued vegetarian dishes: grilled mushrooms brushed with a little garlic olive oil served simply with fresh ripe sliced tomatoes and basil; kebabs of baby new potatoes and feta cheese with black olive tapenade; grilled haloumi cheese with roasted pepper and red onion salsa. Using a little imagination and some colourful fresh produce, you can create an endless variety of delicious treats.

Most vegetables have no natural fats so will need to be brushed with a little oil or marinated. While harder vegetables like potatoes and broccoli can be grilled, they need to be par-cooked beforehand. The freshest ingredients don't need much dressing up – a few fresh herbs, some sea salt and black pepper, and a brush of good olive oil.

Meat, fish and marinades

Barbecuing is a particularly healthy way to cook meat and fish as it requires very little extra fat. Most meats will benefit from a pre-grill marinade, which will add terrific flavour and help to tenderise and keep them moist.

A marinade can be made up of many different spices and flavourings. A Thai dish will be enhanced by a marinade of Asian spices or sauces such as rice wine vinegar, ginger and soy sauce. Use chillies, lime zest and coriander for a Latin flavour. A simple vinaigrette made with olive oil and balsamic vinegar will work especially well with vegetables. If time is a problem, there are some really good ready-made marinades on the market.

You can also use a dry rub made with spices such as cumin, coriander, fennel and dried chilli flakes. Gas-grill users love these dry spices as they don't drip onto the flames to cause flare-ups that can burn the food. Whichever you use, always keep your marinating meat and fish in the refrigerator (in warm weather, meat shouldn't be kept out of the fridge for longer than an hour). As little as one hour of marinating time will start to add flavour, but you'll get better results if you can marinate for longer. Take your dish out of the refrigerator 30 minutes before cooking to bring meat to room temperature.

Salads and side dishes

A salad can be almost anything, from dressed mixed lettuce leaves to grilled vegetables tossed with couscous, or pasta with olive oil and lemon juice. Mix a drained tin of white beans or chickpeas with fresh herbs, feta cheese and cherry tomatoes, or simply combine boiled new potatoes with fresh herbs (mix them while the potatoes are still warm for best results) and drizzle with a little good olive oil. Hummus and tzatziki go well with grilled lamb or pork and you can make a simple sauce by blending fresh herbs with Greek yogurt or crème fraîche.

Food safety

We tend to be more casual about cooking on the grill, but in fact barbecuing demands extra food safety precautions.
- Keep raw meat separate from other ingredients.
- Wash your hands before and after handling uncooked meat, as well as before eating.
- Use separate utensils for cooked and raw food and avoid putting cooked meat back into the dish in which it was marinated. If you want to use a marinade for basting, boil it for at least five minutes to kill off any bacteria.
- Clean all cooking surfaces and utensils thoroughly, and make sure they are free of old food residues before cooking.
- Cook meat thoroughly as raw or undercooked meat can cause food poisoning; you may want to pre-cook larger joints before adding them to the barbecue. Check meat is cooked all the way through by slicing it open – juices should be clear in colour, with no traces of pink or red.

Sweet endings

Delicious grilled fruits can be dressed with cream and fresh berries, served over ice cream, or dished up with meringues and thick cream. For a really decadent treat, cut a lengthwise slit in an unpeeled banana, insert pieces of dark chocolate, wrap the banana in foil, barbecue and serve with a little crème fraîche or ice cream.

You can do it...

Treats for kids

Baby-sized burgers and halves of grilled corn on the cob will go down a treat with children, and skewers of mixed grilled fruit can be served with a delicious dipping sauce of yogurt sweetened with honey.

B&Q

Barbecue
accessories

Most barbecue cooks stick to the simple tools like skewers and tongs, but there are many other accessories that will help you make the most of your barbecue.

Using skewers

Skewers are the most useful and versatile barbecue accessories. Your main decision will be whether to choose metal or wood. Metal costs a little more but can be used again and again, while wooden skewers are thrown away after just one use. Longer skewers can help you avoid burning your fingers on the heat as you turn them. You can buy metal skewers in a rack that sits directly on the grill, making them easier to manage. Wooden skewers need to be soaked for an hour before you use them to keep them from catching fire on the grill. Think about what your kebabs will look like when cooked; use a variety of colours and textures but select foods that need roughly the same cooking times.

Tools for grilling vegetables and fish

A hinged grill basket will prevent small items such as slices of vegetables slipping through the grill. It's also a useful tool for ingredients such as haloumi cheese that might stick. You can even use a hinged grill basket to create whole dishes: slices of cooked potato and asparagus layered with basil, or Thai fish fillets marinated with lime leaves and lemongrass. The basket allows fish to absorb much more flavour and prevents it sticking to the grill. You can also easily turn a grill basket over to cook the other side.

Brush your grill basket with a little olive oil before you load it to keep the food from sticking. Fish may need a little extra oil as it becomes very delicate when cooked and can flake if it sticks to the basket. Placing thin slices of lime or lemon around the fish can help eliminate this problem, and will also keep it moist.

Basting for added flavour

A basting brush is a useful tool for creating big taste. Food can be basted throughout the cooking process to keep it moist and to add flavour. You can buy a variety of basting brushes, or mops for slopping on sauces, or you can make your own by tying a hearty herb like rosemary into a brush with kitchen twine. If your basting sauce is sugary, apply it in the last 10 minutes of cooking time to avoid burning.

Tongs or prongs?

All barbecue utensils and tools should be metal. Tongs are indispensable – no barbecue chef should be without them. They are generally easier to control than a spatula, and you can use them for turning almost anything (though nothing can replace a metal spatula for flipping stubborn burgers or delicate foods that may stick). Choose tongs to turn steaks and other pieces of meat as a pronged fork may release juices and dry out the meat. There are versions available to suit any budget, and while there is no science to choosing the right pair, you may find it useful to keep a long pair handy for hot fires, and a shorter one for more control.

You can do it...

Planning ahead

Before your guests arrive, set your table, make sure your meat is marinating, your salads are assembled (in the case of a green salad, hold back the dressing until the last minute or the salad leaves will wilt) and your drinks are chilled. This will give you more time to relax and chat to your guests while the food cooks.

B&Q

Outdoor cooking fun for kids

While it's not safe practice for your smaller children to help with the barbecuing, you can get them involved in the preparations. Kids love to make their own kebabs. Cut up some fruit and some courgettes, mushrooms and par-boiled new potatoes, then arrange them in different bowls. Avoid raw meats when laying out the skewer options, or throw out any vegetable leftovers: children tend to be messy and are liable to cross-contaminate ingredients. Skewer tips can be very sharp, so choose ones that are less so – such as a wooden variety – and warn the children before they start skewering.

ideal tool

Grill wok

A grill wok allows you to grill smaller items easily. You won't get the grill lines, but you will get the barbecue taste. Try grilling green beans or courgettes with a little basil olive oil.

A garden is the ideal place to escape from the stresses and strains of life. Some people find an hour or two spent weeding or deadheading to be therapeutic, while for others, relaxing in the outdoor room means nothing more than sitting or lying in the sun or shade, reading or snoozing, eating and chatting with friends.

relax outdoors

An outdoor room can be your chill-out zone, a place to de-stress mind and body. Adding light and heat will create an oasis of comfortable calm surrounded by the sights, sounds and scents of nature.

An outdoor retreat

Your garden should reflect your lifestyle – and that includes how you choose to relax. If you want to practise yoga or meditation, read a good book or simply lie back and gaze at a starry sky, then make a space in your outdoor room in which you can indulge yourself. Find a spot in which you can let go and forget your cares, and install a comfortable lounger, swing seat or hammock.

If your garden lacks privacy, install some trellis panels or an arbour or pergola that will screen you from prying eyes. Although the sun and its warmth are always welcome, on a hot summer day the dappled shade provided by tree branches can be a relief. If you don't have any overhanging trees in your garden you can introduce some shade and privacy with a parasol. Seats arranged in a spot that is sheltered from the wind will provide a cosy haven. A well placed outdoor heater will take off any chill in the air, and a mug of hot soup or a glass of mulled wine will be warming on a crisp autumn day.

Tapping into nature

If you look after nature it will look after your garden: tits and thrushes, hedgehogs and toads, and aphid-devouring insects such as lacewings and ladybirds will all help keep the garden free of pests. Encourage birds and their song into your garden with nesting and feeding boxes and attract bees and butterflies with scented plants that will fill the air with colour and perfume.

One way to block out the noise of neighbours or road traffic is to introduce soft, pleasing sounds that give your ears something to focus on and push other noise into the background. A gently bubbling water feature, the breeze through long grasses or a delicate wind chime are surprisingly effective at dampening outside noise and are attractive additions to the garden in their own right.

If the conditions are right (see page 298), lavender is a good choice in pots or beds around your relaxation zone as the perfume has relaxing properties and will also keep moths away at night. Peppermint and chrysanthemums will repel ants, so plant plenty around your dining area. At night, candles scented with lavender or citronella will keep flying insects at bay.

Outdoor lounging

The key to relaxation is comfort and there is a huge range of outdoor furniture in styles and materials to suit every garden. Before you buy a sofa you sit on it to try it out; do the same with the seating for your outdoor room.

Choosing furniture

When deciding which type of furniture you want for your outdoor room think about styles and materials: traditional styles will complement traditional gardens, while modern or sculptural forms may look better in a contemporary setting. Materials will affect the weight as well as the finish of furniture, so if you want the option of portability, choose models with castors or wheels, or consider pieces that are made from lightweight aluminium tubing or plastic, or that fold up or stack easily for storage.

A good rule of thumb with regard to outdoor furniture is the more lightweight the piece, the more solid and level the surface beneath it needs to be, otherwise you'll end up with annoying wobbles and potentially dangerous capsizes.

Relaxing in style

One of the most popular pieces for outdoor relaxation is the sun lounger. As well as retro versions of the original hardwood steamer chair designed for ocean liners, loungers are now available in metal and plastic so there is one to suit every sun worshipper. Try out a lounger for size before you buy: make sure it's long enough and wide enough and that it has enough support for your back. Don't forget that you can add a mattress and plenty of cushions to make it really comfortable, but you'll need to remember to store fabric items under cover to protect them from rain and the damp night air. You could keep them in a shed or summerhouse, or even invest in an outdoor storage box; it's always much easier to keep clutter out of view when there's somewhere to tidy it away.

Lying in a hammock, gently swaying beneath the dappled shade of a tree, is possibly the best way of all to relax in the outdoor room. Hammocks are readily available and are easy to hang. When you buy one, make sure that it is safe and sufficiently strong to take the weight of the heaviest person who is going to use it. If you plan to leave a hammock out all summer long, then choose one made of non-rotting nylon rather than natural fibres. In a small garden it is unlikely that there will be two conveniently located trees from which to hang your hammock. You could mount strong brackets on walls or other sturdy structures as supports, but by far the simplest solution is to buy a hammock with its own self-supporting frame which can be sited anywhere in the garden.

Fixed or movable?

The great advantage of freestanding pieces of outdoor furniture is that they can be moved around relatively easily: if you are a sun worshipper, you can follow the sun around the garden all day just by moving to a new position. Alternatively, furniture can be placed in a quiet, secluded area, among scented flowers and herbs, or in a spot from where you can admire an uninterrupted view of the garden.

Fixed furniture, such as a tree seat or garden bench, not only offers the sitter a place to relax and view the garden, but, when unoccupied, can become a decorative feature in its own right. It could be surrounded by an arbour of sweet-smelling flowers or positioned at the end of a pathway, inviting you to sit down and relax for a while.

Wooden furniture

Wooden furniture is always a good choice in the garden, where its natural tones harmonise with the surroundings. Many hardwoods are tough enough to require little or no treatment, although other timber furniture does require a periodic rub-down with a wire brush to remove algae or lichen, and an annual application of timber preservative. Natural wooden furniture ages and weathers beautifully, though it can also be painted or stained. Do your bit for the environment and check the labels on wooden furniture carefully: only buy timber products guaranteed to have come from a well-managed, sustainable source.

Other materials

Moulded plastic furniture is inexpensive, surprisingly comfortable and available in many different colours. It is also tough and durable. Lightweight cane furniture is often relatively inexpensive and is easy to move around but it must be stored when not in use or it will quickly deteriorate. Because of its vulnerability to the weather, cane is ideally suited to sheltered areas such as conservatories, summerhouses and permanently covered terraces. Rattan and wicker furniture will require a similar level of protection. Metal furniture, especially that made of alloys, requires little or no maintenance, but anything made of iron or steel will require anti-rust treatment from time to time. Any furniture that folds up is likely to have metal hinges: these should be regularly inspected for signs of wear and tear, and oiled to keep the movement free.

Tree and turf seats

If you have an established tree in the garden, building a seat around it can make a very attractive feature. Tree seats are available in kit form, but if you have basic woodworking skills it is not too difficult to build your own – just remember to allow enough space between the seat and the tree trunk so that the tree can grow.

A turf seat is an unusual feature. It is simply a mound of earth covered in turf with the sides, back and front supported by planks of treated wood (deck boards would be ideal), brick or stone walls, or thin sticks woven together to form a wattle wall. Instead of turf you could plant the soil with chamomile (*Anthemis nobilis*) which produces a wonderful fragrance when you sit on it. Alternatively, you could plant a fragrant creeping thyme (see page 81), but be careful not to sit on it when it's flowering as it is likely to be full of bees!

Inside out

Where space is restricted it's worth considering dual-purpose furniture for use indoors and out. The director's chair, with its canvas sling seat and back, is a modern design classic, while lightweight and portable bean bags are ideal for sunny terraces, patios, balconies and roof gardens.

On a sunny afternoon or balmy evening few things are more satisfying than having a few friends around. This might mean simply sitting chatting and enjoying some food, but if kids are present it may involve more energetic activities – a treasure hunt, a nature trail by torchlight, jumping around in a bouncy castle or even splashing about in a swimming pool.

fun outdoors

An outdoor room that provides adults with a tranquil oasis does not have to be at odds with a child-friendly space. Even so, you may have to be realistic: those exotic specimen plants and flower-filled borders might have to wait until the urge to kick footballs around diminishes.

A kids' paradise

Children – our own and other people's – often use a garden more than anyone else. After school, at weekends and during the school holidays, it's their kingdom, a place where they can let off steam and make some noise, a venue for birthday parties and other celebrations. The garden is an ideal place for children to play as long as it is secure, keeping them within a defined space and in sight of adults. Any access points like gates need to be secure and constructed so that little ones can't slip through the bars or climb over the top to reach a busy road. Make sure you can see younger children at all times; place some comfortable adult seating alongside children's play areas so you too can relax while they play. There's a huge range of play equipment available to keep them entertained, from traditional see-saws, swings and slides to trampolines and inflatables. Doing things together – sweeping up autumn leaves, watering flowers, watching butterflies and birds, enjoying family meals – will encourage kids to see the outdoor room as an extension of the house, a safe and healthy place for them to play and learn.

Grown-up kids

Adults love to play too, and when grown-ups join in with children's games the fun for everyone increases. Some games that can involve everyone require little more than a lawn – and it doesn't matter if it's a bit rough. Badminton is one: the lightness of the shuttlecocks means that even young children can often make a hit, while stronger and more aggressive players will still find it difficult to send the shuttlecock flying into the neighbours' garden.

The ultimate plaything for all ages has to be a swimming pool, and it's now possible to have one even in a small garden. If you have the space, a permanent sunken swimming pool is the ultimate garden accessory for water-lovers. But there are also many raised pools to choose from, big and small. Some of these are permanent, while others can be dismantled for the winter. Or consider a spa: just imagine the luxury of wallowing at the end of a long day in a steaming, bubbling hot tub under the stars (see page 143).

Kids' zone

Kids love the challenges and freedoms of being outdoors. Here, in relative safety, they can run around and let off steam, play messy games without being told off, and even learn about nature, gardening, and the food they eat.

Green-fingered kids

Children enjoy getting involved in gardening. If you have the space, you could set aside a small patch of ground or some containers in which they can grow their own flowers, fruits and vegetables under adult supervision (see page 117). They could compete to grow the tallest sunflower or the biggest pumpkin. Encourage them to help out by providing them with child-sized hoes, rakes and wheelbarrows.

Keep your garden free of poisonous plants and also any thorny or spiky plants that could cause injury. Even so, you need to make sure that children understand from a young age that they should not eat things they find in the garden other than plants that have been specifically grown as food.

Playthings

Swings, slides, trampolines, climbing frames and activity centres are all great for adventurous play that will also develop your children's coordination and fitness. Anything kids could fall from should be placed on a safe surface. A lawn is preferable to a hard patio, though you may have to live with a worn patch of grass. Alternatives include rubber mats, pellets made from recycled rubber, or natural bark chippings. Rake the chippings over occasionally so that there is a consistent depth of no less than 150mm over soil, more on harder surfaces. Large play structures should be anchored or concreted into the ground to prevent them tipping or shifting (see page 116).

Garden buildings for kids

From simple playhouses to grand timber buildings, there are outdoor structures of all shapes and sizes where kids can play and give free rein to their imagination. Young children enjoy the sense of privacy and ownership that a low picket fence or some dwarf hedging surrounding their playhouse will bring, but you'll still be able to keep an eye on them. In early years, the playhouse will be a venue for teddy bears' picnics, but if it is large enough for sleeping out in, the kids will continue to identify with it right into their teens.

Tree houses and tower playhouses can also be terrific fun but they must be very solidly constructed, and younger children should be supervised by an adult at all times to avoid dangerous falls. Before you invest in a tree house or tower playhouse, it's advisable to approach the Planning Department of your local council, as there may be restrictions on the height of garden structures in your area (see page 373).

Sandpits

Sandpits are great fun, and young children armed with toy buckets and spades will spend many happy hours constructing magnificent sand cities. When the kids grow out of sandcastles, the pit can easily be filled in and turfed over, or even excavated and turned into a pond.

A portable sandpit can be moved around to follow the sun or shade and stored away when not in use. A permanent sandpit will need a cover to keep the sand dry and prevent it being fouled by cats; this can be easily made from deck boards, which have the advantage of being pressure-treated against rot. Unlike builder's sand, play sand is classified as a toy: it is light in colour, won't stain clothes, and is non-toxic and lime-free so should not irritate children's skin or eyes.

Fun with water

Children of all ages love water and a paddling pool is invaluable during hot spells. However, it's essential that toddlers and children are not allowed to play in paddling pools unattended. A safer alternative can be a garden hose and water toys: kids will love to chase each other under the spray. But do watch out for them tripping over the hose, or for the ground beneath becoming slippery.

Special occasions

The outdoor room is the perfect venue for dining and dancing or simply decorating to a festive theme. Whether you're celebrating a birthday or anniversary, Christmas or Diwali, Hannukah, Eid or the New Year, give free rein to your imagination and transform the outdoor room with colourful lights, decorations and music to celebrate the festival and share good times with your friends, family and neighbours.

Seasonal touches

With a little advance planning, the outdoor room can be themed to create a gorgeous festive setting: nighlights set in pumpkins carved into gruesome grinning lanterns provide the perfect backdrop to a spooky fancy dress Halloween party; weatherproof fairy lights strung through trees and over arbours create a magical look after dark in summer and winter alike. Bonfire night doesn't need to involve an enormous towering pyre: a small fire in a stove or chiminea is safer and equally fascinating for youngsters as they wave their sparklers in the November evening. Celebrate the winter solstice by decorating the space with elegant wreaths of evergreen foliage bedecked with gold and red ribbons. No indoor Christmas scene is complete without a beautifully decorated tree adorned with lights and baubles; why not light up an outdoor tree too? Children in particular will love looking at an illuminated winter garden, and there are plenty of novelty lights to help create a fun- and light-filled winter wonderland. Use your imagination to turn any occasion – a birthday, festival, engagement, wedding anniversary, the end of exams – into a really special event.

A party in the garden

A party can mean many different things. The key to any great party is planning. How many people will you invite – and how many will fit into your outdoor room? Do you want to eat, cook, talk or just dance the night away? Once you have decided how simple or elaborate you want it to be you can begin to plan your perfect party.

Dressing the scene

If you are serving food and drink outdoors, attractive tableware will add to the sense of occasion: look out for unbreakable acrylic and melamine tableware that is perfect for informal meals such as picnics and barbecues, and means you can dine in style without worrying about plates or glasses getting broken if they are accidentally dropped.

Flowers, both fresh and dried, add colour and ornament. You can move pots and containers around for visual impact, or arrange interestingly shaped branches in large urns for a stylishly minimal effect. Paper lanterns hung from tree branches, or from wires strung well above head height, create a wonderful party mood.

Lights, music and consideration

Along with plenty of good food, music and atmospheric lighting are essential ingredients in any celebration. But do be aware that your neighbours may be trying to sleep: don't let your garden lights interfere with their darkness. Outdoor lights on a dimmer switch are useful: you can control the strength of the lights and dim them as the evening wears on. Solar lights weaken naturally during the evening as their sunlight-charged batteries run down.

Such consideration is even more important with music: be aware of your neighbours and remember that sound carries. Keep the volume low – especially the base beat. If you are worried about disturbing your neighbours, encourage guests to use the outdoor room as a chill-out zone rather than a dance floor: put out chairs, bean bags, plenty of cushions, even a rug on the terrace or deck to create a relaxed and intimate atmosphere. Always inform your neighbours of your party plans well in advance. Even better, invite them along!

information

Outdoor security

Securing the garden

Garden tools, furniture, ornaments and even plants can provide rich pickings for thieves. Fortunately, there are many measures you can take to safeguard not only your belongings, but your home too.

The back garden

Ideally, the back garden should be surrounded by a tall barrier that is difficult to climb over. Fencing, railings or walls should be at least 1.8m high. Be aware of planning regulations (see opposite) – you may need permission for a barrier taller than 2m. Sadly, however, even a high wall or fence is not enough to stop many burglars, so you should think about additional deterrents. Dense, thorny shrubs or hedges are off-putting to intruders. You could fix trellis panels, 300–400mm high, to the top of the fence or wall. These should be strong enough to support a climbing plant but not a climbing intruder: the risk of breaking it, leading to injury or discovery, will make many burglars think twice. Secure the trellis with screws from the garden side of the fence.

Front garden

Burglars will hesitate to break into your home from the front if they will be visible from the road or seen by neighbours. So keep boundaries to a front garden under 1m high – this will ensure that the front door and windows remain on view. If you want a taller barrier, erect railings or an open fence that you can see through. Remember too that low-hanging trees and large shrubs can provide cover for an intruder, so keep them trimmed and tidy.

Gates

A gate should be the same height as your wall or fence and strongly constructed. Make sure the hinges, bolt and padlock are secured on the garden side. If possible install two different locks on a gate. Wrought-iron gates are more difficult to scale than solid wood, and their open structure does not provide cover for an intruder.

Safeguarding property when away
You can secure your garden ornaments and furniture with specially designed kits. Screw the bracket to a solid surface, then wrap the cable tightly around the item and padlock it to the bracket.

Lighting the garden

Thieves prefer to operate under cover of darkness, so illuminating the garden at night is a good deterrent. Most effective are movement-activated floodlights, which you could install on the front and back of the house; these will also light the way for evening visitors. As with all garden lighting, make sure your lights will not annoy neighbours or dazzle road users. Security lights should be positioned so they are difficult to reach and the bulbs hard to tamper with.

Berberis frikartii 'Amstelveen' Barberry

Paths

Consider using gravel on a path – it is noisy to walk on and so you will hear a visitor approach.

Sheds

A garden shed is often an easy target for petty thieves. All opening windows require good locks, or you could screw them permanently shut if ventilation is not a concern. Secure the door with two sturdy padlocks on hasps and staples fixed through both door and frame where possible.

Even if there is not much of value in the shed, the tools stored there might be of use to break into your home. Make sure ladders or stepladders are locked up; securely chain and padlock them to a post or wall. A garden spade is an effective implement for forcing doors and windows: you could either padlock it to a heavy bench or frame, or consider investing in a strong lockable box where you can store tools and also any potentially harmful garden chemicals.

Furniture and ornaments

Large or expensive items will be of interest to a thief – and that includes newly planted trees or other expensive plants.
- Mark valuable items with your postcode and house number.
- Check that your household insurance covers sheds, outbuildings and thefts from the garden.
- Use security brackets to protect hanging baskets.
- Anchor your furniture or ornaments to a patio or hard surface with cables and padlocks (below).

Kit for securing garden belongings

ideal plants

For deterring intruders

Osmanthus
A family of very prickly evergreen shrubs and trees.

Pyracantha (Firethorn)
An evergreen shrub barbed with spiny thorns, complete with brightly coloured autumn berries. Easy to grow and very effective as a hedge.

Chaenomeles (Quince)
A deciduous thorny shrub with spring flowers that will also thrive as a hedge.

Crataegus monogyna (Common hawthorn)
This fast-growing shrub makes an impenetrable thorny hedge with white spring flowers and red berries in autumn.

Berberis (Barberry)
A dense evergreen shrub with spiny stems that will form a bushy hedge.

Ilex (Holly)
Prickly rather than spiny, there are over 300 species of holly trees and shrubs.

CCTV home security

CCTV protection

Protect your garden and its contents with a CCTV system. This is simple to install, with a camera fitted outside that connects to your television. Pictures can be recorded via a video or DVD recorder. When an intruder is detected the camera automatically begins recording, and an audio buzzer may sound.

Planning regulations

Check first

Planning restrictions differ widely from one area to another. This table is a general guide to planning regulations in England and Wales, but you should also consult the Planning Department of your local council before going ahead with larger-scale garden improvements. This is especially true if you live in a Conservation Area, National Park, or similar.

If planning permission is necessary, your Planning Department will require an application together with fairly detailed plans and a fee. They will write to your neighbours and publish your application in the local press. The whole procedure can take up to two months or more. Even if formal planning permission is not required, it is always a good idea to talk to your neighbours about your plans, and let them know when you intend to start the work.

The website of the Office of the Deputy Prime Minister contains up-to-date information and advice about planning regulations (www.odpm.gov.uk).

seeking permission for garden improvements

		Planning permission not needed	Planning permission needed
Houses and bungalows	Fences, walls and gates	• For a fence, wall or gate under 2m tall, or under 1m tall next to a highway used for vehicles	• The house is listed • The fence, wall or gate is over 2m tall • The fence, wall or gate is next to a highway used for vehicles and is over 1m tall
	Patios and drives	• For any size of patio or other area of hard standing that is for domestic purposes	• For a raised patio or elevated deck that could overlook a neighbour's property • For a new driveway that will cross a pavement or verge, you will need permission from your council's Highways Department • For a new or wider access onto a trunk or other classified road you will also need Highways Department permission and possibly planning permission as well
	Garden buildings and structures	For a: • Garden shed or small summerhouse • Swimming pool • Tennis court • Greenhouse • Cabin for sauna • Kennel or other animal enclosure • Garden pond	• The house is listed • The building or structure will be nearer to any highway (inc. bridleways, footpaths and byways) than the nearest part of the house (unless it will still be more than 20m from the highway) • More than half of the area of land around the house will be covered by the structure • The structure will be used for any commercial purpose, including parking a commercial vehicle • The structure is over 3m high (4m for a ridged roof)
	Hedges and trees	• To plant a hedge or tree, provided there are no restrictions in the deeds to your property (but if they block a neighbour's light, you may be required to cut them back)	• To prune or fell a tree that is subject to a Tree Preservation Order • For hedges and trees next to a highway used for vehicles and over 1m tall
Flats and maisonettes			• For any garage, garden shed or greenhouse; hard standing such as a patio; wall or fence • For any work that would materially alter the appearance of the property

Electricity outdoors

Changes to Building Regulations

As of 1 January 2005, changes to the Building Regulations affect domestic electrical installations in England and Wales. You don't need to be a qualified electrician to make changes to your home's electrical system, but the work must be done in accordance with the standards in the Regulations.

Before you start any electrical work (other than repairs or replacements) outdoors (eg. installing garden lighting or sockets, etc.) you must notify your Local Authority Building Control Department, which has responsibility for ensuring the work is inspected and tested.

Where you have any work done by an electrician who is a member of a competent person self-certification scheme, the electrician will be able to certify that the work complies with the Regulations and you do not need to notify your Local Authority.

It is recommended that you make yourself aware of the Regulations before you undertake any work and if you require any clarification you should contact your Local Authority Building Control Department. Or visit www.odpm.gov.uk

Make certain your system is safe

If at any time you are uncertain of your ability, or you suspect that your system has been adapted or extended in an unorthodox way, always seek the advice of an electrical contractor registered with the NICEIC (the National Inspection Council for Electrical Installation Contracting), the ECA (Electrical Contractors' Association) or the Electrical Contractors' Association of Scotland (trading as SELECT).

RCD protection

Any electrical appliance used outdoors must have the protection of an RCD (residual current device) rated at 30 milliamps. This will cut off the power in a split second as soon as it detects an earth leakage, preventing injury from electric shock.

Working safely

If you do undertake any kind of work on an electrical installation in the home or garden, always isolate the circuit first by removing the circuit fuse or switching and locking the circuit breaker. Double-check it is dead with a socket tester or voltage tester. Never take risks with electrical safety.

Selecting the right electrical fittings for outdoor use

Electrical fittings have an IP rating to tell you what environment they can be safely used in. IP stands for 'ingress protection' and is followed by two numbers: the first tells you how easily objects or dust can penetrate the fitting, the second how easily water can get in. The numbers run from 0 (or X), meaning wholly unprotected, to 6 (objects) or 8 (water). So a rating of IP68 would mean totally dust-proof and submersible.

The second number in an IP rating – the level of protection from water – is critical when selecting fittings to be installed outdoors. The table below is for guidance only; always read and follow the manufacturer's advice.

IP water protection ratings

1		Protected against vertical drops of water	5	💧💧	Jet-proof: protected from water projected from a nozzle from any direction (under stated conditions)
2	💧	Drip-proof: protected against drops of water falling at an angle up to 15° from vertical	6		Watertight: protected against conditions on ships' decks, etc
3	💧	Rain-proof: protected against rain falling at an angle up to 60° from vertical	7	💧💧	Submersible under stated conditions of pressure and time
4	💧	Splash-proof: protected from water splashed from any direction	8		Indefinitely submersible under stated conditions of pressure and time

Building materials

Estimating quantities

Building materials for garden projects can be delivered in a variety of ways – in bags or sacks weighing up to a tonne, or even by the lorry load. Once delivered you won't want to move these materials any more than necessary. Often they cannot be returned and disposal may be laborious – compelling reasons to estimate how much you need with care.

- Consult the supplier for advice on estimating the amount of material or materials you need.
- Measure the volume or surface area carefully and recheck your measurements.
- Always add 10% to the estimated quantity to allow for error and unforeseen circumstances.

Measuring surface area

Measure the width and length of the area in metres. Multiply these measurements together to discover the surface area in square metres (m^2).

- For example: (width) 2m x (length) 6m = 12m^2

Measuring volume

Measure the width, length and depth of the area in metres. Multiply these measurements together to discover the volume in cubic metres (m^3).

- For example: (width) 2m x (length) 6m x (depth) 0.15m = 1.8m^3
  If buying concrete, you would round that up by 10% to 2m^3

Weight

The table below is a useful but rough guide: always check with your supplier for an accurate conversion of volume to weight.

volume to weight	
Soil	1m^3 = approximately 1.4 tonne
Gravel	1m^3 = approximately 1.6 tonne
Cement	1m^3 = 1.4 tonne
Sand and ballast	1m^3 = 1.7 tonne

Buying and storing building materials

Select your materials with care, and check the quantity and condition upon delivery.

Follow the manufacturer's recommendations regarding storage. Some materials will be unfit for use if spoilt by moisture or contaminated by other materials – kiln-dried sand and cement are obvious examples. Small quantities of sand and loose materials can be stored in heavy-duty plastic sacks. Larger quantities are best stored on a solid base; if on earth, lay an impermeable ground sheet first. Cover the pile when not in use – this will deter fouling by pets and prevent materials being washed away. Do not let the pile get too dry and compacted, or it may become unusable.

Measuring circular shapes

To measure the area of a circle, use the formula πr^2 (π = 3.14 and r^2 = the radius of the circle squared; the radius is the measurement from the middle of the circle to the outer edge).

- For example: (π) 3.14 x (radius) 2m x (radius) 2m = 12.56m^2

To find the volume of a circular area, multiply the area by the depth (in metres).

Measuring irregular shapes

To work out the area of an irregularly shaped site, measure it carefully and draw it to scale as accurately as possible on graph paper. Each square should represent 1m^2 of the site. Count the whole squares covered and roughly add up the part squares. Round the figure up by 10%. To find the volume, multiply the area by the depth (in metres).

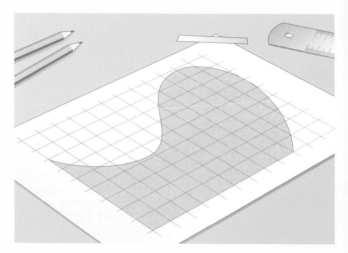

Bricks

Bricks come in different shapes, sizes and levels of durability. The standard size brick is 215mm x 102.5mm x 65mm, but this can vary by a few millimetres.

Bricks are graded according to their levels of frost-resistance and durability. Only fully frost-resistant bricks are suitable for most landscaping work. Lower salt levels reduce the likelihood of efflorescence – powdery salt deposits that form on the surface of the brickwork. However, salt can also enter bricks from mortar, concrete or ground water.

brick grading and durability	
F	Fully frost-resistant
M	Moderately frost-resistant
N	Normal levels of salt
L	Low salt levels

Facing bricks

Available in a wide variety of different colours and textures, these are the type of brick most likely to be used for a garden wall.

Common bricks

Generally cheaper and less attractive than facing bricks. Usually used where they won't be visible, though they can't be laid below ground.

Engineering bricks

Dense, strong bricks that are usually used underground, particularly for foundations or manhole construction.

Timber

Use exterior-grade timber for all outside projects. This is pre-treated with preservative to combat the destructive effects of exposure to the elements. Timber – usually softwood – that has been treated with preservative under pressure is described as tanalised or pressure-treated.

Buying and storing wood

Select your timber with care. Reject any lengths of timber that are not straight, or are weakened by large knots or show moisture damage. Store your timber under cover.

Cutting and preserving timber

When you cut treated timber, always paint the cut ends with wood preservative or end-grain preserver.

Decking timbers

Remember to allow for a 3mm drainage and expansion gap between deck boards when calculating the amount of decking timber you require.

Paving and block paving

Measure the surface area in square metres for your paving and then consult the supplier's information to determine how many paving stones you require. You may need extra stones for a complex shape requiring a lot of cutting.

Aggregates and sand

You are likely to use a variety of aggregates for landscaping projects. Bear in mind that builder's sands and aggregates are not suitable for horticultural use as they may contain elements and chemical characteristics that are unsuitable for, or damaging to, plants.

aggregates and sand	
Type 1	Short for MOT (Ministry of Transport) Type 1 Granular Sub-base Stone. Crushed stone that is compacted to form a solid sub-base beneath paved areas.
Cleanstone	A grit- and dust-free aggregate predominantly used for drainage purposes, such as in soakaways and land drains, or in constructions through which water needs to drain, such as retaining walls.
Ballast	Aggregate consisting of various sized particles from sand to small stones. Graded in mm according to the size of the largest stones. Used for concrete mixes.
Sharp sand	A gritty sand used for coarse work such as concreting or rendering floors.
Builder's sand	Finer than sharp sand, this is smooth and non-gritty. Used in mortar, for bedding paving slabs and for rendering walls. Also known as building sand.
Kiln-dried sand	Fine-graded sand for brushing over block paving to fill the joints without staining the stone.
Play sand	Clean and dry sand specifically for children's sandpits and play areas.
Gravel	Small stones, usually 5–30mm in diameter and rounded. The gravels most commonly used as loose surface dressings are in the 6–20mm size range: 6–10mm is recommended for paths; 10–18mm gravel for driveways. Coverage rates for gravels are typically 15–20m³ per tonne when laid to a depth of 35mm.

Fixings

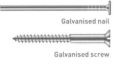

Galvanised nail

Galvanised nails or screws

Rust-proof galvanised fixings should always be used for exterior projects.

Galvanised screw

Deck screws

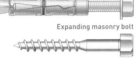

Deck screw

These are cross-head screws specifically designed for driving into decking timbers with a power drill or driver without the need to drill pilot holes first.

Expanding masonry bolt

Heavy duty fixings

Use coach screws or coach bolts for securing wood to wood. For fixing into walls – a fence post to a masonry wall, for instance – use an expanding masonry bolt.

Coach screw

Damp-proof membrane

Damp-proof membrane (DPM) provides a barrier to the passage of moisture and water vapour. DPM is sold in strip and sheet form for building walls or laying under floors, and self-adhesive jointing strips are available to join sheets together. Always install DPM with care so as not to puncture or damage it. Also available in liquid form for application with a brush.

Landscaping fabric

This sheet material, available in a variety of thicknesses and strengths, is used for suppressing weed growth in beds and borders, beneath areas of gravel or play bark, and under decks. You can grow plants through it (see page 33) as it is permeable to water, air and nutrients. The most durable geotextile landscaping fabrics are strong enough to stabilise surfaces under heavy-traffic drives and paving, and are used to line land drains and soakaways (see page 197). When using landscaping fabric to control weed growth, always clear all surfaces of weeds before you lay the fabric – either dig them out or spray with a glyphosate-based weedkiller. Lay the fabric as soon as the ground is cleared to reduce the risk of seeds germinating. Cover the fabric with a 50mm layer of mulch (such as bark, cocoa shells or stone chippings) to protect it from direct sunlight. Any weeds that do germinate will be easy to remove, as their roots will only be as deep as the mulch layer.

Exterior paints and finishes

Select from a wide range of exterior paints, stains, preservers, oils and varnishes.

paint finishes	
Multisurface colours	All-weather protection for wood, metal, masonry and terracotta.
Masonry paints	Long-lasting protection for masonry and walls – brickwork, stone, concrete, render, pebbledash and terracotta. Choose between smooth and textured finishes.
One-coat exterior gloss	Suitable for all exterior wood and metal.
Deck and furniture oils	Available in clear or coloured finishes, oils protect and replenish the natural beauty of wood.
Wood varnish	Available in a high-gloss or satin finish, coloured or clear.
Wood stains and preservers	Colour and preserve the wood at the same time. Some are formulated for spray application – ideal for sheds and fences.
Decking stains	Specifically formulated for decks. Choose from hardwood tones as well as more unusual colours.

Building materials

Concrete

Concrete is made up of cement, aggregate (particles of stone) and sharp sand mixed with water. In different proportions, these materials produce concrete of different strengths for different uses. It's important to get the proportions accurate: if there is too much aggregate, you will have difficulty producing a satisfactory finish; too much sand will mean that the mix will be weak and the finished surface could be damaged by the elements.

Plasticiser

Adding plasticiser to cement or mortar makes the mix more pliable and easy to work with.

concrete mixes	
Ingredients	Amounts required for approx. 1m³ of concrete
Paving mix (strong mix suitable for exposure to all weathers, including frost), using separate aggregate	
1 part cement	16 x 25kg bags
1.5 parts sharp sand	0.5m³
2.5 parts 20mm coarse aggregate	0.75m³
Paving mix (strong mix suitable for exposure to all weathers, including frost), using all-in aggregate	
1 part cement	16 x 25kg bags
3.5 parts all-in aggregate (ballast)	1m³
Footing or foundation mix (and for concreting in fence posts), using separate aggregate	
1 part cement	11.2 x 25kg bags
2.5 parts sharp sand	0.5m³
3.5 parts 20mm coarse aggregate	0.75m³
Footing or foundation mix (and for concreting in fence posts), using all-in aggregate	
1 part cement	11.2 x 25kg bags
5 parts all-in aggregate (ballast)	1m³
For garage or garden shed bases (not exposed to weather), using separate aggregate	
1 part cement	12.8 x 25kg bags
2 parts sharp sand	0.5m³
3 parts 20mm coarse aggregate	0.75m³
For garage or garden shed bases (not exposed to weather), using all-in aggregate	
1 part cement	12.8 x 25kg bags
4 parts all-in aggregate (ballast)	1m³

Mortar and render

Mortar sticks bricks or blocks together in a wall; render is a thin layer of mortar for coating the exterior of a wall. General-purpose mortars are a mix of builder's sand, cement and water, plus either lime or plasticiser. Plasticisers and frost-proofers create small pockets of air in the mix, making it smoother. Frost-proofer gives some protection against freezing but only against slight frosts. One 25kg bag of sand, with the other ingredients mixed in the proportions shown below, is enough to lay approximately 55 bricks.

mortar mixes	
General-purpose mortar (moderate conditions)	1 part cement, 1 part lime and 6 parts builder's sand
Strong mortar (severe conditions)	1 part cement, 6 parts builder's sand and plasticiser
Very strong mortar (exposed to snow, heavy wind and rain)	1 part cement, 4 parts builder's sand and plasticiser
Render	1 part cement, 3 parts builder's sand and plasticiser

Post-fix concrete

Ready-mixed, quick-drying post-fix concrete is very convenient for fixing posts for decks, fences etc. Place the post in the hole, add the mix, and then pour on the recommended quantity of water. (Or pour in the water, followed by the mix: check the manufacturer's instructions.) It sets in about 10–15 minutes.

Cement dyes

Cement can be coloured with a special cement colouring agent, which is added to the dry mix. When mixing more than one batch, be careful to use the same dosage of dye for a consistent colour. Some dyes act as a plasticiser too.

Mixing concrete and mortar

Always wear safety goggles, gloves and a dust mask when handling cement.

Mixing by hand

For small amounts, mixing concrete by hand is the only real option. Mix thoroughly and methodically – a longer job than you might think – until it is an even consistency, neither too dry nor too sloppy. When you pick up a shovelful, it should stay on the shovel.

Using a mixer

Start by pouring about a quarter of a bucket of water into the mixer. Add half the aggregate and half the sand (or half the all-in aggregate), and all the cement, then check the mix to see if you need to add more water. Add the rest of the aggregate (and sand, if using it), and more water if necessary. If the final mix is too sloppy, add more aggregate and cement in proportion.

Ready-mixed concrete

If you are planning to lay a large area of concrete or have little time, ready-mixed concrete is worth considering. Depending on the access to your site, the concrete is delivered in lorries and either poured directly on to the area or wheelbarrowed from the lorry to the site. Ready-mixed is ordered by the cubic metre: add 10% to allow for wastage and specify the job you are doing so the right mix can be prepared.

Waste removal

When you need to remove debris from demolitions or excavations, consult your local council and waste removal companies to find out the most appropriate method in your area. In principle there are two choices, skip hire or muck away.

Skip hire

Skips are available in many different sizes to suit all manner of projects and are hired for a period of time. You need a licence from your local council to site a skip on a public highway and must also abide by the relevant byelaws, such as lighting the skip at night.

Muck away

It may be more economical and effective to use the services of a 'muck away' lorry, especially if you have the space to amass waste material. These lorries are either loaded by hand or are equipped with a hydraulic arm to scoop up the waste into the lorry. They are particularly useful for one-off, end-of-project clearance.

Plant index

General index

Acknowledgments

Project director Nicholas Barnard
Consulting editor Ken Schept
B&Q project manager Geoff Long
Project manager Katie Murphy
Assistant project manager Kate Barnes
Photography Lucy Pope, Dan McNally, Ginny Jory, David Eno
Garden design Alan Emery
Illustrations Peter Bull – Art Studios, Stuart Blower,
Drazen Tomic
Horticultural and technical advice Alan Emery, Tom Eno,
David Eno, Ron Hayden, Charles Dowding, Tricia Tuttle
Contributing writers Felicity Jackson, Dawn Fisher,
Maria Costantino, Charles Dowding, David Eno,
Tricia Tuttle, Nicholas Barnard
Index Hilary Bird

Project gardens

Design Alan Emery, David Eno
Management Katie Murphy, Josie Lewis
Landscaping Tom Eno
Building John Dennett, Dayrell Bishop, Luke Bishop,
Alan Tyler, J Dennett Builders (Essex)
Rendering Terry Taylor
Carpentry Oliver Marlow, James Bowthorpe, Jack Richold,
Tom Bowthorpe
Electrical Trevor Silvester, Specialist Services (Electrical) Ltd
Gardening David Eno, Jo Younger, Jo Chater, Ed Cannon, Dan Cross,
Guy Clark, Julian Gibb, Amelia Slater, Keith Simm, Ryan Jones,
Mark Young, Oliver Bayley, Clare Grady, Jane Booth, Frances Juckes

Garden owners

Aaron and Paula Hayden; Nicholas Barnard and Camilla Blench; Sudip
and Liz Ray; Mark Lane and Jasen Cavalli; Jim Hooper; David Eno;
Charles Dowding; Caroline Gathorne-Hardy; Sally Mackie; Andrew and
Camilla Heath; Sean and Gillie O'Connor; Chris Morrison; Sue Hassell;
Phil and Dawn Moore; Alan Emery and Lisa Williams; Mo Ellis and Roy
Avis; Diana and Stephen Yakeley; Ed Sayers, Sarah Toogood and Louis
Toogood Sayers; Nori and Sandra Pope of Hadspen Garden, Castle Cary,
Somerset BA7 7NG (open to the public 1 March to 30 September,
10am–5pm, Thurs–Sun and Bank Holiday Mondays)

Additional modelling

George, Thomas and Paula Hayden; Imogen Gibb; Amelia Slater;
Keith Simm; Alice Eno; Kieran and Megan Hunter; Matthew and
Joshua Hardy; Phoebe and Kathryn Cadey; Lucy, Daisy and Michelle
Philips; Josie Lewis; Susie, Rosalie, Jack and Edward Dowding;
Pilar Everington; Gillie, Matt and Poppy Livey; Camilla Waters;
Daisy Gathorne-Hardy; Mabintu Mustapha; Fran Andreae; Sorrel
Packham; James Gloyne; Simon Matthews; Anna Parry;
Luke Emery; Ginny Jory; Peter Dawson; Patrick and Hannah Tilling;
Nastazja Laskowski

With special thanks to

Tim Cullen 360° Innovation
Phil Austin and Andy Sharp Advance Label Printing Services Ltd
Susan Hill, Richard Sadler and Sam Haggan Aggregate Industries
Martin Turner and Rob Peck Appleton Signs
Jim Duncan Bord Na Mona Horticulture
Brian Pinker Burall Floraprint Ltd
Chris Wheatley and Tony Burnett Canadian Spa Company Ltd
Jill Kelly Craig & Rose
Dave Bullivant, Pam Brady and Paul Newton
    Creative Print Solutions Ltd
Mike Horsfield and Ian Wilson Degussa Construction Chemicals (UK)
David Spenser Direct Dialogue
Andrew Butcher Dunure
Kerry Samuel Emplas
Nick Harris Expamet Building Products
Bernie Walker FFA Concept
Ken Reidy Finnforest UK Ltd
Debbie Johnson Gardena UK Ltd
Guy Grimes and Susan Prince Garden Excel Ltd
Rachel Badham Garden Pictures.com
Andrew Mellowes and Chris Richmond Gardman
Louise Mason Grange Fencing Ltd
Keith Cochrane and Steve Chalk Growing Success
Julie Wheeler and Clare Jeffery Hanson Building Products
Ruth Sheard Heissner UK Ltd
Paul Bagnall Henkel
Robin Upton and Sue Capewell Hortipak Ltd
Melanie Brady and David Hamilton Hozelock Ltd
Geoff Gallon HSS
Pam Bradley Imprint
Teresa Chappell Keith Butters
Ian Morley and Ed Reed Keter (UK) Ltd
Chris Cooper Lafarge Cement UK
Scott Trayhorn Lingar Design Ltd
Sarah Uttley and Andy Culhane Master Lock
Debra Brigante and Rob Christian M H Berlyn Co Ltd
Neil Stein and Jamie Heywood Micromark
Andy Bateman Mulu Nurseries, Evesham
Charlotte Feltham and Garry Foley Nationwide Premixed & Aggregates
Bob Ford Nature Portfolio
Andy Parkington, John Payne and Reg Skilton Parker Baines Ltd
Jane Lawler and Robert Smit PBI
Ian Mitchell Pirelli Cables Ltd
Adrian Clarke and Steve Davis Premium Timber Products Ltd
Chris Carr Q Lawns
James Whitmore Richard Sankey
Jim Platt Ronseal
Jonathan Bunbury, Jacqui Arm and Bob Drew The Scotts Company (UK)
Peter Dobson and Martin Hayman Suttons Seeds
John Adams
Graham Rhodes
Lee Rhodes

Photo credits

The following abbreviations are used to identify sources:
BF – Burall Floraprint Ltd, GWI – Garden World Images,
NP – Nature Portfolio

t: top; b: bottom; m: middle; l: left; r: right

Page 14b, 15br, 17tl BF; 18b, 19t Fred Walden/Disability Now Magazine; 30b,
30t, 31bl BF; 39b, 41t David Eno; 72–73 plants 1, 2, 9, 11, 14, 16, 23, 25 David
Eno, plants 3–6, 10, 12–13, 15, 17–22, 24, 27–29, 31, 33 BF, plants 8, 30–32 GWI;
86–87 plants 2–4, 6, 10–21, 24–26, 28–34 BF, plants 5, 8–9 GWI; 108–9 plants
1–3, 5–10, 12, 14–15, 17–20, 22–27, 29–32, 34 BF, plants 4, 13, 16, 21, 28, 33
GWI; 120–21 plants 1–4, 6, 9–10, 12, 15–20, 24–25, 27, 28 BF, 5 GWI; 138–39
plants 1–16, 18, 20–24, 26, 28–29, 31–35, 38–45, 47 BF, plants 19, 27, 30, 36–37
GWI; 148–49 plants 1–3, 6, 8–15, 17–19, 21–27, 30, 33 BF, plants 28–29 David
Eno, plants 16, 20, 31–32, 34 GWI; 164–65 plants 3–4, 6–12, 15, 17–20, 22–23,
25–27 BF; 168–69 plants 2–10, 12–13 BF, plant 11 David Eno; 172–73 plants 1,
4–12 BF, plants 2–3 GWI; 212mr, 213tr, 213 table, t BF; 214tr Deirdre Rooney;
216tl, 217tl BF; 221 second from l David Eno; 236tr, 237tr, 239t BF; 239br
David Eno; 241tr, 242br BF; 242tl David Eno; 249tl, 251tl, 251bl, 251 (Special
sprinkler) Hozelock Ltd; 256 l to r 1 Trevor Sims/NP, 7 Keith Sloan/NP, 2–6,
8 Bob Ford/NP; 257 l to r 1–3, 8, 10–11 Bob Ford/NP, 4 Mike Gale/NP, 5, 9 Mark
Hodsman/NP, 6 Andy Bradley/NP, 7 Mick Scarrott/NP, 12 Elliott Neep/NP;
258 l to r 1, 7, 10–12 Bob Ford/NP, 2 Keith Sloan/NP, 3 Trevor Sims/NP, 4 Mike
Gale/NP, 5 Elliott Neep/NP, 6, 9 GWI; 259 l to r 1–2, 7, 9 Bob Ford/NP, 4 Trevor
Sims/NP, 6 Jim Bradley/NP, 5 Howard Rice/Garden Picture Library, 8, 10 GWI,
11 picture Crown Copyright courtesy of Central Science Laboratory, 12 Mick
Scarrott/NP; 263mr BF; 269 l to r 1, 8 Gary Skinner/NP, 2, 4, 12 Elliott
Neep/NP, 3 Keith Sloan/NP, 5–7, 10–11, 13 Bob Ford/NP, 9 Sally Groucutt/NP;
270tr, 272tl, 274bl, 275bl BF; 292bl David Eno; 294–327 Plant Chooser, plants
1–8, 10–14, 16–21, 23–37, 40–41, 43–45, 47–52, 55–56, 58–59, 61–78, 80, 82–86,
88–96, 99, 101, 103–15, 119–22, 125–28, 131, 134–37, 140–48, 150, 152, 154,
156, 159–60, 163–67, 169–74, 176, 178–89, 191–203 BF, plants 9, 15, 22, 38, 42,
53, 57, 79, 81, 87, 100, 102, 116–18, 124, 129–130, 132, 138–39, 149, 151, 153,
155, 158, 161–62, 168, 175, 190 David Eno, plants 54, 60, 97, 123, 157 GWI;
342tr, 343br Charlie Bettinson

scale
survey
light
planting
design
balance
colour
plan
sketch
space
garden
trees
tomato
lawn
path
grow
spring
compost
herbs
mulch
flowers
mow
seeds
comfort
autumn
scent
organic
summer
apple